William Hope Hodgson:
Voices from the Borderland

HIPPOCAMPUS PRESS LIBRARY OF CRITICISM

Massimo Berruti, *Dim-Remembered Stories: A Critical Study of R. H. Barlow* (2011)
Scott Connors, ed., *The Freedom of Fantastic Things: Selected Criticism on Clark Ashton Smith* (2006)
Gary William Crawford, Jim Rockhill, and Brian J. Showers, ed., *Reflections in a Glass Darkly: Essays on J. Sheridan Le Fanu* (2011)
S. T. Joshi, *Primal Sources: Essays on H. P. Lovecraft* (2003)
———, *The Evolution of the Weird Tale* (2004)
———, *Lovecraft and a World in Transition: Collected Essays on H. P. Lovecraft* (2014)
S. T. Joshi and Rosemary Pardoe, ed., *Warnings to the Curious: A Sheaf of Criticism on M. R. James* (2007)
Ben Szumskyj, ed., *Two-Gun Bob: A Centennial Study of Robert E. Howard* (2006)
Robert W. Waugh, *The Monster in the Mirror: Looking for H. P. Lovecraft* (2006)
———, *A Monster of Voices: Speaking for H. P. Lovecraft* (2011)
Lovecraft Annual
Dead Reckonings

William Hope Hodgson: Voices from the Borderland

Seven Decades of Criticism on the Master of Cosmic Horror

Edited by
Massimo Berruti, S. T. Joshi, and Sam Gafford

Hippocampus Press
New York

Copyright © 2014 by Hippocampus Press

Brian Stableford, "William Hope Hodgson," from *Scientific Romance in Britain 1890–1950* (London: Fourth Estate), copyright © 1985 by Brian Stableford. Reprinted by permission of the author.

Published by Hippocampus Press
P.O. Box 641, New York, NY 10156.
http://www.hippocampuspress.com

All rights reserved.
No part of this work may be reproduced in any form or by any means without the written permission of the publisher.

Cover illustration © 2014 by Daniele Serra.
Cover design by Barbara Briggs Silbert.
Hippocampus Press logo designed by Anastasia Damianakos.

ISBN: 978-1-61498-106-0
First Edition
1 3 5 7 9 8 6 4 2

Contents

Introduction 7
    Sam Gafford

I. Some Studies of Hodgson's Life and Early Reception 9
Houdini v. Hodgson: The Blackburn Challenge.............................11
    Sam Gafford
William Hope Hodgson: In His Own Day......................................27
    A. Langley Searles
Pioneering Essays 34

II. Some Special Topics 43
William Hope Hodgson 45
    Brian Stableford
The Dark Mythos of the Sea: William Hope Hodgson's Transformation of Maritime Legends..56
    Emily Alder
Things in the Weeds: The Supernatural in Hodgson's Short Stories 73
    S. T. Joshi
Against the Abyss: Carnacki the Ghost-Finder..............................84
    Mark Valentine
William Hope Hodgson in the Underworld: Mythic Aspects of the Novels...92
    Phillip A. Ellis
Decay and Disease in the Fiction of William Hope Hodgson 110
    Sam Gafford
Hodgson's Women 117
    Sam Gafford

III. Studies of Individual Tales 129
Things Invisible: Human and Ab-Human in Two of Hodgson's Carnacki Stories..131
    Leigh Blackmore
Sexual Symbolism in W. H. Hodgson 146
    Sid Birchby
The "Wonder Unlimited"—The Tales of Captain Gault 150
    Mark Valentine

The House on the Borderland: On Humanity and Love 157
    Henrik Harksen

IV. Comparative Studies 167
    Time Machines Go Both Ways: Past and Future in H. G. Wells and
    W. H. Hodgson 169
        Andy Sawyer
    The Long Apocalypse: The Experimental Eschatologies of H. G. Wells
    and William Hope Hodgson 182
        Brett Davidson
    Shadow out of Hodgson 193
        John D. Haefele
    Robert H. Barlow's "A Memory" in William Hope Hodgson's
    The Night Land 198
        Marcos Legaria

William Hope Hodgson: A Bibliography 205
    S. T. Joshi and Sam Gafford, with Mike Ashley
    I. Works by Hodgson in English 206
        A.   Books and Pamphlets 206
        B.   Contributions to Books and Periodicals 223
        C.   Media Adaptations 259
    II. Hodgson in Translation 260
    III. Works about Hodgson 284
        A.   Bibliographies 284
        B.   Books about Hodgson 285
        C.   Dictionary and Encyclopedia Articles 286
        D.   Criticism in Books or Periodicals 289
        E.   Academic Papers 299
        F.   Book Reviews 300

    Indexes 303
        A. Names 303
        B. Works by Hodgson 308
        C. Periodicals 318

General Index 321

Introduction

Sam Gafford

It has taken nearly 100 years, but William Hope Hodgson is finally starting to get some respect.

When he died in 1918 during World War I, it looked as if Hodgson was going to be forgotten. His work, although garnering good reviews, was not financially successful. Hodgson was unable to gather the readership of someone like H. G. Wells. Hodgson's last novel, *The Night Land*, was published in 1912 and, as far as he was concerned, was a failure.

Even though all his books were reissued in cheap editions in 1921, Hodgson's legacy seemed on the verge of disappearing until an unexpected revival began with the Arkham House edition of *The House on the Borderland and Other Novels* in 1946, the culmination of years of work by H. C. Koenig to bring Hodgson to the attention of readers of weird fiction. In the decades since, Hodgson has enjoyed more prosperity than he knew in life, to the point where the majority of his work is either in print or available online. This effort has culminated in Night Shade's five-volume edition of Hodgson's *Collected Fiction* (2003–07) and other recent editions of Hodgson's poetry and other works.

After all, a writer has to be read before he can be studied.

The first critical piece about Hodgson was by H. C. Koenig and appeared in the December 1934 issue of the *Fantasy Fan*. It was a beginning. Slowly, other pieces would appear. H. P. Lovecraft, inspired by his friend Koenig, discussed Hodgson in the revised version of his essay "Supernatural Horror in Literature," and by this means many readers became aware of this forgotten master of the weird. Although both R. Alain Everts and Sam Moskowitz wrote various articles, the bulk of these would be biographical with limited critical content.

The first significant collection of articles about Hodgson and his work came in 1987 with Ian Bell's *William Hope Hodgson: Voyages and Visions*. This was a pamphlet with limited release, but it showed that there was an interest in studying Hodgson's works.

Over the next few decades, Hodgson would be the subject of several entries in various encyclopedias of science fiction, fantasy, and horror. Like a slow-moving tide, critical attention was growing.

Hodgson has since been the subject of doctoral theses as well as scholarly articles in a number of different publications. In 2013, I established the first regular magazine devoted to the study of Hodgson and his works, entitled *Sargasso*, which brought together articles by many of the leading figures in weird fiction criticism. Papers about Hodgson are now being presented at literary symposiums. In many ways, everything has been leading up to this volume you're reading now.

Several years ago, Massimo Berruti first approached me about this anthology. I immediately saw not just the need for such a collection but the importance of one. Many of the articles that have appeared in the past have been in small magazines and are not easy to find. Now, many of the most important pieces are being preserved here for further research and study.

No author can be properly studied without a thorough grasp of the extent of his publications and of the criticism he received during and after his lifetime. This book presents the first comprehensive bibliography of Hodgson ever published, a years-long effort by S. T. Joshi, Mike Ashley, and myself, with contributions by many other hands. In some ways this bibliography is itself provisional, but it exhibits for the first time the full range of Hodgson's writings—books, short stories, essays and reviews, poetry—and of what has been written about him, including books, encyclopedia and newspaper articles, criticism in books and periodicals, academic papers, and book reviews.

The field of Hodgson studies is still a relatively new one, even though he died nearly a century ago. In so many ways, critical study of Hodgson has been hampered by difficulties such as the unavailability of material and of access to previous criticism. At last, we are providing a solid foundation for further study and exploration of Hodgson's work. It is finally time to shed some light on that Night Land.

I. Some Studies of Hodgson's Life and Early Reception

Houdini v. Hodgson:
The Blackburn Challenge

Sam Gafford

When Harry Houdini took the stage at the Palace Theatre in Blackburn, England, on the night of October 24, 1902, little did he expect that he would face a challenge that would scar him for the rest of his life. That would come at the hands of a small, stocky man named William Hope Hodgson, who was the owner and operator of a local school of "physical culture" and would go on to become a major author in science fiction and horror. This confrontation would become a milestone in the lives of both men.

By 1902, Harry Houdini had been working very hard on building his act and his reputation. Since receiving his big break in 1899, Houdini had been touring the Orpheum vaudeville circuit and playing to packed houses. Although he originally started with card tricks, Houdini's manager Martin Beck had convinced the magician to concentrate on escape acts and booked Houdini on a European tour in 1900. Although the tour began slowly, Houdini had elicited the interest of the manager of the prestigious Alhambra Theatre in London. After a flamboyant escape from handcuffs at Scotland Yard, Houdini played the Alhambra for six months.

His tour launched, Houdini would now be billed as "the Handcuff King" and went on a whirlwind tour of many cities in England, Scotland, the Netherlands, Germany, France, and Russia. But it was his ego and over-confidence that would nearly lead him to ruin in Blackburn in 1902.

> Houdini arrived in Blackburn, a major cotton manufacturing town in the north-east of Lancashire with a population of just under 130,000 at that time, to play the Palace Theatre for the week beginning 20th October, 1902. The Palace was the newest of Blackburn's four theatres, having been erected in 1899. It was a magnificent building which could seat 2,500 people. (Woods-Lead 11)

It had become Houdini's custom to try to create publicity in the various cities in which he performed, and Blackburn was no different. The theatre's advertisement of the upcoming appearance ran in the local *Blackburn Standard and Weekly Express* paper on October 18. It was a short notice as was common for the time and read:

> THE PALACE THEATRE. BLACKBURN
> Proprietor............Mr. FRANK MACNAGHTEN.
> Manager............Mr. CHARLES SCHUBERTH.
>
> ———————
>
> MONDAY NEXT, Oct 20th, 1902 and Every Evening
> During the Week:
> Special Expensive Engagement of
> HOUDINI
> World-famous Jail Breaker and Handcuff King.
> He is the originator of this Act.

The remainder of the ad announced a Soprano Vocalist, an "exponent of quaint comedy," an "artistic musical act," a team of "comedians, vocalists, & dancers," swimmers, a "vocalist and step dancer," and "Chinko, the astounding boy juggler." It was obviously a very full bill.

As usual, Houdini created his own publicity as well. On October 21, 1902, an interview with Houdini appeared in the local Blackburn paper, the *Daily Star*. Houdini's career as a public relations mastermind was well underway and is reflected in his manipulation of the interviewer. Houdini "deliberately distorted certain facts about his history to make himself more of a romantic and appealing character to the public at large" (Woods-Lead 11). Houdini was in the habit of claiming that he had been born in Appleton, Wisconsin, when, in fact, he had been born in Budapest, Hungary. The magician also increased his age by a year.

In addition, Houdini claimed to have been a professional locksmith who had been fired after opening "one of his employer's so-called 'burglar-proof' locks in the presence of a customer!" (Woods-Lead 12). He also stated that he had been the unwitting accomplice to a burglary in Germany by unlocking a house for people he thought were the owners but that the local police had known Houdini's "good reputation" and let him off with a warning.

When asked how he developed his act, Houdini spun yet another yarn.

> Houdini gave an account that whilst playing a small variety theatre in the States, Mike W. Telling, a bank robber with still a fortnight of his sentence to serve, was allowed out of jail in the Sheriff's custody to watch the show. Telling was handcuffed to a chair whilst the Sheriff helped to tie Houdini for a rope trick. Houdini remarked that if the convict knew what he knew he would be able to escape. The result was that Houdini was tested by having

the handcuffs placed on him and he escaped from them in ten minutes. This feat, he claimed, led to his re-engagement and his subsequent handcuff act with challenges to police and gaolers of every nationality. (Woods-Lead 12)

All interesting tales but, as Woods and Lead point out, there is nothing in any of the established biographies of Houdini to verify the account. In fact, Houdini had been working in a tie factory before beginning his magic career. But, as with so many others, Houdini's charm overwhelmed the reporter.

The first night of Houdini's engagement at the Palace Theatre on October 20 was well received. A report issued in the *Northern Daily Telegraph* the next morning described Houdini as escaping from various handcuffs that were locked upon him, although it does not state whether those shackles were supplied by spectators or by Houdini himself. The article also reports that a "private sitting" had taken place earlier that morning for a select number of Blackburn townsmen. During that special performance, Houdini was bound with a variety of handcuffs and leg irons and, naked, was placed behind a curtain while he escaped from the shackles.

Houdini had already gotten into the habit of issuing a challenge when performing in a new city, and this had become part of his "performance" mystique. Houdini offered a £25 reward if he failed to escape from "regulation restraints as used by the police of Europe and America" (Woods-Lead 14). Blackburn was no different and, on October 24, his challenge was accepted.

The *Northern Daily Telegraph* printed the challenge as follows under the Palace's advertisement of Houdini's engagement:

CHALLENGE TO THE "HANDCUFF
KING" AT BLACKBURN
HODGSON v. HOUDINI

Interest in the visit of Houdini, the handcuff magician, to the Palace Theatre, Blackburn, this week is intensified by the acceptance of his challenge by Mr. W. H. Hodgson, of the School of Physical Culture, Blackburn. Letters have passed between the parties to the following effect:

(Copy.)

The School of Physical Culture
 Ainsworth-street, Blackburn
Mr. Harry Houdini.
Sir,—
 Being interested in your apparently anatomically impossible handcuff test, I have decided to take up your challenge to-night (Friday) on the following conditions:
  1st—I bring and use my own irons (so look out).
  2nd—I iron you myself.

3rd—If you are unable to free yourself, the £25 to be given to the Blackburn Infirmary.

Should you succeed, I shall be the first to offer congratulations. If not, then the infirmary will benefit.

W. HOPE HODGSON
(Principal)

P.S.—Naturally, if your challenge is bona-fide, I shall expect the money to be deposited.

W. H. H.

HOUDINI'S REPLY

I, Harry Houdini, accept the above challenge, and will deposit the £25 at the "Telegraph" office. Match to take place to-night (Friday).
H. HOUDINI

Hodgson's challenge to Houdini altered the usual rules by not only insisting that he bind Houdini himself but that he would be the one to supply the irons. By this point, Houdini had performed hundreds of escapes, so it is possible that he had grown over-confident and perhaps had begun to believe his own press releases. In any case, the events of that night would lead Houdini to reconsider his "challenges" in the future.

If Houdini had known Hodgson, it is likely that he might have reconsidered.

Born in 1877, the son of an Anglican priest, William Hope Hodgson (called "Hope" by friends and family) spent a childhood mesmerized by the ocean. By the time he was thirteen, Hope had already tried to run away to sea, and it was only through the intervention of an uncle that he was finally apprenticed. Hodgson would spend the next eight years at sea and would leave it with a venomous hatred that would color the rest of his days.

Hodgson himself has written of the cruelty of life on the sea in his essay "Is the Mercantile Navy Worth Joining":

> Why am I not at sea?
> I am not at sea because I object to bad treatment, poor food, poor wages, and worse prospects. I am not at sea because very early I discovered that it is a comfortless, wearyful, and thankless life—a life compact of hardness and sordidness such as shore people can scarcely conceive. I am not at sea because I dislike being a pawn with the sea for a board and the ship-owners for players. (*Demons of the Sea* 52)

Shortly after joining the Mercantile Navy, Hodgson had an encounter that changed his life. It resulted in his interest and devotion to physical culture, and he related it in an interview published in the *Blackburn Weekly Telegraph* on September 7, 1901:

> "You see, I was driven to the development of my muscles at a very young age. I went to sea when thirteen, and being a little chap with a very ordinary physique, had the misfortune to serve under a second mate of the worst possible type. He was brutal, and although I can truthfully say I never gave him just cause, he singled me out for ill-treatment. He made my life so miserable that in the end I summoned sufficient courage to retaliate and I 'went for him.' It was for all the world like a fight between a mastiff and a terrier, for he was powerful, and knew how to punish. Of course I received an unmerciful thrashing, but I remember how proud I was the next day, when I was arraigned before the captain for insubordination, to see that I had dealt him a lovely black eye.
>
> "Well, from that day I resolved to go in for muscular development, and I worked hard and made a study of physical culture, and at the end of my eight years life on the sea I had the satisfaction of transforming myself into what you see me now." (*Uncollected William Hope Hodgson* 1.12-13)

As Sam Moskowitz relates, Hodgson took to this program of exercise with great vigor: "He did not stop at mere exercise, but delved into the interaction of muscles and made body development an obsession. The primary motivation of his body development was not health, but self-defense" (*Out of the Storm* 18). Moskowitz goes on to state that Hodgson may have had a cruel streak as well: "There is strong evidence that throughout his life one of his most delightful diversions was to pound sailors into jelly at the slightest provocation" (18).

Hodgson's interest in physical culture would extend beyond his time at sea. In 1899, he opened "W. H. Hodgson's School of Physical Culture" in Blackburn. In the 1902 interview, Hodgson claims to have had "between 300 and 350 pupils in the past eighteen months" (*Uncollected William Hope Hodgson* 1.13) and that several members of the Blackburn police force have been among his pupils (1.14).

It is entirely possible that this "interview" was entirely written by Hodgson himself. Starting with the publication of his article "Dr. Thomas' Vibration Method *versus* Sandow's" in *Sandow's Magazine* in 1901, Hodgson had begun to turn his attention toward writing. He would also show a gift of publicity nearly equal to that of Houdini when he rode a bicycle down a steep street that had been converted to a narrow flight of stairs. The feat was reported in the *Blackburn Weekly Telegraph* on August 30, 1902. "There are some men, however, to whom fear is an unknown quantity and danger merely an element to be conquered and one of these is Mr. W. H. Hodgson, the well known professor of physical culture, who has this week cycled down the 'Steppy' precipice without breaking his neck" (Frank 59).

The bicycle incident is undoubtedly an attempt at some free publicity for his school, which makes one wonder if the picture was not as rosy as Hodgson had painted it in 1901. It is certainly probable that, once Hodgson learned of Houdini's challenge, he saw another opportunity for publicity.

Ian Bell notes an interesting prequel to the confrontation:

> As he had explained in his newspaper interview, Hodgson numbered amongst the customers of his School the borough police force. Consequently, when the famous escapologist Harry Houdini visited the area and, as a publicity exercise, escaped with considerable ease from Blackburn Gaol, it was only natural that the local constabulary should turn to Hodgson for assistance. (2)

Bell does not give the reference for this incident. Neither does Sam Moskowitz when he repeats the anecdote in his essay "William Hope Hodgson," which introduces his collection *Out of the Storm*. It is possible that an article about this event may still exist in an old paper yet to be found. Given that Houdini was in the habit of doing such escapes as publicity in the cities on his tour, it is not entirely impossible that this did, in fact, happen. But, at this point, I submit it only as an unverified anecdote.

What we do know is that the confrontation took place at the Palace Theatre on Friday evening, October 24, 1902.

The challenge had generated so much publicity that the theatre was completely packed. The *Daily Star* reported that "the crowd ... crammed the theatre ... from floor to ceiling, even standing room being ultimately unobtainable." Remember that a previous account gave the Palace Theatre a seating capacity of 2,500 (Woods-Lead 11). The result of the challenge was reported by three newspapers: the *Blackburn Standard and Weekly Express*, the *Northern Daily Telegraph*, and the *Daily Star*. They are, by and large, similar. In their excellent book, *Houdini the Myth-Maker: The Unmasking of Harry Houdini*, Roger Woods and Brian Lead use these three accounts to piece together an accurate representation of the event, and I use this as the best source of the encounter.

Houdini gave two performances that night. The first was at 7 P.M. and the second at 9 P.M., with a slight break between the two. Shortly after the finish of the second show, around 10 P.M., the challenge was announced. Hodgson produced six pairs of heavy irons "furnished with clanking chains and heavy padlocks" (*Star*, October 25, 1902). Upon inspecting the shackles, Houdini claimed that his challenge was that he would escape from any "regulation restraints" and that Hodgson's had been tampered with. "Houdini at the outset raised a protest against the irons which were to make him a prisoner, as he urged that the locks had been tampered with and had been wrapped with twine, which was against the spirit of the competition" (*Blackburn Standard and Weekly Express*, October 25, 1902). The crowd showed their disappointment until Hodgson announced that he had stipulated that he would bring his own irons and use them himself. As this was the wording of his challenge and as it had been accepted by Houdini, Hodgson must have felt himself justified in his actions.

After consideration, Houdini replied that he would be "willing to go on, if only the audience would give him a little time in which to deal with the extra difficulties" (*Star*). The crowd cheered and the work of binding Houdini began.

Hodgson, with the aid of another man (presumably one of his students), started by fixing a pair of irons over Houdini's upper arms and passing them behind his back. They pulled the chains tight, which pinned Houdini's elbows to his sides. Hodgson and his assistant then ran another pair in a similar fashion and padlocked them both behind Houdini's back. Next, they affixed a pair of cuffs on Houdini's wrists "so that the arms, already pulled stiffly behind, were now pulled forward. The pulling and tugging at this stage was so severe—the strong man [Hodgson's assistant] exercising his strength to some purpose—that Houdini protested that it was not part of the challenge that his arms should be broken" (*Star*).

At this point, Houdini reminded Hodgson that he had stated that *he* would bind Houdini himself. The crowd agreed and Hodgson's assistant left the stage. Yet Hodgson was not quite finished with the magician.

Next, Hodgson fixed another pair of cuffs on Houdini's wrists and padlocked them. "Houdini's arms were now trussed securely to his sides. Any escape seemed impossible" (Woods-Lead 18). And still Hodgson was not done.

"Getting Houdini to kneel down, he passed the chain of a pair of heavy leg irons through the chains which bound the arms together at the back. These were fixed to the ankles, and after a second pair had been added, both were locked, and Houdini now seemed absolutely helpless" (*Star*).

A canopy was placed over Houdini, who was in the middle of the stage. Now the waiting started and the tension grew by the minute. Meanwhile, Hodgson and others kept a sharp watch on Houdini's wife and brother (Hardeen), who were also on the stage.

"Often Houdini was to play on an audience's excitement by deliberate delay but, in this case, there was no need to sham" (Woods-Lead 18). Houdini was facing the challenge of his life.

After fifteen minutes, the canopy was raised and revealed Houdini lying on his side, still completely bound. At first it was thought that he had fainted, but Houdini motioned that he wished to be lifted up. "This Mr. Hodgson refused to do, at which the now madly excited audience hissed and 'booed' him for his unfair treatment, and Hardeen lifted his brother to his knees" (*Star*). The canopy was lowered again and the orchestra played current music selections.

When another twenty minutes had passed, the canopy was raised again. Houdini was still bound and, this time, asked that the irons be unlocked "for a minute" as his arms were "bloodless and numb owing to the pressure of the irons" (*Star*).

Hodgson's reply was simple. "This is a contest, not a love match. If you are beaten, give in." The crowd, appalled at this treatment, began shouting. "The audience was close to violence" (Woods-Lead 19). A Dr. Bradley stepped forward to examine Houdini. "Dr. Bradley, after examining Houdini, said his arms were blue, and it was cruelty to keep him chained up as he was any longer" (*Star*).

Neither Hodgson nor Houdini would give in. "Houdini said steadily that he would continue. He again asked for time and the audience screamed their approval" (Woods-Lead 19).

Feverish activity could be seen under the canopy and, after fifteen minutes, Houdini appeared to announce that his hands were now free and that he would take a short rest. This was met with cheers and some hostile voices, to which Houdini replied: "You must remember, ladies and gentlemen, that I did not state the time it would take me to get them off. These handcuffs have been plugged" (*Blackburn Standard*). The canopy was lowered again.

The time continued to pass and the audience was growing restless; "in the hearts of most people it was felt that Houdini had met more than his match" (*Evening Standard*). But Houdini appeared to announce that that it would not be long now before he was entirely free. The audience was still unhappy, especially when Hardeen approached the canopy. Houdini was given a drink and continued to appeal to the audience for more time. "Hodgson said something about seeing a key in one of the locks and shortly after left the building" (Woods-Lead 19).

Shortly after midnight, Houdini appeared, free of the locks and chains. "He came out with torn clothing and bleeding arms, and threw the last of the shackles on the stage, the vast audience stood up and cheered and cheered, and yelled themselves hoarse to give vent to their overwrought feelings. Men and women hugged each other in mad excitement. Hats, coats, and umbrellas were thrown up into the air, and pandemonium reigned supreme for 15 minutes" (*Star*). It is interesting to note that the description in the *Blackburn Standard* is significantly more restrained, merely stating that the crowd stood up and cheered. The *Star*'s description may just be journalistic hyperbole.

Houdini had the look of a man who had been tortured. His shirt was torn from shoulder to cuffs and, in places, his flesh was raw. He stood and addressed the audience when it had calmed. "Ladies and gentlemen, I have been in the handcuff business for fourteen years, but never have I been so brutally and cruelly ill-treated. I would just like to say again that the locks have been plugged" (*Blackburn Standard*).

The crowd now looked around for Hodgson. "A voice: 'Where is Hodgson? Why is he not here to offer his congratulations?'" (*Blackburn Standard*). Hodgson had left the theatre some time earlier. "It was as well for Hodgson that he had left the theatre, apparently according to the *Northern Daily Telegraph* on the advice of a police sergeant fearing a disturbance" (Woods-Lead 19–20). The crowd eventually dispersed, aware that they had seen something historic.

The aftermath of the conflict came quickly.

The next morning Houdini was interviewed by a reporter from the *Daily Star*, and his indignation was clearly evident. "'I was like a trussed fowl,' he said, 'and it was more than half an hour after being pinioned before I was able to do anything, my fingers being practically dead'" (Woods-Lead 20).

Houdini claimed that he had never been bound so tightly as to lose his circulation before. When the reporter asked if Houdini felt that he was not manacled according to the agreement, Houdini claimed: "'I was manacled too much to say the truth'" (Woods-Lead 20). Houdini described the cuffs as not being regulation and containing "pully-blocks" that he had never seen on cuffs before. He also repeated his assertion that the keyholes on the locks had been plugged.

To demonstrate the painful results of his escape, Houdini showed the reporter his arms. "They were red and swollen and pieces of flesh were torn out. He said that this was partly due to the fact that his flesh had been fastened in with the locking of the fetters and he had been forced to wrench a piece of flesh to get away. He explained that Dr. Bradley had told him that a few minutes more might have left his arms paralyzed. He praised the doctoring given to him the night before by Dr. Bradley" (Woods-Lead 20).

Not one to allow such an accusation to go without answer, Hodgson responded to the *Northern Daily Telegraph* that the irons had not been plugged and that he acted fairly according to the terms of the challenge. To enforce his position, Hodgson wrote a letter to the *Blackburn Times*, which was published on Saturday, November 1, 1902:

THE HOUDINI EXHIBITION

Sir — The allegations made by Mr. Houdini to the effect that the "irons" used were plugged is not correct. Those who were in the Palace at the time will remember that the "Handcuff King" thoroughly examined each of the "irons" (with which I confined him) before he consented to be fastened up, and it is absurd to suppose a detail of such importance would have escaped his practiced eye. With regard to his charge of brutality, I must explain that so long as Mr. Houdini kept still he was in no danger of suffering; it was his own struggles which caused him any painful degree of inconvenience. The "irons" used were of the regulation pattern, with the addition of a couple of padlocks to keep them in position; though even had I made use of cuffs of an usual [sic; presumably 'unusual' was intended] design Mr. Houdini had no grounds for grumbling, as he consented to the trial after having examined them. It was obviously against the rules of fair play that Mr. Houdini's brother and wife should have been allowed to go near him at any time during the contest. I maintain that only the committee, Mr. Houdini and myself had any right to be on the stage during the trial. One word more; I stood to win nothing, having promised to devote the £25 (in the event of my winning) to the Blackburn Infirmary, and I trusted to Blackburnians to see fair play, stead of which many allowed themselves to be carried away by mawkish appeals to sentiment which had little or not true basis. I entered for a contest; I found, too late, the public wanted an exhibition.

W. HOPE HODGSON

The School of Physical Culture,
Ainsworth-street, Blackburn,
October 25th, 1902
(Woods-Lead 21)

A postscript to this letter appeared in some editions: "In his letter which appears in another column, Mr. Hodgson omitted to state that he offered to withdraw from the contest if Houdini was suffering any pain whatever" (Woods-Lead 21).

Woods rightly questions the validity of this postscript. By all accounts, Hodgson refused to give in even when Dr. Bradley stated that it was cruel for the contest to continue.

It is difficult to determine how much impact this encounter had on Hodgson. Due to the lack of letters or other primary sources, we do not know how Hodgson felt about Houdini or if he ever realized the important part he had played in the magician's life.

We do know, however, that Houdini never forgot that night in October or Hodgson.

Houdini was back in Blackburn a mere three weeks later, playing the Palace Theatre again in November. Although no "handcuff challenge" took place, Houdini was challenged to escape from a straitjacket provided by a Mr. George Hardman from yet another school of physical culture in Blackburn. It took only sixteen minutes for Houdini to escape from the straitjacket; afterward, he "made a short speech congratulating Mr. Hardman on the sportsmanlike manner in which he had carried out his part of the challenge"

(Woods-Lead 25). This is clearly a thinly veiled insult against Hodgson and the way the last challenge had been conducted.

Throughout most of his life, Houdini would produce souvenir booklets that he would use as publicity material. He would often make reference to the Blackburn encounter in these pamphlets and, as Woods notes, "the accounts are embroidered in Houdini's favor." This is to be expected from such a master of publicity, and it is not unusual that he would turn the story to his favor. In fact, Houdini could be said to be one of the earliest examples of what we have come to call "spin doctors."

Houdini would return to the Blackburn area several times and, in 1911, he visited Burnley in Lancashire, which was nearby. As usual, he made the rounds of the local papers and, when interviewed by the *Burnley Express* on April 15, would claim:

> His most nerve-racking ordeal was undergone at Blackburn in 1902 where a physical culture expert so manacled him that he was two hours in releasing himself, and then his bleeding arms and wrists testified to the punishment he had gone through. (Woods-Lead 22)

When interviewed for the *Hull Daily Mail* in 1914, Houdini discussed retiring because his health was suffering from his many escape feats, and mention is made once again of the Blackburn incident.

The confrontation had begun to take on a life of its own, even outliving both of its participants.

Spanning the years 1953–54, the Blackburn incident made the papers once again. In the December 10, 1953, edition of the *Northern Daily Telegraph*, an article on the Palace Theatre mentioned briefly that Houdini had not freed himself that night in 1902.

A rebuke was published in the December 12 edition in a letter from Mr. A. E. Shaw of Blackburn, who "added the information that Hodgson had admitted that the irons he used were not of a regulation type but were used for mutineers at sea" (Woods-Lead 23). Shaw also confirmed that Houdini had freed himself and that Mrs. Houdini had called out loud to him to ask if he was all right.

In the December 19 edition, another letter was printed. Signed anonymously as "Interested," the writer confirmed that Houdini freed himself and that Hodgson had left the theatre before Houdini had completed his escape. This implied that Hodgson could not have known if Houdini had help because he did not stay until the end.

The discourse became larger when a new article entitled "Was Houdini Helped Free That Night in Blackburn?" appeared in the *Northern Daily Telegraph* on January 12, 1954. The article detailed the story of Mr. Richard

Clegg, of Dixon Street, Blackburn, who claimed to have acted as Houdini's "bodyguard" during the magician's engagement in 1902 and was on the stage at the Palace Theatre on that fateful night. Clegg said that he had remained on stage even after Hodgson had left. Also, Clegg stated:

> But before long his brother, who travelled with him, went to him with a glass of water, and when I went to them, Houdini was telling his brother that he couldn't get free. I said if Houdini wanted anything I could get it. His brother went to him later on, and either then or when he took the water, must have given him some sort of tool.
>
> Houdini did eventually come out and say he was free but the curtain came down before the audience could get a proper look at him. He still had one of the irons on, and the other, from which he had got free, had been filed. (Woods-Lead 24)

Clegg then goes on to state that the irons that were used were afterwards displayed in the window of a local store where everyone could see them.

Not to be outdone, the same Mr. A. E. Shaw who had written previously fired back a rebuttal. In it, Shaw rebuked Clegg's claims and reaffirmed his previous comments. Shaw also referred back to the newspaper's own reports of October 25, which contradicted Clegg's and pointed out that the deposit check had been returned to Houdini. This, surely, was proof that it was considered that Houdini had freed himself. Shaw shows contempt for Clegg's account and barely restrains himself from calling Clegg a liar.

In addition, Shaw declares that Hodgson's leaving the entire matter in Clegg's hands is "ridiculous" and states that he has several witnesses ready to back up his claims. Finally, Shaw points out that the irons used were not displayed in the shop that Clegg had indicated but another shop altogether—one that, Shaw claims, was a newsagent well known to Hodgson. Shaw concludes by stating that he had ample opportunity himself to examine the irons while they were on display and that, while they were scratched, they showed no evidence of having been filed or cut.

As might be expected, Hodgson does not fare so well in various Houdini biographies. Woods states that several biographers may have depended upon Houdini's own press booklets, which were less than trustworthy and certainly created to play up Houdini's role.

William Kalush and Larry Sloman's biography of Houdini gives little detail about Hodgson and omits the fact that the challenge had been agreed previously through the newspaper. The implication is that Hodgson had "ambushed" Houdini, and the authors later describe Hodgson as "laughing derisively" when Dr. Bradley suggests that the irons be removed.

Surprisingly, Kenneth Silverman's Houdini biography suffers just as much. Once again, the newspaper challenge and acceptance is not mentioned, and there is a suggestion that Houdini was goaded into the challenge. Strangely, Silverman quotes more about Hodgson than most of his fellows, as he paraphrases several facts that appear to have been gleaned from Moskowitz's introduction. No mention is made of Hodgson's assistant and, amazingly, Silverman not only has Hodgson agreeing to let Houdini be set upright but doing the act himself!

Silverman details the after-effect of Houdini's escape:

> After escaping from cuffs Houdini often soothed his mangled hands with lotion; while working in Bradford he had even ruptured a small vein in his left arm. But this time his arms were swollen and discolored with welts where the irons had nipped them, bleeding where he had had to tear flesh to get free, looking, a reporter said, "as though some tiger had clawed him." The physician speculated that a few more minutes of compression might have left the arms paralyzed. (56)

But Silverman goes even further with Hodgson:

> Houdini's shredding did not impress the physically cultured Hodgson. Interviewed a day or two later by the *Blackburn Star*, he denied that he had locked Houdini in crabbed cuffs or roughed him up, much less nearly paralyzed him: "absolute nonsense," he said. He maintained that he had passed his fingers around the inner ring of each cuff to be sure it did not squeeze Houdini, and knowing something of anatomy, he had been careful not to compress his brachial artery. He griped about the suspicious presence onstage of Bess and Dash, and exhibited a pair of handcuffs he had locked on Houdini. One iron link had been cut through and others showed deep file marks. The slicing suggested that Houdini had gotten hold of some tools, and used them. The *Star* backed up Hodgson, remarking that four other irons he had put on Houdini had not been returned to him. (56-57)

I have been unable to verify the accuracy of this interview. Silverman then describes Houdini's return to Blackburn three weeks later in a different light. Houdini had "returned just to show up Hodgson's 'miserable falsehoods' and defy taunts from his supporters that he 'dared not come back.' Speaking from the footlights of the same Palace Theatre, he accused Hodgson himself of having cut the handcuff links after the event, in order to discredit him" (57).

According to Silverman, Houdini's later returns to Blackburn were never welcomed by the magician. "It remained a 'wretched' place to him, its gallery the worst of 'all the hoodlum towns I ever worked.' Hodgsonites did not fancy him either, or forget him" (57). Silverman goes on to imply that a later appearance in Blackburn that featured another "handcuff challenge" unconnected to Hodgson had, in fact, been either engineered or inspired by Hodgson in some way.

Even Silverman acknowledges that the confrontation with Hodgson never left Houdini "and he privately referred to it as 'that terrible 'Hodgson' night.'"

In her Houdini biography, Ruth Brandon correctly makes the statement that both men were fighting for their lives that night. Houdini was fighting for his professional life. He could not be seen to be bested by anyone, anywhere if he was to retain his professional and personal pride. Insightfully, Brandon notes that Hodgson was fighting for the life of his school and his livelihood. If he could present himself as "the man who beat Houdini," he would have had hundreds of new pupils. (Interestingly enough, Brandon is the only Houdini biographer who would even mention that Hodgson would go on to become a pioneer writer in horror and science fiction.)

Brandon was unfortunately correct. Hodgson closed his school soon after the Houdini incident. By 1904, he was unemployed and starting on his career as a writer. Although no longer an instructor, Hodgson would remain a devotee of physical culture all his life. It is likely that it was this condition that enabled him to survive his devastating injury when thrown from a horse while serving as a lieutenant in the Royal Field Artillery in 1915. As a writer, Hodgson would become a highly imaginative and prolific author. Unfortunately, he did not receive either the financial or critical acclaim he deserved. After his death in World War I in 1918, Hodgson's work would go on to become considered a classic example of the form and, as we approach the hundredth anniversary of his death, Hodgson's name is more widely known than ever before.

Although we cannot analyze the effect upon Hodgson, we know that the confrontation made a vast impact on Houdini. It is included in many Houdini biographies and Houdini himself used it in his publicity material. As several writers have pointed out, this was a turning point for Houdini in that, from that point onward, he was more careful about what he agreed to do. The encounter with Hodgson in Blackburn had taught Houdini that he was not perfect and that he had come too close to being beaten to risk it again.

Houdini would, of course, go on to become one of the most famous magicians in history. He would die of peritonitis, secondary to a ruptured appendix, in 1926. He remains a figure of mystery and magic to many, and his legend grows every year.

The Palace Theatre went through several changes, including becoming a cinema and a bingo hall at one time (Woods-Lead 26). Sadly, it was demolished in 1999 and a parking lot now takes its place.

The Hodgson/Houdini confrontation remains a significant incident in the lives of both men. It enables us to see a side of Hodgson that we would have never known but for these newspaper reports. We can debate the actual facts that occurred that night. Was Hodgson as mean-spirited and despicable as Houdini claimed? Did Houdini escape fairly? It is impossible to know at this point. It is likely that there is a little bit of truth in both accounts. Hodgson possibly did alter the locks and Houdini may very likely have had assistance in his escape. It is unfair to both men to consider the other completely blameless in this affair. It was to the benefit of each man to claim a moral superiority. Certainly Houdini comes off better if he is the victim of a vicious, bitter man who cheated and was unfair. Hodgson would suffer embarrassment and shame in his community if he appeared to be anything other than an "honest Englishman" who was cheated of his victory by an "underhanded American." Each man had reasons to cast shadows on the other.

When we examine the Blackburn challenge, we find two men who are intent upon winning. The stakes are high for each and, eventually, Houdini comes out on top as he parlays the escape into part of his personal mythology. Beaten, Hodgson eventually loses his school and becomes a writer and never challenges Houdini again, even though the magician appears several times in Blackburn and environs. Hodgson has left that part of his life behind and is concerned with his writing. If Houdini had been beaten, who knows what would have happened to Hodgson? Would he have continued to run his school and never write the many masterpieces he penned in later years? In some strange way, could we consider that Hodgson escaped that night as well? Escaped to become the masterful writer that he needed to be and that we all remember.

(The author wishes to acknowledge appreciation to Roger Woods, who supplied the Hodgson portion of his book, *Houdini the Myth-Maker: The Unmasking of Harry Houdini*. This excellent volume provided a great deal of information and was instrumental in the writing of this article.)

Works Cited

Bell, Ian, ed. *William Hope Hodgson: Voyages and Visions*. Oxford, UK: I. Bell & Sons, 1987.

Brandon, Ruth. *The Life and Many Deaths of Harry Houdini*. New York: Random House, 1993.

Hodgson, William Hope. *Demons of the Sea*. Ed. Sam Gafford. West Warwick, RI: Necronomicon Press, 1995.

———. *Out of the Storm: Uncollected Fantasies*. Ed. Sam Moskowitz. West Kingston, RI: Donald M. Grant, 1975.

———. *The Uncollected William Hope Hodgson*. Ed. Sam Gafford. Bristol, RI: Hobgoblin Press, 1992–95. 2 vols.

———. *The Wandering Soul: Glimpses of a Life: A Compendium of Rare and Unpublished Works by William Hope Hodgson*. Ed. Jane Frank. Harrogate, UK: PS Publishing/Tartarus Press, 2005.

Kalush, William, and Larry Sloman. *The Secret Life of Houdini: The Making of America's First Superhero*. New York: Atria, 2006.

Silverman, Kenneth. *HOUDINI!!! The Career of Ehrich Weiss*. New York: HarperCollins, 1996.

Woods, Roger, and Brian Lead. *Houdini the Myth-Maker: The Unmasking of Harry Houdini*. N.p.: Leads & Woods, 1987.

Newspaper Sources:

Blackburn Standard
"Announcement," October 18, 1902.
"The Handcuff King," October 25, 1902.

Daily Star
"Manacled by a Strong Man," October 25, 1902.

Northern Daily Telegraph
"The 'Handcuff King' at Blackburn," October 21, 1902.
"Challenge to the Handcuff King," October 24, 1902.

William Hope Hodgson: In His Own Day

A. Langley Searles

The scanty amount of critical and descriptive material which has appeared in this country on William Hope Hodgson and his writings, together with the lamentable scarcity of his published works, both here and in England, have resulted in a general impression of the matter which is not altogether in keeping with the facts. Hodgson has been variously classed as a forgotten genius and a writer of no moment; the truth of the matter obviously lies somewhere between these extremes, and it is my intention in mentioning the subject to give a clear account of what is known about this author and a definitive critique of his extant writings. In this, the first of two planned articles, I shall deal solely with Hodgson's place in the literary world as seen by his own generation; I hope in a second to evaluate his work as it appears today, some three decades later.

The best method for appraisal of the literary opinion coeval with the author appears to be consultation of reviews of his works then current. One may generalize, first, by stating that the tone of all of these is distinctly favorable; in fact, I have yet to find one which is moderately critical of Hodgson's productions. To particularize, I have chosen for quotation a series of reviews that appeared in the English literary publication the *Bookman*. The general tone of this magazine may be described by comparing it to our own *Saturday Review of Literature*, although it was far more pretentious, both in scope and format, than the latter periodical. But like it, the *Bookman* clearly and accurately mirrored the literary trends of its day, and was noted for its fair and unbiased critical opinions. These latter may, therefore, be given the weight of authority.

It is typical of its caution that neither of Hodgson's first two novels received the *Bookman*'s reviews. That they were known and evaluated, however, is obvious from the context of the review of *The Ghost Pirates*, which was published in the October 1909 number (vol. 37, p. 54):

> There can be no need to call to memory two such remarkable works as Mr. Hodgson's *Boats of the "Glen Carrig"* and *The House on the Borderland*. They are books of the kind that, once read, cannot be easily forgotten. *The Ghost Pi-*

rates forms the last volume of the trilogy, for, as the author points out, "though very different in scope, each of the three books deals with certain conceptions that have an elemental kinship." The next sentence in his preface is a disappointment to us: "With this book, the author believes that he closes the door, so far as he is concerned, on a particular phase of constructive thought." We can only hope that Mr. Hodgson may be induced to reconsider his decision, for we know of nothing like the author's previous work in the whole of present-day literature. There is no one at present writing who can thrill and horrify to quite the same effect. *The Ghost Pirates* does not display Mr. Hodgson's wonderful qualities of imagination to such good effect as did *The House on the Borderland,* nor is it so terrifying a book to read. Nevertheless, it is a very remarkable story, told in a matter-of-fact manner that materially increases his "grip." The author particularly excels in the creation of "atmosphere," but he is also possessed of a vigorous style and a wonderful ingenuity in the concoction of terrifying detail. Mr. Hodgson has his faults; his exaggerated treatment of the Cockney dialect of one of the minor characters is unsatisfactory, and his punctuation is annoying. But when all is said *The Ghost Pirates* is a book of high literary qualities and a worthy member of a memorable trilogy.

Let the reader reflect for a moment on Mr. Hodgson's competitors in the field of imaginative writing. Though such literary giants as Arthur Machen and M. P. Shiel, tramping behind, were not receiving the praise that was to be their due in coming years, he still had to compete with two recognized masters: Algernon Blackwood and Montague Rhodes James. The former's fantasy *Jimbo* was being published in the same year (1909), and the proceeding three years had witnessed the appearance of a trio of that master's works—*The Empty House, The Listener, John Silence*—that definitely established Blackwood's reputation. And with the publication of his initial collection *Ghost-Stories of an Antiquary* (1904) M. R. James had but recently gained a following as a writer of the supernatural that he has not lost to this very day. Arthur C. Benson's *Hill of Trouble* (1903) was still being read and reprinted, as was Robert Hugh Benson's equally worthy collection of supernatural happenings *A Mirror of Shalott* (1907). The fact that he could gain recognition in the face of such opposition speaks volumes in itself for Hodgson's abilities as an exponent of the outré.

The next three years were not idle ones for him. His reputation made, he occupied himself with the production of several smaller works which were eagerly sought after by British magazines, and some of which were to appear abroad in American periodicals, as well as to be collected in book form at a still more advanced date. It was in this period, too, that that literary gargantua, nearly 200,000 words in length, *The Night Land* was completed. With its publication (in 1912) the author received but slightly qualified praise from all quarters. "It cannot be denied that *The Night Land* is a wonderful effort," said the *Manchester Courier*. The *Pall Mall Gazette* called the work "an extraordinary love tale" and added that the author was "gifted with a strong imagination." "A remarkably fine piece of narrative . . . a *tour de force*," stated the *Morning Leader*. Said *Vanity Fair*:

> The book is in every sense remarkable. . . . The style in which it is written, the theme of which it treats, and the eerie imaginative quality which abounds in it are all exceedingly rare and fascinating, so that when once it has been taken up one cannot leave it for any length of time.

Country Life, the *Morning Post*, and the *Occult Review* were other periodicals, all of which spoke in complimentary terms of the novel. The *Bookman* likewise noted its appearance; I quote in full the review which appeared in its June 1912 number (vol. 42, p. 137):

> You may say that in *The Night Land* Mr. Hope Hodgson's reach exceeds his grasp, that his story in some of its details is obscure and difficult to follow, that he tells it in a quaint, archaic language that does not make for easy reading, but at least you cannot say that he has not aimed at doing a big thing. He has set himself to unfold a love tale that is not bounded by the limits of a lifetime, but continues and is renewed again at last in a strange dream-life after many centuries. His hero is a man of two hundred years ago who loses a woman he loves not long after she is married to him; in utter grief and despair all his thoughts go yearning after her—they carry him far on down the ages yet to be, and he seeks her and cries out for her through new and newer planes of existence until, at length, in a miraculous trance state he finds himself at the close of some million of years living in the latter days of the world when the powers of evil have grown so potent, so aggressive, so almost all-conquering that the survivors of the human race are gathered for self-defence into one enormous pyramid, building their city tier above tier within it, and on every hand all around this Last Redoubt stretches the Night Land, inhabited by primeval, material giants and loathsome monsters and sinister dreadful immaterial beings of the spirit world that have power over the souls of mortals. Here, in this place of refuge, that man of two hundred years ago is continually sending his eager thoughts out across the grim wastes of the Night Land in search of the woman he loved and lost; and a time comes when out of the vast and unknown darkness her thoughts answer him, and after some broken fashion they are able to communicate with each other. Suddenly this communication fails; he tries in vain to renew it; and fearful that she may have set out across that fiend-haunted dayless wilderness to find him, he takes all due precautions, arms and fits himself for his enterprise, quits the shelter of the Pyramid and begins to make his way in the direction whence he believes she may be coming. From this point onwards the story grows rapidly

in power and interest. Whatever Mr. Hodgson lacks it is not imagination, and his description of that fearsome journey by trackless ways and through perils undreamt of before, and of the meeting of the two lovers, and the adventures, by turns grim, terrible, charmingly idyllic, through which they passed together give him scope for painting some of the most eerie, wildly horrible and pleasantly dainty pictures that have ever come from his pen. We shall not attempt to give any full outline of Mr. Hodgson's romance; it runs to nearly six hundred pages and is crowded with incident and alive with inner significances and undercurrents of meaning. You may read it as a cloudy and elusive allegory, if you have a liking for that form of literature, but in its allegorical aspect it is not simple enough, it needs too much explaining, and you will do better perhaps to read it simply as a daring imaginative love story, and as such you will find it a very original and sufficiently remarkable book.

This, then, is indicative of the reception *The Night Land* met with on its publication. A brief glance at the literary scene of the time shows that in no sense could an imaginative story of the future be lauded on the basis of its theme alone; H. G. Wells had produced *The Sleeper Awakes* just before the turn of the century, and had, in fact, published it anew in a revised version but a year before (1911). Nor was Wells, of course, the sole exponent of the novel of the future—many works upon such a theme had already appeared before that master had set his hand to it. Still, reviewers remembered his works, and stories of the future were frequently compared with *The Sleeper Awakes, A Story of the Days to Come,* and *The Time Machine,* as well as Bellamy's *Looking Backward* and a few other lesser-known excursions into futurity. Again it is seen that Hodgson must have possessed something more than an active imagination to impress leading literary periodicals of his day.

In 1910 Hodgson for the first time presented the book-reading public with a selection of his short stories. *Carnacki the Ghost-Finder* was its title, and it proved popular enough to be reprinted within a year. The author had laid the groundwork by the publication, in this country, of *Carnacki, the Ghost-Finder, and a Poem* (1910), a small board-bound brochure which gave rough synopses of those episodes which were thoroughly treated in the larger volume. On the whole, reviewers reacted even more favorably to *Carnacki* than had they to the author's previous writings. The *Westminster Gazette* dubbed it "A collection of admirable ghost stories"; the *British Weekly* complimented Hodgson's ability by calling it "a book of thrills which should not, perhaps, be taken up by nervous readers too late in the evening"; "There is not one of this collection of ghostly episodes which does not grip with its weird fascination," remarked the *Globe.* Said the *Daily Express:* "Some ghosts are real, some are not, but from both kinds Mr. Hodgson . . . gets a maximum of blood-curdling thrills. Better stories of haunted houses have not been told in our day . . ."

For a more complete account, the *Bookman* may be once more referred to; in its June 1913 issue (vol. 44, p. 142) there appeared this:

> Mr. Hope Hodgson's new novel comprises half-a-dozen of the "creepiest" experiences imaginable. Carnacki, the hero or victim of these experiences, narrates them to a privileged circle of friends with an artistic sense of cumulative horror calculated to create the sensation known as gooseflesh in your veriest skeptic. Whether you believe in ghosts or not, you are sure to find something to your taste in Carnacki's thrilling reports of his investigations; for in some cases the mysterious forces at work prove to be merely ingeniously contrived tricks of human origin, while in other cases strange and horrific Beings take threatening shape and have to be dealt with according to the laws of supernatural "science." Read after nightfall in a dimly lighted room peopled with uneasy shadows, those tales carry with them a haunting atmosphere of terror and an ever-present sense of the unknown powers of darkness. Take for example the phenomenon of "The Whistling Room" in an old Irish castle. The room at nights was wont to give out a weird whistling sound "like a monster with a man's soul." Carnacki climbing in by moonlight to the window from the outside looks in. "And then, you know, I saw something. The floor in the middle of the huge, empty room, was puckered upwards in the centre into a strange, soft-looking mound, parted at the top into an everchanging hole, that pulsated to that great, gentle hooning. . . . And suddenly, as I stared, dumb, it came to me that the thing was living. I was looking at two enormous, blackened lips, blistered and brutal, there in the pale moonlight . . ." Mr. Hope Hodgson plays deftly on the strings of fear, and his new novel stamps him a fascinating panic-monger with a quick eye for all the sensational possibilities of ghost lore.

Again let it be borne in mind that such a complimentary review involves a tacitly favorably comparison of Hodgson's ghost stories with not only those mentioned earlier in this article, but with M. R. James' second collection *More Ghost Stories of an Antiquary* (1911)—which, incidentally, contains that master's finest work—and with Blackwood's *Lost Valley* (1910), as well as the sterling work of three newcomers to the field, F. Marion Crawford, represented by *Wandering Ghosts* (1911), Oliver Onions's *Widdershins* (1911), and E. F. Benson, whose *Room in the Tower* (1912) had appeared in the following year. And yet, coming on the heels of these notables, Hodgson was actually characterized by the *Liverpool Courier* as "probably our best writer of Ghost stories, whether he finds them afloat or ashore . . ."

In 1914 a second collection of short stories put in its appearance. It was titled *Men of the Deep Waters*, and consisted of tales which had mostly been printed previously in magazine form. The London *Times* termed it "a serious contribution to literature" and further remarked, "Its quality is excellent . . ."

"In these stories of the sea Mr. Hodgson worthily maintains a well-won reputation of strength in the qualities of imagination, mystic beauty and spiritual force," was the opinion of the Glasgow *Herald*; and the *Liverpool Courier* said: "Mr. Hodgson is a writer on whom the mantle of Poe has fallen." Complimentary indeed! And no less so was the *Bookman*; in the November 1914 number of that periodical (vol. 47, p. 54) this review is to be found:

> Mr. Hodgson has not gone to work in the orthodox way and put his best stories first in this book; but that is not the only sense in which he is unorthodox. "On the Bridge" is a very vivid sketch—a brilliant bit of imaginative realism, and "The Sea Horses," which has second place, is a story of no little charm, though the sentiment is now and then in need of a restraining touch; it is when you come to "The Derelict" and "From the Tideless Sea" that you find Mr. Hodgson right at home, where he belongs; these, with "The Voice in the Night," "Through the Vortex of a Cyclone," and "The Mystery of the Derelict," are stories that, in their kind, would add something to the reputation of any living novelist. They grip you, as Poe's grim stories do, by their subtle artistry and sheer imaginative power. In fashioning his most uncanny, most supernormal occurrences his imagination so completely realises them that he describes them, and what has led up to them, and all their environment with a minuteness in detail that makes them convincingly real to a reader's apprehension. The fury and terror of storm at sea has never been more impressively pictured than it is in Mr. Hodgson's wonderful description of how the four-masted bark, *Golconda*, was drawn into the mighty vortex of a cyclone; and of the mystery, the perils, the loneliness of the sea, the almost unthinkable horrors that lurk waiting for the castaway in its unknown places, we have read few stories equal to the others named. No lover of tales of mystery and imagination that are also good literature should miss this book.

William Hope Hodgson followed this volume with a third collection of his shorter works, *The Luck of the Strong*, two years later. It was as favorably received as his first. Said the *Daily Telegraph*: "Mr. Hodgson more than once has been paid the compliment of being likened to Poe. It is not a compliment carelessly paid. Among it all there is not a dull paragraph." And the *Bookman* rated the book as favorably; in its August 1916 issue (vol. 50, p. 142) the following account of it appeared:

> "Rum things! Of course there were rum things happen at sea—as rum as ever there were. I remember when . . ." This alluring introduction to what perhaps is the best yarn in the book might have served equally well as an opening formula for the rest of the thrilling sea stories that make up the greater part of this entertaining volume of "rum things." Mr. Hope Hodgson is certainly an expert raconteur of "rum things," whether of the sea or the

land. He is an adept in the art of giving you the "creeps", and he sees to it that you extract the last ounce of fearful delight from the thrill before he lets you down with a comfortable explanation. In "The Stone Ship," an excellent example of the author's skill, the crew of a windjammer, becalmed on a misty night a thousand miles from the nearest land, are astounded to hear the sound of a brook running down a hillside! Next, they become aware of a frightful stench and a strange, fitful glow; and the mystery culminates in the discovery of a ship built wholly of stone, manned by a stone crew, and to all appearances floating on the Atlantic in the defiance of the laws of buoyancy. And the explanation, while destroying none of the glamour of the mystery, is remarkably concise and satisfying. Hidden gold and rare sea monsters play important parts in many of the stories. In Captain Jat's quest for the island pearls, a mammoth man-eating crab figures prominently, while one of the biggest thrills in "The Stone Ship" is afforded by a giant sea-caterpillar. Another story tells of the ingenious ruse whereby Captain Gunbolt Charity smuggled "The Painted Lady" into the U. S. A. Ingenious too is the explanation of the ghostly ringing of the bell on the derelict *Laughing Sally*—a story noteworthy also for its amusing sketch of Dot-and-Carry-One Cargunka, ship owner and saloon keeper. The author spins his yarns cleverly and neatly, has a crisp, racy style, and a bold imagination with a flair for the macabre and horrific that will always appeal to a wide public.

Hodgson followed *The Luck of the Strong* with yet a fourth collection of short stories, *Captain Gault*. In this latter volume, however, he abandoned the supernatural theme entirely, and therefore a detailed discussion of this work is outside of the scope of this article. It may be noted in passing, however, that this venture into the realm of playful romance and detective-work proved, in the eyes of literary periodicals then current, as successful as his earlier attempts in the field of fantasy and the supernatural. The influence of the sea is still patent in this work, as might be guessed from inspection of its title.

Besides his prose works, Hodgson had, over a period of the decade preceding his death, dabbled frequently in poetry. Examples of his poems had appeared in his other books as prefatory and epilogic additions, as well as in the three American-published works: *Cargunka, and Poems and Anecdotes*; *Carnacki, the Ghost-Finder, and a Poem*; and "Poems" and "A Dream of X." The collected editions of his poetry appeared under the titles *The Calling of the Sea* (1920) and *The Voice of the Ocean* (1921). The influence of the author's years spent on shipboard on this phase of his work is patent throughout. Closer consideration of these two volumes is likewise beyond the pale of this discussion, but it may be mentioned that the former received a reasonably favorable review in the *Bookman* in which Hodgson was referred to as "a true poet as he is a true novelist of the sea."

Pioneering Essays

H. P. Lovecraft: "The Weird Work of William Hope Hodgson"

Mr. H. C. Koenig has conferred a great service on American "fandom" by calling attention to the remarkable work of an author relatively unknown in this country, yet actually forming one of the few who have captured the illusive inmost essence of the weird. Among connoisseurs of phantasy fiction William Hope Hodgson deserves a high and prominent rank; for, triumphing over a sadly uneven stylistic quality, he now and then equals the best masters in his vague suggestions of lurking worlds and beings behind the ordinary surface of life.

Despite a tendency toward conventionally sentimental conceptions of the universe, and of man's relation to it and to his fellows, Mr. Hodgson is perhaps second only to Algernon Blackwood in his serious treatment of unreality. Few can equal him in adumbrating the nearness of nameless forces and monstrous besieging entities through casual hints and significant details, or in conveying feelings of the spectral and the abnormal in connexion with regions or buildings.

In *The Boats of the "Glen Carrig"* (1907) we are shewn a variety of malign marvels and accursed unknown lands as encountered by the survivors of a sunken ship. The brooding menace in the earlier parts of the book is impossible to surpass, though a letdown in the direction of ordinary romance and adventure occurs toward the end. An inaccurate and pseudo-romantic attempt to reproduce eighteenth-century prose detracts from the general effect, but the really profound nautical erudition everywhere displayed is a compensating factor.

The House on the Borderland (1908)—perhaps the greatest of all Mr. Hodgson's works—tells of a lonely and evilly regarded house in Ireland which forms a focus for hideous other-world forces and sustains a siege by blasphemous hybrid anomalies from a hidden abyss below. The wanderings of the narrator's spirit through limitless light-years of cosmic space and kalpas of eternity, and its witnessing of the solar system's final destruction, constitute something almost unique in standard literature. And everywhere there is manifest the author's power to suggest vague, ambushed horrors in natural scenery. But for a few touches of commonplace sentimentality this book would be a classic of the first water.

[*The Ghost Pirates* (1909), regarded by Mr. Hodgson as rounding out a trilogy with the two previously mentioned works, is a powerful account of a doomed and haunted ship on its last voyage, and of the terrible sea-devils (of quasi-human aspect, and perhaps the spirits of bygone buccaneers) that besiege it and finally drag it down to an unknown fate. With its command of maritime knowledge, and its clever selection of hints and incidents suggestive of latent horrors in Nature, this book at times reaches enviable peaks of power.][1]

The Night Land (1912) is a long-extended (538 pp.) tale of the earth's infinite future—billions of billions of years ahead, after the death of the sun. It is told in a rather clumsy fashion, as the dreams of a man in the seventeenth century, whose mind merges with its own future incarnation; and is seriously marred by painful verboseness, repetitiousness, artificial and nauseously sticky romantic sentimentality, and an attempt at archaic language even more grotesque and absurd than that in "*Glen Carrig*".

Allowing for all its faults, it is yet one of the most potent pieces of macabre imagination ever written, and it is said to have been the author's favourite among his works. The picture of a night-black, dead planet, with the remains of the human race concentrated in a stupendously vast metal pyramid and besieged by monstrous, hybrid, and altogether unknown forces of the darkness, is something that no reader can ever forget. Shapes and entities of an altogether non-human and inconceivable sort—the prowlers of the black, man-forsaken world outside the pyramid—are *suggested* and *partly* described with ineffable potency; while the night-bound landscape with its chasms and slopes and dying volcanism takes on an almost sentient terror beneath the author's touch.

Midway in the book the central figure ventures outside the pyramid on a quest through death-haunted realms untrod by man for millions of years—and in his slow, minutely described day-by-day progress over unthinkable leagues of immemorial blackness, there is a sense of cosmic alienage, breathless mystery, and terrified expectancy unrivaled in the whole range of literature. The last quarter of the book drags woefully, but fails to spoil the tremendous power of the whole.

Mr. Hodgson's later volume, *Carnacki, the Ghost-Finder*, consists of several longish short stories published many years before in magazines. In quality it falls conspicuously below the level of the other books. We here find a more or less conventional stock figure of the "infallible detective" type—the progeny of M. Dupin and Sherlock Holmes, and the close kin of Algernon Blackwood's

---

1. This paragraph was added in "Supernatural Horror in Literature."

John Silence—moving through scenes and events badly marred by an atmosphere of professional "occultism." A few of the episodes, however, are of undeniable power; and afford glimpses of the peculiar genius characteristic of the author.

Clark Ashton Smith: "In Appreciation of William Hope Hodgson"

Among those fiction writers who have elected to deal with the shadowlands and borderlands of human existence, William Hope Hodgson surely merits a place with the very few that inform their treatment of such themes with a sense of authenticity. His writing itself, as Mr. Lovecraft justly says, is far from equal in stylistic merit: but it would be impossible to withhold the rank of master from an author who has achieved so authoritatively, in volume after volume, a quality that one might term the realism of the unreal. In some ways, Hodgson's work is no doubt most readily comparable to that of Algernon Blackwood. But I am not sure that even Blackwood has managed to intimate a feeling of such profound and pervasive familiarity with the occult as one finds in *The House on the Borderland*. Hideous phantoms and unknown monsters from the nightward gulf are adumbrated in all their terror, with no dispelling of their native mystery; and surely such things could be described only by a seer who has dwelt overlong on the perilous verges and has peered too deeply into the regions veiled by invisibility from normal sight.

However, *The House on the Borderland,* though probably the most sustained and least faulty of Hodgson's volumes, is far from being his most unique achievement. In all literature, there are few works so sheerly remarkable, so purely creative, as *The Night Land*. Whatever faults this book may possess, however inordinate its length may seem, it impresses the reader as being the ultimate saga of a perishing cosmos, the last epic of a world beleaguered by eternal night and by the unvisageable spawn of darkness. Only a great poet could have conceived and written this story; and it is perhaps not illegitimate to wonder how much of actual prophecy may have been mingled with the poesy.

The books above mentioned are, in my opinion, Mr. Hodgson's masterpieces. However, the first portion of *The Boats of the "Glen Carrig"* maintains a comparable level of imaginative power; and one regrets that the lost mariners should have escaped so soon from the malign and mysterious dimension into which they were carried. One must also accord a more than formal praise to *The Ghost Pirates*, which is really one of the few successful long stories dealing with the phantasmal. Its rout of ghastly and persistent specters will follow the reader long after they have seized the haunted ship!

It is to be hoped that work of such unusual power will eventually win the attention and fame to which it is entitled. Beyond doubt, accident and fatality play a large part in such matters; and many meritorious books and works of art are still shadowed in obscurity. Hodgson, though little known, is in good company. How many, even among fantasy lovers, have heard of the great imaginative artist, John Martin, or the equally great and macabre imaginative poet, Thomas Lovell Beddoes?

H. C. Koenig: "William Hope Hodgson: Master of the Weird and Fantastic"

In 1931 Faber and Faber published an anthology of ghost stories under the title, *They Walk Again*. The tales were selected by Colin de la Mare. Most of the stories included in this splendid anthology were by well-known writers such as Blackwood, Dunsany and Bierce. Many of them were familiar to the inveterate reader of ghost stories—"The Monkey's Paw", "Green Tea", and "The Ghost Ship." However, one new story was included in the book; one comparatively new name was included in the list of authors. The story was "The Voice in the Night", a horrifying and yet pathetic tale of human beings turned into fungoid growths; the author was William Hope Hodgson.

Who was William Hope Hodgson? I had a vague recollection of some short stories in old pulp magazines. I dimly remembered a book of short stories about a ghost detective. That was all. But it was sufficient to start me on the trail of one on the great masters of the weird story. Letters to various readers and collectors of fantasy in this country produced negligible results. Except for one or two of the older readers of weird stories, the name of Hodgson meant nothing.

I consulted Edith Birkhead's excellent study of the growth of supernatural fiction in English literature, *The Tale of Terror* (1921) in an effort to get some information about Hodgson and his writings. I found references to Pain, Jacobs, Le Fanu, Stoker, Marsh, Rohmer and a host of other writers of weird tales—but no mention of Hodgson. I searched through H. P. Lovecraft's informative essay "Supernatural Horror in Literature" (in its original form) without success. Hundreds of titles were covered. Among them I found "Seaton's Aunt", "The Smoking Leg", *The Dark Chamber*, "A Visitor from Down Under" and many other tales—familiar and unfamiliar. But not a single one of Hodgson's stories was discussed—or even mentioned. I paged through numerous anthologies—by Bohun Lynch, Dashiell Hammett, Dorothy Sayers, Montague Summers, T. Everett Harré and Harrison Dale—but the name of Hodgson was conspicuous in its absence. Then followed a period of time during which I traced him through innumerable bookstores in England. Percy Muir of Elkin Matthews, London, took an interest in my search and obtained several of Hodgson's first editions for me. He also put me in touch with Dennis Wheatley, the writer of English thrillers and an admirer and collector of

Hodgson. As a result of these contacts, I learned that Hodgson had written a number of stories which compared very favorably with any of our modern weird stories; tales which ranked high in the fantasy field and which deserved far more popularity and publicity than they had ever received.

Hodgson was the son of an Essex clergyman. He left home as a youngster and spent eight years at sea. During that time he voyaged around the world three times, visiting all sorts of places. Incidentally, he received the Royal Humane Society's medal for saving a life at sea. For some time before the World War he and his wife lived in the south of France. When war broke out he returned to England (at the age of 40) and was granted a commission in the 171st Brigade of Royal Field Artillery. Two years later, in 1917, he went to France with his battery and was soon in the thick of the fight; his brigade doing splendid work at Ypres. At the time the Germans made their great attack, in April, 1918, he with a few other brother officers and non-commissioned officers successfully stemmed the rush of an overwhelming number of the enemy. Shortly thereafter, Hodgson volunteered for the dangerous duty of observation office of the brigade. On his first missions, he was killed by a shell. And thus, a most promising literary career came to an abrupt ending.

I never could understand why his work was so little known to the general public. It was curious and unfortunate that he had become so engulfed in oblivion. And so, I started my campaign to obtain recognition for Hodgson in this country. For over ten years I have preached the gospel of William Hope Hodgson; by word of mouth, by letters and in articles. For years I have circulated my little collection of Hodgson's first editions all over the country. California to Rhode Island, Oregon to Florida, Wisconsin to South Carolina. To readers and writers and editors. Year after year I have kept up the campaign. Slowly but surely I began to get results. Hodgson's name began to appear in the amateur fantasy magazines. Requests for Hodgson's stories began to creep into the readers' columns of the professional magazines. And, requests for a loan of Hodgson books began to multiply. Then came the break for which I was waiting patiently. An appeal for Hodgson's stories came from Miss Gnaedinger of *Famous Fantastic Mysteries*. A copy of *The Ghost Pirates* and several short stories were soon in her hands. Then followed months of anxious waiting. Copyrights had to be settled. Mrs. Hodgson had to be located, a far from easy matter. A splendid cover, illustrating one of Hodgson's novels, and painted by Lawrence, was being held, pending the settlement of copyrights.

Unfortunately, due to the long period of delay, this illustration was never used in *Famous Fantastic Mysteries*. I had just about given up hope when Mrs. Hodgson was located and the copyright obstacles were removed. Then, in the December 1943 issue of *Famous Fantastic Mysteries*, Miss Gnaedinger published Hodgson's short story "The Derelict". This was followed by the novel *The Ghost Pirates* (cut by 10,000 words) in the March 1944 number.

I am extremely grateful to Miss Gnaedinger and her associates for taking the lead in reprinting some of Hodgson's stories. But I am not so easily satisfied. I will not rest content until I have seen every one of his books reprinted in some book or magazine in this country. Until that time comes, however, we will have to be content with those of his books which we are able to locate in the second-hand book shops. (It is not an easy matter.) A complete list of Hodgson's books may be of some assistance to the weird fan. For the benefit of the collector I am also giving the name of the publisher and the date of publications.

The Boats of the "Glen Carrig", a novel published by Chapman & Hall, 1907.
The House on the Borderland, a novel published by Chapman & Hall, 1908.
The Ghost Pirates, a novel published by Stanley Paul, 1909.
The Night Land, a novel published by Eveleigh Nash, 1912.
Carnacki, the Ghost-Finder, short stories, published by Eveleigh Nash, 1913.
Men of the Deep Waters, short stories, copyrighted in U.S.A., 1906, first English edition published by Eveleigh Nash, 1914.
The Luck of the Strong, short stories, copyrighted in the U.S.A., 1912, first published by Eveleigh Nash in England, 1916.
Captain Gault, short stories, copyrighted in the U.S.A., 1914, first English edition published by Eveleigh Nash, 1917.
The Voice of the Ocean, poems, published by Selwyn & Blount, 1921.
The Calling of the Sea, poems, published by Selwyn & Blount, no date.

As indicated earlier in this article, one of his short stories, "The Voice in the Night", will be found in Colin de la Mare's collection of ghost stories *They Walk Again*, published by Faber and Faber in 1931. And Dennis Wheatley included three of Hodgson's short stories in his splendid collection of horror tales, *A Century of Horror Stories*, published by Hutchinson & Co. The titles were "The Island of the Ud" from *The Luck of the Strong*; "The Whistling Room" from *Carnacki, the Ghost-Finder*; and "The Derelict" from *Men of the Deep Waters*.

The first three books listed above in the short bibliography form (in Hodgson's words) "what perhaps may be termed a trilogy; for though very different in scope, each of the three books deals with certain conceptions that have an elemental kinship." A few chapter headings will give some idea of the treat in store for fantasy fans fortunate enough to locate these three books—"The Thing that Made Search", "The Island in the Weed", "The Noise in the Valley", "The Weed Men", "The Thing in the Pit", "The Swine Things", etc.

The Night Land is one of the longest fantastic romances ever written, running close to six hundred pages. It is a story of the world in the future when the sun has died and the "Last Millions" are living in a large redoubt, a huge pyramid of gray metal nearly eight miles high and five miles around the base. Beyond the pyramid were mighty races of terrible creatures, half-beast and half-man, night hounds, monstrous slugs and other horrible monsters. As a protection against all these evils a great electric circle was put about the pyramid and lit from the Earth Current. It bounded the pyramid for a mile on each side and none of the monsters were able to cross it due to a subtle vibration which affected their brains.

Carnacki, the Ghost-Finder is a series of six short ghost stories in which Carnacki investigates ghostly phenomena in various homes. One or two of the tales are somewhat weakened by a natural explanation of the ghosts, but each of the stories is well worth reading.

Hodgson's tales may well have served as source books for many of the stories now being read in our present day pulp magazines. The whole range of weird and fantastic plots appears to have been covered in his books—pig-men, elementals, human trees, ghosts, sea of weeds, thought-transference, intelligent slugs, and in *The Night Land* the men are equipped with a hand weapon called a Diskos. This consists of a disk of gray metal which spins in the end of a metal rod, is charged from earth currents and capable of cutting people in two.

To me, Hodgson will always be remembered as one of the great masters of the weird and fantastic. And I, for one, will always be grateful for the slim list of books he left behind him.

August Derleth: "William Hope Hodgson"

William Hope Hodgson is one of the most neglected men in the field of the mystic and weird. Certainly the *Famous Fantastic Mysteries* publication of Hodgson is a step in the right direction, even if the stories have been woefully cut in some cases. I think it is not far wrong if it is wrong at all to suggest that no one else has quite the same approach and effect as Hodgson, particularly in such novels as *The Night Land* and *The House on the Borderland*. He manages to convey an extra-sensory perception to his readers, and that is no small accomplishment. I am hoping to see published soon in this country an omnibus of the important Hodgson novels; if Arkham House does not do it, perhaps some other, first-line publisher can be persuaded to take such a book on. He deserves to be far better known among the aficionados, but manifestly out-of-print books across the sea give no comfort to the would-be reader and collector. Hodgson's sense of other worlds (decidedly not in the science-fiction tradition), his feeling for horror of the soul or spirit as apart from grue, his sometimes commonplace but always insidious manner of writing—all these aspects are distinctly his own, and it is all the more regrettable, this being so, that he has had no worthwhile publication in the U.S.

Ellery Queen: "William Hope Hodgson and the Detective Story"

Too few people in America are familiar with the work of William Hope Hodgson; and even this fortunate minority, who know Mr. Hodgson as a writer of weird and supernatural stories, have to be reminded that he also wrote two books in the detective-crime field.

One is *Captain Gault*—ten short stories about a modern smuggler. The other is *Carnacki the Ghost-Finder*—six short stories about a ghost-breaker: a unique detective who investigates haunted houses and similar phenomena.

Readers, writers, and students of supernatural fiction deplore the fact that at the end of five of the Carnacki stories, Carnacki produces a tangible, real-life explanation for the ghostly manifestations. For example, H. P. Lovecraft, one of the great modern masters of weird fiction, once expressed the opinion that the Carnacki stories were "weakened" by the realistic solutions. Well, one man's meat is truly another man's poison. To your Editor the sane, of-this-world explanations *strengthen* rather than weaken the stories. These *natural* elucidations, frowned on by devotees of the weird, must be applauded by devotees of the detective story; they transform Carnacki from a mere dabbler into the unknown to a legitimate and authentic detective.

But let's not quarrel over Carnacki. He's a 24-carat "find" both for lovers of the "invisible" and addicts of the "visible." Let's rejoice that EQMM can bring you one of Carnacki's strange and fascinating adventures which, to the best of your Editor's knowledge, is here printed for the first time in the United States.

Fritz Leiber: "William Hope Hodgson: Writer of Supernatural Horror"

William Hope Hodgson achieved his greatest success in a literary form which most masters of supernatural horror have avoided because of its exceptional difficulty—the weird story of book length. He did this without recourse to the stereotyped plot-elements of the Gothic novel (except for the love story which mars rather than embellishes *The Night Land*) or to the adventure or detective settings that modern authors have used to provide sufficient action to space out an eerie concept over some 75,000 words.

Undoubtedly the chief reason for his success in this field is the extreme, even naive, seriousness with which he went to work. He never succumbed to, perhaps never felt, the temptation to add facetious or whimsical touches in order to assure adult readers that he "did not really believe this stuff." Nor did he, for similar reasons, provide alternate scientific explanations or sophisticated psychological analyses of the spectral events he narrated. His novels are presented in the guise of actual documents, "found by so-and-so" or "as told by so-and-so," and are written, at a white heat of inspiration, in the directest possible way. Note, for example, the abrupt opening of *The Boats of the "Glen Carrig"*—"Now we had been five days in the boats, and in all this time made no discovery of land."—or of *The Ghost Pirates*—"He began without any circumlocution. 'I joined the *Mortzestus* in 'Frisco.'" This outstanding ability of Hodgson, to plunge into a dream world and stay there for a book-length sojourn, fits with his seriousness and lends to his tales a straightforward, desperate convincingness. He is never apologetic, never inclined to provide cushioning explanations, no matter how bizarre the concepts he introduces. (Such as those magnificent black landscapes looming with mountain-beast-idols—the "Watchers" of *The Night Land* and *The House on the Borderland*. It would be interesting to know the imaginative antecedents of those landscapes—perhaps an early interest in Egyptian and Babylonian, or Mayan, or Indian, architecture.)

Hodgson shows as much freedom from traditional patterns and editorial demands in his choice of subject-matter as in his plot-structure. He wrote before science-fiction had become a separate and widely-explored field, and, for example, did not hesitate to introduce into *The House on the Borderland* that chilling vision of Earth's future, made possible by time-acceleration, which anticipates the impressive vistas of Olaf Stapledon. To achieve the effects he desired, he combined supernatural terror, mystical speculations, and science-fiction, in a way peculiarly his own.

These various abilities enabled Hodgson to write such a novel as *The Ghost Pirates*, which to my mind fulfills at book length all the canons of the spectral tale laid down by Lovecraft, James, and others. It is painstakingly realistic—consider the earthy, pungent conversations of the sailors—except when touching on the central supernatural phenomenon. That phenomenon is unified and handled with adequate impressiveness. There is no "scientific" explanation to let you down. Nor is the story itself marred by romantic concessions—there is a steady progress toward doom, in which the suspense builds with an almost unparalleled uninterruptedness. (Incidentally, Sime's frontispiece for the book is magnificent and—oh, rare virtue!—magnificently faithful.)

II. Some Special Topics

William Hope Hodgson

Brian Stableford

William Hope Hodgson was born on 15 November 1877 in the Essex village of Blackmore End. His father, Samuel Hodgson, was a rather unorthodox Anglican clergyman, with whom he quarreled fiercely. The family was a large one—there were twelve children in all, although three died in infancy—and was always poor; it also moved around a great deal as Samuel Hodgson was continually posted to different parishes all over the British Isles. Hope, as he was optimistically called within the family, ran away from home and school on more than one occasion, and became determined to get away permanently by going to sea. He was eventually apprenticed as a cabin boy in 1891 and remained at sea for eight years, in spite of appalling conditions that made his early years aboard ship almost unbearable.

Because his family was in desperate straits following the death of his father in 1892, Hodgson was eventually forced to assume much of the burden of supporting his siblings. He studied for his "mate's papers" in Liverpool and received the qualification enabling him to serve as an officer in 1897. Having been bullied during his apprenticeship, he took up body-building and became physically powerful; he remained an enthusiastic propagandist for physical culture for the rest of his life. He also took up photography and achieved some notable successes in connection with that hobby, taking remarkable pictures of storms at sea.

His return to the sea did not last long; by 1899 he had had enough of that life and turned to his other skills in search of a means of support. He opened a School of Physical Culture in Blackburn, in Lancashire, but it never became commercially successful. He had always been an avid reader, especially of fantastic material, and an early fascination with the supernatural had partially given way to an enthusiasm for scientific romance. In the early 1900s, therefore, he began to investigate the possibilities offered by the popular magazines. He launched his new venture by writing articles, illustrated by his own photographs, for a magazine of physical culture, but rapidly moved on to the general periodicals. He joined the Society of Authors and became an enthusiastic member, often contributing to its journal, the *Author*. Although he lived a long way from the literary world of London, he began corresponding with other writers, including H. G. Wells.

Hodgson's early fiction sales included a far-fetched murder story, "The Goddess of Death" (1904), for Arthur Pearson's *Royal Magazine*, and a sea-serpent story, "A Tropical Horror" (1905). He was initially more successful, though, with his articles about the sea, and he began giving lectures built around the photographs that he had taken aboard ship. It was for the American *Monthly Story Magazine*—later retitled *Blue Book*—that he started writing fantastic stories in some quantity. His first story published there was "From the Tideless Sea" (1906), a story of life aboard a ship trapped in the floating weed of the Sargasso Sea, which is menaced by various creatures of the deep, including giant octopodes. The story was reprinted in Alfred Harmsworth's *London Magazine* in 1907.

"From the Tideless Sea" established a template that Hodgson was to reemploy in many later stories. He did more than any other writer to popularize the myth of the Sargasso Sea: a mid-Atlantic region clogged with weed, where sailing ships could be trapped permanently. The idea was not introduced into popular fiction by Hodgson—Thomas A. Janvier's novel *In the Sargasso Sea* had appeared in 1898, and Jules Rengade's *Voyage sous les flots* (as by "Aristide Roger"; tr. as *Voyage Beneath the Waves*) had featured it in an early Vernian pastiche in 1867—but Hodgson was the writer who developed the legend into its most engagingly fantastic form. The first story was followed up by a sequel, "More News from the *Homebird*" (1907; retitled "The Fifth Message from the Tideless Sea" for English publication in 1911), and by an unconnected but very similar story, "The Mystery of the Derelict" (1907).

All these stories are essentially accounts of hauntings, but not by ghosts: the monstrous things that lurk in the damp darkness on and around these stricken ships are living creatures, exaggerated in size and ferocity far beyond their natural counterparts. "More News from the *Homebird*" features giant crabs, "The Mystery of the Derelict" giant rats. In these early stories, Hodgson was simply ringing the changes, after the fashion of writers connected with an earlier boom in Victorian ghost stories that had suffered something of a resurgence in the new periodicals, but his imaginative range soon expanded very considerably.

Hodgson's enthusiasm for physical culture seems to have been correlated, not unusually, with a preoccupation with hygiene. Certainly, the psychology of his horror stories is based very strongly in anxieties about personal pollution. Attention is frequently called in his stories to noxious odors and to the discomfiting presence of slimy substances. That aspect of his work is particularly clear in three works published in the latter part of 1907. In "The Terror of the Water-Tank" a series of puzzling deaths turns out to be due to a ribbon-like monster that emerges periodically from a filthy water tank. "The Voice in the Night"—which became Hodgson's most famous short story—is a strange traveler's tale of a castaway and his wife forced by hunger to eat a strange addictive fungus, whose appearance and texture their own flesh gradually acquires.

In between those two short stories Hodgson published his first novel, *The Boats of the "Glen Carrig."* The story is yet another account of the adventures of a group of castaways, written in a mock-archaic style supposedly reflective of the antiquity of their exile. When the *Glen Carrig* is wrecked, the survivors drift for some time through weed-choked waters. The first land they reach appears to have no animal life, although the plants crowding it seem to have animal forms embedded in their flesh. Even human faces can be found, perhaps those of people absorbed by the plants. The plants attack the castaways, and scream and bleed when their attack is repelled.

That section was presumably intended originally as a short story, but Hodgson elected to continue it to novel length. Having left the first island, the shipwrecked sailors drift on through the Sargasso, encountering derelict ships, giant crabs, octopodes, and a beaked humanoid face. Eventually, they come upon a second island, which proves to be the home of the beaked creatures: "Weed Men" reminiscent of "human slugs" with slimy bodies and tentacles instead of fingers. Another ship has run aground off the island long before and has been fortified against the Weed Men; the men of the *Glen Carrig* succeed in reaching it before their final climactic battle with the monstrous creatures.

The Boats of the "Glen Carrig" is primarily an exercise in teratology, made highly effective by the careful combination of the realistic details derived from Hodgson's own experiences at sea and the horrific *frissons* connected with the mingling of human and animal characteristics. Tales of wolf-men and ape-men were already commonplace in fantastic fiction, but slug-men were something new; man-eating trees were also familiar, but not man-*absorbing* trees.

Hodgson was now enthusiastic to become a novelist, and also to develop his ideas much more elaborately. In his next short stories of the sea he abandoned teratology in favor of a peculiar mysticism. In "The *Shamraken* Homeward-Bounder" (1908) he made elaborate use of his experience of the meteorological phenomena associated with cyclones to color an eerie story about a ship whose crew sense that the Day of Judgment is at hand. In "Out of the Storm" (1909) a man aboard another ship that is doomed to sink feels that the world he is in has been deserted by God and that the sea itself is a monstrous cruel force whose dominion is absolute. Hodgson's creative efforts in those years were, however, almost wholly devoted to novel-length stories that display a much less conventional mysticism. The next ones to be published, although they were probably not the first to be written following the stitching together of *The Boats of the "Glen Carrig,"* were *The House on the Borderland* (1908) and *The Ghost Pirates* (1909).

The story told in *The House on the Borderland* mostly consists of a manuscript purportedly found by two tourists in the west of Ireland, discovered in the ruins of an almost-obliterated structure on the brink of a great chasm beneath a waterfall. It turns out to be an account of the visionary experiences of a man who lived in the building when it was whole, with his sister and his dog. Part of the story deals with the writer's attempts to protect himself and his companions from the effects of forces of decay associated with swine-like humanoid creatures that invade his environment from below. In the end, though, he is infected by the decay in question by the dog, which has been in contact with the swine-things.

The story also includes several visionary sequences. In the first of them, the writer describes a vast and desolate plain surrounded by high mountains, where there is a transfigured version of his house and the chasm it overlooks. Behind the mountains the apparitions of ancient gods, including Kali and Set, appear; the swine-things appear to be avatars of a member of this evil pantheon. Other visions carry the writer to a more peaceful place, the Sea of Sleep, where he can renew contact with a long-lost loved one, but one of these episodes gives way to a sensation of accelerating time, which seems to hurtle him into the distant future.

Although the house itself remains inviolate within this vision, all the things in it crumble to dust and the Earth dies too as the sun fades and cools. The disembodied writer retains his consciousness, however, and watches the house taken over by the swine-things before being consumed by a pillar of flame. The solar system collapses and falls into a giant Green Sun, from which white globes then emerge, transporting the writer with joy to the Sea of Sleep and a reunion with his beloved. Then a Dark Sun appears to separate the lovers again, and more globes emerge from a dark nebula, this time infused with sorrow and anguish; one of them engulfs the writer and returns him to the plain of his earlier vision. Entering the house there, he is finally brought back to its "real" counterpart. It is after this episode that the "infection" from without is brought into the house to destroy him.

This story seems to be a radical break from Hodgson's previous work, although he was later to suggest that it ought to be viewed as the centerpiece of a trilogy begun and ended with the much more conventional novels that preceded and succeeded it. It also seems to be radically different from previous generic scientific romances, although its visionary element has strong affinities with Humphry Davy's *Consolations in Travel* as well as echoes of Edgar Allan Poe's visionary essay *Eureka* (1848).

Although the novel borrows imagery from Lord Kelvin in the same fashion as *The Time Machine*, offering a more detailed representation of the "meteoric hypothesis" favored by Kelvin as an explanation of the sun's heat, the cosmic vision is more allegorical than literal. As such, it is bleaker in its import than Davy's dream, envisaging no interplanetary path of progress toward any kind of perfection. The story's spatiotemporal sweep is even greater than that of *The Time Machine*, but Hodgson's purpose in doing that is not simply to push the genre's imaginative horizons further back; its allegory, although vague and uncertain, is as elaborate and as eccentric as that embodied in Shiel's *The Purple Cloud*.

Hodgson added an introduction to the novel in which he assumes the guise of editor in order to call attention to the allegory and suggest how it might be decoded:

> From a *seeming* 'fantasia' there grew, to reward my unbiased concentration, a cogent, coherent scheme of ideas that gripped my interest more securely than the mere bones of the *account* or *story*. . . . I found a greater story within the lesser—and the paradox is no paradox. . . .
>
> I cannot but look upon the account of the Celestial Globes as a striking illustration (how nearly had I said "proof"!) of the actuality of our thoughts and emotions among the Realities. For, without seeming to suggest the annihilation of the lasting reality of Matter, as the hub and framework of the Machine of Eternity, it enlightens one with conceptions of the existence of worlds of thought and emotion, working in conjunction with, and duly subject to, the scheme of material creation. (*House on the Borderland* 108)

The world into which Hodgson's writer is carried by his visions is a quasi-Platonic world of Ideas, where the innate moral order of the cosmos is displayed in a series of physical representations and transactions. The house is the home of consciousness—the psyche—which exists both in the mundane world and, in a more grandiose form, in the world of Ideas. The "two central suns of creation," the Green and the Dark, are neither Good and Evil, nor Life and Death, but rather Growth and Decay, the former associated with love and ecstasy and the latter with pain and anguish.

This redefinition of fundamental opposition is not so very different from Shiel's characterization of "the black and the white" that are at war in Adam Jeffson's soul, but in Shiel's evolutionary scheme both the black and the white are the instruments of progress; the forces of destruction, however one might regret the suffering they bring, are ultimately to be construed as positive. Hodgson, by contrast, embraces a deep pessimism. The oasis of consciousness is set in a bleak Plain of Silence, behind whose protective boundaries lurk the forces of Decay, symbolized by the malevolent gods of ancient pantheons—

Kali from the Hindu pantheon, Set from the Egyptian, and others.

Evil is here represented physically as swinishness, and in the mundane world it seeks to invade consciousness from below. It is opposed by affection, whose power is weakened by the dream-like quality of erotic passion, which tends to attach itself more to images than to real people. In the end, humankind, like every individual, is bound to be consumed by the forces of decay, and so are the Earth and the Sun; even the world of Ideas must suffer decrepitude and dereliction.

There is an obvious danger in attempting to psychoanalyze an author by means of complicated interpretations of his work, but, in connection with Hodgson's association of love with remote objects of memory rather than real individuals, certain other points might warrant mention. One of his early stories, "The Valley of Lost Children" (1906), is a sentimental story about an imaginary land where dead children are preserved, and tempts speculation as to whether, like J. M. Barrie, Hodgson had found himself competing on uneven terms for his mother's affection against his siblings who died in infancy.

Hodgson did not marry until five years after he published *The House on the Borderland*, and might well have had little experience of love in 1908. His devotion to physical culture suggests a determination to resist the ravages of bodily deterioration, but any such victory can only be temporary. All humans die, and the life and death of every individual can be seen as a microcosm of the *kalpa*—a term that Hodgson borrowed from Hindu metaphysics to describe the entire cosmogonic cycle that is witnessed by his visionary.

In this sense, Hodgson is in total opposition to Shiel; whereas Shiel saw individuals as being unimportant within the great scheme of things, the morality of matter being concerned only with the progress of the entire race, Hodgson took the individual as his measure of all things, the Moral Order of the universe reflecting the inevitable death of the individual in the ultimate victory of the archetypes of malevolence.

The explication of the "greater story within the lesser" in *The House on the Borderland* helps to illuminate some of the features of *The Ghost Pirates* that might otherwise seem puzzling. Hodgson's preface to the latter work, in which the claim is made that it concludes a trilogy begun with *The Boats of the "Glen Carrig"* and continued with *The House on the Borderland*, also contains the observation that "though very different in scope, each of the three books deals with certain conceptions that have an elemental kinship." The elemental kinship in question has not been obvious to commentators on Hodgson's work, but it does exist.

The Ghost Pirates is, like its predecessors, a tale of a Borderland separating but also linking two worlds. It is the most elaborate of Hodgson's tales of haunted ships, telling the story of the last voyage of the *Mortzestus*—the name has an obvious significance—which is first invaded by humanoid creatures that rise up out of the sea, and then sails out of the mundane world altogether, into a peculiar zone of separation. There, the narrator—who is telling his story to the captain of another vessel, having been picked up as the sole survivor of the disaster that ultimately overwhelms the *Mortzestus*—sees a fleet of ghost ships sailing in a "mirror world" beneath the reflective surface of the sea. Eventually, the humanoid denizens of that world swarm forth in force to slaughter the crew of the *Mortzestus*.

Although *The Ghost Pirates* is a relatively simple tale of parallel worlds, seemingly not too different from other such tales, Hodgson's deliberate association of it with *The House on the Borderland* suggests that the "other dimension" inhabited by the malevolent humanoids is to be given more significance. The monsters emerging from the "underside" of the sea are easy to associate with the swine-things that menace the house in the earlier novel. They are not simply nasty creatures, but embodiments of the forces of decay and destruction. The ship takes the same symbolic role here as the house in the earlier novel, and the sea the same role that it has in "Out of the Storm." Hodgson apparently intended this symbolism to extend retrospectively to the ships in *The Boats of the "Glen Carrig"* and, by implication, to all his other stories of vessels doomed to dereliction and destruction by their entrapment in slimy weed and their invasion by monstrous creatures.

Hodgson had begun his writing career as a relatively hard-headed professional, but the direction he had taken in 1908 had carried his writing far away from the world of the popular magazines. None of his novels was serialized, and it appears that none of them made a significant amount of money. In 1910, therefore, Hodgson made an evident conscious effort to change his policy, and to shape his work thereafter according to strictly commercial priorities. He became a prolific producer of short pieces, including numerous non-fantasy stories of life at sea.

For the *Idler* he produced a series of stories about Carnacki, a consulting detective specializing in supernatural visitations. Carnacki is clearly modeled on Algernon Blackwood's "psychic detective" John Silence, several of whose adventures had been assembled in an eponymous collection published in 1908. The Carnacki stories Hodgson published in 1910 are mediocre, but Hodgson wrote others that did not sell at the time. These did not appear in the book *Carnacki, the Ghost-Finder* that was published in 1913, but are in the similarly titled collection published by Mycroft & Moran in 1947. The last—and by far the best—of them, "The Hog," is an inter-dimensional fantasy clearly associated with the allegory of *The House on the Borderland*.

Some of the stories Hodgson churned out in this period, including "The Thing in the Weeds" (1912), are lackluster pastiches of his earlier sea-monster stories, but in the main, the short stories of 1910-12 were of a markedly different character from his early fantasies. Two of them—"The Island of the Ud" (1912) and its sequel, "The Adventure of the Headland" (1912)—seem to be attempts to write sea stories in the jocular vein of Cutcliffe Hyne's stories of Captain Kettle. In the same year, however, Hodgson published his final novel, which he had certainly begun and might well have completed several years before, and was not in the least commercial, in the composition of which he had permitted himself to be absolutely self-indulgent. This was *The Night Land* (1912), one of the most bizarre and eccentric fantastic novels ever produced.

The novels of the earlier trilogy are all set in the past. Both of the sea stories are set in the eighteenth century (although there are no dates in *The Ghost Pirates*, the fact is evident) and although the manuscript in *The House on the Borderland* is said to have been found in 1877, it was obviously composed much earlier, probably, once again, in the eighteenth century. Hodgson adopted a deliberately archaic style for all of them, and in *The Night Land* he took that affectation further. The story begins in an unspecified time, in an apparently medieval setting, and the narrator tells the story of his love affair with one Mirdath, whom he married after saving her from an attack by a mad dog, although she subsequently died, after giving birth to a child, thus condemning the narrator to "an utter and dreadful pain of longing" from which he is liberated only in sleep, when he experiences an astonishing vision of the distant future. In that dream, he and she can be mysteriously reunited, as the narrator puts it, "in the Womb of Time." The main body of the text—which is longer than the three earlier books put together—is an account of this far-futuristic vision.

Millions of years in the future, the last remnants of humankind live in the 1,320 cities contained in a single huge pyramid nearly eight miles high, called the Great Redoubt, or the Last Redoubt. The Fields producing food for the pyramid's population are deep underground, illuminated by courtesy of the Earth-Current, which appears to draw energy from the planet's core. The humans of the pyramid are physically similar to those of the twentieth century, but they have telepathic abilities—particularly powerful in the narrator—which are disciplined and protected by some kind of cryptographic key that allows deceptive transmissions to be filtered out.

The future society is governed benevolently by the vigilant Monstruwacans. The pyramid is defended by the Electric Circle, and needs to be, for in this decadent Earth the barriers separating the planetary surface from other dimensions have long since broken down, and the forces of destruction are free to roam the world in a multiplicity of physical forms, ranging from the gargantuan immobile Watchers to tiny serpentine creatures, all of which are hidden by the cloak of perpetual darkness.

The inhabitants of the Last Redoubt discover that their refuge is ill-named when they receive a call for help from a Lesser Redoubt, whose existence they had not suspected. Naani, who is a "reincarnation" of Mirdath, appeals for rescue, and the narrator's dream-self sets out in response across the haunted landscape, carrying supplies of food and water in pill form and armed with a spark-spitting weapon called a diskos. The journey is very long and arduous, and is described in such detail that its countless bizarre incidents ultimately fuse into a rather monotonous catalogue.

The narrator eventually arrives at his destination, only to find the Lesser Redoubt has already been breached, although Naani is still alive. They begin the equally long-drawn-out return journey, the menace of the monsters from the eternal night now punctuated by their decorous love-making, in a series of sentimental scenes awkwardly reflective of Victorian moral assumptions and conventions. Naani is ultimately killed, struck down by an evil spiritual Force, but she is then resurrected by the Earth-Current. The story ends with an archetypal happy ending, displaying its moral in praise of the power of love like a triumphant banner.

The Night Land is a literary curiosity. Such are the idiosyncrasies of its style that it seems virtually unreadable to many readers—Everett Bleiler dismisses it with unusual brutality as "pseudo-archaic gibberish" (365)—but it also has an imaginative intensity that could belong only to an extremely personal book. It is highly enigmatic, disdaining even the token gesture of explanation that is to be found in the introduction to *The House on the Borderland*, and presents a puzzle to would-be commentators that few have even tried to solve. The book has its fervent admirers, however; Sam Moskowitz's biographical account of Hodgson quotes several favorable press notices that the book received (95-96), and H. P. Lovecraft spoke very highly of it in his classic essay on "Supernatural Horror in Literature" (396-97).

The broad outlines of the plot of *The Night Land* fit in well enough with the allegory in *The House on the Borderland*. The novel imagines the world approaching the end of a *kalpa*, with the forces of decay all but triumphant, although their ravages can still be held at bay by the careful cultivation of the forces of growth: physical culture, love and the benevolent force of the Earth-Current. The optimistic note on which the story ends seems to contrast with the pessimism of the earlier novel, but it results from a change of perspective rather than a change of mind. *The House on the Borderland* brooded on the inevitability of death; *The Night Land* accepts that, and concentrates on the personal triumphs that can be won in spite of it.

A condensation of *The Night Land*, less than a tenth of the length of the original, was published in America as *The Dream of X*, in a volume containing some other material, mainly poetry. This might have been done in order to obtain an American copyright for the book, but it seems highly probable that Hodgson had to pay for the publication himself. The book made no money to speak of, and Hodgson continued to churn out hackwork for the magazines, mainly for Alfred Harmsworth's *London Magazine* and *Red Magazine*.

Some of the stories in question try recapture the spirit of his early works, including "The Derelict" (1912), about the spontaneous generation of life aboard a decaying ship, and "The Stone Ship" (1913), about a petrified vessel thrown up from the sea-bed with a monstrous collection of deep-sea creatures by an underwater volcanic eruption. The only really significant story of the period, however, was one that the popular magazines would not take at the time, although it eventually appeared posthumously in 1919 as "The Baumoff Explosive." Originally entitled "Eloi Eloi Lama Sabachthani"—under which title it is reprinted in the collection *Out of the Storm* (1975)—it tells the story of a chemist who reproduces the meteorological anomalies that occurred at the time of the crucifixion, and crucifies himself in order to form a psychic link with Christ. The alien consciousness that invades him as the experiment reaches its climax, however, is a bestial one; it is the swinishness of the dark gods that possesses him, not the loving spirit of Christ. Thus Baumoff learns, in the cruelest possible fashion, the metaphysical intuition that Hodgson had long ago found to justify his own apostasy.

Hodgson married in 1913, and went to live for a while in the south of France. In the next few years he published several collections of his short stories, but wrote little new material. He did begin another novel—another sea story involving faces in the water that belong to monstrous humanoids—but did not get far with it. When the Great War began, he and his wife returned to England, and he enlisted in 1915, receiving a commission in the Royal Field Artillery. While serving in France in 1916 he was thrown from a horse and badly injured, but he returned to the front when he had recovered. He was killed in action in April 1918, near Ypres.

As a writer, Hodgson was a remarkable amalgam of hard-headed professional and inwardly driven amateur. Historians of science fiction usually regard him as a marginal figure, primarily interesting as a writer of horror stories rather than as a writer of speculative fiction, but that judgment neglects important elements of kinship that link his works to the endeavors of H. G. Wells, M. P. Shiel, and J. D. Beresford. There is nothing in his work that is authentically supernatural; his metaphysics is as thoroughly disenchanted as Wells's, although it is as baroque as Shiel's.

What distinguishes Hodgson from the three named writers is that they all built their new metaphysical systems around ideas derived from evolutionary philosophy. Their cosmic schemes, whether optimistic or pessimistic, dealt with possibilities of change in the human species. Hodgson was not an evolutionist, and did not think in such terms; his model of change was taken from the life-history of the individual, and his macrocosmic visions embody the occult principle of "As above, so below." His idea of the fundamental, impersonal Force that stands in for God is therefore very different from the one formed by Shiel. In Shiel's view, that basic Force imported a progressive *élan vital* into the history of life and the career of mankind; in Hodgson's view the agent that is ultimately bound to triumph is the counteractive force of decay and dissolution, and the individual's battle is to win an essentially temporary and partial victory.

Had Hodgson been familiar with the concept of entropy, and had he had a clearer consciousness of the manner in which the order of life on Earth is dependent on the influx of energy from the sun to mount its temporary defiance of the entropic decay of the universe, he would probably have made much more use of scientific language in his work, rather than borrowing ideas and images from Hindu mythology, but the ultimate effect is the same. His self-education was presumably too selective to make such ideative resources available to him, and that lack limited his mode of expression, but the limitations in question do not obscure the underlying spirit of his endeavors.

Works Cited

Bleiler, E. F., and Richard Bleiler. *Science-Fiction: The Early Years*. Kent, OH: Kent State University Press, 1990.

Hodgson, William Hope. *The House on the Borderland and Other Novels*. Sauk City, WI: Arkham House, 1946.

Lovecraft, H. P. "Supernatural Horror in Literature." In *Dagon and Other Macabre Tales*. Sauk City, WI: Arkham House, 1965.

Moskowitz, Sam. "William Hope Hodgson." In *Out of the Storm: Uncollected Fantasies by William Hope Hodgson*. West Kingston, RI: Donald M. Grant, 1975.

The Dark Mythos of the Sea: William Hope Hodgson's Transformation of Maritime Legends

Emily Alder

William Hope Hodgson's characteristic, Lovecraftian worldview of cosmic horror is familiar to readers of *The Night Land* (1912) and *The House on the Borderland* (1908). In these novels, human life is pitted against unfathomable and overwhelming "outward powers" (*Night Land* 328), forces from other dimensions which manifest in both material and immaterial forms. The marine environment and maritime context of Hodgson's sea fiction lend a particular richness to this narrative, grounded in his own sailing experiences and his gift for evoking the texture, detail, and atmosphere of seafaring. In the fictions examined here, Hodgson transforms traditional legends and superstitions of ghosts, ship spirits, phantom ships, and the world beneath the waves to create his own corpus of sea horror literature.

Hodgson is one of many writers who adapted, rewrote, or recorded legends, superstitions, and folklore of the sea either as fiction or as cultural record. I will draw on some of these texts, such as William Jones's *Credulities Past and Present* (1880), Allan Cunningham's *Traditional Tales of the English and Scottish Peasantry* (1887), and Angelo S. Rappoport's *Superstitions of Sailors* (1929), as sources of the forms in which traditional legends were transmitted into the nineteenth and twentieth centuries and which thus help to inform our examination of Hodgson's sea fiction. Hodgson also taps into a literary and artistic tradition using supernatural tropes of the sea: examples include Coleridge's *The Rime of the Ancient Mariner* (1798), Marryat's *The Phantom Ship* (1839), and Wagner's *The Flying Dutchman* (1843). The sea's literary popularity and symbolic diversity is extensive and well documented (see, e.g., Carlson, Klein, and Landow). Carlson argues that the sea produced a series of archetypes for writers: "the ship as microcosm; the phenomenal beast; a cosmology of constant flux; the uneasy division between order and chaos; . . . the conflict between human and non-human" (Foreword). These archetypes, as we will see, help to shape Hodgson's sea horror fiction. The sea's eternal, unknowable quality, its identification as "the untamed, the formless, and the unpredictable" (ibid.), lends itself to the unfathomable terrors, hallmarks of Hodgson's writing, in which humans come face to face with the incomprehensibility of what lies beyond the limits of human experience. Hodgson's stories, therefore, resonate with a rich history of symbolism of the sea through both literature and traditional legend.

Legends and superstitions about the sea date back to the earliest maritime cultures and appear globally, sometimes in surprisingly similar ways.[1] While rational modern eras dispelled supernatural beliefs to an extent, certain superstitions lingered on in maritime culture (Baker 9). By the late nineteenth century, when Hodgson was a sailor, the rise of spiritualism and the occult in Western culture offered a recasting of the supernatural within a new materialist framework (see, e.g., Noakes and Owen). In the sea fiction discussed here, Hodgson reworks old legends with a modern worldview, often transforming traditional tales into stories of horror, revising legendary encounters with sea monsters, ghosts, and ghost ships for terrifying effects. Maritime legend is varied, but a few key themes are evident. These include beliefs in a world beneath the waves, sightings of phantom ships such as the *Flying Dutchman*, visions of ghosts of the drowned, and spirits that haunt the structure of ships themselves. Relocating these tropes in a modern world of materialist science, Hodgson imbues them with new horrors—prophetic meanings of legends of ghost ships, for example, are stripped away and replaced with the terror of a meaningless universe.

Another set of legends surround sea monsters such as serpents, mermaids, or kraken; although these form a vital part of Hodgson's sea mythos, monstrosity in his fiction represents a study in itself and, to an extent, engages with some different cultural and scientific contexts.[2] Here, therefore, I focus on what we might term Hodgson's "supernatural" sea fiction or ghost stories, rather than those primarily characterized by physical monstrosity (such as *The Boats of the "Glen Carrig"* [1907], "From the Tideless Sea" [1906], or "The Derelict" [1912]).

---

1. See Brown, *Phantoms*. Brown notes that the superstition of drowned souls going down to the domains of the sea was "almost universal" (155) and notes the dispersal of fragments of old myths among the world's sailing cultures. "Individual superstitions fragmented into complete identities of their own to be disseminated amongst the world's sailors. Sometimes the sailors of one nation might take up the superstitions of another without realising they had done so" (155).

2. See Hurley for discussions of the morphic, undifferentiated bodies in Hodgson's fiction; and Alder for discussions of Hodgson's representations of monstrosity.

It is nevertheless important to note that some of these ghostly sea stories aim to debunk the supernatural and superstition. In some cases, the supernatural element is predicated at least partly on late nineteenth-century naturalized explanations for spiritual existence and, as we will see, some overlap exists between ghostly and physical terrors in these stories. This paper will first explore the use of maritime superstitions and legends in several of Hodgson's short stories and how traditional tales are transformed into tales of terror, followed by a detailed examination of *The Ghost Pirates* and its unification of key tropes of legends of the sea. This paper does not attempt to comprehensively map Hodgson's use of sea legends, a futile task given the general fragmentation, dispersal, and variety of sea lore in literature generally, but explores certain legends reworked by Hodgson that contribute significantly to his construction of a dark mythos of the sea.

Ghostly Stories of the Sea

Hodgson, as a sailor, writer, and avid reader with at least a passing interest in spiritualism (see Everts), was familiar with legends of ghost ships and ship spirits. He works several of them into his fiction in different ways. Ship hauntings are often deployed, presented as either actual (*The Ghost Pirates*), imagined ("The Ghosts of the *Glen Doon*" [1911]), or ambiguous ("Old Golly" [1919]). Derelicts appear as ghost ships ("Demons of the Sea" [1923]), or misty ship-shapes signal impending disaster (*The Ghost Pirates*). Meteorological phenomena house departed spirits ("The Riven Night") or act as portals to the other world ("The *Shamraken* Homeward-Bounder" [1908]). In each case, the narrative shifts between signals of the supernatural and signals of rational or material explanation.

Several of Hodgson's stories exploit sailors' reputations for superstition and tendency to conjure up imaginary ghosts. In doing so, they elaborate on familiar anecdotes of the sort recounted by William Jones; in *Credulities Past and Present*, he describes two stories in which the "smell" of a ghost turns out to be a dead rat, and the remains of a mast from a wreck resembles a moving figure on the surface of the sea (86–87). This type of mystery appears in several Hodgson stories, sometimes rationally resolved, sometimes left ambiguous. In "The Ghosts of the *Glen Doon*," for example, tapping noises in an iron derelict believed to be the hammers of ten sailors who had drowned in her turn out to be the sounds made by a gang of illegal coin-punchers. "Old Golly," however, plays on the ambiguity inherent in superstitions of ship-haunting. Golly's murder by the captain is followed by a series of accidents in the ship's rigging, which the crew begin to attribute to Golly's ghost. Eventually the furious captain, ascending the rigging to investigate, hears the words "Golly! Golly!" and falls to his death. The first mate later discovers the cause to be a broken pump echoing the sound of gurgling water up the hollow steel mast, but the crew maintain their belief in the ghost: "Old Golly'd never have rest til he got level. If he hadn't got him that time, he'd have got him in the end!" (270). The question of supernatural haunting is left open; the narrative fully endorses neither the rational worldview of the officers nor the staunch superstition of the sailors.

Other stories deal critically with such superstitious invention, highlighting its potential damage. In "The Wild Man of the Sea" (1926), prejudice against a clever and talented but eccentric seaman leads to the crew blaming him for mishaps on the voyage. This eventually leads to his murder and the murder of a young cabin boy by members of the crew, who later out of guilt abandon the ship without pay when they reach San Francisco. The superiority of the "Wild Man," the innocence of the cabin boy, the ignorance and "dull minds" (225) of the crew, and the "wholesome" (231) nature of the officers are all made clear—an indictment of prejudice and superstition, but with no suggestion of the supernatural.

In his most interesting short stories, however, Hodgson draws on specific sea legends and transforms them for his own purposes. In his reworkings, the natural and supernatural worlds are knit more closely together than they often are in sea legends, heightening the engagement of the human characters with the mystery facing them, and transforming a benign or passive experience into an encounter imbued with horror. The sea already bears an otherworldly quality and, in Hodgson's hands, becomes the perfect environment for tales of terror. For the sea is a quintessentially liminal region. Situated between political, cultural, and geographical boundaries, it is also physically changeable and unpredictable; to the eighteenth- or nineteenth-century sailor to be at sea was to be isolated and vulnerable, existing between elements, between countries, between life and death. The constant risk and regular occurrence of shipwreck and drowning at sea, while family waited anxious and unknowing onshore, rendered the association of sea and death a close one (see Rediker).

Such themes of borderline existence, isolation, and death resonate in stories of ghosts at sea. In the traditional tale of *La Belle Rosalie*, a grieving bride, Maria Batiste, sees her fiancé returning to the harbor, only for the ship to fade away with the mist at dawn (Rappoport 223-25). Such a vision signals the loss of the ship at sea, of which no definite news could be brought by conventional means. In other stories, it is sailors who receive visions of the death through glimpses of ghosts at sea. Rappoport describes a Scottish legend in which

> a sailor is said to have suddenly seen the ghost of his murdered bride. She appeared in the shape of a brilliant light over the water. The nearer she came the more distinctly appeared the human shape. At last she called him by

name, and both seaman and bride disappeared in the brilliant light. The dead bride had come to claim her affianced from the living. (244)

Hodgson adopts two features of this legend in an unpublished (until the 1970s) short story, "The Riven Night." Here, as in "The *Shamraken* Homeward-Bounder," odd meteorological effects generate an expectation of the supernatural, emphazising the sea's capacity for mysterious phenomena as well as its position on a borderline between life and death.

Hodgson weaves into his fiction many of his real-life experiences of sailing, some of which he also wrote up as nonfiction vignettes or for lectures and slide shows. In "Through the Vortex of a Cyclone" (1909; illustrated with his own photographs of the occasion), Hodgson describes an unnatural glare to the sky preceding the cyclone, stalk lightning manifesting itself as "flickering streaks and tongues of flame rising apparently out of the sea," and a "curious luminous quality" to the advancing water-spout (121). The description of the cyclonic storm points to the capacity of marine weather to produce uncanny effects and a sense of strangeness. Hodgson makes good use of such experiences to establish atmosphere and suspense in his sea stories, sometimes in anticipation of a storm, sometimes in preparation for a supernatural intrusion.

"The Riven Night" incorporates this sort of experience while tracking the legend of the murdered bride closely. An unnamed ship, becalmed midvoyage, drifts into a "valley" or "chasm of violet light" (158). The luminous rift is "strange," "spectral," "unearthly," and reflects no light; it "rose right up into the midnight sky" while "the point of the shimmering wedge seemed to drive far below the surface of the silent deep" (159). Thus the night is riven, and the rift bridges the world above the waves and the world beneath. Furthermore, as the frightened sailors drift into the mist, they find themselves "submerged in an ocean of violet shades that gleamed wondrously" (160). The ship enters a borderland region where the two worlds overlap, simultaneously drifting on the surface and submerged underneath. With the ship encased by the luminous billows, ghostly shapes appear from the fog: "shapes clothed mistily, that watched us with great sombre eyes . . . not clouds, but legions upon legions of those spirit forms" (161). Some of the sailors recognize wives and family members among these ghosts and are drawn from the ship to their destruction; on hearing the entreaty of his dead wife, the captain throws himself into the sea, and the narrator sees "a shadowy form with a face like that of the Captain's, float upwards into the violet twilight" (162–65). The captain's spirit joins the "legions": thus the riven night bridges the worlds of living and dead as well as those above and beneath the sea, aligning the world beneath the waves with the spirit world.

"The Riven Night" opens with an account of the captain's happy marriage and tragic loss, but another sailor, Langstone, has a different encounter with the ghost of his lover. Out of the shrouds of the mist emerges "the face and figure of a lovely young girl":

> [She] put one ghostly hand to her heart, and I saw the handle of a sailor's sheath-knife showing starkly. . . . Langstone's voice rose shrilly, "Mary! Mary! Forgive . . ." He stopped abruptly. The girl-spirit after that one accusing gesture had turned away coldly and unforgivingly . . . with a cry of "God help me," [Langstone] leapt away out into the purple billows. (161–62)

In Rappoport's account of the legend, the murderer of the bride is not clearly identified; Hodgson's version, through the detail of the sailor's knife and the behavior of spirit and sailor, points more explicitly to Langstone's guilt. Significantly, Langstone's suicide produces, the narrator notices, "from miles beneath my feet . . . a far distant splash, and then a long dread silence" (162). Langstone's spirit does not rise to join the captain's. Again, Hodgson's retelling aligns the world beneath the waves with the world of the dead, and this incident emphasizes the punishment and retribution brought by the encounter, as the captain's suicide suggests consolation and reunion.

On the surface, as Sam Moskowitz claims, "The Riven Night" "is a bonafide fantasy almost to an extreme, leaving no room for ambiguity as to the other-worldliness of what is occurring" (155). However, the story's close suggests a more uncomfortable possibility, enabled by Hodgson's play on sea legends. The story's apparent reliance on familiar sea tales—the phenomena of strange clouds and lights, the world beneath the waves, the encounter with spirits of dead loved ones—leads the reader into a complacency about the story's underlying premise that makes the final event all the more shocking. "The Riven Night" is not simply a retelling of legends of the sea but hints at something far more dreadful.

To do so, Hodgson deploys many layers of representation of the sea. The sea has long been a region of mystery, traveled by sailors unable to penetrate more than a few meters below the surface. "The belief has always prevailed," writes Angelo S. Rappoport, "that the depths of the sea were the abode of a particular world and inhabited by various beings either graceful or monstrous, terrible or benevolent" (141). Later, he comments that in early history "men were still unacquainted with the various phenomena and meteorological laws and, as in a glass, they saw darkly many things not only upon the waves, but beneath them. . . . The sea repeated in its mirror the sky and the shore and the land beyond" (146–47). Rappoport uses the metaphor of the dark mirror from 1 Corinthians, which suggests a dark reflection of the real world, dimly understood, in the sea. In the world beneath the waves, animals and plants were supposed each to have their counterparts (Rappoport 157). Hodgson turns this longstanding tradition of a world beneath the waves into a source of terror, by revealing a glimpse of what might abide there.

In "The Riven Night," the ship drifts through the mist for "silent aeons"; the narrator loses track of time, but at last sees a new light, "a cold malicious gleam that frightened me" (165). The gleam resolves into "two transparent pillars through which played a shiver of lambent flame," and a dark wave drives toward the ship, swamping it in "a surging blackness" that renders the crew unconscious: "Yet ere it reached us, my eyes had seen something, something terrible—eyes that blazed out of mystery, and beneath, lips—white, vast and slobbering had opened, disclosing the blackness of an everlasting night" (165). The narrator glimpses the real terror on the far side of worldly boundaries. As elsewhere in his fiction, Hodgson presents such horrors as hellish and unreal, yet material and physical.

Perhaps the narrator has glimpsed, magnified by his own terror, a pale deep-sea serpent like the one cast up by an underwater eruption in Kipling's "A Matter of Fact" (1893). Yet, considered alongside other stories of Hodgson's such as "The Habitants of Middle Islet" (1908), "Out of the Storm" (1909), and "Eloi Eloi Lama Sabachthani" (1919; first published as "The Baumoff Explosive"), this sequence also bears the characteristically Hodgsonian touch of monstrous otherworldly hostility, against which humans have very little power. In "The Habitants of Middle Islet," the appearance of the ghost of a dead sweetheart similarly lures the narrator's companion into the sea to drown. However, it is unclear whether it really is her ghost or merely a malicious entity wearing her appearance, since she returns to threaten the remaining sailor (510). In "Eloi Eloi Lama Sabachthani," a scientist's attempt to re-create the experience of Christ's crucifixion leads, arguably, to his possession and destruction by "a Christ-apeing monster of the void" (218). Reading "The Riven Night" in this way, the glimpse of the night-mawed entity casts new doubt over the earlier spirits: Are they really what they appeared to be, the ghosts of human beings, or should they be considered as projections of the sailors' heartache and guilt, or as the malicious tools of a demonic intrusion into our world? As part of Hodgson's modern mythos of sea horror, the narrative leaves such questions open.

Such an encounter forms the center of "Out of the Storm." In this story, the experience of a passenger on a sinking ship is transmitted by a sort of radio telegraph to a scientist in a laboratory. Once again, Hodgson transforms traditional representations of the sea environment for horror, destabilizing the boundary between life and death by destabilizing the boundaries between the world of the sea and the world above it. Which world the ship now occupies seems uncertain; as if already underneath, the passenger describes sky the color of mud and looks *up* at clouds like "monstrous, mildewed-looking hulls" that "show solid, save where the frightful wind tears their lower edge" (142). This image serves to invert the two worlds and render the passenger's experience as both a voice from the liminal region represented by the sea and a voice from beyond the world of the living. The ship is sinking and the passenger describes himself as "already one among the dead" (142).

Like the narrator of "The Riven Night," the passenger glimpses unspeakable horrors, intended only "for the doomed and the dead . . . say the alive-in-death, those upon the brink" (143). The use of "alive-in-death" invokes Coleridge's *Rime of the Ancient Mariner* and thus a long literary, as well as superstitious, tradition of representing the sea as a liminal space in which transforming encounters between life and death can take place. Hodgson's emphasis, of course, is unashamedly on the pure horror of such an encounter. The passenger reports of forbidden secrets: "I have no right to tell of it to you; to speak of it to one of the living is to initiate innocence into one of the infernal mysteries" (143). Yet technology enables him to "expose, in all its hideous nakedness, the death-side of the sea" (142) through the communication instrument. Thus not only are the untold experiences of people and ships lost in ocean storms relayed, but, as part of Hodgson's sea mythos, so are the unseen terrors to which death at sea leads. The ship is being destroyed by a "hungry thing" resembling the horror glimpsed in "The Riven Night," inasmuch as both are represented as voracious mouths and seem both material and supernatural. In "Out of the Storm," the Thing eats and has teeth, but also seems supernaturally demonic; it spreads "an infection of sin" (144); the remaining people aboard are driven mad, fighting their own children and lovers for a safe hold on the deck.

The Thing represents both death and the sea. With a voice "like Satanic thunder," assailing the ship with "shrieking foam" and "gigantic billows," it behaves like a personified storm: "It roared about them, churning and growling; then surged away" (143-47). The sea itself has become monstrous. The passenger's final words report that "It is coming! The Sea has come for me! It is rushing down through the companionway! . . . I am drowning! I—am—dr—" (149). Here, the Thing and the Sea are conflated as the approaching "it" is left unspecified. Whether we are to understand the Thing as "real" or as a representation of human insanity and terror during a fatal storm is left ambiguous. The sea is a literally and conceptually unstable region, not only between life and death but also between a world of normality and sanity and a world of horror and madness. In his ghostly sea stories, Hodgson offers glimpses of terrors beyond the known boundaries, physical or metaphorical, of the world. The inversion and transformation of established archetypes of the sea in this way is most cohesively demonstrated in his 1909 short novel, *The Ghost Pirates*.

The Ghost Pirates

The Ghost Pirates draws on many different sea legends and superstitions. The story of the windjammer *Mortzestus* is told by Jessop, a sailor picked up by another ship, the *Sangier*.[3] As the *Mortzestus* journeys between San Francisco and Britain, a series of events that begins with accidents and glimpses of strange figures and ghostly vessels finally results in the ship's invasion by the eponymous ghost pirates, who draw it down into the ocean. In a novel set in the contemporary sailing environment of his own experience, Hodgson draws on tales of ship spirits, phantom ships, and strange inhabitants of a world beneath the waves to create a modernized myth using the language and arguments of late nineteenth-century spiritualism and psychical research.

The Ghost Pirates begins as a story of a haunted ship. Jessop, a new hand, is warned by an old sailor, Jaskett, that "There's too many bloomin' shadders about this 'ere packet; they gets onto your nerves like nothin' as ever I seen before" (208). Jessop's early glimpses of "shadows" about the *Mortzestus* seem at first to suggest a simple story of haunting, but Hodgson's novel is in fact much more complex. Some of the early mysterious incidents aboard the *Mortzestus* recall legends of ship spirits much as Jessop's glimpses of ghostly ships echo traditional tales. One example is the ship spirit legend of the North and Baltic Seas, known as the Klabautermann. It is mostly a protective spirit, but has a mischievous temper: "If he is in a bad humour, he makes an awful noise, throws about the fire-wood, spars, and other things, knocks on the ship's sides, destroys many things, hinders those at work, and unseen gives the sailors violent cuffs on the head" (Thorpe 3.50). The first accident on the *Mortzestus* happens as a loose sail, apparently caught by wind although there is none, "thrashed right over the after side of the yard, . . . knocking Tom clean from off the foot-rope" (29). In these early incidents, *The Ghost Pirates* clearly alludes to superstitions and legends of ship haunting.

In *Northern Mythology* (1851), Benjamin Thorpe records that the Klabautermann is often supposed to take the form of "a little fellow with yellow breeches, horseman's boots, a large, fiery-red head, green, teeth, and a steeple-crowned hat" (3.49), but, like the *Flying Dutchman*, the Klabautermann's form varies. Jessop's "shadders" resemble some of these closely: the ghost pirates are gray and man-shaped figures, and in other accounts the ship spirit sometimes appears as an "old gray man" or a "man in gray clothes" (Buss 44). Reinhard Buss records one "memorat" of a "Captain on heavy seas" who "sees gray man come toward him and jump overboard" (74) (other memorates listed here include dogs who appear and jump overboard, or gray men who

---

3. Windjammer is the name given to the steel merchant sailing ships of the 1890s.

speak or simply are seen). Similarly, Jessop is startled to observe "nothing less than the form of a man stepping inboard over the starboard rail" which later "made three quick strides to the port rail, and *climbed over it into the sea*" (209, 210; emphasis in text). In *Superstitions of Sailors*, Rappoport describes an incident prior to a murder on a ship called the *Pontiac*: a steersman sees "a strange-looking man, of ghostly appearance," whom the mate cannot see (245). This causes some of the crew to believe the ship haunted, portending some calamity; not long after, the murder takes place. In *The Ghost Pirates*, the associations the narrative forges with such tales mean that the glimpses of the shadowy ghost pirates already hint at disaster to come.

Buss records that in some cases the ship spirit is supposed to have entered the ship when she was being built, or sometimes when she was launched (39). The Klabautermann is sometimes generated from the wood as the ship was being built (for example, the first chip hewed, or the last piece used), and sometimes is already present in the wood if it comes from a tree that, for whatever reason, has a spirit inside it. In one example, "In building a ship, wood was used from a tree which had killed a lumberjack. When the tree was cut into planks, blood could still be seen on them and consequently the Klabautermann has entered the ship" (36).[4] Jessop's theory—as he recounts to Tammy, the cabin-boy—that the ship is "open to be boarded by those things" can be read in this context: according to such tradition, the wood of the ship is open to spirits because of the condition of the trees, or the timber, from which it was constructed (238).

Jessop's explanation, however, uses a modern rhetoric that resists superstition and the supernatural: the ship is open not to ghosts but to "the attacks of beings belonging to another state of existence" (238). Jessop's language echoes *fin-de-siècle* spiritualist and occultist arguments not for a supernatural explanation for communication with spirits, but for the rational existence of another world (see Oppenheim). When Tammy asks him if "you *really* think they're ghosts," Jessop concedes only that "I don't think they're our ideas of flesh and blood" (239). Rather, "The earth may be just as *real* to them, as to us . . . but neither of us could appreciate the other's realness" (239). In this way, the traditional ship spirit is transformed, accorded an independent existence equal to that of humans and thus recast as a serious threat. As *The Ghost Pirates* progresses, it becomes increasingly clear that there is more to the mystery of the *Mortzestus* than malicious haunting. Hodgson begins to weave the

---

4. This particular story also evokes the anthropophagic trees of *The Boats of the "Glen Carrig,"* which display human faces on their bark and bleed when cut.

legend of ship spirits into legends of phantom ships, another popular topic of traditional tales of the sea.

Ghost ships can take various forms: lights that are seen and vanish, ships that do not respond to attempts at communication, or long-lost ships like *La Belle Rosalie* making a brief return in ghost form to their home ports. Ghost ships appear to living land-dwellers to make them aware of disaster at sea, or to sailors themselves as omens of shipwreck. Allan Cunningham's *Traditional Tales of the English and Scottish Peasantry*, published 1887, for example, relates the story of "The Last Lord of Helvellyn." The narrator experiences a vision of a ghost ship that portends a catastrophe a day later. He sees

> a low dark mist arise from the middle of the Solway; which, swelling out suddenly came rolling huge and sable towards the Cumberland shore. Nor was fear or fancy long in supplying this exhalation with sails and pennons. . . . I observed it become more dark, and assume more distinctly the shape of a barge, with a shroud for a sail. It left the sea, and settled on the beach, maintaining still its form, and still sending forth the merry din of mariners. In a moment the voices were changed from mirth to sorrow; and I heard a sound, an outcry like the shriek of a ship's company whom the sea is swallowing. The cloud dissolved away, and in its place I beheld, as it were, the forms of seven men, shaped from the cloud, and stretched black on the beach; even as corses are prepared for the coffin. (206)

The next day the eponymous Lord's new barge is launched, but one of the mariners later reports "a ship formed of a black cloud, sailing beside us, which moved as we moved, and tacked as we tacked . . . the spectre shallop of Solway, which always sails by the side of the ship which the sea is about to swallow" (208). The new barge is destroyed by a whirlwind, and the bodies of the Lord's son and six mariners are duly washed up on the same spot where the narrator saw his vision. Thorpe describes a related Scandinavian legend: "It often happens that mariners in the wide ocean see a ship—in all respects resembling a real one—sailing by, and at the same instant vanishing from their sight. It is the spectre-ship, and forebodes that a vessel will soon go to the bottom on that spot" (2.276). Phantom ships warn of disaster, and their appearance and disappearance is often accompanied by mist or smoke.

La Belle Rosalie, as we have seen, fades into the mist, and Begg quotes a 1648 account by New Englander John Winthrop of "The Spectre of New Haven":

> There appeared over the harbor at New Haven in the evening, the form of a keel of a ship with three masts, to which were suddenly added all the tackling and sails . . . Then from the side of the ship which was toward the town arose

a great smoke, which covered all the ship, and in that smoke she vanished away; but some saw her keel sink into the water. (121)

Hodgson uses tropes and rhetoric familiar from phantom ship legends to signal the impending disaster that will overtake the *Mortzestus*. Thus, one sunset, Jessop observes the appearance of a misty ship on the water:

> away on the starboard bow, a faint mist drove up out of the sea. . . . as I watched, the weird mistiness collected and shaped and rose into three towers. These became more definite, and there was something elongated beneath them. The shaping and forming continued, and almost suddenly I saw that the thing had taken on the shape of a great ship. (290)

This description distinctly echoes tales like "The Last Lord of Helvellyn" and "The Spectre of New Haven," in which a ship is observed to take shape out of mist or cloud. Hodgson's extended treatment of tropes like this in *The Ghost Pirates* enables him to manipulate and invert them for the production of suspense and terror.

Jessop's next vision of a ghostly ship is underneath the surface of the sea. As two of the ghost pirates' victims, Svensen and Jock, are buried, Jessop and Tammy watch the sail-wrapped bodies sink into the sea and notice the "shadow of a ship rising out of the unexplored immensity beneath our keel" (284). Later Jessop detects more clearly, "after a few moments staring, the shadow of a royal-yard, and, deeper, the gear and standing-rigging of a great mast. Far down among the shadows, I thought, presently, that I could make out the immense, indefinite stretch of vast decks" (297). The ship under the waves resolves itself into visibility to the observers in the same gradual way as the misty version above.

Although the *Mortzestus*'s experience is thus aligned with phantom ship legends in which the glimpse of a ghost ship foretells disaster, the underwater vessel invokes the world beneath the waves, rather than the mist or cloud above, as the source of such specters. Since the earlier misty ship sank into the sea, the location of this one under the surface serves to connect above and below, to relate visions of ghost ships above the waves to the mysterious and potentially hostile world beneath it. Mist indicates that conventional boundaries are blurred, and is also used to suggest that the *Mortzestus* now inhabits a liminal world as Hodgson casts her as a phantom ship herself.

The name of the ship, *Mort-zest-us*, suggests its position between living and dead, recalling, as in "Out of the Storm," the alive-in-death of *The Rime of the Ancient Mariner*. From the beginning, then, the liminality of the *Mortzestus* is signaled. She is also closely associated with mist, not only used to shape visions of ghost ships but also to mark her passage into a liminal realm. Jessop observes that "the whole ship was surrounded by a thinnish haze that quite hid the horizon" (240). Once the mist has faded, the *Mortzestus* is apparently sailing on "the blank surface of the sea, reaching everywhere to the empty horizon" (242); other ships that had been in sight have now vanished. Later, the sudden appearance and vanishing of another ship from Jessop's view at first suggests to him that he is looking at an imaginary ship, as he might a specter ship, but he gradually concludes that the peculiarity is about the *Mortzestus* herself: "It was nothing about the other packet that was strange. The strangeness was with us" (243). Jessop feels as though "I had looked at her [the other ship] from out of some other dimension," looking out of, not into, a ghost-world (243). Similarly, later, at night, Jessop and other sailors sporadically sight ships' lights: lights that ought to be warning the oblivious *Mortzestus* to get out of the way, but instead leave them puzzled. The danger is not merely from the ghostly pirates, but there is also a real risk to, and from, other shipping as the *Mortzestus* lingers half in one world and half in another. From the point of view of the other ships, it is the *Mortzestus* that appears and disappears like a ghost ship.

The *Mortzestus*'s phantom-like existence in some borderland dimension is reinforced in the novel's epilogue, which recounts the *Sangier*'s view of the *Mortzestus* shortly before Jessop is rescued: "I saw the sails fill bang up with wind," relates the mate, "and yet, you know, ours were slatting" (304). The *Mortzestus* sails to alternative winds in an alternative existence. To an extent, she represents a reworking of elements of the most famous phantom ship legend, the *Flying Dutchman*, the subject of a range of texts from Marryat's novel *The Phantom Ship* and Wagner's opera to Disney's *Pirates of the Caribbean* (2006). The *Dutchman* is supposedly the ship of a Dutch captain cursed to sail eternally, usually seen off the Cape of Good Hope. A glimpse was famously recorded by Prince Albert Victor and Prince George of Wales in 1881:

> July 11th—At 4 a.m. the *Flying Dutchman* crossed our bows. A strange red light as of a phantom ship, all aglow, in the midst of which light the masts, spars, and sails of a brig 200 yards distant stood out in strange relief . . . [The midshipman] was sent forward at once to the forecastle; but upon arriving there was no vestige nor any sign whatever of any material ship was to be seen either near or right away to the horizon. (George 551)

In common with other ghost ships, the *Dutchman* is mysteriously glimpsed and associated with wreck and destruction. It appears in Sir Walter Scott's *Rokeby* (1813) as a "Demon Frigate" famous as a "harbinger of wreck and woe" (canto 2.11). In some cases, the *Dutchman* is less a ghost than cursed ship with unnaturally extended existence, neither belonging to the living world nor a part of the dead: in Marryat's *The Phantom Ship*, the *Dutchman* is variously represented as insubstantial and as solid. Through the sightings of ghostly ships above and below the waves, and the *Mortzestus*'s liminal position as modern windjammer, haunted ship, and phantom behavior, Hodgson blends different representations of the phantom ship into a single narrative.

He also draws on other, related legends. A tale sometimes conflated with the *Flying Dutchman* is the legend of the *Libra Nos*, said to be sailed by skeletons (Begg 119). Thomas Moore's "Written on Passing Dead-man's Island" (1804) describes a phantom ship with a skeletal crew:

> See you, beneath yon cloud so dark,
> Fast gliding along, a gloomy bark?
> Her sails are full, though the wind is still,
> And there blows not a breath her sails to fill!
> [. . .]
> To Dead-Man's Isle, in the eye of the blast,
> To Dead-Man's Isle, she speeds her fast;
> By skeleton shapes her sails are furl'd,
> And the hand that steers is not of this world! (279)

Like the *Mortzestus* as observed by the *Sangier*, Moore's gloomy bark is moving under full sail, although "there blows not a breath her sails to fill," somewhere between this world and another.

However, the "skeleton shapes" that finally sail the *Mortzestus* are not the remnants of the original crew, but, apparently, the invading crew of the underwater ghost ships. In the final scene, a "moving greyness resolved into hundreds of strange men" like "the inhabitants of some fantastic dreamworld," which "swarmed in upon us in a great wave of murderous, living shadows" (300–301). The pirates sail the ship down into the sea: "The jibboom was plunged right into the water, and, as I stared, the bows disappeared into the sea" (302). Those sailors not already killed by the pirates are drowned, and Jessop alone survives. In Hodgson's novel, ghost ships are doubly threatening: not only harbingers of wreck and woe, but also the perpetrators.

Hodgson's original ending to *The Ghost Pirates* is published in Moskowitz's 1991 collection *The Haunted Pampero* as "The Silent Ship" and provides a more detailed description of the *Mortzestus*'s last hours from the viewpoint of the *Sangier*. The silent ship once again hoists its sails to alternative winds, and during the ghost pirates' attack sound escapes the *Mortzestus* only sporadically. Like the "shriek of a ship's company whom the sea is swallowing" given by the dissolving specter of Cunningham's "The Last Lord of Helvellyn," the *Sangier*'s mate hears the screams of the *Mortzestus*'s crew as the ship is sailed into the water: "a gust of crying swept up to us for one dreadful instant, and then only the boil of the sea as it closed in over all" ("The Silent

Ship" 166). In this version, the sailors themselves are positioned as a ghostly crew returning to the world beneath the waves, yet at the same time remain entirely mortal as they are swept to dreadful deaths. Hodgson's specters, both ship and pirates, resolve into a material threat able to realize itself in the physical world. Traditional legends contrasting separate worlds of above, below, living, dead, material, immaterial, are inverted, to produce instead a narrative in which the human world does not merely glimpse the other side but is fatally and inextricably woven into it.

Thus through ghosts, ship spirits, phantom ships, and the liminal world of the sea, Hodgson constructs a cohesive mythos of sea horror that blends and transforms traditional tales and legends. Rather than simply rework old sea ghost stories, across his sea fiction Hodgson offers his narratives on revised terms of explanation, an alternative, modern premise for the spiritual and dimensional borderland of the sea. In *The Ghost Pirates*, Hodgson's horror mythos cumulates: conventional anthropocentric meanings inherent in legends of the sea, of ghosts and ghost ships as warning, punishment, or consolation, disappear and are replaced only with a heightened awareness of the meaningless horrors that lie beyond human boundaries of knowledge and thought. In *The Ghost Pirates*, as in the short stories discussed earlier, Hodgson creates a new mythos around the sea as a portal, an area of weakened boundaries, a place where the human world overlaps with something unthinkably terrible.

Works Cited

Alder, Emily. "William Hope Hodgson's Borderlands: Monstrosity, Other Worlds, and the Future at the *fin de siècle*." Ph.D. diss.: Edinburgh Napier University, 2009.

Baker, Margaret. *Folklore of the Sea*. Newton Abbot, UK: David Charles, 1979.

Begg, Paul. *Mary Celeste: The Greatest Mystery of the Sea*. Harlow, UK: Pearson, 2007.

Brown, Raymond Lamont. *Phantoms, Legends, Customs, and Superstitions of the Sea*. London: Patrick Stephens, 1972.

Buss, Reinhard J. *The Klabautermann of the Northern Seas: An Analysis of the Protective Spirit of Ships and Sailors in the Context of Popular Belief, Christian Legend, and Indo-European Mythology*. Berkeley: University of California Press, 1973.

Carlson, Patricia Ann, ed. *Literature and Folklore of the Sea*. Amsterdam: Rodopi, 1986.

Coleridge, Samuel Taylor. *The Rime of the Ancient Mariner*. 1798. Ed. Walter Dent. London: Blackie & Son, 1895.

Cunningham, Allan. *Traditional Tales of the English and Scottish Peasantry.* London: Routledge, 1887.

Everts, R. Alain. *William Hope Hodgson: Night Pirate, Volume 2: Some Facts in the Case of William Hope Hodgson: Master of Phantasy.* Toronto: Soft Books, 1987.

George, Prince of Wales, and Prince Albert Victor. *The Cruise of Her Majesty's Ship "Bacchante," 1879–1882.* Edited by John Neale Dalton. London: Macmillan, 1886.

Hodgson, William Hope. *The Boats of the "Glen Carrig."* In *The House on the Borderland and Other Novels.* London: Gollancz, 2002. 3–103.

———. "Demons of the Sea." In *Terrors of the Sea: Unpublished Fantasies.* Edited by Sam Moskowitz. Hampton Falls, NH: Donald M. Grant, 1996. 72–85.

———. "Eloi Eloi Lama Sabachthani." In *Out of the Storm: Uncollected Fantasies.* Edited by Sam Moskowitz, 189–220. West Kingston, RI: Donald M. Grant, 1975. 189–220.

———. "The Ghosts of the *Glen Doon.*" In *The Haunted Pampero.* Edited by Sam Moskowitz. Hampton Falls: Grant, 1991. 101–22.

———. *The Ghost Pirates.* In *The House on the Borderland and Other Novels.* London: Gollancz, 2002. 203–305.

———. "The Habitants of Middle Islet." In *The Ghost Pirates and Other Revenants of the Sea.* Edited by Jeremy Lassen. San Francisco: Night Shade Books, 2005. 499–510.

———. *The House on the Borderland.* In *The House on the Borderland and Other Novels.* London: Gollancz, 2002. 108–203.

———. *The Night Land.* In *The House on the Borderland and Other Novels.* London: Gollancz, 2002. 307–637.

———. "Old Golly." In *The Haunted Pampero.* Edited by Sam Moskowitz. Hampton Falls, NH: Donald M. Grant, 1991. 260–70.

———. "Out of the Storm." In *Out of the Storm: Uncollected Fantasies.* Edited by Sam Moskowitz. West Kingston, RI: Donald M. Grant, 1975. 139–59.

———. "The Riven Night." In *Terrors of the Sea: Unpublished Fantasies.* Edited by Sam Moskowitz. Hampton Falls, NH: Grant, 1996. 155–67.

———. "The Silent Ship." In *The Haunted Pampero.* Edited by Sam Moskowitz. Hampton Falls, NH: Donald M. Grant, 1991. 156–69.

———. "Through the Vortex of a Cyclone." In *The Wandering Soul: Glimpses of a Life: A Compendium of Rare and Unpublished Works.* Edited by Jane Frank. Leyburn, UK: Tartarus Press, 2005. 119–35.

———. "The Wild Man of the Sea." In *The Haunted Pampero*. Edited by Sam Moskowitz. Hampton Falls, NH: Donald M. Grant, 1991. 260-70.

Hurley, Kelly. *The Gothic Body: Sexuality, Materialism, and Degeneration at the Fin-de-Siècle*. Cambridge: Cambridge University Press, 1996.

Jones, William. *Credulities Past and Present: Including the Sea and Seamen, Miners, Amulets and Talismans, Rings, Word and Letter Divination, Numbers, Trials, Exorcising and Blessing of Animals, Birds, Eggs, and Luck*. London: Chatto & Windus, 1880.

Klein, Bernhard, ed. *Fictions of the Sea: Critical Perspectives on the Ocean in British Literature and Culture*. Aldershot. UK: Ashgate Publishing, 2002.

Landow, George. *Images of Crisis: Literary Iconology, 1750 to the Present*. London: Routledge & Kegan Paul, 1982.

Marryat, Frederick. *The Phantom Ship*. 1839. Edited by David Hannay. London: Macmillan, 1897.

Moore, Thomas. "Written on Passing Dead-man's Island." 1804. In *The Poetical Works of Thomas Moore, Collected by Himself*. Edinburgh: Gall & Inglis, 1859.

Moskowitz, Sam. "Introduction: The Riven Night." In *Terrors of the Sea: Unpublished Fantasies*. Edited by Sam Moskowitz. Hampton Falls, NH: Donald M. Grant, 1996. 155.

Noakes, Richard J. "Natural Causes? Spiritualism, Science, and the Supernatural in Mid-Victorian Britain." In *The Victorian Supernatural*, ed. Nicola Bown, Carolyn Burdett, and Pamela Thurschwell. Cambridge: Cambridge University Press, 2004. 23-43.

Oppenheim, Janet. *The Other World: Spiritualism and Psychical Research in England, 1850-1914*. Cambridge: Cambridge University Press, 1985.

Owen, Alex. *The Place of Enchantment: British Occultism and the Culture of the Modern*. Chicago: University of Chicago Press, 2004.

Rappoport, Angelo S. *Superstitions of Sailors*. London: Stanley Paul & Co., 1929.

Rediker, Marcus. *Between the Devil and the Deep Blue Sea: Merchant Seamen, Pirates and the Anglo-American Maritime World, 1700-1750*. Cambridge: Cambridge University Press, 1987.

Scott, Walter. *Rokeby*. In *The Poetical Works of Sir Walter Scott*. Edinburgh: Black, 1855. 289-348.

Thorpe, Benjamin. *Northern Mythology, Comprising the Principal Popular Traditions and Superstitions of Scandinavia, North Germany, and the Netherlands*. London: E. Lumley, 1851-52. 3 vols.

Things in the Weeds:
The Supernatural in Hodgson's Short Stories

S. T. Joshi

William Hope Hodgson's substantial output of short stories appears to have received short shrift from readers and critics alike, and for reasons that are not entirely clear. To be sure, Hodgson's four novels are all so distinctive of their kind—and, at a time when the "horror novel" was by no means a recognisable commodity, so noteworthy as harbingers of things to come—that they have perhaps justifiably attracted a significant proportion of the critical attention given to Hodgson. The mere fact that Hodgson wrote short stories with such prodigality and made relatively little attempt to gather them in collections—only four, *Carnacki the Ghost-Finder* (1913), *Men of the Deep Waters* (1914), *The Luck of the Strong* (1916), and *Captain Gault* (1917), appeared in his lifetime, and only a small proportion of this material was reprinted in such later volumes as *Deep Waters* (1967) and *Out of the Storm* (1975)—has made an assessment of his short fiction an unusually difficult prospect. Only now, with the ongoing publication by Night Shade Books of Hodgson's *Collected Fiction*,[1] is it becoming possible to gauge the full extent of Hodgson's work as a short story writer beyond such anthology chestnuts as "The Voice in the Night" or the well-known Carnacki stories.

That work has both its virtues and its drawbacks. Like many short story writers, Hodgson wrote a bit too much, and his tales are in some instances marred by repetitiousness of conception, slipshod writing, and a certain monotony of setting, as he overused the sea topos that forms the most recognisable feature of his overall output. Hodgson appears to have had a relatively small body of distinctive short story ideas, and he often wrote several tales on the

---

1. In spite of certain deficiencies—notably an unacceptably high number of typographical errors and an absence of the highest professional standards of text editing and copyediting—this edition does make available a substantial proportion of Hodgson's short stories in a convenient edition, and it will be cited here where possible, under the abbreviation *CF.*

same basic premise with only slight variations in tone, setting, and execution. Moreover, his tales fall into several discrete categories, with relatively little overlap. The Carnacki stories, utilising the "psychic detective" scenario popularised by Algernon Blackwood's *John Silence–Physician Extraordinary* (1908), form a class by themselves, as do the lesser-known Captain Gault stories, recounting the adventures of that genial smuggler. Other tales are purely stories of adventure, whether on sea or land. But a substantial residue feature the core element that infuses at least three of his four novels (*The Night Land* being put aside as an unclassifiable cosmic fantasy): the supernatural. More specifically, a number of short stories provocatively address whether the supernatural does or does not come into play, and do so in such a way as to fall variously into such rubrics as the clearly supernatural, the "explained supernatural" (where purportedly supernatural phenomena are explained away as the product of trickery or of perceptual error on the part of the protagonists), the ambiguously supernatural (where, as in *The Turn of the Screw*, it is not possible to determine whether the apparently supernatural phenomena are actually supernatural or the products of mental aberration), and even a few proto-science fiction specimens.

That the great proportion of Hodgson's tales, of whatever type, take place in a maritime setting suggests that Hodgson saw in such a setting a convenient means for effecting that "willing suspension of disbelief" so critical to the success of a supernatural tale. Because the sea—especially in its more remote stretches, as in the immensities of the Atlantic or Pacific Ocean—is a relatively unknown quantity to most readers, and because of the known existence of unusual creatures lurking in the depths of the ocean, a sea setting can be the locus of horrors that, on land, might appear too incredible for belief. "I will expose, in all its hideous nakedness, the death-side of the sea" (*CF* 3.180), says the narrator of "Out of the Storm" (1909)—a statement that is emblematic of much of Hodgson's work. In "The Stone Ship" (1914) we learn that "some mighty strange things do happen at sea, and always will while the world lasts" (*CF* 3.299). The technique is no different in kind from other weird writers' use of remote locales—Blackwood's employment of the Canadian wilderness in "The Wendigo" and other tales; Lovecraft's setting many of his tales in the backwoods of New England or, in *At the Mountains of Madness*, in the frozen wastes of Antarctica—and Hodgson incorporates within his zone of mystery not only the inaccessible reaches of the sea itself but those hapless islands of humanity, ships, that dare to venture upon it.

One of the means by which Hodgson seeks to convey a sense of the supernatural, even if in the end the supernatural does not actually come into play, is by the seemingly elementary use of the word *Thing*. The fact that Hodgson would use such titles as "The Thing in the Weeds" and "The Thing

Things in the Weeds: The Supernatural in Hodgson's Short Stories

Invisible" points to the importance of this formulation in his aesthetic of the weird. What might seem like a kind of cop-out—an inability or unwillingness to describe in detail the entity in question—becomes instead a device for the segregation of the non-human (or the no-longer-human), or even the non-animal, from the known animate species that populate the earth. It is exactly in the *indefinability* of the "Things" encountered by Hodgson's protagonists that is the source of terror in these tales; they inspire fear because, at least initially, they resist easy classification within the realm of biology, and their almost uniform aggressiveness and hostility to humanity renders them a far from abstract intellectual conundrum.

To be sure, Hodgson is variously successful at conveying the inimical qualities of his "Things." In the early tale "A Tropical Horror" (1905) an immense monster that comes on board the deck of a ship is labelled a "Thing" (CF 3.146), but later it is identified as a "serpent" (3.147). It is not entirely clear whether the serpent is actually a supernatural entity or merely a large sea-snake: Hodgson, as frequently in his tales and novels, relies on the increased dramatic pace of his narrative—many of his tales become adventure stories in which frenetic action must be taken against the hostile force, whether natural or supernatural, that is menacing the protagonists—to distract the reader from questioning too closely the reality or plausibility of the entity in question. In "A Tropical Horror" the entire absence of any plausible rationale for the serpent's existence renders the tale unconvincing and preposterous. Similarly, in "The Call in the Dawn" (1920) the "Thing" (CF 1.227) encountered by a ship in the Sargasso Sea proves to be "some kind of devil-fish or octopus" (1.227)—presumably non-supernatural, even if "The thing was enormous" (1.228).

The Sargasso Sea stories, indeed, engage in a subtle dance between supernaturalism and non-supernaturalism. In several tales the supernatural does not appear to come into play, unless we are to assume that the very existence of this weed-choked realm is itself a supernatural phenomenon, a matter directly addressed in "The Call in the Dawn":

> To those who have cast doubt upon the reality of the great Sargasso Sea, asserting that the romantic features of this remarkable sea of weed have been greatly exaggerated, I would point out that this mass of weed lurking in the central parts of the Atlantic Ocean is a fluctuating quantity, not confined strictly to an area, but moving bodily for many hundred of miles according to storm and prevailing winds, though always within certain limits. (CF 1.221)

This pseudo-scientific explanation is, in fact, not especially helpful, but it suggests that there is a kind of double remoteness associated with the site—not only is it in an unknown stretch of the Atlantic Ocean (where, theoretically, almost anything can breed and emerge), but those all-pervading weeds themselves provide an added layer of obscurity beneath which "Things" can lurk. In the two-part "From the Tideless Sea" (1906-07) we learn that "There was some dread Thing hidden within the weed" (CF 1.148), but this turns out to be an octopus. The hapless Arthur Samuel Philips, who, with his wife, is trapped aboard a derelict caught in the weeds, states, "I have grown to believe this world of desolation capable of holding any horror, as well it might" (1.156); but there is little justification for his alarm until he discovers that a pig that he had on board has been killed by "some monstrous thing" (1.165). But even this baleful entity proves to be "a gigantic crab, so vast in size that I had not conceived so huge a monster existed" (1.172). But when Philips, seeing an entire herd of crabs large and small, remarks that "the mystery [was] solved" and that "with the solution, departed the superstitious terror which had suffocated me" (1.172), we are to understand that no actual supernatural phenomenon has occurred.

Something similar happens in the other Sargasso Sea stories. In "The Mystery of the Derelict" (1907) the derelict encountered by the crew of the *Tarawak* proves to be filled with "giant rats" (CF 1.184), but no suggestion of supernaturalism is necessarily conveyed by this description. At the end of the story the narrator reflects on the matter:

> . . . of the rats that evidently dwelt in [the derelict], I have no reasonable explanation to offer. Whether they were true ship's rats, or a species that is to be found in the weed-haunted plains and islets of the Sargasso Sea, I cannot say. It may be that they are the descendants of rats that lived in ships long centuries lost in the weed-sea, and which have learned to live among the weed, forming new characteristics, and developing fresh powers and instincts. (1.186)

The implication is that the existence of these rats could be encompassed by science, if sufficient information about their nature and origins were available.

"The Thing in the Weeds" (1912) opens with the dramatic statement, "This is an extraordinary tale" (CF 1.187), which might lead one to suspect supernaturalism, as might the later comment that "out there in the darkness there surely lurked some Thing of monstrousness" (1.191). The narrator, looking out over the prow of his ship at night, contemplates the situation: "I remember how the lamps made just two yellow glares in the mist, ineffectual, yet serving somehow to make extraordinarily plain the vastitude of the night and the *possibilities of the dark*" (1.193). Hodgson's emphasis on that last phrase suggests that, just as anything can be imagined coming out of the sea, so can horrors of all sorts be conceived to emerge from the darkness. Indeed, in this tale the monster is much more frequently *heard* and *smelled* before it is actually *seen*. When it finally makes itself visible, it proves to be nothing more than a giant "squid" (1.198), one that is dispatched with guns and knives. The same fate overtakes the aquatic creature in "The Finding of the *Graiken*" (1913), which is finally identified as a cuttlefish (CF 1.219).

The ambiguity of the ontological status of Hodgson's monsters—are they supernatural or natural?—is maintained in a great many of his non-Sargasso Sea stories as well. "The Silent Ship"—evidently a variant ending of *The Ghost Pirates*—presents entities that are manifestly humanoid but, also, manifestly supernatural, in keeping with the nautical ghosts of the novel: "I saw Things coming out of the water alongside the silent ship. Things like men, they were, only you could see the ship's side through them, and they had a strange, misty, unreal look" (CF 1.138). In "The Stone Ship" (1914) the eponymous ship appears to be the locus of a succession of supernatural phenomena: members of the crew that lands on the ship seem to see immense faces peering at them underwater, are pursued by what seem to be strings of red hair, and the like. But the narrator, Duprey, systematically explains all these phenomena: the strings of red hair prove to be nothing more than "some kind of big-hairy sea-caterpillar" (CF 1.302), while the faces are those of drowned men whose tissues have been swollen by what is explicitly noted as a "natural process" (1.303). All this lends credence to Duprey's expostulation, "The natural wonders of the sea, beat all made-up yarns that ever were!" (1.301).

An exquisite ambiguity as to the nature of the supernatural phenomenon is maintained in "The Haunted *Pampero*" (1918). Captain Tom Pemberton agrees to take the *Pampero*, a ship that has a bad reputation, on a commercial voyage. His derision at the notion that the ship is cursed ("She's no more haunted than I am!" [CF 1.377]) does not reassure his wife, who insists on accompanying him. Shortly after a man, Tarpin, is picked up as a castaway, strange things begin to happen on the *Pampero*: the pigs on the ship are attacked, and appear to be suffering from shark-bites; a mysterious snarling creature appears to be on board. There is some suggestion that the entity is after the captain's wife; and there is the further suggestion that Tarpin is a kind of shape-shifter. After the latest attack, Tarpin is missing—and something is seen swimming away from the ship: "He saw the Thing again. The fish had two tails—or they might have been legs" (1.389). In the end the matter remains unresolved: the narrator quotes from an unnamed writer who has written about the phenomena aboard the *Pampero*, and who suggested that Tarpin might have been a "sea ghoul"—"some abnormal thing out of the profound deeps" (1.390). And yet, this writer also maintains that

> he did not believe the *Pampero* to be "haunted." It was, he held, simple chance that had associated a long tale of ill-luck with the vessel in question; and that the thing which had happened could have happened as easily to any

other vessel which might have met and picked up the grim occupant of the derelict whaleboat. (1.391)

And the final bit of supernatural deflation comes from Pemberton's recollection that "the marlinspike which Tarpin always carried was sharpened much to the shape of a shark's tooth" (1.391).

Another sea legend is recounted in "The Mystery of the Water-Logged Ship" (1911)–the legend of the sailor's light. The captain of the *White Hart* explains:

> "It's always give as a warnin'. My father, as was fifty-five year at sea, an' died there, seen it three times, an' if he hadn't took notice he'd have smashed up his shop every time. He always said it was the spirits of them that's drowned warnin' the sailors. I half believes it, you know, and half don't." (CF 2.357)

This legend appears to be, at the start, the only way to explain the lights seen on an apparently abandoned derelict in the North Atlantic. Later, as further bizarre phenomena occur, another member of the crew states, "There's something devilish aboard that craft, you mark my word; but whether carnal weapons is any use, the Lord He knows. I don't" (1.362). Certainly, something awesome and mysterious appears to be involved, especially when five members of the *White Hart*'s crew disappear. But here the resolution of supernaturalism is traced not to unusual natural phenomena but to human trickery: it is discovered that the derelict has a secret underground compartment where its crew had been hiding, having robbed an immense quantity of gold bullion from another ship. The crew was deliberately staging the lights and other mysterious events to scare off potential detection.

Quite similar is "The Ghosts of the *Glen Doon*" (1911), whose very title suggests the supernatural. But the opening sentence of the story–"The *Glen Doon* was reputed to be haunted–whatever that somewhat vague and much abused term may mean" (CF 1.369)–already equivocates on the matter. The *Glen Doon* had capsized and was anchored in San Francisco Bay. Larry Chaucer accepts a bet to spend a night aboard the ship. He hears a strange tapping or hammering on board the ship, then disappears. His father, the chief of police, investigates: "He had no belief at all in the supernatural" (1.377), and quickly gets to the bottom of the affair: the ship has a hollow steel mast that leads down to a large room, formed by a series of boilers, housing counterfeiters.

It is, however, difficult to deny that the entities in "Demons of the Sea" (1923) are supernatural. The narrator writes:

> . . . crawling about the barque's deck were the most horrible creatures I had ever seen. . . . Their bodies had something of the shape of a seal's, but of a dead, unhealthy white. The lower part of the body ended in a sort of double-curved tail on which they appeared to be able to shuffle about. In place of

arms they had two long, snaky feelers, at the ends of which were two very human-like hands equipped with talons instead of nails. Fearsome indeed were these parodies of human beings! (CF 1.479-80)

And yet, these loathsome entities are dispatched—or, at any rate, dispersed—with cutlasses and pistols; but the fact that they are not entirely extirpated makes the narrator ponder uneasily: "Perchance on some dark, fog-bound night, a ship in that wilderness of waters may hear cries and sounds beyond those of the wailing of the winds. Then let them look to it; for it may be that the demons of the sea are near them" (1.482).

The two Captain Jat stories are of some interest in this context. Told from the point of view of Pibby Tawles, a cabin-boy for whom the gruff captain has developed a fondness, the tales appear merely accounts of adventure on the high seas, as Captain Jat searches for treasure in far-off corners of the world. In "The Island of the Ud" (1912) Jat comes to that island, whose name he explicitly declares to mean "Devil" (CF 2.423). Pibby and Jat first hear "a far, faint inhuman howling" (2.421), then see "something that was half a woman and half something else" (2.421). Later several of these women are seen; a later description is striking:

> They had faces so flat as to be almost featureless. At first, if he thought at all, he supposed that they were wearing some kind of mask; but as they ran, the nearest woman opened her mouth and howled, the same disgusting sound that he had heard earlier that night. As she howled, she brandished both the hand that held the torch, and the other hand, above her head. But she had no hands; her arms ended in enormous claws, like the claws of a giant crab. (2.422)

This seems spectacular enough, but later Pibby "saw plainly that [the claws] were no more than cast-off shells of some huge sea-reptile" (2.428). But just as the supernaturalism of the tale seems to be deflated, Pibby sees another sight: "But the second woman gave him a horrible feeling; he could not see where her arms ended and the claws began" (2.428). And there the matter is left unresolved: do these women merely put on the claws of some sea creature for the purpose of frightening their enemies, or do their arms actually grow into claws? Much the same ambiguity is maintained in "The Adventure of the Headland" (1912), in which Jat and Pibby encounter creatures called Iils, or sacred dogs "near big as donkeys" (CF 2.450), as Jat remarks. Other creatures found running with the dogs, who "whined and snarled like dogs, yet certainly were not dogs" (2.452), prove to be the priests of the cult, covered with dog-skins and running on all fours.

There is little reason to doubt that "The Voice in the Night" (1907) is Hodgson's most accomplished tale of supernatural horror. What distinguishes this story, aside from the gradualness and subtlety of its supernatural manifestation, is an element of religious criticism that is rare in Hodgson's work. We learn that the protagonist—named only John—and his fiancée (never named), having survived the sinking of the *Albatross* (a name that immediately recalls Coleridge's *The Rime of the Ancient Mariner,* a poem of supernatural horror that is itself heavily laden with religious imagery), find themselves stranded on a lagoon. Initially they "thanked God" (CF 3.160) for their apparent salvation, especially when they found that there were edible foodstuffs on a foundered ship near the lagoon, at which point John "thanked God in my heart for His goodness" (3.161). But the lagoon is nearly entirely covered with a curious grey fungus, which also grows on the foundered ship. A short time later a bit of the fungus is found growing on John's fiancée's hand—then on John's own face. At this point the couple seem resigned to their fate ("God would do with us what was His will" [3.163]), but after several months in which their food has been reduced to virtually nothing, the woman takes to eating the fungus. Later John encounters a hideous creature—perhaps a man—covered with the fungus. Finally, John capitulates and eats some of the fungus himself. . . . As in Lovecraft's "The Colour out of Space" (1927), which features a somewhat analogous phenomenon, we are left to wonder at both the physical and the psychological degradation of the couple—and we are not surprised that John, in seeking help from a ship that has sailed nearby, refuses to allow the crew members to catch a glimpse of him. What is puzzling, however, is John's insistence that "it is God's wish that we should tell to you all that we have suffered" (3.159). The motivations of a God who would allow the creatures of his special care to experience such a loathsome fate can only be wondered at.

"Out of the Storm" is somewhat similar in its implicit religious criticism. A scientist has apparently managed to establish some kind of mental communication with a man who is on board a sinking ship. This man sees "the tentacles of some enormous Horror" (CF 3.180) and, in his terror, delivers a rebuke to God: "Oh! God, art Thou indeed God? Canst Thou sit above and watch calmly that which I have just seen? Nay! Thou art no God! Thou art weak and puny beside this foul *Thing* which Thou didst create in Thy lusty youth. *It is now* God—and I am one of its children" (3.180). Although the man later admits that he has blasphemed (3.182), it is his condemnation, not his sheepish apology, that remains in our minds.

"The Derelict" (1912) appears to be somewhat of an expansion or revision of "The Voice in the Night." Whereas in the earlier story the exact biological status of the grey fungus is never clarified (is it animate? or is it merely a kind of virus or plague?), "The Derelict" is much more explicit. What appears to be a kind of half-animate mould is found on an ancient derelict:

All about him, the mould was in active movement. His feet had sunk out of sight. The stuff appeared to be *lapping* at his legs; and abruptly his bare flesh showed. The hideous stuff had rent his trouser-legs away, as if they were paper. He gave out a simply sickening scream, and, with a vast effort, wrenched one leg free. It was partly destroyed. The next instant he pitched face downward, and the stuff heaped itself upon him, as if it were actually alive, with a dreadful savage life. It was simply infernal. (CF 3.249)

Horrible as this is, it is not the end of the story. The culmination occurs when the strange noises accompanying the horrors on the derelict—specifically a "Thud! Thud! Thud!" heard at regular intervals—are explained: they are the beating of the heart of the derelict itself, which by some means has become a living entity. In the end a doctor who had introduced the narrative concludes that it exemplifies his notion that "so eager [is] the Life-Force to express itself, that I am convinced it would, if given the right Conditions, make itself manifest even through so hopeless-seeming a medium as a simple block of sawn wood" (3.235). In the case of the derelict, the doctor continues,

> "If we could know exactly what that old vessel had originally been loaded with, and the juxtaposition of the various articles of her cargo, plus the heat and time she had endured, plus one or two other only guessable quantities, we should have solved the chemistry of the Life-Force, gentlemen. Not necessarily the *origin*, mind you; but, at least, we should have taken a big step on the way." (2.257)

Whether this pseudo-scientific explanation is convincing is not to the point; it is the gesture of making such an explanation at all that matters. Just as in some of the Sargasso Sea stories, we are led to believe that it is merely the absence of adequate scientific information that prevents the seemingly supernatural phenomena from being entirely explained in natural terms.

A different kind of "scientific" explanation is found in a number of the stories involving Thomas Carnacki, the psychic detective—but it is an explanation based largely upon unconvincing occultist presuppositions. Although perhaps the best known of Hodgson's short stories, the Carnacki tales as a group do not rank high in his overall output, as they are marred by the crude stylistic formulae customary in popular fiction—the mechanical use of a recurring character, a verbose drawing out of the plot beyond its natural parameters, certain irritating habits of speech by Carnacki himself (especially his repeated query, "Can you understand?" when dealing with apparent supernaturalism), the contrived use of occultist mumbo-jumbo ("electric pentacles," the "Saaamaaa Ritual," etc.), and so forth. That Hodgson was attempting to capitalise on the success of Blackwood's best-selling *John Silence* (1908) is evident, as the Carnacki tales began appearing in the *Idler* only two years after the appearance of that volume.

And yet, where the Carnacki tales gain their interest is in their constant fluctuating, exactly as Hodgson's other tales do, between supernaturalism and non-supernaturalism. In the first story, "The Thing Invisible," Carnacki declares that "I am as big a sceptic concerning the truth of ghost tales as any man you are likely to meet" (CF 2.138). Carnacki goes on to say that he is an "unprejudiced sceptic," by which he means that "I am not given to either believing or disbelieving things 'on principle', as I have found many idiots prone to be . . . I view all reported 'hauntings' as un-proven until I have examined into them; and I am bound to admit that ninety-nine cases in a hundred turn out to be sheer bosh and fancy" (2.138). The proportion is not by any means quite that high in the nine Carnacki tales, but a surprising number of them resolve themselves non-supernaturally: in "The Thing Invisible" it turns out that the dagger that has apparently hurled itself through the air and nearly killed a man has been operated by a secret mechanism; in "The House among the Laurels" the seemingly supernatural phenomena in a deserted castle have been staged by a group of squatters who may have lived in the place for years; "The Find" is an explicitly non-supernatural story of a forged rare book. Conversely, "The Gateway of the Monster," "The Whistling Room," "The Haunted *Jarvee*," and "The Hog" are unequivocally supernatural, although several are spoiled by incomprehensible occultist pseudo-science.

This leaves the two stories, "The Searcher of the End House" and "The Horse of the Invisible," in which *many* but not *all* of the "supernatural" phenomena are resolved naturally: Carnacki, at the end of both stories, insists that a slim residue of genuine supernaturalism may still remain. The first tale is set in a house being rented by Carnacki himself and his mother; and it is plagued with strange odours, inexplicable rappings, and so forth. Although Carnacki discovers that many of the occurrences were engendered by a Captain Tobias, a smuggler, he is unable to identify Tobias as the source of the most striking phenomena—the ghosts of a woman and a child, seen variously by Carnacki himself and others. Carnacki is compelled to conclude: "I can only suppose that *fear* was in every case the key, as I might say, which opened the senses to an awareness of the presence of the Woman" (CF 2.230). Similarly, in "The Horse of the Invisible," while it is determined that a man named Parsket has dressed up as a horse in order to scare away a naval officer named Beaumont who is engaged to Miss Hisgins (Parsket being in love with her himself), Carnacki believes that "there was something more at work than [Parsket's] sham-haunting" (CF 2.252), and concludes tentatively that "Parsket had produced what I might term a kind of 'induced haunting,' a kind of induced simulation of his mental conceptions, due to his desperate thoughts and broodings" (2.254). The suggestion in both stories is that intense emotions can of themselves produce quasi-supernatural phenomena even when other phenomena are convincingly explained away as the product of deceit and trickery.

In other tales by Hodgson we find the pseudo-supernatural ("The Goddess of Death" [1904], in which the apparent movement of a marble statue of Kali is explained away as a mechanical contrivance), the mystical ("The Riven Night," in which spirits of the dead are seen in a purple fog), a touching religious fantasy ("The Valley of Lost Children," which explains what happens to little children who die prematurely), and even a curious proto-science fiction tale to prove a religious point ("The Baumoff Explosive"). The posthumously published "The Room of Fear" appears to be one of Hodgson's earliest tales, and is a gripping narrative of the effects of fear upon a small boy who is made to sleep in a lonely bedroom and is terrified of the shadows he encounters there. In many ways this story is emblematic of the entire corpus of Hodgson's short fiction, which exhibits the manifold effects of fear upon the varied protagonists—ranging from grizzled sea captains to learned scientists, from hapless passengers adrift on derelicts to uneducated and superstitious sailors—who people his tales. Even if few of the short stories can be said to have the substantive effect of his novels, especially such a fantastic epic as *The Night Land,* and even if they are marred by a certain repetitiveness of setting and incident, the best of Hodgson's tales comprise an important contribution to the literature of terror; and in large part they gain their significance by exhibiting a multiplicity of gradations between pure non-supernaturalism and pure supernaturalism, with some of the most provocative of them failing to resolve definitively into the one mode or the other. While the obscurity into which much of Hodgson's work fell for a generation following his death may have precluded its exercising a notable influence upon his successors in the weird tale, the refusal of that work to fade away bespeaks an inner core of aesthetic merit that augurs well for its endurance.

Works Cited

Hodgson, William Hope. *The Boats of the "Glen Carrig" and Other Nautical Adventures.* The Collected Fiction of William Hope Hodgson, Volume 1. Edited by Jeremy Lassen. San Francisco: Night Shade Books, 2003. [CF 1]

———. *The House on the Borderland and Other Mysterious Pieces.* The Collected Fiction of William Hope Hodgson, Volume 2. Edited by Jeremy Lassen. San Francisco: Night Shade Books, 2004. [CF 2.]

———. *The Ghost Pirates and Other Revenants of the Sea.* The Collected Fiction of William Hope Hodgson, Volume 3. Edited by Jeremy Lassen. San Francisco: Night Shade Books, 2005. [CF 3.]

Against the Abyss: Carnacki the Ghost-Finder

Mark Valentine

William Hope Hodgson wrote nine episodes in the career of "Carnacki, the Ghost-Finder," probably (though we do not know for certain) during 1908-10. Two of them at least, "The Whistling Room" and "The Hog," are among the most powerful and intense depictions of personal terror in the face of supernatural evil by any author in the twentieth century. Some of the other stories have effective passages of chilling description, and all of them, even those that end up with a rational explanation, offer plenty of narrative satisfaction, from the unusual ideas, strongly realized central character, and energy in the telling.

The collection has become a classic in the occult, or psychic, detective field, much reprinted and evidently relished by readers. As Gerald Suster pointed out, in the (UK) Sphere paperback 1980 edition, the book once set a sort of record. In 1973, sixty years after it first appeared, it was in print from three publishers at once. The author's early death in World War I meant that his books went out of copyright in the mid-1960s, and that certainly helped publishers to risk a reprint. But many other books are also out of copyright: few have been so enthusiastically reissued. Individual episodes have also been anthology favorites. Despite this popularity, though, *Carnacki the Ghost-Finder* is not always well regarded, and in this essay I propose to suggest the stories merit more attention.

Detective stories were of course well established in the story magazines and publishers' lists of the Edwardian period: the great success of Sherlock Holmes had assured that. And authors were alert to the possibilities of engaging the reader's interest with unusual variations on the form: hence, Ernest Bramah wrote about a blind detective in his Max Carrados stories, Victor L Whitechurch about a railway detective, Thorpe Hazell, Baroness Orczy about a woman detective, Lady Molly of Scotland Yard, and so on. E. W. Hornung also hit upon the astute idea of telling a crime story from the villain's perspective, in his popular Raffles yarns.

At the same time, stories in which detectives encounter the eerie, macabre, and seemingly supernatural had been part of the techniques for building up mysterious atmosphere ever since the genre had begun—the cases of Poe's M. Dupin and Wilkie Collins's *The Woman in White* and *The Moonstone* being striking examples. Even Van Helsing, in *Dracula*, if not exactly a detective, is certainly a combative investigator who pursues the Count as any crimefighter would a master-criminal; while Dr. Hesselius, in Sheridan Le Fanu's supernatural tales, is a medical man whose casebook also resembles that of a detective.

Moreover, the strong late Victorian interest in spiritualism and apparent evidence of paranormal phenomena had led to the foundation of the Society for Psychical Research in 1882 and the beginning of independent investigations into purported "real-life" hauntings, manifestations, poltergeists, possessions, and other phenomena. A further important piece of background, in view of Hodgson's frequent use of the "haunted house" format, may have been the eager reception given to Elliott O'Donnell's accounts of supposedly authentic supernatural visitations, in *Some Haunted Houses of England and Wales* (1908), *Haunted Houses of London* (1909), and others, a publishing success for Nash, who were to become Hodgson's publisher too.

The stage was therefore set for the creation of a character that would draw together all these strands and seize the public imagination with fictional accounts of supernatural investigation. A few such attempts had been made, of which perhaps the most notable were the Flaxman Low stories of E. & H. Heron (1899). But none had quite established themselves as the real exemplar and prototype for the form, with widespread public recognition.

Algernon Blackwood was the first to earn fame in this way, with his *John Silence*: when the book was published in 1908, it was advertised on billboards and omnibuses, and soon became a great success. In his introduction to a reprint edition (1942), Blackwood reveals that these tales of his indomitable psychic investigator "were originally separate studies of various 'psychic' themes, and it was on the suggestion of Mr Nash, who had already published two books for me, that I grouped them under the common leadership of a single man, Dr John Silence." It was a shrewd suggestion, that gave a new shape and force to the author's otherwise somewhat diffuse studies in the supernatural.

It may have been the recollection of this success that prompted William Hope Hodgson, still determinedly finding his way as a working writer, to produce the series of Carnacki the Ghost-Finder stories for the *Idler* magazine, where five of them appeared from January 1910 onwards. Hodgson wrote for the *Idler* in what was to prove to be its last full year of existence: it folded in March 1911. Whether the stories had been devised with the *Idler* specifically in mind or not, they matched its mood well. It has been observed that its "basic mood" was "the gentleman at leisure." The framing of the Carnacki stories was therefore exactly apt for the *Idler*: a group of gentlemen gathered for dinner in comfortable and fashionable rooms on Cheyne Walk, The Embankment, Chelsea, to hear yarns from a host who is evidently himself a gentlemanly amateur.

The first published story, in the January 1910 issue, was "The Gateway of the Monster," followed in consecutive months until April by "The House among the Laurels," "The Whistling Room," and "The Horse of the Invisible." At the same time as the January publication, Hodgson produced a condensed version of these four tales, in one narrative, issued as a paper-covered booklet in London and New York, evidently for copyright purposes. As the other Carnacki tales (five more) were not included, it is reasonable to assume they had not then been written, or presumably Hodgson would have wanted to safeguard them too.

There was a gap of one month before "The Searcher of the End House" appeared in the *Idler* for June 1910, and that break may also suggest the story was written a little later than the first four. The sixth tale, "The Thing Invisible," did not appear until it was published in the *New Magazine* for January 1912, by which time the *Idler* was no more. Interestingly, in late 1909, Hodgson had inquired at the *Bookman*, for which he was reviewing, after a review copy of Anthony Dyllington's novel *The Unseen Thing*. This now rare novel concerns a deformed human creature kept in the attic by his brother: its cries and paroxysms are taken to be a haunting. The similarity of title to Hodgson's story "The Thing Invisible" is striking, as is the theme of concealed family madness in both works. Did Hodgson write the story after reading the book and draw upon elements of it for inspiration? Or had his story already been written, and he simply wanted to check what that this book with the similar title was about? The former may seem more likely, because if "The Thing Invisible" had already been written by January 1910, it would surely have been included in the copyright volume and perhaps in the *Idler* series.

However that may be, it was these six that were collected by the same publisher as for *John Silence*, Eveleigh Nash, in 1913. (Three others, "The Hog," "The Find," and "The Haunted *Jarvee*," were added for the Mycroft & Moran edition of 1947, edited by August Derleth.) "The Thing Invisible" was chosen as the opening story for the Nash collection. Was this simply for some practical reason, such as that it was nearest to hand, having been most recently published? Or did Hodgson consider it the best?

The Carnacki stories were written at what might be called a transitional point in Hodgson's writing career. He had three published books already to his name: *The Boats of the "Glen Carrig"* (1907), *The House on the Borderland* (1908), and *The Ghost Pirates* (1909), all written, most probably, when he had time to himself at Glaneifion, the house at Borth, mid-Wales, overlooking the sea, that the family rented. They had won some acclaim but had not been the great literary or commercial success Hodgson had anticipated. So now he was turning his attention more toward the demands of the market. Indeed, he never wrote another full-length novel (*The Night Land*, published in 1912, had been written earlier). Instead, he aimed his work more at the periodicals, which would pay for a striking short story. It is likely that the Carnacki stories represent the first signs of an increased understanding on Hodgson's part about the best way to enter these literary markets, and the need to place his far-flung visions into a form readers could more readily understand. They were followed by a regular supply of stories, especially to the *Red Magazine*, including a further series character in the shape of the nautical Captain Gault.

In devising the Carnacki stories, Hodgson made sure they would contain many elements that would be endearingly familiar to enthusiasts of the more usual sort of detective fiction. The hero appears to be of private means and his reputation is such that clients call upon him from all corners of the British Isles. He has an understanding with the police that enables him to draw on their help when needed (although what they make of the more genuine supernatural occurrences is not recorded: can one imagine, by analogy, Lestrade vs. the Hog?). We are made aware that there are many more cases to tell of, through passing references with intriguing hints—"the Black Veil," "the Silent Garden," and so on. And, as so often in the field, the hero has a Boswell—or Watson—to set down his adventures for him. But Carnacki's chronicler is by no means as active as Watson. He is either indolent or incurious or both, since he merely turns up when summoned by the great man, enjoys dinner, and listens to the tale. He never evinces the lightest inclination to join in on an adventure. Instead, he contents himself with retelling what he (and a trio of other summoned friends) hears from Carnacki.

In "The Gateway of the Monster," the first-told story, Hodgson deploys a significant number of elements that would also accord with readers' expectations of occult or supernatural sources. The hero is learned in a secret ancient grimoire, the fourteenth-century Sigsand Manuscript, knows the "Second Sign of the Saaamaaa Ritual" (we are not told if there is a First), and, in constructing a circle of power around himself as a defense, uses sacred herbs, holy water, and a chalked sign. Despite all these precautions, the manifestation of a giant, shadowy, clawing hand, which pounces repeatedly at Carnacki, is powerfully done. Strangest of all, though, is Hodgson's invention of a modern protective force, the Electric Pentacle, with its softly glowing blue tubes. It is just possible he may have got the idea for this from a stage magician, Dr. Walford Bodie, who performed many shows in the North of England, easily accessible from Blackburn, Lancashire, then Hodgson's home, during about the same period as Hodgson's notorious Houdini challenge. Bodie used electrical apparatus to striking effect in his act, trusting to the public's imperfect knowledge of how electricity works to give the impression that he was immune to huge shocks and surges of power.

As shown in the exciting narrative thrust of "The Gateway of the Monster," the Carnacki stories provided a format and framework well-suited for channeling Hodgson's personal energy, robustness of character, and striking imagination. It has been suggested that the stories drew on real incidents from Hodgson's life; but whether this is an important element or not, they certainly capture an attitude of courage, curiosity, and determination that we recognize in the author himself, from his tough upbringing at home and at sea, his enthusiasm for his body-building trade, his youthful exploits, his challenge to Houdini and braving of the hostility of the audience, and his later pluck at war. Although the stories' narrator is called Dodgson, and the similarity of name suggests we are to read this as meaning Hodgson, we also cannot doubt that there is much of the author in the character of Carnacki himself.

The character's name is interesting. It was probably selected to fit in with readers' expectations that exotic characters with unusual skills must have a name and background to match. The trend was perhaps started by M. P. Shiel's refulgent *Prince Zaleski* (1895), a detective who, if he does not encounter the supernatural, certainly deals in the occult; and Guy Boothby's enormously popular hero-villain Dr. Nikola (in five novels starting with *A Bid for Fortune*, 1895) who (like Carnacki) is enmeshed in both conventional villainy and supernatural evil. It is also likely that the stage names adopted by magicians and stage performers—indeed such as Houdini, whom Hodgson challenged in 1908—were an influence.

There have always been those who are unhappy about the hybrid that is the occult detective. When Ronald Knox put forward his "Ten Commandments" of detective fiction in 1928, he stipulated that there should be no supernatural element. The Detection Club put it more forcefully, ruling out "Mumbo-Jumbo, Jiggery-Pokery . . . or the Act of God." On the other hand, neither have weird fiction savants been entirely happy that the sleuthing format works best for their field. H. P. Lovecraft said of the Carnacki volume: "In quality it falls conspicuously below the level of [Hodgson's] other books. We here find a more or less conventional stock figure of the 'infallible detective' type—the progeny of M. Dupin and Sherlock Holmes, and the close kin of Algernon Blackwood's John Silence—moving through scenes and events badly marred by an atmosphere of professional 'occultism.'"

In fact, those distinctions are not quite as straightforward as they appear. A surprising number of the Holmes stories start with strong hints that some supernatural or uncanny agency is in play (*The Hound of the Baskervilles* most obviously, "The Sussex Vampire," etc.), even if in the end these are always rationalized. Most of the Carnacki stories adopt a similar approach—a strong whiff of sulphur is only used to disguise the common stench of villainy. And as in the Holmes stories, one is sometimes unpersuaded by the lengths villains will go to create the semblance of the supernatural and disguise their more worldly concerns. Hodgson is always potent and compelling when he evokes the supernatural: paradoxically, it is the lesser infamies that make the reader skeptical.

Despite this weakness, Hodgson makes the stories succeed through a number of strong qualities that are his particular hallmark. His main character is not quite the superhuman figure Lovecraft evoked; he is not, indeed, "infallible," since he fails in the case of "The Haunted *Jarvee*." He is not as aloof from the common run of the world as either Zaleski or Silence—or the moody aesthetical Holmes, for that matter. He is a practical, methodical individual, more like R. Austin Freeman's always well-prepared exemplar of "medical jurisprudence," Dr. Thorndyke. Whereas the latter's black bag might contain chemicals, test tubes, and other analytical equipment, Carnacki's carries the tools of *his* trade: candles, herbs, talismans, charged symbols, holy water, and of course his Electric Pentacle. And just as Thorndyke is well versed in the niceties of the law and the developments of forensic science, Carnacki is a deep student of esoteric and occult literature. Although unpaid, he is not an amateur in the sense of a mere dabbler, but is profoundly committed to his unusual vocation.

This hard-headed, unflinching approach to his craft makes Carnacki's encounters with the supernatural all the more compelling. In the four or five "pure" occult cases, where what Hodgson calls the "Ab-Normal" is either the sole or strongly the uppermost element, we feel Carnacki's isolation and vulnerability as grotesque forces push at the boundaries of this world, their power the more fearful because we see they are confronting a man of courage who knows his work. In this scene, for example—"There came a sense as of dust falling continually and monotonously and I knew that my life hung uncertain and suspended for a flash in a brief, reeling vertigo of unseeable things" ("The Whistling Room")—the image of the dust falling is a finely desolate hint at the insignificance of humanity within the fall of ages, and at the same time conveys silence and ominousness: we think, "What happens when the dust stops?"

Or, again, in "The Gateway of the Monster," Carnacki's vulnerability is stressed: "I had for a moment that feeling of spiritual sickness as if some delicate, beautiful, inward grace had suffered." In that simple, poetic phrase, Hodgson conveys to us that Carnacki is not simply the muscular hero who depends upon physical prowess nor a calculating machine of cold intelligence, as in some detective fiction of the period. The sense of personal violation in the phrase strikes the reader forcibly. The character is more human, more a prey to emotions and sensations than is common in the genre. His mortal fear, which he freely acknowledges, is suppressed only by his sheer determination and his deep understanding of the forces he faces.

This powerful element of the stories helps them transcend the suggestion that they work only as cheap suspense thrillers. Several commentators, as well as Lovecraft, have implied that *Carnacki the Ghost-Finder* is an aberration in the Hodgson canon, motivated mainly by commercial considerations. Peter Tremayne (*Masters of Terror, Volume 1*, 1977) contrasts the stories with his other work and implies they were meant to be merely "money-making." Ian Bell calls the stories "considerably inferior" to Hodgson's other work (in an article for *Antiquarian Book Monthly Review*, December 1985). Sam Moskowitz (*Out of the Storm*, 1975) says they are "deliberate pot-boilers" with a "weak" story-frame and an almost totally unvisualized lead character. But I suggest these assessments do the author a serious injustice. They may have been shaped to appeal more to a popular readership, but that is not their only motivation: Hodgson puts himself and his fervid imagination into all his work. There are a number of good reasons for regarding the Carnacki stories as an integral part of his vision.

Firstly, they retain and bring into sharp focus the sense of a vast cosmic battleground that Hodgson conveyed so strongly in *The Night Land* (1912). The image of the "night-black, dead planet, with the remains of the human race . . . besieged by monstrous, hybrid and altogether unknown forces," as Lovecraft memorably evoked, is quite literally brought down to earth in the Carnacki adventure of "The Hog," where "the monstrosities of the Outer Circle" have "desires regarding us which are incredibly more dreadful to our minds when comprehended than an intelligent sheep would consider our desires towards its own carcass." The faltering Electric Circle that, for the time being, protects the last humans in the Night Land is found in microcosm in Carnacki's personal psychic safeguard, the Electric Pentacle. Yet there is a difference. In the far-future Night Land, humanity has all but lost; in the Carnacki stories, all is still to fight for, and the protagonist is our warrant that the voracious elemental forces can be staved off. We should regard the stories as providing a tauter, more disciplined evocation of the vision Hodgson lays out at greater length in his novels, with a greater concentration on the possibilities of human resistance.

Secondly, the stories do tell us something more about Hodgson himself. There are obvious parallels between him and his lead character, such as the familiarity with photography and seamanship, and more implied references, such as the absence of a father in the Carnacki family home (Hodgson was less than fifteen years old when his own father died). In "The Searcher of the

End House," the unaccountable knock on the banister at the beginning of the story is said to have been a recollection of a genuinely inexplicable happening that happened when Hodgson was living with his mother (according to R. Alain Everts, in *Some Facts in the Case of William Hope Hodgson*, 1987). Carnacki is credited with having an "inward, unused sense" in "The Gateway of the Monster," and an "extraordinary and peculiar nervousness" in "The Searcher of the End House," and it has been suggested that Hodgson himself experienced these too, and was something of a psychic "sensitive." We know also that Hodgson was angered and disturbed by the physical abuse he suffered as a boy aboard ship in his Merchant Navy days, and something of that proud resistance to attack is surely to be seen in the way Carnacki fights back against the gross intrusions from cosmic monstrosities. It is certainly arguable that no other character in all Hodgson's fiction possesses so many of his own attributes.

We should be wary, therefore, of dismissing the Carnacki stories as simply commercial episodes. Julian Symons (*Bloody Murder: From the Detective Story to the Crime Novel–A History*, revised edition, 1985) has suggested the detective story is "The Folk-Myth of the Twentieth Century," its ritual order and archetypes satisfying our instincts and longings in the same way as the traditional oral tale. He notes, however, that while "at their best crime writers can illuminate the condition of society . . . they never move . . . in mystical regions where spiritual truths are being considered." That is precisely what the occult detective story, at its best, does achieve; and the Carnacki stories are real exemplars of that.

There is a case, I therefore propose, for treating the stories with some of the respect accorded to *The House on the Borderland* and *The Night Land*. Although he is described as a "Ghost-Finder," Carnacki does not deal merely with the pallid wraiths of Gothic tradition, but rather with the same vast dark gulfs and predatory abominations envisioned in the two novels. Moreover, much more so than in the longer narratives, we are drawn to admire the urge to repel evil. Carnacki is a combatant. Even when he is faced with one of "Hell's mysteries," against which "there is no protection," he pits himself against it, though he knows it is "a crazy thing to do" ("The Whistling Room"). And when, accompanied by his client, he is being sucked into an abyss that "no human has any right to be near, for his soul's sake" ("The Hog"), he is sustained by "a feeling of furious anger." Why does Carnacki have this will to resist? Why, when he believes that humanity is an insignificant physical condiment compared with the immense and rapacious forces of the "Outer Circle," does he continue to do battle? While the Carnacki stories may not have the rambling, rhapsodical majesty of Hodgson's major novels, they are in their own way a lucid testament of existential defiance against the abyss.

William Hope Hodgson in the Underworld: Mythic Aspects of the Novels

Phillip A. Ellis

The quest is one of the basic themes of human narratives. It underlies mythology and literature as diverse as the Trojan War and *The Lord of the Rings*. And it underlies, and unites, the four novels of William Hope Hodgson. When we look at the quest, we see that it is usually set in an underworld of sorts. The hero enters the mythic underworld, faces its denizens, and returns with a boon. One question is: How is this underworld constructed in a given narrative or narratives, and what is its nature? When we look at Hodgson's novels, we find some interesting aspects of the underworld, and the way that they unite the four novels into a tight, focused body of work. For example, the nature of the underworld, and the reactions of the hero toward it, are mirrored in the denizens, the inhabitants. In addition, looking at the call to adventure, the spur to the quest proper, as well as the boon, is also illustrative. These are important because they enable a fuller appreciation of the novels and their essential unity, as well as providing us with a framework for approaching other, related texts.

Before proceeding further, it must be remarked that there are some aspects of the underworld that are not covered in this essay. First, the mythological nature of the underworld is not discussed. That has been covered adequately by Joseph Campbell, among others. Second, the nature and progression of the hero's journey into and out of the mythic underworld are also unremarked upon. To do so would be little more than to paraphrase the plot of the novels, even though the call to adventure is the next topic of discussion. Third, how and why Hodgson employed the quest motif will be largely glossed over. What is of primary concern is the nature of the underworld, and of its inhabitants, and of the boon derived therefrom. Finally, the degree to which the novels are analogues of myths is not studied here. Thus the parallels and divergences of *The Night Land* (hereafter referred to as *Night*) from the Orpheus myth, for example, is not discussed.[1] There is insufficient space to address these and other issues arising from the examination of the mythic underworld in Hodgson's novels, so that what is addressed must form the core of our current investigation. And the point to start with is with the call to adventure, as it is present among them.

The call to adventure, as the initial stage of the journey into the mythic underworld, is an important part of myths and the quest motif. It serves as the inciting act of Freytag's Pyramid, the stage of the narrative whereby the hero is compelled to enter into the mythic underworld upon the quest proper. In Hodgson, we find that this stage is not always present in the narrative. In *The Boats of the "Glen Carrig"* (hereafter referred to as *Boats*), for example, it is glossed over in the subtitle; this reads, in part, "*after the foundering of the good ship* Glen Carrig" ([3]). It is precisely that foundering which constitutes the call to adventure for the narrator. In *The House on the Borderland* (hereafter referred to as *House*), it is marked by visions. The initial vision itself is marked by color, first green, then red, in relation to the change of the candles (118). This helps foreshadow the later visions and leads to the first glimpse of the house in the arena. The call is most fully present in *Night*. This occurs in the initial contact by telepathy of Naani and the narrator. Here, we read how from "out of all the everlasting night a whisper was thrilling and thrilling upon my more subtle [sic] hearing" (333), signifying the re-establishment of contact between the Greater and Lesser Redoubt. This marks the sudden efflorescence of the Earth-Current in the Lesser Redoubt, leading to its failure, and it is this failure that helps spur the rescue attempts (347). The overall result is that the story proper starts: the quest begins, and the hero enters into the mythic underworld itself. What that mythic underworld is, what its nature is, forms the next area of inquiry.

Before going into greater detail about the nature of the mythic underworld, some general remarks need to be made. The mythic underworld is, basically, a place set aside from the otherwise mundane world, in both myth and in the novels of Hodgson. One way of marking this is by appeal to the imagination and the emotions. We read, for example, of the abandoned gardens in *House*, that "One could imagine things lurking among the tangled bushes" (113). We also find the appeal to the emotions soon thereafter, where we have Tonnison remarking, "'There's something queer about this place; I feel it in my bones'" (114). In myths, too, we find that the underworld is apart,

---

1. The main divergence is the substitution of a eucatastrophic ending for a catastrophic one, which is in common with the Middle English treatment of "Sir Orfeo"; cf. Ovid 10.1-85 and Sisam 13-31.

separate from the otherwise mundane world. Hades' realm, for example, is beneath the world; he must arise from the abyss to capture Persephone as she is entranced by the flower.[2] Keeping in mind this separate nature of the mythic underworld, we can make some remarks upon its nature: it is elsewhere, unmappable, yet it is also physical. There are other qualities, too, associated with it: it is uncertain in nature, unique yet unnatural. It is also a wild place, it is repulsive, and it is marked by both sound and silence. Starting, then, with its elsewhere nature, we can begin to understand the mythic locus that is the underworld.

That the quest proper takes place "elsewhere" is important to our understanding of its nature, and to the narrative. The quest occurs outside of normal existence. In *Boats*, we read in the subtitle how the events occur *"in the unknown seas to the Southward"* ([3]). The mythic underworld is literally not knowable to the mundane world. Likewise, in *House*, we read how "no map that I have hitherto consulted has shown either village or stream" (110). Again, this sense of being unknown is remarkable; the mythic underworld is literally unmappable. With *The Ghost Pirates* (hereafter referred to as *Ghost*), the underworld is on the ship itself, literally separated from the external world in part by its nature, in part by the mist. As the narrator remarks, "The strangeness was with us" (243). With *Night*, the underworld is the Night Land, and the rift through which the narrator passes. As it appears, as it were, in the narrator's dreams, it too is unmappable. All these share, in some way, a sense of reality beyond that of the mundane world. This reality is, usually, physical.

Even where there is a sense of immateriality about them, the mythic underworlds are described as physical places, or involving physicality. Note, for example, the description of the central narrator's self in the first vision: "a fragile flake of soul-dust" (*House* 119). Though the soul is immaterial, it is approached through the conceit of "dust," bringing to mind images of dust floating in a shaft of sunlight. At the same time, the narrator expresses physical feelings; he feels "lightness and cold discomfort" (119), and this note of physicality and immateriality, of sensation and soul, is readily apparent in *Night*. There, the narrator remarks how he has "at night in [his] sleep, waked into the future of this world, and seen strange things and utter marvels" (321). The Night Land, which forms the bulk of that novel, is at once dream, vision, and reality (witness the importance of eating and drinking in relation to time and movement in the narrative).[3] There is in this physicality, then, a sense of cer-

---

2. The standard treatment is the Homeric hymn to Demeter; cf. Cashford xxviii-xxxii, 5-2.

3. This forms a motif in some myths, such as that of Persephone, for example.

tainty: the mythic underworld is a real place, accessible even if only to the hero of *Night* or to ancillary characters in the three other books. Yet since the underworld is a place of paradoxes, there is an element of uncertainty to it.

An element of uncertainty certainly colors the nature of the mythic underworld.[4] For example, we read how, in *Boats*, of the first sighting of land that "none could tell whether it was land or but a morning cloud" (4). In the same book we read of an uncertainty between life and lifelessness. The narrator expresses this when he says: "I am scarce correct when I speak of life as being extinct in that land: For, indeed, now I think of it, I can remember that the very mud from which it sprang seemed veritably to have a fat, sluggish life of its own, so rich and viscid was it" (7).

Uncertainty, too, occurs in the language used. We read in *House*, for example, that "there seemed something uncanny" (113). We read, again in the same book of a "twirling and undulating rapidly, with a horrid suggestiveness" (164). Further, we find how the narrator "seemed to see . . . the world . . . revolving visibly against the stars" (164), and that "it seemed to me that I could see the very furniture of the room rotting and decaying before my eyes" (167). Note the language used: "seemed," "suggestiveness," "seemed," "seemed." There is an element of indeterminacy here, as if the narrator is struggling to understand the reality or otherwise of the underworld and its visions. This uncertainty occurs elsewhere, of course; note the telling remark "it seemed to me like the shadow of a ship" (284) in *Ghost*.

This notion of uncertainty, as it appears in language, has relations with the visceral nature of the mythic underworld. The narrator of *House* remarks that he "had . . . seen, vaguely, things that puzzled [him, and, perhaps, had felt more than [he] had seen" (118). In relation to the first vision of the house in the arena, he notes: "In my mind, a question formed, reiterating incessantly: 'What does it mean? What does it mean?' and I was unable to make answer" (121). This inability to answer highlights the uncertainty; he can no more give an answer than say with certainty whether what is witnessed is real. (Note, too, the question in the circumnavigation of the underground pit: "'What does it all mean?'" [154].) This uncertainty of language, of the language used in apprehending the reality of the mythic underworld, extends to the reality of the mythic underworld.

---

4. This sense of uncertainty, which runs through Hodgson's work, also reminds us of the themes of vagueness and ambiguity that run through Lovecraft's work. It is highly possible that there is, after all, a degree of influence from one to the other, as if Lovecraft were deriving part of his literary palette from Hodgson's, or was emphasizing it in part from his example.

This uncertainty of the mythic underworld's nature is clearly seen in *Ghost*. Although the ship is rumored as haunted, its exact nature remains uncertain. The narrator, early on, remarks how "When I asked fellows to give it a name, they generally could not" (207). This existential uncertainty extends to the denizens of the underworld. Briefly, we read of the first sighting of weed-men that "they were all at a loss to know whether I had fallen asleep, or that I had indeed seen a devil" (31). In *House*, "It seemed to me that the woods were full of vile things" (116); and, in the Pit: "I thought I heard a sound of breathing" (127). Finally, in *Ghost* the narrator notes: "I . . . saw something peering over the taffrail. It had eyes that reflected the binnacle light, weirdly, with a frightful, tigerish gleam; but beyond that, I could see nothing with any distinctness" (292). This uncertainty is more than just linguistic: it is phenomenal, real. And it is compounded by a sense of the uniqueness of the underworld.

The uniqueness of the mythic underworld is, essentially, beyond normal knowing. Of the vegetation of the first island in *Boats*, for example, the various elements "were like unto nothing which ever I had set eyes upon before" (4). Likewise, the island in the weed-choked sea's "strange vegetation" (31) is compounded by the "ground of strange and spongy texture" (32) in the island's center. In *House*, we find that the narrator's sense of time is affected: "It was as though time had been annihilated for me; so that a year was no more to my unfleshed spirit, than is a moment to an earthbound soul" (162). This is repeated in the central cosmic vision, where, of the initial speeding up of nature, it is remarked: "It was a strange sight" (163). This question of uniqueness is reflected in the unnaturalness, the divorce of the underworld (and its inhabitants) from the known world.

For the most part, the concept of the unnaturalness of the mythic underworld is expressed in *Ghost*. True, the narrator of *Night* does call the darkness of the Night Land "monstrous" (418), but it is primarily in the former book that expressions of unnaturalness occur. We read, for example, that "it was common talk among the other fellows, that there was something queer about the ship" (207). An example of this is the tendency of "sails that . . . had been properly stowed, were always blowing adrift *at night*" (207-8). This is clearly meant to be taken as contrary to the nature of things as they should be. Further, one character notes to the narrator how "'There's too many bloomin' shadders about this 'ere packet'" (208). Again, the overabundance of shadows is considered unnatural. Another example: the death of Williams is considered "damned queer" (233) by Stubbins; the note of unnaturalness is again emphasized. Finally, regarding the mist, the narrator remarks: "I had a sudden, queer feeling that the thing was not right" (241). As can be seen from these examples, the expression of this unnaturalness relies in large part upon the word "queer," emphasizing the strangeness of the unnaturalness. This brings to mind a related concept: of the underworld as a wild place, a concept again largely expressed through one book.

If the natural, settled world is ordered, the "other" place, the mythic underworld, must be wild, disordered. We read of this concept largely in *House*, but it also occurs in *Night*; there we find the narrator saying, "surely all before me was utter wildness of a dark desolation" (417). Although the linkage of wildness is related almost solely to the uncultivated gardens, there is a sense of a paradox: gardens are cultivated, ordered places, yet this one has been left to ruination, disorder, wildness. We see this clearly when the narrator says, "This house is . . . surrounded by . . . wild and uncultivated gardens" (*House* 126). And it is earlier described as "a wilderness of bushes and trees" and "the riot of a great and ancient garden" (113). The narrator also remarks: "What a wild place it was, so dismal and sombre!" (113). Yet the plain, too, is considered a wild place. It is described as a "great waste of loneliness" (119), and this linkage with being alone, solitary, reminds us that, in the wild place, we are divorced from civilized discourse. The underworld, then, is in part wild, just as it is in part unnatural and in part repulsive.

The repulsiveness of the mythic underworld is in part physical, but mainly it is a manner of psychological reaction on the part of narrators. In *Boats*, for example, we read of the initial island as being of an "abominable flatness" (4). The sides of creek are "composed of a vile mud," and the trees have "what might be described as an unwholesome look" (4). Note, too, the reaction inherent in the note of the "grotesque shadows . . . cast from the trees" (5). The narrator continues his discussion of the island by saying that "it gave [him] a sense of dreariness to look out upon it" (5). Further, the noise of the sobbing provokes certain key terms; we read, notably, the terms "curious," "awesome," "fearfully," "extraordinary," and "strange" (6). Note, too, the following: "we hoped presently to come upon a country . . . where we could put foot to honest earth" (7). These terms and phrases are not just applied to the initial island; of the island in the weeds it is said, "the valley had a very unholy fascination for me" (69). In *House*, too, there is a clear sense of repulsiveness. One of the narrators remarks, for example, of "the haunting dread that had followed me among the trees" (116). We also read the following remark, which indelibly conveys the link between repulsiveness and the unholy nature of the place: "There is something unholy–diabolical about it" (116). Even the speeding up of time in the central vision bears a sense of repulsiveness. The storm is described as being "like a monstrous black cloth . . . twirling and undulating rapidly, with a horrid suggestiveness" (164). "It seemed hideous and insupportable" (170), the narrator says elsewhere, and, shortly thereafter, he says that "It was palpable, and hideously brutal to the sense" (177); and he also mentions a "great and overwhelming distress of uneasiness" (177). Finally, in *Night*, concerning the region of the Night Land near House of Silence, it is remarked that "there did a seeming of Unholiness to brood in the air" (615). This emotive use of language is also closely related to the central vision in *House*. We read of how "The sun leapt upon me with a frightening abruptness" (164), and how "I experienced all the time a most profound awe" (165). We also read the following: "there was in it . . . a strange and awful clearness, and emptiness" (167), where the word "awful" clearly reveals the narrator's reactions to what is witnessed. Then, too we read how "a strange tremor of fear took me, and a fresh sense of wonder" (187). Further, the use of such language is important: it conveys, succinctly and powerfully, the emotional reactions of the narrators. Since all four novels are narrated in the first person, this narrative "I" that is common to all helps lend a greater sense of unity among them. This leads in turn to a final consideration of the underworld as a place, before the denizens, too, are looked at: the role of sound and silence.

Noise and the absence thereof is representative of the mythic underworld, and the dialectic between the two typifies the various examples. In *Boats*, for instance, the initial island is one characterised by silence; the narrator states, for instance, that his "spirit was put in awe by the extreme silence of all the country around" (5). Further, when the grounded boat hails the wreck, the "*silent* trees took on a little quivering, as though his voice had shaken them" (8; my emphasis). The noises themselves, when they occur, are unusual. There was the "curious, low, sobbing note" that then "died, and the silence of the land was awesome by reason of the contrast" (5). The growling, too, "seemed demoniac" (10), a description that fits in with those applied to the residents of that underworld.

In *House*, "a strange wailing noise" (116) is heard in the enveloping narrative, and also a "rustle of stirring leaves" (116). Note, too, how the arena is silent, until the swine-thing spots the narrator: "for the first time, the stillness of that abominable place was broken, by a deep, booming note, that sent an added thrill of apprehension through me" (123). The use of sound to announce the denizens is also notable here. At the Pit, at first rocks are dislodged, then there is sound: "a loud, half-human, half-pig-like squeal sounded" (127), followed by "jabbering" and "a semi-human yell of agony." This emphatic use of sound marks the start of the siege by the swine-things of the house on the borderland. During that siege, too, we read of a "noise of something rubbing and fumbling against the back door" (129). Notable, too, is the early appearance of the subterranean noises. There is, for example, the "muffled, but hideous chorus of bestial shrieks. It appeared to rise from the bowels of the earth" (129). And, finally, from the same book, there is the evocative statement that "the oppressive stillness is broken by a little eldritch scream of wind" (195).

The use of noise and silence in *Ghosts* is less notable than in the other books. There are two points, however, worth noting. First is the occasion when there "wailed down through the darkness a weird, sobbing cry. What it was, I do not know; but it sounded horrible" (270). That this noise is associated with the ghost pirates themselves cannot be doubted. Of the ghost pirates, though, the more striking note is of silence, striking since it is emphasized only once, really; we read how the "silent figure . . . *climbed over* [the port rail] *into the sea*" (210). In *Night*, however, sound and silence are more noticeable. There are, for example, the Silent Ones, for example. Further, sound and silence help define the Night Land's geography; we can easily list, among the various regions of the Night Land visible from the Great Redoubt, the Country of Wailing (329), The Place Where The Silent Ones Kill (330), and the Road Where The Silent Ones Walk (330). As can be seen, sound and silence have their parts to play in characterizing the various underworlds of the novels. What remains, then, are some concluding remarks about the nature of the mythic underworld, some notes on the denizens, and on the boon retrieved.

As noted, the mythic underworld is set aside, set apart from the mundane world. It does not, properly, exist so as to be mapped: it is unmappable. It is also a physical place, approached in physical terms, yet an aura of uncertainty persists within it. Too, the mythic underworld is beyond mundane knowing; it is unique, and also unnatural, unlike the mundane world. Unlike the mundane world, it is associated with wildness, repulsiveness, and, finally, unusual aspects of noise and silence, all in direct contrast with the mundane world. Overall, the effect given us is that the mythic underworld, the locus for the adventures of the narrator and the narrator's comrades, is a place set apart in numerous, telling ways from the ordinary, mundane world of our existence. That the hero enters in and returns with a boon is the "natural" result; that this hero is also the narrator helps strengthen the immediacy of the underworlds of the four novels, nowhere, perhaps, more so than in the hero's dealing with their inhabitants.

In looking at the inhabitants, the denizens, of the mythic underworld, we come to an understanding in part of Hodgson's literary conceptions of the abnormal and unnatural. It would be a mistake, without explicit proof, to read these as actual beliefs held, either in nature or number; however, there are a number of points that can be made regarding the inhabitants. First, there is a degree of reticence about them, a degree to which human elements have been absorbed and characterize them, yet at the same time there is an element of bestiality. The denizens are, in a sense, hybrid, just as many of the denizens of mythology are hybridized (such as the harpies and sirens—both part woman, part bird—or the centaurs, satyrs, hippocampoi, mermaids, and so on). There are also other notions present regarding the denizens. Noteworthy is the way in which familiar forces and beings are used, figuratively or apocryphally, to help convey something of the denizens' nature; some, moreover, are familiar from the arena. Also, some are first noted by animals, and the emotional reaction of the characters to the underworld is mirrored in their reaction to the denizens. Then, the repulsiveness of underworld that is mirrored in its denizens is examined. Afterwards we look more closely at both the weed-choked sea and the ghost pirates, to elucidate some final considerations. These comprise the basic areas of interest regarding the inhabitants of the underworld, and they help convey the nature of the experiences of the novels' heroes. First, though, the reticence with which the inhabitants are approached must be examined.

There is, to a degree, a sense of reticence about the inhabitants, where they are not described, as in the weed-men, and the swine-things (both of these occurring in the later books of the four; see Gafford). In the other two, however, there is a degree of reticence. In *Ghost*, for examples, the nature and description of the ghost pirates remain sketchy, almost allusive. Only their name really gives a clue as to their nature: they are ghostlike, elusive, and defying an easy comprehension or categorization. In *Night*, too, there is a reticence about the nature of most beings. They are chiefly known through descriptive names: Ab-humans, the Silent Ones, the Thing that Nods, the Watchers, giants, Night-Hounds, Strange Things. But there is a slightly greater emphasis upon description, albeit a description fragmented into key aspects of their physicality. Size is one such, their abnormality remarked upon by an emphasis in height. Hair is another characteristic that is remarked upon here and there. This reticence does not forbid some key factors in our understanding of the inhabitants. We still gain a sense of humanlike qualities, for example, which is next to be discussed in further details.

There is, to a degree, some absorption of human elements by non-human entities in the description of the underworld's inhabitants. For instance, the inhabitants of the Night Land are described as "half men and half beast, and evil and dreadful" (328). With the Humped Men, for example, "the eyes of the men did shine like the eyes of beasts" (434). In *Boats* we can note a degree of humanity in the sounds produced. Note, especially, the following: "there was in it a curious sobbing, most human in its despairful crying" (6). As the narrator notes: "it seemed that we harked to the weeping of lost souls" (6). The face on the tree is likewise abnormal; it is described as an "excrescence" (19), which emphasizes the abnormality of its nature. Chiefly, though, in that book the most humanlike of the inhabitants are the weed-men. Their "white demoniac face [is] human save that the mouth and nose had greatly the appearance of a beak" (30). They are called, for good reason, "human slugs" (70).

In *House*, the greater swine-thing at the house in the arena is remarked to have "moved with a curious lope, going almost upright, after the manner of a man" (123). It retains its swinelike nature, yet it apes humans. With the swine-things in general, what is emphasized is their speech-like noise. We read of a "half-human, half-pig-like squeal" (127), for example. And we also read of how "there sounded a noise of confused jabbering" (127). Shortly after this passage, the narrator notes: "The mouth kept jabbering, inanely, and once emitted a half-swinish grunt" (128). The swine-things also give a "semi-human yell of agony" (127), and when struck by butt of gun one of them "dropped, with an almost human groan" (129). Finally, there is, at the study door, "a sound of whispering" (132). This emphasis upon the swine-things' speech is not the only area in which comparisons to humans are made. We read how one "had run upright, or nearly so, . . . with a motion somewhat resembling that of a human being" (127). And the close description of one notes how it "had a grotesquely human mouth and jaw; but with no chin of which to speak" (127). Its eyes "seemed to glow, at times, with a horribly human intelligence" (128), a point that underscores the unnaturalness of the thing; a swine, compared to a human, is unintelligent. In addition, one physical mark of humanity, its hands, is stressed: the swine-thing's "two claw-like hands . . . bore an indistinct resemblance to human hands" (128).

When we turn to *Ghost*, we find that the first sight of a ghost pirate reveals how it was in "the form of a man" (209). This is reinforced by the statement that "It was a human figure" (210). Yet, paradoxically, this serves to heighten the abnormal nature of the ghost pirate. Such a reading is supported by the following: "It was such a beastly confirmation of the *unnaturalness* of the thing" (210). This reminds us of the following passage that occurs soon thereafter: "I saw something that looked like a man; but so hazy and unreal, that I could scarcely say I saw anything" (212). Finally, in *Night*, the Abhumans preserve in name the human element (325). That they are humans who had evolved to adapt to the Night Land is evident. Yet the description of one reminds us that "it was not properly a man" (407). Their monstrous nature is emphasized. We read of a "grey monster, that was a Great Grey Man" (383), and of giants, which are a "very man-monster filled of unwholesome life" (486). Further, we read how "many and diverse were the creatures that had some human semblance" (329). Finally, we read of the Humped Man, who "gave out a strange howling, that did be half seeming of an animal and half of an human" (573). This last point, the emphasis of the human with the bestial, reminds us of another aspect of the underworld's inhabitants: their bestial nature. This is the next aspect of them to be examined.

The notions of the bestial nature work against their identification with rational, human forces. They are not so much humanlike as inhuman, beasts, brutes, more mere animal than thinking clay. There are two books that focus on the beastlike nature of the inhabitants. The first of these is *House*, where we read in the vision of the house in the arena that "The mountains were full of strange things—Beast-gods, and Horrors, so atrocious and bestial that possibility and decency deny any further attempt to describe them" (122). Of the greater swine-thing that approaches the house, "it was the face that attracted and frightened me the most. It was the face of a swine" (123). This emphasis upon the swine as a creature of horror reminds us of "The Hog." Greater description is given to the swine-things themselves. One is described as having a "skin like a hog's, only of a dead, unhealthy white colour" (127). This is reinforced by the extended description of the one that peered into the study window. Its "nose was prolonged into a snout; this it was, that, with the little eyes and queer ears, gave it such an extraordinary swine-like appearance. Of forehead there was little, and the whole face was of an unwholesome white colour" (127-28). Adding to this, the hands are "webbed up to the first joint, much as are a duck's," and the nails are "more like the talons of an eagle than aught else" (128). Further, its grunt is described as being "half-swinish" (128). There is a later description of a "confused murmur of swine-voices" (137), which reinforces this description. Of their speech itself, it is remarked how it "might have been mistaken, by a casual listener, for the grunting and squealing of a herd of pigs. But . . . it came to me that there was a semblance in it to human speech" (133), a reading reinforced by the statement that "From the Pit, came a deep, hoarse Babel of swine-talk" (135).

Recall, too, how in *Night*, it is said of some of the men that "they to have tusks like to the tusks of pigs" (626). In contrast to *House*, in *Night* we find a wider variety of bestial references. For example, the inhabitants of the Night Land are at one point called "Infernal sharks" (329); note the emphasis of the adjective: they belong to the underworld as real sharks belong to the ocean. Note, too, how it is said later that "these [Evil Forces] . . . were congregate and gathered about the Mighty Pyramid, being attracted thereto by the great spiritual essence . . . , even as sharks do come after the ship that hath bullocks within" (432). Of the specific races that inhabit the Night Land, the giants are said to be "fathered of bestial humans and mothered of monsters" (329). And we also read how "their strength and brutishness was like to that of odd and monstrous animals of the olden world; yet part human" (354). Indeed, some are described as "seeming to be haired like to mighty crabs" (353). The Grey Man, for instance, spies "along the earth, in a strange and Brutish fashion"; it went "as a very nasty beast might go, wanton" (384). It is also called a "great and horrid monster" (385). Likewise, the yellow Man-Beast is explicitly called a "Beast" (498), thereby dehumanizing it, and the Humped Man "gave out a strange howling, that did be half seeming of an animal and half of an human" (573). Thus notions of bestiality help counterpoint those earlier, regarding the sense of humanity in the inhabitants. Ultimately, they are neither wholly human nor wholly bestial; they are composite, the one leavening the other and making them unnatural, as unnatural as the underworld itself. Yet these two extremes are not the only means of apprehending the inhabitants. Other notions exist, to which we must now focus our attention.

These other notions present about the inhabitants involve comparisons in *Night* to unliving things. We read how the Watcher of the South is called a "living hill of watchfulness" (327), and how the other Watchers are called "mountains of living watchfulness and hideous and steadfast intelligence" (329). Again, the Northeast Watcher is referred to as a "Mountain of Watchfulness" (618); this description reinforces the gigantic aspect of the beings, and their unnatural size in turn emphasizes their unholiness. These are not the only comparisons of this kind. The Yellow Thing is referred to "as it had been a low hillock that did live" (402), for example. Similarly, the slug-thing in the gorge is referred to as "like to the hull of a great ship" (451). This reminds us, perhaps, of the description of the beached airship, but it also enables a strong image to form, so that we may comprehend more fully the being's nature and appearance. In these ways is the repertoire of associations broadened. There is another way of broadening the repertoire, through associations with known, recognizably unnatural beings.

To some extent, familiar forces are used figuratively, in relation to the denizens of the underworld. We see this in the statement that the growling "seemed demoniac" (*Boats* 10); it becomes comprehensible to the reader by analogy to a familiar concept of the unnatural. Likewise, the lady who had been shipwrecked in the first island invokes a similar result by "declaring . . . that she was haunted by a devil" (13). This is echoed in the later description of the face on the tree by stating that "whether it was a part of the tree or not, it was a work of the devil" (19). In *House*, we get a sense of origins by recourse to a familiar figure: the house and its environs are an underworld because "there is an old story, told amongst the country people, to the effect that the devil built the place" (117). Similarly, the infrequent mentions of vampirism reinforce this tendency. In *Boats*, "vampires are said to inhabit the nights in dismal places" (11). Similarly, in *Night*, of the yellow Man-Beast the narrator states that "I knew that it did never eat of aught that it did slay; but to drink as a vampire" (498). The precise nature of the swine-things is questioned by another appeal to supernatural entities. It is asked, for example: "Had they life, as we understood life, or were they ghouls?" (159). The question is, basically, were they natural by our standards or unnatural? One final example: in the prelude to one of the visions, the narrator notes how it seemed "more as though the ghost of each table and chair had taken the place of the solid article" (160). This usage reinforces them all: we understand by appeal to commonly accepted conceptions of the unnatural. We gain, through our culture and shared cultural expressions, a knowledge of what is demoniac, vampiric, ghoulish, or ghostly; and by apprehending these we come in some way to comprehending the inventions of Hodgson's narratives. This is reinforced by the fact that, in *House* at least, Hodgson uses some readily recognizable figures, and not just in analogies or other rhetorical figures.

Hodgson definitely employs some familiar figures in the arena of the central visions. The giant being with an "ass-like head, with gigantic ears" (*House* 121) is recognized as Set (122), "the Destroyer of Souls." The narrator also recognizes Kali, "the Hindu goddess of death" (121), and other unnamed figures are mentioned as being present. What is immediately evident is that these figures represent evil forces, and they watch the central house in much the same manner that the Watchers keep guard of the Greater Redoubt. Note, too, their antiquity, reinforcing the vast stretches of time covered in the central visions. Again, as in the reference to the swine-things as ghouls, this appearance leads to questions on the nature of life. The narrator clearly states this in his speculations regarding their nature: "There was . . . an indescribable sort of dumb vitality, that suggested . . . a state of life-in-earth—a something that was by no means life, as we understand it; but rather an inhuman form of existence, that well might be likened to a deathless trance" (122). All this leads us to begin to grasp, in familiar terms, the nature of the living beings of the underworld. The totality of the comparisons—to living beings, to non-living items, and to familiar supernatural beings—and the employment of familiar mythological figures of evil all point to the means whereby the reader can begin to understand. Hodgson allows us to make analogies, by referencing the unfamiliar to the familiar, and in doing so he reinforces their evil nature and their utter unnaturalness to the mundane world.

What remains now are a number of relatively brief observations about the inhabitants of the underworld, before the boon is finally discussed. First, in *House*, we note that the incursions of the underworld's denizens are first noticed by animals. Note how, for example, the initial vision is marked by Pepper's cowering (118). Again, at the Pit, Pepper's continued barking signals the appearance of the swine-things; and it is deemed "most unusual behaviour on his part" (126). Note, too, toward the novel's end, the reaction of Tip: "it stood, rigid, as though frozen in an attitude of extraordinary terror" (192). This heralds the final monster's appearance, the same where we read of how "the dog moaned, strangely" (192). All these details reflect a common conception that incursions of the supernatural are often first noticed by animals. It is a function of the denizens' unnatural nature; the animals detect them because, unlike rational humans, they are somehow "closer" to a pure, natural state, and are, therefore, more attuned to the unnatural.

The next area of note is the degree to which the narrators' emotional reaction to the underworld is mirrored in that of the underworld's denizens. We see this most clearly in the language used, and in *House* in particular. Of the swine-thing, the narrator states how he "stood looking at the thing, with an ever growing feeling of disgust, and some fear" (128). The swine-things are later tellingly described by a number of significant words: "hideous" and "monstrous" (131), for example, "brute" (131, 137, 138, 139, 147, 150), and "infernal" (141). The rubbing against the back door provokes, in the narrator, an "indescribable feeling of terror" (129), and, later, the narrator notes how a "peculiar sense of fear thrilled through me—a fear, palpitant and real" (129); what is important is the emotional reaction. This reaction, the disgust of the narrator, is clearly emphasized in this following passage about the swine-thing: "it was more a sensation of abhorrence; such as one might expect to feel, if brought in contact with something superhumanly foul; something unholy—belonging to some hitherto undreamt of state of existence" (128). What is important is the language, and the way the first-person narrative enables the narrator's reactions, emotional and otherwise, through the medium of language. Hence the importance of style in approaching the four novels, especially in relation to their perceived fictional settings. This leads, in turn, to the way that the repulsiveness of the underworld is mirrored in its denizens.

The repulsiveness of the inhabitants of the underworld mirrors that of the underworld itself. This is understandable. Both are equally unnatural, and this inspires a similar response: repugnance and disgust. Note that of the weed-men, for example, particular attention is drawn to their "sudden, hateful reek . . . foul and abominable" (*Boats* 30). This visceral response is important: the weed-men are, in a sense, evil, and this is reflected in the response to their very being. Note, too, how later the narrator "was near sickened with the abomination of it" (45), and how he remarks upon the "horrible stench" (46) and the "hateful stench" (72). There is a point, too, in *House*, where the narrator remarks on being "filled with a terrible sense of overwhelming horror and fear and repugnance" (122) at the watching beings in the arena. He speaks, also, of a "legion of unholy things" (180); those familiar with the Gospels should remember that Legion is the name of the demon cast out and thrust into the Gadarene swine (Mark 5:9). Note too, how in *Ghost* Tammy the 'Prentice's "movement had shown such terror" (211); the emotional reaction is not just limited to the narrator, but to the narrator's associates as well. What remains, before consideration is given to the boon retrieved from the underworld, are aspects of the weed-choked sea, then the ghost pirates.

The core of *Boats* occurs in the weed-choked sea, and upon the island trapped therein. It is notable because of the unnatural nature of the inhabitants. Some, for example, are unnatural because of their size. Thus, the giant crab is called "a very monster" (27). The giant octopus, too, is at one point called "so great a monster as ever I had conceived" (28–29). Note the term itself used: "devil-fish" (29 *passim*). The most unnatural inhabitants are the weed-men; they are the most fantastic, and the most repugnant. Remember how the first glimpse by the narrator was of a "white demoniac face" (30); this is echoed elsewhere by the terms "devil face" and "demon" (31). They are called "foul ghouls" (75), "hideous things" (69), and "vile things" (60). This last mention allows us to recall the later description: "something slimy and vile" (70). Elsewhere, they are described as "white and unwholesome" (69), which reminds us of the description of the swine-things in *House*. We are also reminded of the ancients' equation of the beautiful with the good and the ugly with the evil. The weed-men are repugnant, ugly, and this mirrors their essentially evil nature. Further, there is a sense of immateriality in the description of the weed-man's "two flickering hands" (30). They seem unreal and unnatural, an echo of which is found in the phrase "one misshapen hand fluttered" (30) that occurs close by. Finally, there is the statement that, swimming, the weed-men "made a queer appearance" (64), and this term, "queer," sums up the utterly outré nature of these beings. This reminds us of the ghost pirates and their unnaturalness; for they are our next subject of inquiry.

The ghost pirates are not described literally. They are not ghosts, but something else. The narrator makes an attempt to fathom their nature, articulating, perhaps, the clearest conception of what they are (238–39). He uses the term "ghost," but it is clear that they are otherwise. They are inhuman, and this is reflected in the text: the first sight is of "something altogether extraordinary and outrageous. It was . . . the form of a man" (209). Note: not a man but the "form of a man," a "thing whatever it was" (209). Shortly thereafter, we read that "It was a human figure. And yet . . . I was unable to say more than that" (210). That is, it appears like a human, but its precise nature is ungraspable. Later, too, we read of a "dim, shadowy form" (210); we should remember the statement of "too many shadows" (209) on board the ship, which is made about this time. Further, the narrator admits how he "saw something that looked like a man; but so hazy and unreal, that [he] could scarcely say [he] saw anything" (212). This last point reminds us that, just as there is a degree of uncertainty with the underworld, there is a degree of uncertainty that mirrors that of the wider underworld itself.[5] It is marked through the vocabulary used. The narrator states: "it seemed to me that I saw something shadowy" (257), for example, and one appearance of a ghost pirate resolves into the "figure of a man" (257). Note: the figure, the semblance, and not a real man himself. Finally, when the narrator is attacked in the rigging, observe how he states: "It is queer, but I cannot say with certainty that I struck anything; . . . and yet it seemed to me that my foot encountered something soft" (265). All this reflects similar themes and responses in the nature of the wider underworld and adds to a fuller picture of the underworld's inhabitants.

Before addressing the boon, it would help to recap some of the salient points about the inhabitants of the underworld. First, the incursions of the underworld's denizens are initially noticed by animals, being closer than humans to the natural sphere and, hence, more attuned to occurrences of the unnatural. Second, there is a degree to which the narrators' emotional reaction to the inhabitants reflects that toward the underworld itself. Third, and finally, there is the way that the repulsiveness of the inhabitants also reflects that of the underworld. Both the inhabitants of the weed-choked sea and the ghost pirates were also examined in greater detail, as case studies, as it were. What is most obvious from this examination is the way that the inhabitants, and the responses they trigger, are akin to those of the greater underworld. This is not surprising. Both are equally unnatural, and both share a similar nature. Both are, in essence, apart, other than the natural world (there is a sense of alterity within the novels, and rarely do we see the natural world, except parenthetically, as a framework for the most part of the underworld itself). This leads us, then, to consider the boon which is retrieved from the underworld.

The boon is, perhaps, the most important part of the quest. It is the reason for the quest, the goal and reward that the hero must find and return

---

5. It could be argued that this sense of vagueness and ambiguity, as well as the sense of alterity mentioned elsewhere in this essay, are essential to the practice and composition of cosmic horror. I would point out that these things are not necessarily unique to this type of weird literature, nor necessarily integral to it. Rather, they reflect a subtlety and deftness of handling seen in the best proponents of any type of weird literature, of which weird cosmicism is an important, if underdeveloped, part.

with. And, remarkably, perhaps, there are two consistent boons that recur among the four novels. I shall not discuss in detail the first: the awareness of spheres of existence other than the purely mundane. Whether these be classed as alternatives of reality, as in *Ghost* or *Boats*, or whether they be more spiritual, as in *House* and *Night*, what is important is that they challenge the basic materialism and scientific ethos of Hodgson's world. The presence of the otherworlds, that is, points toward a unified worldview underlying all four novels. This is not the place to explicate this worldview, nor is it to discuss the nature of these other places, except to note this: the underworlds all form an integral part of these other realms, whether as the realms themselves (*Boats*, *House*, and *Night*) or as thresholds or liminal spaces to these realms (*House* and *Ghost*). What remains is the second of these two boons, and, fittingly, in three of the four, this is revealed as love. The hero becomes the "Spirit of Love, searching for its mate" (*Night* 340); he becomes the lover, and the Beloved is in a sense the goal. The reason for staying in the House on the Borderland is not intransigence, but this sense, this vision of love that the hero returns with. In a sense, the use of frame narratives supports this; we enter the world of the central narrator, just as we enter into his visions, and we return with a sense of love and its place in the cosmos. Note, too, how love is "announced" to us. The theme of love is foreshadowed in *Boats* through the use of the poem "Madre Mia" as an epigraph. It is also echoed in the use of "Grief" in *House*. Most tellingly, *Night* opens with a passage that is literally repeated in the narrative itself; this announces, clearly and noticeably, the theme, and the importance of love to the narrative. The handling, too, is of note. It is handled with tact, reticence (*Boats, House, Night*), and we never, in these three novels, read the names of the protagonists, but we do, for the most part, of their loves: Mistress Madison in *Boats*, Mirdath/Naani in *Night*. The beloved is more important in this respect than the lover. Finally, what remains above all is a knowledge of the basic theme of the novels. This is best illustrated in the material quoted twice in *Night*, where we read, first,

> in verity, THIS to be love, that your life shall bound in you with abundance, and joy dwell round you, and your spirit to live in a natural holiness with the Beloved, and your bodies to be a sweet and natural delight that shall never be lost of a lovely mystery that doth hold a perfect peace each unto the need of the other; and all to be that there go round about you a wonder and splendour all the days and the nights that you shall be—the Man with the Woman, the Woman with the Man. And Shame to be unborn, and all things to go natural and wholesome, out of an utter greatness of understanding; and the Man to be an Hero and a Child before the Woman; and the Woman

to be an Holy Light of the Spirit and an utter Companion and in the same time a glad Possession unto the Man. (587-88)

And where we read, also: "for this to be the especial glory of Love, that it doth make unto all Sweetness and Greatness, and be a fire burning all Littleness, so that did all in this world to have met The Beloved, then did Wantonness be dead, and there to grow Gladness and Charity, dancing in the years" (595).

A fuller appreciation of the novels, and their essential unity, is obtainable. We can do so by examining the mythic underworld and the underworlds of the novels, and their inhabitants, as well as the call to adventure, and the boon. Knowing how, for example, uncertainty, uniqueness, and unnaturalness operate as aspects of the underworld is important to this appreciation. So too is the emotional reaction, and the repulsiveness engendered. Understanding how the boon, in part a knowledge of other realms, but for the main part love, helps to unite the novels is also important. In doing so, we see that the four novels are a tight, focused body of work. They become, as it were, more intertextual by virtue of this common heritage of setting, theme, and underworld. As a result, we have an important body of work in the field of weird literature, one that explores one of the basic themes of human narratives.

Works Cited

Cashford, Jules, trans. *The Homeric Hymns*. Harmondsworth, UK: Penguin, 2003.

Gafford, Sam. "Writing Backwards: The Novels of William Hope Hodgson." *Studies in Weird Fiction* No. 11 (Spring 1992): 12-15.

Hodgson, William Hope. *The Boats of the "Glen Carrig."* In *The House on the Borderland and Other Novels*.

———. *The Ghost Pirates*. In *The House on the Borderland and Other Novels*.

———. *The House on the Borderland*. In *The House on the Borderland and Other Novels*.

———. *The House on the Borderland and Other Novels*. London: Gollancz, 2002.

———. *The Night Land*. In *The House on the Borderland and Other Novels*.

Sisam, Kenneth, ed. *Fourteenth Century Verse and Prose*. Oxford: Oxford University Press, 1921.

Decay and Disease in the Fiction of William Hope Hodgson

Sam Gafford

As with many great writers, there are many interesting themes that run through much of the fiction written by William Hope Hodgson. Chief among these, of course, is the theme of the oceans, which in Hodgson's stories takes on many guises. There are, however, other concepts in his fiction if one looks closely enough.

It is difficult to get a grasp of Hodgson the man, due to the lack of such primary sources as letters. As such, we need to depend upon the work of previous scholars like Sam Moskowitz. In his ground-breaking essay in *Out of the Storm*, Moskowitz provides many anecdotes about Hodgson and his life. One of the most interesting is this:

> He [Hodgson] was a hypochondriac, always gargling because his father had died of cancer of the throat. After opening letters and reading them, he would wash his hands to kill any germs received in the mail. When, years later, his youngest brother, Chris, was leaving for Canada and asked for a word of advice from his brilliant older brother, he received in dead seriousness: "Advice? Well, yes, never sit on a public toilet seat." (*Out of the Storm* 25)

In more modern times, Hodgson might have been diagnosed with obsessive-compulsive disorder. Hodgson's preoccupation with health and cleanliness is shown both in his fiction and in his devotion to exercise and what was known as "physical culture." At thirteen, Hodgson had been apprenticed into the Merchant Marine and, soon after, discovered the need to improve his strength when he was abused by a second mate. From that point onward, Hodgson was an advocate of physical conditioning and health, of which, it is safe to assume, cleanliness and proper diet were essential components.

In one of his exposés of sea life, Hodgson describes the type of food that was often available: "I have known the beef and pork so putrid and their smell so offensive as to prohibit their being brought into the Berth. In such case they would be left on deck, and any youngster who had the temerity was at liberty to go out and get a cut for himself. Hunger covereth a multitude of sins!" (*Wandering Soul* 170). Consider how this passage echoes Hodgson's classic story "The Voice in the Night." Even though Hodgson frequently points out the economic wastefulness of a life at sea, one has to wonder how much poor food and the unclean living conditions contributed to his dissatisfaction.

Taken from this viewpoint, the themes of decay and disease occur quite frequently in Hodgson's work. Probably the most significant example of this symbolism comes from the aforementioned story, "The Voice in the Night."

Commonly hailed as Hodgson's masterpiece, the story concerns a ship becalmed at sea that is suddenly hailed by a lone voice from out of the dark. The speaker tells how he and a woman have been shipwrecked and are in need of supplies but, oddly, refuses to come close to the ship. After receiving the supplies, the voice rows away but returns a short while later to tell his story.

When their boat, the *Albatross*, sinks, the man and woman are left abandoned by the crew and have to take to the sea in an open raft. They come upon an island cove where a strange derelict lies:

> "Yet I had much ado to make my way up, because of a kind of grey, lichenous fungus, which had seized upon the rope, and which blotched the side of the ship, lividly.
>
> "I reached the rail, and clambered over it, onto the deck. Here, I saw that the decks were covered, in great patches, with the grey masses, some of them rising into nodules several feet in height; but at the time, I thought less of this matter than of the possibility of there being people aboard the ship. I shouted; but none answered. Then I went to the door below the poop-deck. I opened it, and peered in. There was a great smell of staleness, so that I knew in a moment that nothing living was within, and with the knowledge, I shut the door quickly; for I felt suddenly lonely." (CF 3.160-61)

The two take residence on the ship and proceed to clean off the fungi but their results are not lasting:

> "Yet even thus early, we became aware that our lot was even less to be desired than might have been imagined; for though, as a first step, we scraped away the odd patches of growth that studded the floors and walls of the cabins and saloon, yet they returned almost to their original size within the space of twenty-four hours, which not only discouraged us, but gave us a feeling of vague unease." (CF 3.161)

Taking a more aggressive stance, they use carbolic on the growth. "'Yet, by the end of the week, the growth had returned in full strength, and, in addition, it had spread to other places, as though our touching it had allowed germs from it to travel elsewhere'" (CF 3.162). When they find spots growing on their linen and clothes, they decide to abandon the ship for the island, only to find that the conditions there are actually much worse.

> "Yet, as we drew near to it, I became gradually aware that here the vile fungus, which had driven us from the ship, was growing riot. In places it rose into horrible, fantastic mounds, which seemed almost to quiver, as with a quiet life, when the wind blew across them. Here and there, it took on the forms of vast fingers, and in others it just spread out flat and smooth and treacherous. Odd places, it appeared as grotesque stunted trees, seeming extraordinarily kinked and gnarled—The whole quaking vilely at times." (CF 3.162)

After finding a small stretch of sand that is untouched by the fungus, the couple camp there for several months until they discover that gray spots are appearing on their flesh. Rigorous scrubbing with carbolic and water have little effect, and they silently realized that they are infected and "it would be unallowable to be among healthy humans, with the thing from which we were suffering" (CF 3.163).

Their supplies begin to dwindle and, when he returns from scrounging the derelict for food, the man finds his sweetheart eating some of the dreaded fungus. Appalled, he gets her to agree to never eat it again "however great our hunger" (CF 3.164). Later, he walks further inward among the fungus than he had dared before and notices a large mass of fungus.

> "Abruptly, as I stared, the thought came to me that the thing had a grotesque resemblance to the figure of a distorted human creature. Even as the fancy flashed into my brain, there was a slight, sickening noise of tearing, and I saw that one of the branch-like arms was detaching itself from the surrounding gray masses, and coming towards me. The head of the thing—a shapeless grey ball, inclined in my direction. I stood stupidly, and the vile arm brushed across my face." (CF 3.165)

Overcome with hunger, he falls upon the fungus and eats ravenously. Remembering how he had admonished his love only that morning, he throws the fungus away and runs back to her where she can tell what he has done. The couple vow to resist the foul food, but the harm has already been done as the fungus grows over them every day. He knows that the mass of fungus that had attacked him in the jungle will be their final fate.

His tale done, the speaker rows away, giving the men on the ship a final glimpse as the sun pierces the mist. "Indistinctly, I saw something nodding between the oars. I thought of a sponge—a great, grey nodding sponge—The oars continued to ply" (CF 3.166).

The symbolism is obvious almost to the point of predictability. The fungus is either a manifestation of a disease or a symptom of one. Beginning from their first exposure on the derelict, the victims become more and more infected despite their attempts to return to cleanliness. When they seek a false cure, i.e., the escape to the island, it makes their disease even worse.

The disease certainly appears to be bacterial in origin, as the narrator even mentions carrying it via germs despite their cleaning. They are under attack by the disease just as a healthy host is from a pestilence. But there is another aspect to this symbolism: guilt.

When they submit to their hunger and eat the fungus, finally accepting it, they feel guilty and unclean. The narrator even says that his moment of clarity after gorging on the fungus comes from God. What then are we to make of this? Normally, patients do not feel guilt from contracting cancer or tuberculosis, and this leads us to another conclusion: the fungus is a representation of syphilis.

Consider that they are an unmarried man and woman, struggling against something that is attacking them relentlessly. Their desire for each other is mirrored in the fungus that surrounds them and which, try as they might to resist, keeps coming back over and over again. When they finally give in to consuming the forbidden fungus, they lose their innocence and are overwhelmed with guilt. Despite their refutation of their new desire for the fungus, their single indiscretion dooms them and they eventually become nothing more than physical manifestations of their disease and sin.

In this story, Hodgson shows the couple's moral decay by means of their bodies giving way to the fungus and, therefore, their own desires. We do not know much about Hodgson's personal or romantic relationships. Moskowitz states that Hodgson was a bit of a "ladies' man" but offers no proof of this statement. It is, however, worth noting that he did not marry until 1913, when he was thirty-five years old. And, of course, we must remember that he went to sea at the tender age of thirteen, so we must assume that he received something of a "worldly" education in his youth.

The concept of disease is closely connected with the theme of horror. The human psyche has a natural repulsion to disease and illness, as shown in the historical aversion to victims of the plague and leprosy. As such, readers have a visceral reaction to such scenes; it is, however, not just the depictions themselves that have impact but what they have come to represent.

In "The Derelict," Hodgson once again uses these scenes to capture not only an effect but an emotion as well. A doctor relates a tale about yet another becalmed ship discovering yet another odd derelict. When they row over to inspect the derelict, they encounter an unnatural ring of scum that surrounds it. As they get closer, the scum thickens to the point where it physically impedes their progress.

When they finally get to the derelict, they find that the wood has become incredibly soft, almost like a sponge. After climbing on board, they find that the situation is even worse:

> "I climbed over the rail, with the Second Mate close behind and stood upon the mould-covered decks. There might have been no planking beneath the mould, for all that our feet could feel. It gave under our tread, with a spongy, puddingy feel. It covered the deck-furniture of the old ship, so that the shape of each article and fitment was often no more than suggested through it." [. . .]
>
> "I turned this way and that, staring, as I have said. Here and there, the mould was so heavy as to entirely disguise what lay beneath; converting the deck-fittings into indistinguishable mounds of mould, all dirty-white, and blotched and veined with irregular, dull purplish markings." (CF 3.242-43)

They find that the mold does not break under their feet but "merely indented it." There is a strong smell on the derelict that the Doctor likens to something "animal-like"; a musk that is similar to that of rats but there are no rats aboard.

On board, they stumble upon a weird creature: "'I stooped over his shoulder, and saw what he meant; it was a clear, colorless creature, about a foot long, and about eight inches high, with a curved back that was extraordinarily narrow. As we stared, all in group, it gave a queer little flick, and was gone'" (CF 3.245). The "thing" is identified as a giant "sea-lice"—an external parasite that feeds on the mucus, epidermal tissue, and blood of host fish. Of course, the sea-lice are usually very small, but Hodgson uses their giant size to instill disgust in the reader.

The adventure soon becomes terrifying when the ship itself seems to be attacking the men. This is shown in one of Hodgson's most horrific scenes:

> "The man who had run from us, was standing in the waist of the ship, about a fathom from the starboard bulwarks. He was swaying from side to side, and screaming in a dreadful fashion. He appeared to be trying to lift his feet, and the light from his swaying lantern showed an almost incredible sight. All about him, the mould was in active movement. His feet had sunk out of sight. The stuff appeared to be *lapping* at his legs; and abruptly his bare flesh showed. The hideous stuff had rent his trouser-legs away, as if they were paper. He gave out a simply sickening scream, and, with a vast effort, wrenched one leg free. It was partly destroyed. The next instant he pitched face downward, and the stuff heaped itself upon him, as if it were actually alive, with a dreadful savage life. It was simply infernal. The man had gone from sight. Where he had fallen was now a writhing, elongated mound, in constant and horrible increase, as the mould appeared to move towards it in strange ripples from all sides." (CF 3.249)

The remaining men barely escape with their lives. Later, the doctor who has been narrating the story concludes that the boat itself had become alive through the "'juxtaposition of the various articles of her cargo, plus the heat and time she had endured, plus one or two other only guessable quantities, we should have solved the chemistry of the Life-Force, gentlemen'" (CF 3.257).

The life form they had encountered attacked the men in the same way that the human body attacks invading disease: it either absorbs the invader or expels it. To an invading microbe, the host would seem terrifying in its attempts to protect itself. In this instance, humans have become the disease.

In a sense, much of Hodgson's fiction is concerned with different variations of decay and disease. They are interchangeable in his world. Much of the horror in his fiction springs from these concepts, as they are violations of the "natural" order. The world is subject to an "ab-normal" influence from these forces, which seek to violently destroy humanity through any means possible. Such concepts take more bodily form in such instances as the "Watchers" in *The Night Land* and the loathsome swine creatures in *The House on the Borderland*. The titular house, of course, is representative of a healthy body under attack from "outside" and below. Psychologically, the swine-creatures are breaking out from below, showing the explosion of the subconscious to the conscious level.

In virtually all Hodgson's best weird fiction, we are dealing with attacks from the "outside." This accounts for much of the "siege" mentality present in the stories, as the characters are both literally and figuratively under siege from these forces. The people are the symbols of health, epitomized by young, strong men and women who face death and decay from the "outside." Given this viewpoint, is it any wonder that many of the concepts in Hodgson's fiction appealed to H. P. Lovecraft? Both writers were consumed with the "outside," even if they interpreted it differently.

It is often argued how much of an author's choices are made deliberately. When considering Hodgson's fiction, it is doubtful that he sat down and purposefully decided that he was going to focus so strongly on this concept. It is far more likely that this developed over time as he turned to the ideas and themes that meant the most to him and which he could write about most convincingly. When we consider how important health appears to have been to Hodgson throughout his life, should we really be surprised that he would write so often and so powerfully about those things which destroyed health?

Works Cited

Hodgson, William Hope. *The Ghost Pirates and Other Revenants of the Sea*. The Collected Fiction of William Hope Hodgson, Volume 3. Edited by Jeremy Lassen. San Francisco: Night Shade Books, 2005. [CF 3.]

———. *Out of the Storm: Uncollected Fantasies*. Edited by Sam Moskowitz. West Kingston, RI: Donald M. Grant, 1975.

———. *The Wandering Soul: Glimpses of a Life: A Compendium of Rare and Unpublished Works by William Hope Hodgson*. Edited by Jane Frank. Harrogate, UK: PS Publishing/Tartarus Press, 2005.

Hodgson's Women

Sam Gafford

It is not possible to know the mind of William Hope Hodgson. Because of the lack of surviving letters, we do not know much about Hodgson's views, attitudes, thoughts, or literary intentions in his work. The best that we can do is to analyze his writings and attempt to put them into some sort of perspective. Often, however, we can determine threads that run throughout Hodgson's work; not surprisingly, one of these threads is his portrayal of women.

Hodgson had an interesting personal history with women. He was born the second son of twelve children, and four of his siblings were women. Hodgson's relationship with his mother was especially close and was likely the inspiration for several of his more sentimental stories. Although he was described as handsome, it is unknown what, if any, relationships Hodgson had with women outside his family during his youth. His biographers, R. Alain Everts and Sam Moskowitz, only mention one serious romantic relationship before his marriage, but no details about the duration, ending, or even the name of this early love interest remain.

It was not until 1913 that Hodgson would finally marry at the age of thirty-five. Everts speculates that part of the reason for this might be because Hodgson's "major drawback [was] his fits of temper, and like all of the Hodgson boys, he was spoiled" (20). His wife, Bessie, was the same age as Hodgson and had also been working in the publishing field. At present, only one photo of Bessie is known to exist. This is fortunate as it counters Hodgson's statement, in a letter to his sister Mary, where WHH announces his wife as "not at all good-looking" (20). This callous remark is particularly curious and makes us question Hodgson's attitude not only toward his wife but toward women in general.

There are no records about Hodgson's marriage or family anecdotes. Shortly after their wedding, the couple moved to France, apparently in order to save money. When England entered the Great War in 1914, they returned and Hodgson joined the Officer Training Corps of the University of London while Bessie went to stay with Hodgson's mother and sister, Lissie, in Borth.

Bessie would remain there until Hodgson's death in 1918, when she returned to her own family in Cheshire.

It is safe to say that Hodgson had three major relationships with women in his life: his mother, Lissie, and Bessie. His mother was a deeply religious woman who had lost several children in their infancy. Her devout faith may have been behind the break with her oldest son, Chad, who married a divorced woman. The family broke all ties with Chad, who disappears from the family history, never to return. Lissie, in her favor, was described as a strong-minded woman who was responsible for shaming the community into building a house for the family after the death of their father, Samuel, in 1892 had plunged them into poverty. Granted that much of Hodgson's writing (including his four novels) was completed well before his marriage, we can presume that his relationship with his mother and sisters influenced how he depicted women in his work.

Previous scholarly research has concluded that Hodgson's four novels were written by 1905 (see Gafford). In addition, there is speculation that much of his short fiction (including the Carnacki stories) was completed early in his writing career. Although the publishing history of Hodgson's work is not a definite resource for determining when he wrote what, it can be used as a guideline. For the sake of this article, we can speculate that the novels came first, followed by various short stories, and ending with the Captain Gault stories.

Hodgson began his writing career with various "physical culture" articles; when his School of Physical Culture failed in 1902, he decided to become a full-time writer. The results were not economically impressive. From the period 1902–1906, Hodgson published very few items. We know that he was working feverishly but with little success.

It is likely that *The Night Land* existed in at least a rough form by 1905 and could possibly be the first major literary work of Hodgson's career. In this novel, a man of the seventeenth century is able to propel his mind into the far future to a world where the sun has burnt out and humanity lives in huge metal pyramids called "Redoubts." The narrator telepathically communicates with his "reincarnated" lover in a distant Redoubt and, when she falls silent, resolves to brave the Night Land to rescue her.

An astounding feat of imagination and vision, *The Night Land* has nonetheless been criticized as much as it has been praised. One of the reasons for this is the "love story" that is at the heart of the plot. H. P. Lovecraft describes this aspect of the novel as "artificial and nauseously sticky romantic sentimentality" (78). C. S. Lewis considers this romance to be a "sentimental and irrelevant erotic interest" (71). When Lin Carter edited a two-volume reprint for his legendary Ballantine Books Adult Fantasy series, he proclaimed that the

"High Victorian love scenes and romantic dialogue are excruciating to the modern taste and hurt the strength of the book" (xi).

What makes *The Night Land*'s love story so unsatisfying is the fact that, even for a fantasy/science fiction novel, it is blaringly unrealistic. It goes beyond the idea of a beginning author finding their voice to the very heart of the plot's conception. Hodgson approaches the "love story" with the type of romantic idealism of someone who has never been in love himself. It can only be equated to the example of a travel guide about a distant, exotic land written by an author who has never walked beyond his front door.

The novel begins in a Victorian setting with the love story between a man and a beautiful, young woman (his cousin) named Mirdath. Despite a series of mishaps more fitting to one of E. F. Benson's *Lucia* novels than a science fiction story, they marry, only for Mirdath to die in childbirth. Later, the man mind-travels to the future, where he believes Mirdath lives again.

The characters represented by the couple are horribly one-dimensional. The man is strong, brave, and fearless, while the woman is beautiful, passionate, and in peril. During an early meeting, the man defends Mirdath from three roughs (with undeclared but probably unsavory intentions) and displays his strength and courage. This would become a common thread in much of Hodgson's early writing. This primitive chest-beating impresses Mirdath, and the couple begin "dating," if one can call it that. When he spots Mirdath with another man, much smaller and weaker than he, the narrator decides to break off his "romance."

Later, he discovers that his rival was actually Mirdath's lady friend who had posed as a man as part of a joke they were playing on her friend's suitor. Because of the narrator's reaction to her friend, Mirdath cruelly schemes to "hurt" him. Mirdath later admits, "And this to be all of it, save that they had planned to punish me, and had met every evening at the gap, to play at lovers, perchance I should pass, so that I should have greater cause for my jealousy, and truly they to have a good revenge upon me; for I had suffered a very long while because of it" (CF 4.16). Mirdath is portrayed as a callous, capricious girl who thinks little of "punishing" the narrator. Her episodes of dancing with the townsfolk and attitude at her birthday ball show an immature socialite the likes of whom would be just at home in a Jane Austen novel.

This perhaps could be at the core of Hodgson's viewpoint toward women in his early writing. Rather than having personal experiences to draw from, he may have based his depictions of romantic relationships from other novels. Certainly this would explain why Hodgson's writing rings so hollow when he writes about people. His early work only comes alive when he is writing about dangers and life at sea because those are events he knows and has experienced first-hand.

But this superficial treatment of women is not limited to *The Night Land*. Many of Hodgson's short stories carry this theme as well.

In "The Smugglers" (1911), the narrator, Mr. Faucett, is the "Preventive Officer" in a small village on the South Devon coast. What this means is that he is in charge of catching smugglers bringing in contraband. Faucett is at odds with a local family, the Rossets, who are the largest offenders. Once again, the situation comes to a head when Faucett is attacked by three men whom he dispatches easily and somewhat cruelly.

> I broke the jaw of one with my fist, and one of the others I pitched bodily over the cliff, where he was found at daylight with both legs broken. The third man ran; but I meant that the smugglers should learn that this sort of thing was not going to be tried without certain pains attaching. And so I chased that man for three miles. When I caught him I beat him with his own stick until he cried like a child. (CF 4.421)

Despite his certainty that the Rossets are continuing their smuggling activities, Faucett becomes entranced with one of the daughters in the family, Ruth, who is cold toward him. The father, Squire Rosset, invites Faucett to dinner and attempts to befriend the government agent, but his daughters are frigid and rude. Although Faucett believes the Squire to be ignorant of his son's activities, it is clear that the smuggling is supported and approved by his daughters and much of the town.

After dinner, Ruth plays the harp and sings but, when Faucett asks her to sing a love song, her true nature is revealed.

> In a moment I saw that I had made a mistake in supposing that there was either grace or courtesy in the girl; for she said no word but looked silently up at me with a kind of white scorn. Abruptly she got to her feet and went over to her harp. Then, sitting down, she sang the "Hanging of the Spy," with such deliberate and deadly insult, considering my request and the circumstances, that I quietly took my leave without more ado. (CF 4.423)

Later, it appears that Ruth has changed her feelings about Faucett, as she agrees to go on daily walks with him while the rest of her sisters bathe in the ocean undisturbed. Faucett quickly falls in love with Ruth and believes that she feels the same until the day that he catches Ruth speaking to her brother, Tom, the head of the smuggling ring:

> They evidently did not hear me as I came along on the soft grass bank bordering the lane; and even as I puzzled a moment how to let them know that I was near, I heard my name, and knew that Tom was accusing his sister bitterly of being in love with me. I paused eagerly listening to her answer, for it was what my heart had been aching yet dreading to hear for all the past

weeks. Then, like a bitter, unbelievable slap in the face, her laughter came hard and scornful, and I heard her tell her brother that she had done no more than she had agreed to do, which was to hold me from the shore whilst the cargoes were run; that she loved me as little as he did, and that if he did not approve of her methods, he had better take me country walks himself, and so combine courtesy to the enemy—thereby obeying their father—and assistance to the smugglers all at the same time; and she hoped he would have as much or as little entertainment out of it as she had gained! And all this with a fresh and bitter accompaniment of scornful laughter, so that my heart was cold and sick and hard within me. (CF 4.426)

At this, Faucett confronts the pair and, typically, beats Tom brutally. Looking at Ruth, sobbing, Faucett makes a cruel accusation: "'Oh!' I said, looking at her, and speaking between my gasps, 'he's a brute, but he's a man. But what are you?'" (CF 4.427).

Faucett discovers that Ruth has been distracting him while her sisters retrieve smuggled cargo left sunken in the ocean by the thieves at night. Now thinking clearly, Faucett traps the sisters in the cove and leads them, shackled, back to town. The sisters beg Ruth to intercede on their behalf. Humbled, Ruth asks Faucett to let her and her sisters go, for they had "learned their lesson"; if any should be punished, he should punish Ruth and let her sisters go free.

Astonishingly, Faucett agrees to let them all go free and unlocks their handcuffs. Ruth stays behind to talk to Faucett and reveals that she could have slipped out of the handcuffs at any time but that she is "still his prisoner." Sobbing, Ruth says, "I shall never be free again. Never, never, never!" (CF 4.431). She professes her love for Faucett, and it is there that the story ends. Although Hodgson means for us to conclude that Ruth is sobbing with joy, she could just as easily be sobbing with despair at the knowledge that she is now Faucett's "prisoner of love."

That "The Smugglers" fails as a story rests primarily upon Hodgson's usual "romanticized" view of relationships. Despite Faucett's dedication to his job, he lets the sisters go free without anything more than a stern warning. This, coupled with the typical "macho" scenes of Faucett beating Tom and the smugglers with his bare hands, combine to show what Hodgson considers to be the "ideal" man. He is strong, moral, capable of surviving any danger, and smarter than all his enemies. But what is his "ideal" woman?

Based on many examples like these in Hodgson's fiction, she is weak, helpless, often in danger, but, most importantly, untrustworthy. Mirdath and Ruth show themselves to be deceiving and duplicitous. Indeed, in "The Smugglers," the only time Ruth is truthful with Faucett is when she snubs him at dinner and insults him with her choice of song.

In Hodgson's world, women are untrustworthy *until* they are conquered by the hero's love. Once they realize that they are truly in love, they become beautiful, supportive, and the "ideal" woman. In short, it only happens because they submit and "fall in line" with the man's wishes.

Hodgson would be a feminist's nightmare.

Consider the deeper implications of "The Smugglers." Ruth and her sisters are not only supportive of the smugglers but actively help them. When they are caught, they are naked in the cove. In essence, they are being "baptized" into the new faith of lawful living. When they walk out of the water, one at a time (just as new believers are baptized singly), they are allowed to dress privately and then present themselves to Faucett, who chains them. They are being brought to him as supplicants in a submissive position. In chains, they are brought before their conqueror.

Only when she has been thus defeated does Ruth admit her "love" for Faucett. But she does not do it proudly or joyfully but in a state of shame and degradation. "She, on her part, looked only downward, and I saw that her hands were trembling a little" (CF 4.431). Ruth does not even go to Faucett. Instead, she stands there and Faucett goes to her. "I came over to her with three quick steps . . . I had her in my arms . . . And I said nothing; for she was still in my arms" (CF 4.431). Ruth has been well and truly dominated.

What would a psychologist make of such an exchange?

Perhaps we can consider this to be, in part, due to the social attitudes and conventions of the period in which Hodgson was raised. Women were expected to submit to their husbands who ruled their households with often extreme ferocity. We could also consider this to be a sort of "wish-fulfillment" on Hodgson's part. Perhaps it is a reaction to his own failed relationship(s)? Was he perhaps stymied or frustrated by a woman who did not allow her personality to be overwhelmed by his?

We begin to see another side of Hodgson's view of women in "Kind, Kind and Gentle Is She" (first published in 1913). Set in some sort of British station in a foreign country, possibly India, the story concerns common soldier Jell Murphy, who is a "big man" with a soothing singing voice. The sister of the commanding colonel's wife, Lady Mary Worthington, is visiting and organizing a concert. Upon hearing Jell's beautiful voice, Lady Mary decides she must have him perform, which begins a series of rehearsals during which Jell, naturally, falls in love with Lady Mary. Jell's voice brings Lady Mary to tears but, in the end, she is only toying with the big soldier. It is implied that she considers his attentions as but another in the tributes she has received over the years.

Even though she feels emotion growing for Jell, she remembers the more socially suitable Captain Harrison whom she loved and "had gone to the extent of admitting as much frankly to herself" (CF 4.462). And so she keeps Jell at a distance while Jell, for his own part, has ignored the longing attentions of Maggie, the Colonel's wife's maid, because he has fallen for Lady Mary.

At the last practice, Lady Murphy is nearly overcome with her emotions: "Murphy sang his song with a quality of voice and passion that brought strange tears into the woman's eyes. She felt herself to be intensely moved; the man's love was so real, and there was so much force of manhood at the back of all. And, also, he really did look splendid" (CF 4.464). Maggie, listening outside, cries with the knowledge that the love Jell sings is not for her. At the end of the song, overcome with emotion, Jell kisses Lady Mary, "at first madly, and then with an infinite tenderness that the woman appreciated with gentle thrills in every fibre" (CF 4.464). But when Lady Mary thinks of Captain Harrison, she pulls away from Jell and runs out of the room. Shattered, Jell wanders through the night, ending up in the hospital with an attack of fever.

It is at this time that the regiment is called away to stop an insurgence of "'Scurries" or hillmen. Captain Harrison is left at the station with a small group of men when, naturally, a sneak attack occurs. What follows is an exciting episode as Harrison and Jell defend the station and the women against an army of attackers. The hillmen are held off virtually single-handedly by Jell, who, in his fever, continually sings the song he had practiced with Lady Mary for so long. Eventually, even the big soldier falls under the weight of numbers but not until he had held the station long enough for the regiment to return.

Months later, Lady Mary weds Captain Harrison:

> At breakfast, a few mornings after the wedding, Captain Harrison remarked:
> "I see the men still keep Murphy's grave covered with flowers."
> "I'm glad of that," replied Lady Mary. "He deserved it. Is your coffee right, dear?" (CF 4.472-3)

The cynicism is plainly evident. Jell gives his life to defend the station and Lady Mary, based on the brief domestic scene shown, dismisses him with barely a thought. Once again, we see the faithlessness of women. Despite her feelings for Jell, she has now completely submitted to Harrison. Lady Mary does not retire to a nunnery, spending the rest of her life grieving over her dead love, but continues with the life she had already planned. Jell and his sacrifice end up meaning less than nothing to her. It is interesting that Hodgson decided upon this ending, as it puts Lady Mary in an exceedingly unfavorable light and, by implication, all women as well.

Had Jell accepted the "pure" love of Maggie, he would not have fallen victim to the fever and, therefore, would have been with the regiment when they left the station. It is his "love" that kills Jell. Already Hodgson is moving away from a dreamy romantic concept of "love" to one that is not only capricious but deadly as well.

Contrast this against "The Captain of the Onion Boat" (first published in 1910), where Marvonna Delia *has* committed herself to a nunnery when she receives the erroneous news that her lover, John Carlos, is dead. Eventually, Carlos manages to "rescue" her from the nunnery and they sail away in the onion boat to begin a new life together. Marvonna has a quality of love that shames that of Lady Mary. If we accept this to be an earlier story, then Hodgson's attitude toward women has definitely changed. The events that an author chooses to include in the plot of a story can often be as revealing as any interview or letters. Hodgson could have easily chosen to have Lady Mary make the same sacrifice as Marvonna, but does not. Is he making a statement about the restrictions of Victorian society or about Lady Mary's fickle concept of love? Based on the fact that Hodgson does not describe regret on Lady Mary's part but instead a dismissive nature, we are led to conclude that the fault here is with Lady Mary, not society.

Few of the other women in Hodgson's fiction provide much insight into his attitudes or much of a contribution to the plot. These women are virtually "stock" characters with barely one dimension. They provide the stereotypical "damsel in distress" for the hero to rescue. The women in *The Boats of the "Glen Carrig,"* "From the Tideless Sea," "The Voice in the Night," and others are little more than decoration or instruments that Hodgson uses to get the plot moving. This fact could be said to indicate that Hodgson himself may not have had much respect for a woman's ability to handle a crisis. Although this is a typical attitude in Hodgson's time, it is curious to consider that it was Hodgson's *sister*, not Hodgson or any of his brothers, who managed to convince the church to build a house for the family after his father's death. It was his sister who provided a place for their mother to live out the rest of her life, not Hodgson, who, near as can be told, was never a financial success in any of his endeavors.

Probably the strongest woman character in Hodgson's fiction was the title character of "Judge Barclay's Wife." In this odd tale, Hodgson presents a story set in the American West. Although a date is not given, it can be assumed that this is a tale of the Old West that, even in Hodgson's time, had faded into the past. The story begins with Judge Barclay presiding over the murder trial of Jem Turrill, accused of killing a man over a game of cards. Although the Judge feels that Jem is not as guilty as the evidence shows, he has no choice but to pass a sentence of death on the young man.

During the night, Jem escapes with the help of his mother but is captured the next day by the sheriff who follows Jem's mother to his hiding place. Just as the sheriff and his posse are about to hang Jem, his mother's yells and screams of protest bring the judge and his wife to the scene. Seeing Jem's mother prostrate on the ground, the judge's wife steals the sheriff's gun and holds off the men while she cuts Jem down and allows him to escape.

It is an unusual story for Hodgson, especially as it is entirely out of his environment. The character of the judge's wife's transformation drives the story. She begins as an overbearing shrew with little regard for her husband:

> On her part, Mrs. Judge Barclay was trying to catch the Judge's eye, to "stiffen his backbone," as she would have phrased it, for she had dealt with him often and bitterly concerning his undue tendency to mercy. A hard-faced, big-boned, childless woman of sixty she was, vigorous and a ruler of men, her husband in particular, except in this one point which pertained to mercy. [. . .]
>
> Too often she would listen with a sort of impatient half-contempt in her heart at old Judge Barclay's constant tempering of justice with good human mercy; and always after any special evidence of this trait in him she would consider it her duty to "stiffen his backbone," as she termed it—a process which occasionally included the unloading upon the Judge of some rather brusque comments, bordering almost on the contemptuous. (CF 5.23-24)

The judge's wife is obsessed with justice and, unlike her husband, does not see the human cost behind the justice. The judge is well aware that "the precursor of that dread scene where a rope and too often a fine man, kicking his life away, formed a dreadful conjunction in his memory" (CF 5.23). It is this reality that causes the judge to temper his justice with mercy, but this is not acceptable to his wife.

After one attempt to explain this to his wife, she responds with a scathing reply that "'evil-doers must take their physic, or else quit their bad ways;' and further, that if he had not the 'stomach for his duty, he would be better employed doing other work, 'maybe nursin' babies!'" (CF 5.24). Yet, when the judge's wife sees Jem's mother pleading for his life and the boy about to be strung up, something changes within her:

> Old Mrs. Barclay stared, suffering at last in understanding of the stern and deathly intention that informed the group of men "about their business," and her heart sick with the horror of human pain that seemed suddenly to emanate from that one plague-spot of tragedy and fill all the earth. Her grim old face had grown ghastly under its pale, tan color. This was justice, the justice that she had so constantly hammered into her husband the need for dealing without shrinking. . . . This was what she—she, Anna Barclay, had urged her husband toward, many and many a time. She had never known; never! Never—NEVER! (CF 5.30)

The judge's wife comes to the realization of the human cost of justice and changes her beliefs. Although we do not know what becomes of these characters later in their lives, we can assume that she becomes more reasonable and kinder in her own judgments. Still, the portrayal of Anna Barclay is not flattering. She begins the story as an overbearing, dominating shrew who looks down on her husband for being "weak." It is not until she realizes that she has been wrong all this time and, by implication, her husband has been right, that she changes. Like Ruth from "The Smugglers," Anna Barclay submits to the superior wisdom of a man. And, as in many of Hodgson's stories, the woman is often the cause of the trouble. Unlike other women in his fiction, Anna Barclay is strong-willed and capable but in the *wrong* sense. It is interesting to note that she is wrong because she does not agree with the men. Her sense of justice is at odds with the judge and, when she realizes her error, she is still shown to be at odds with the sheriff and his posse who want to hang Jem.

According to Jane Frank, Hodgson completed this story in 1911 (*Wandering Soul* 45). This provides somewhat of a bridge between the earlier novels and the Captain Gault stories.

Originally appearing in magazines in 1914–16, the Captain Gault stories are adventure tales featuring the title character outwitting customs agents and even German spies. One of the most revealing Gault stories is "My Lady's Jewels" (1916). Although this is one of the last Captain Gault stories to appear in magazines, it leads off the collection *Captain Gault* (1917), which shows the esteem in which Hodgson held the story.

During a voyage to America, Gault is asked by a wealthy widow, Mrs. Ernley, to help smuggle a million-dollar diamond necklace past customs. Despite his better judgment, Gault agrees and, although he offers to do it for free, Mrs. Ernley insists on giving him a reward of two and half percent for his trouble. However, when she learns that the percentage actually translates to $25,000, Mrs. Ernley balks at the cost and conspires to trick Gault and smuggle the necklace through herself. She fails, of course, but Gault manages to save the day and presents the necklace to her at her home later that day. Humbled, Mrs. Ernley tries to give Gault his reward, but he tells her to give it to the old sailor's home instead.

A typical example of Gault's adventures, it is also very revealing in how Hodgson portrays Mrs. Ernley. Even worse than many of Hodgson's other characters, Mrs. Ernley is not only untrustworthy but greedy as well. She is as much a villain as the custom agents. But, even before she asks Gault to smuggle her necklace, he is cautious and wary of her:

You see, there are women who are more honest than you'd think a woman could be, considering just what a woman is.

I make it a general rule, though, to say "No" to these requests, for it's bad policy to mix up business and pleasure; and I've no use for a woman when it comes to sharing a secret with her. She's so apt to be a bit mixed in her ideas of fair play.

It's all rot to say a woman can't keep a secret. She can! She could keep a secret till Old Nick turned gray, begging for it, *if it suited her*. But that's just the trouble! You never know when it's going to stop suiting her to keep mum. If she gets the notion there's more cash for her in talk, than in keeping quiet, she'll pull the lid off and let the secret pop out, regardless of the hole you may get shoved into as a result. (CF 1.363)

The attitude expressed by Gault is astonishing. Not only is he saying that if a woman is honest, it's against her nature, but that she essentially has no honor. He contrasts this with Gault's sense of honor by having Gault not only *not* betray Mrs. Ernley but smuggle the necklace for her anyway. Gault even confronts Mrs. Ernley about her duplicity before they reach shore:

"And now you have shown not only meanness, but, a thousand times worse, you have lied to me, lie after lie; and with every lie you hurt me badly; for you blackened not only yourself in my eyes; but, at the same time, you blackened all of your sex; for a man judges women through the goodness or badness of the women he gets to know personally. I tell you frankly, Mrs. Ernley, I wish your necklace had been at the bottom of the sea before you had let it be a lever to further lower my general opinion of all that you stand for!" (CF 1.371)

His opinion of women already low, Gault has it not only confirmed by Mrs. Ernley but lowered even further. Shamed, Mrs. Ernley walks away from Gault, who can only comment by writing in his log; "I am getting a sick fear that every woman I meet is going to turn out mean or treacherous or deceitful or worse. If I have helped one to cure herself, I'm satisfied" (CF 1.372).

When Gault visits Mrs. Ernley later at her home, she is humbled and broken: "'But I guess that's not what I'm feeling worst about now I've got steadied a bit. I showed that I was poor stuff, didn't I, Captain Gault? I guess I've never been so ashamed of myself in my life as I feel right now'" (CF 1.377). Once again, a woman is shown the errors of her ways by a smarter, stronger, and more moral man. We have to wonder: how much do Hodgson's male characters speak for him? Given the fact that we see this refrain over and over again in his work, we have to assume that this is more than coincidence. Does Gault's poor view of women reflect Hodgson's own views? Perhaps. But it is such a narrow, bitter viewpoint that one has to wonder where it came from. Because we have so little in the way of primary sources, we will probably never know the answer.

It *is* clear, however, that Hodgson's fictional conception of women changed over his writing career. The "romantic" view of *The Night Land* gives way to a more "courtship" slant in the short stories and eventually to the extremely cynical depiction of "My Lady's Jewels." Women change from frail creatures who need to be protected to the dishonorable Mrs. Ernley who tries to trick Captain Gault. The transition may have occurred because Hodgson matured from a man with little practical interactions with women to one who has not fared well in love.

If we go by Captain Gault's concept of women, they may have proven to be every bit as dangerous as the mutated, giant monsters in Hodgson's Sargasso Sea and just as deadly.

Works Cited

Carter, Lin. "Across the Shadowy Land." In Hodgson's *The Night Land*. New York: Ballantine Books, 1972. Volume II. vii–xii.

Everts, R. Alain. *William Hope Hodgson: Night Pirate, Volume 2: Some Facts in the Case of William Hope Hodgson: Master of Phantasy*. Madison, WI: Strange Company, 1974.

Gafford, Sam. "9 Letters." In *The Uncollected William Hope Hodgson, Volume 1: Non-Fiction*. Bristol, RI: Hobgoblin Press, 1995. 26–42.

Hodgson, William Hope. *The Boats of the "Glen Carrig" and Other Nautical Adventures*. The Collected Fiction of William Hope Hodgson, Volume 1. Edited by Jeremy Lassen. San Francisco: Night Shade Books, 2003. [CF 1.]

———. *The Dream of X and Other Fantastic Visions*. The Collected Fiction of William Hope Hodgson, Volume 5. Edited by Jeremy Lassen. San Francisco: Night Shade Books, 2007. [CF 5.]

———. *The Night Land and Other Perilous Romances*. The Collected Fiction of William Hope Hodgson, Volume 4. Edited by Jeremy Lassen. San Francisco: Night Shade Books, 2005. [CF 4.]

———. *The Wandering Soul: Glimpses of a Life: A Compendium of Rare and Unpublished Works by William Hope Hodgson*. Edited by Jane Frank. Harrogate, UK: PS Publishing/Tartarus Press, 2005.

Lewis, C. S. "On Science Fiction." In *Of Other Worlds: Essays and Stories*. New York: Harcourt, Brace & World, 1967.

Lovecraft, H. P. *The Annotated Supernatural Horror in Literature*. Edited by S. T. Joshi. 2nd rev. ed. New York: Hippocampus Press, 2013.

III. Studies of Individual Tales

Things Invisible: Human and Ab-Human in Two of Hodgson's Carnacki Stories

Leigh Blackmore

Introduction: Carnacki and the Critics

H. P. Lovecraft considered that the work collected in William Hope Hodgson's *Carnacki, the Ghost-Finder*

> falls conspicuously below the level of the other books. We here find a more or less conventional stock figure of the "infallible detective" type—the progeny of M. Dupin and Sherlock Holmes, and the close kin of Algernon Blackwood's John Silence—moving through scenes and events badly marred by an atmosphere of professional "occultism". A few of the episodes, however, are of undeniable power; and afford glimpses of the peculiar genius characteristic of the author.[1]

Lovecraft also comments on Carnacki in a letter to Clark Ashton Smith (September 30, 1934):

> Well—as you see, I surely have become a premier Hodgson fan! Do you know anything about W. H. H. and his career? Koenig tells me he was killed in the war. All told, I believe that nobody but Blackwood can equal or surpass him in capturing the exact shades of the cosmic horror mood in all their actual details. But he was uneven—again like Blackwood. *Carnacki* is very weak, artificial, and stereotyped as a whole despite the strong points which you justly point out. (*Selected Letters* 5.41)

Lee Weinstein is much more complimentary toward the Carnacki stories in his generally positive 1980 essay on Hodgson, "The First Literary Copernicus":

---

1. H. P. Lovecraft, "The Weird Work of William Hope Hodgson," *Phantagraph* 5, No. 5 (February 1937): 5–7; rpt. *Reader and Collector* 3, No. 1 (June 1944): 5–6. Later incorporated in Ch. 9 of "Supernatural Horror in Literature"; see *The Annotated Supernatural Horror in Literature* 79.

Hodgson's mythos achieves its fullest development in *Carnacki the Ghost-Finder* (1910), a collection of stories about one of the earliest psychic detectives. Carnacki often refers to, in the course of his investigations, a volume called the *Sigsand MS*. This book, or manuscript, is supposed to have been written about the 14th century. Quotations from it, scattered throughout the stories, indicate that it is concerned with "Monsters of the Outer World," and defenses against them. In other words, it is very much like the *Necronomicon*. Using information from the *Sigsand MS.*, Carnacki develops a defensive circle containing a pentacle and certain "signs of the Saaamaaa Ritual." Within this chalk circle he places an electric pentacle, suggested by another fictitious book, Prof. Garder's *Experiments With a Medium*. While standing within these defensive barriers, a person is protected from various "powers of the Unknown World," such as the "Outer Monstrosities" and the "Aeiirii forms of semi-materialization." The defense is not good against "Saiitii phenomena," however, since these can "reproduce (themselves) in or take to (their) purposes the very protective material you may use." They involve "the very structure of the aether-fibre itself," we are told in the story "The Whistling Room." In the same story we learn that the Unknown Last Line of the Saaamaaa Ritual, used by the "Ab-human priests in the Incantation of the Raaaee," may be uttered by the inscrutable Protective forces which "govern the spinning of the outer circle and intervene between the human and the Outer Monstrosities." ... At the end of "The Hog" is a lengthy explanation of the Outer Monstrosities. The Earth is surrounded by an Outer Circle 100 thousand miles up and 5-10 million miles in thickness, which spins opposite to Earth's rotation, and consists of extremely rarefied matter. Out of it breed the Outer Monstrosities, which are million mile clouds of force, in the same way that sharks are bred out of the ocean. These monsters chiefly desire the psychic entity of man. In short, the Carnacki stories are based on scientifically rationalized beings from beyond, causing apparently supernatural phenomena.

Weinstein also points out that

> John Silence is also a psychic detective, but in the five stories in the book, he deals with such stock occult menaces as a fire elemental, a werewolf, and persistent spirits of witches who turn themselves into cats. Most of the stories deal with the persistence of evil thoughts after the death of their perpetrators.

Silence combats them with the power of his own mind, rather than the "scientific" methods of Carnacki.

Mark Valentine has written:

> Carnacki is our near contemporary and our witness "that the blind, elemental, swarming energies from beyond" can be resisted; in the far-future

Night Land, Carnacki and humanity have lost. In short, the Carnacki stories, especially those that depict unadulterated cosmic manifestations, are not merely a panderer's box of tricks, but rather a disciplined evocation of Hodgson's dualistic vision presented in a highly accessible form. (27)

Valentine concludes his article on Carnacki with these words of praise for the tales: "Why does Carnacki have this will to persist? Why, when he believes that mankind is an insignificant physical condiment compared with the immense and rapacious forces of the 'Outer Circle' of space, does he continue to do battle? The answer surely lies in the fact that, while the Carnacki stories may not have the rambling rhapsodical majesty and efflorescence of Hodgson's major novels, they are in their own way just as lucid a testament of existential defiance against the abyss" (28).

Another exception to the general critical disdain for Carnacki is the opinion expressed by "Ellery Queen" that Carnacki is "a unique detective who investigates haunted houses and similar phenomena. . . . These *natural* elucidations, frowned on by devotees of the weird, must be applauded by devotees of the detective story; they transform *Carnacki* from a mere dabbler into the unknown to a legitimate and authentic detective. . . . He's a 24-carat 'find' both for lovers of the '*invisible*' and addicts of the '*visible*.'" Of course, whereas many lovers of the supernatural enjoy most the adventures of Carnacki in which monstrous forces from outside seem to be real and verifiable, Queen praises Carnacki for the opposite reason—that a number of his cases prove to have entirely rational explanations.

Most other modern critics have concurred with Lovecraft's low opinion of these tales. Brian Stableford sees them as "inventive and engaging but calculatedly trivial" (Stableford/Pringle 275) (later restated as "hackwork" and "calculatedly trivial" [Stableford/Joshi-Dziemianowicz 553]). The *BFI Companion to Horror* states that Carnacki is "Hodgson's most conventional book" (157). Ian Bell believes that "generally speaking, these stories are considerably inferior to Hodgson's other work" (465). T. E. D. Klein considers that all these stories "offer a shade too much pseudo-scientific explanation and too little real drama" (204). Nathaniel Katz gives a somewhat more balanced view of Carnacki, pointing to the considerable power the Carnacki stories often contain, while noting that "their absurdity cheapens the atmosphere" and confessing himself disappointed with the number of times Carnacki presents rationalized endings for the supernatural phenomena in the tales.

Ian Sinclair, who has been considerably influenced by Hodgson (his own novel *Radon Daughters* is a semi-sequel to Hodgson's *The Night Land*), says: "You know it's going to be a disappointment, but you have to read the book sometime," depicting Carnacki as "a self-starting lightning-rod for psychic phenomena that has not yet been housebroken," and his narrator, Dodgson, "a cut-price Watson" and "plodding serial narrator." Of the stories themselves, Sinclair believes: "Some of these terse sketches ('The Gateway of the Monster', 'The Whistling Room') have their merits, while others . . . well, they'll look good on television. But basically, we're talking direct sale to video." Sinclair does admit that amidst the "dynamic period bombast" and "tedious evenings of billiards and whisky," the symbolic sexual panic of Hodgson's various occult manifestations is obvious, and that "the genuine hauntings are the living heart of these tales, sparks of certified weirdness that illuminate the artificial backdrops. Unexplained, spine-chilling spasms erupt onto the stage of an otherwise unexceptional melodrama" (257-70).

Carnacki in Popular Culture

On the other hand, enthusiasts of the genre have always enjoyed these tales despite their flaws. Carnacki has now widely penetrated popular culture in various forms. Hodgson's tales of the psychic sleuth are popular enough to have inspired at least two book-length collections of pastiches: *472 Cheyne Walk: Carnacki, the Untold Stories* by A. F. (Chico) Kidd and Rick Kennett (chapbook, five stories, Ghost Story Society, 1992; expanded version, nine stories, Ash-Tree Press, 2002; 500 copies only; now available as a Kindle e-book).

Kidd and Kennett consider that the series' enduring attraction comes more from Hodgson's capacity for world-building than any special appeal of Carnacki himself: "It certainly isn't his dynamic personality. Not much character is evident in Hodgson's creation: he is your generic stiff upper-lip Edwardian Englishman . . . but the exotic landscapes he inhabits are supernatural. . . . It's his exploits, and the carefully constructed milieu in which they take place, that continue to intrigue. They are quite timeless."

William Meikle began a series of fictional Carnacki tributes with his chapbook series *Carnacki: Ghost-Finder: The New Adventures* (Ghostwriter Publications, 2009). He has since published the short story collection *Carnacki: Heaven or Hell*. Meikle has also published standalone Carnacki stories such as "A Parliament of Owls" (Lovecraft eZine). The cover of the Dark Regions Press edition of *Carnacki: Heaven and Hell* features a superb illustration, by Wayne Murray, of Carnacki sitting in the middle of his electric pentacle.

Kim Newman, Barbara Hambly, Guy Adams, Alberto Lopez Aroca, and others have used Carnacki as a character in stories of their own, and Andrew Cartmel even featured Carnacki as a companion to the second Dr. Who in a novella titled "Foreign Devils," published as a standalone volume.

M. S. Corley has a blog on the Internet (Carnacki: Recorder of Things Strange) where he posts his illustrations of Carnacki's adventures. Other artists are also inspired by Carnacki,[2] and at least one comic book series has been devoted to the new adventures of Carnacki—that by Richard Amari.[3]

There is even an electronic album of Carnacki-inspired music, *Music for Thomas Carnacki*, and a Librivox recording by various readers of all the Carnacki stories (running over 5 hours) can be accessed at YouTube. The continuing fame of Hodgson's occult sleuth seems to be assured.

Carnacki and the "Ab-Human"

The term "ab-human," distinguished from the similar term "inhuman," is a descriptor used by Hodgson in both his novel *The Night Land* and his *Carnacki* stories. Hodgson appears to have originated this term in his stories, linking the Latin prefix *ab* (meaning "off, away from") with "human" to produce a term descriptive of the monstrous and mysterious entities that plague the human world in his tales. Just as the word "abnormal" means "Deviating from what is normal or usual, typically in a way that is undesirable," "ab-human" implies "deviating from what is human." Hodgson used the term mainly of those "monstrous, unknown forces from Outside" of which he wrote so frequently. Hodgson's word "ab-human" seems closely akin to words such as "preternatural," meaning "beyond the natural" (from the Latin prefix *praeter*, meaning "beyond"), and the word "praeterhuman," meaning "beyond the human" or "superhuman" (used often by occultist Aleister Crowley in referring to "intelligences" with which he claimed to be in communication), in pointing to manifestations of being far beyond the normal course of human nature and intelligence. Hodgson's coinage of the term is effective because the very unfamiliarity of the word in English jars our senses. It thus awakens the reader to the sense of alienage that Hodgson's work seeks to explore and represent.

In more recent times, philosophy and Gothic literary studies have also used the word "abhuman," though it not clear whether this was directly adapted from Hodgson's terminology. It seems more closely akin to the term "abjection" used by feminist philosopher Julia Kristeva. For Kristeva, the 'abject' is a state that may be briefly summarized as our reaction (horror, vomit) to a threatened breakdown in meaning caused by the loss of the distinction between subject and object or between self and other. In postmodernist literary studies of Gothic fiction, "abhuman" refers to a "Gothic body" or something

---

2. For Carnacki-inspired artwork see http://www.redbubble.com/people/jelarson/works/4502952-the-manifestation-of-thomas-carnacki; http://paulsizer.deviantart.com/art/CARNACKI-THE-GHOST-FINDER-55573584; http://browse.deviantart.com/?qh=&section=&global=1&q=carnacki; and http://terrytaylordrawings.blogspot.com.au/2007/05/carnacki.html.

3. For Richard Amari's Carnacki comics, see http://theghost-finder.blogspot.com.au/.

that is only vestigially human and possibly in the process of becoming something monstrous, such as a vampire or werewolf. Kelly Hurley writes that the "abhuman subject is a not-quite-human subject, characterized by its morphic variability, continually in danger of becoming not-itself, becoming other" (3).

Hurley says that she created the "concept of the abhuman . . . on the basis of Kristeva's notion of abjection." Hurley argues that "through depicting the abhuman," the Gothic genre "reaffirms and reconstructs human identity at the point at which it is dissolved." In this sense, Hurley (following Kristeva) indicates that the "abhuman" of philosophical and Gothic studies is a shapeshifter, perhaps a human subject that morphs from human to "abhuman" and back again. For Hodgson, however, "abhuman" always refers to cosmic horrors beyond human ken and experience, to beings so much larger than puny mankind that they are completely foreign and alien to our concerns.

"The Thing Invisible"

"The Thing Invisible" was the sixth story in the Carnacki series to be published. Unlike the first five tales, which had all appeared in 1910 in the *Idler*, "The Thing Invisible" first appeared two years later, in the *New Magazine* (January 1912). It has been speculated that it may be one of the earliest—or even the first—of the Carnacki tales to be written, for a variety of reasons. Firstly, there is a rationalized (non-supernatural) ending. The "haunting" itself is not as frightening as those in some later Carnacki tales—the main fear comes as Carnacki sits alone in the haunted chapel. Furthermore, though Carnacki is obviously well-informed about the dark arts and arcane matters, there is no mention of his previous cases (as is common in other stories), and no mention of such rituals as the Saaamaaa Ritual or such artefacts as the *Sigsand Manuscript*. His investigative techniques here do involve photography, but are otherwise fairly undeveloped compared to other stories where he uses such devices as placing wires and sealing doors.

It has been pointed out by Marcus L. Rowland that the version of this story printed in book collections has several significant changes from the text first published in the *New Magazine*. The 1912 version includes a major error of British etiquette; early in the story Carnacki repeatedly addresses Sir Alfred Jarnock as "Sir Jarnock," when the correct term would be "Sir Alfred"; and the cast of characters is slightly different in the two versions.[4]

The plot is relatively straightforward. The tale opens with Carnacki inviting his usual London friends over for supper. He tells them of his latest ex-

---

4. The variant texts are available for comparison at http://www.forgottenfutures.com/game/ff4/carnacki.htm

ploit—being hired by the family of Sir Alfred Jarnock of South Kent to investigate the stabbing of their butler by a ghostly dagger. Sir Alfred's estate includes a reputedly haunted chapel. There is a long history behind the bloody reputation of the dagger within the family. Supposedly, if an enemy were to enter the chapel after nightfall, the dagger that rests just over the altar will attack them. The Jarnocks have until now treated the family legend as but a curious folktale; but Carnacki has suddenly been called in because the "waeful dagger" has attempted to take a life.

Carnacki is told that one Sunday the rector had been talking with Sir Alfred and his eldest son; Bellet (the butler) was meanwhile extinguishing the candles. The rector, remembering he had left a small prayer book on the Communion table, called the butler to retrieve it. As the Jarnocks and the rector looked towards the butler, Bellet opened the small chancel gate and was suddenly struck by the dagger before their very eyes: "absolutely alone, and then the *blow*, out of the Void, he described it, and the *force* prodigious—the old man being driven headlong into the body of the Chapel. Like the kick of a great horse, the Rector said. . . ."

We note here that Hodgson's peculiar fascination with the symbol of the spectral horse comes into play. While it transpires that no supernatural agency is involved, the notion that there may be a ghostly horse is clearly suggested here—a fact that links this tale (at least in imagery) to the Carnacki tale "The Horse of the Invisible." This hint of a ghostly presence represents the "ab-human" factor in the story, though it must be admitted the notion of a spectral horse is a fairly conventional one, this motif having appeared in Fuseli's famous painting "The Nightmare," in Celtic lore and legend such as that of the Abbey Lubber, and as a variant in a wide variety of folktales regarding spectral or phantom animals.

The butler does not die due to this blow; he only has his collarbone broken. But the family is so perturbed that George Jarnock, the eldest son, calls in Carnacki to investigate. Sir Alfred is too disturbed and nervous to do anything positive. On arrival at the Jarnock estate, Carnacki conducts an exhaustive investigation of the site, not neglecting to inspect the roof, which takes him three days. (We are reminded of Sherlock Holmes's painstaking investigation of crime scenes for every available detail.) Carnacki comes to the problematic conclusion that none of the witnesses could have hidden in the chapel—thus the mystery of the butler being attacked when no one was near to him is deepened. Is the cause of the attack "human" or "ab-human"?

The dagger itself has a complex shape and legend. Carnacki examines it closely, finding it be "ten inches long, two inches broad at the base, and tapering to a rounded but sharp point, rather peculiar" and "double-edged." Furthermore, "the metal sheath is curious for having a crosspiece . . . with . . . the hilt itself . . . continued three parts up the hilt . . . [giving] it the appearance of a cross." There is a depiction of Christ crucified on one side, whilst on the other is the inscription (in Latin) translating to "Vengeance Is Mine, I Will Repay." On the dagger's blade is engraved in Old English capitals: I WATCH. I STRIKE, and on the butt of the hilt there is carved deeply a pentacle.

Carnacki requests that he be allowed to spend the night in the chapel, but Sir Alfred Jarnock says he locks the chapel every night and is most insistent that Carnacki not be admitted. Carnacki, however, contrives to borrow and duplicate the key. He also sets up his camera gear and photographs the chapel interior by daylight.

Carnacki spends the night in the chapel clad in plate armor, over which is a shirt of chain mail he has borrowed from the Armory at the estate. His camera is at the ready to photograph any mysterious phenomena. And he is armed with a lantern and his gun. All night he hears mysterious noises. Although he considers the legend might be nonsense, he has been careful enough to wear the armour beneath his clothes: "'I can tell you, as I stood there, I could believe that something invisible was coming toward me in the air of the Chapel. Yet, I had got to go through with the business, and I just took hold of my little bit of courage and set to work.'"

Here we see the human at work—Carnacki himself is all too human—not over-courageous and even a bit of a coward at times. This is one of the strongest aspects of the story. Carnacki is no supercool sleuth, never breaking out in a sweat, and with complete confidence in his own abilities to confront the supernatural (or alleged supernatural). He battles his own fears; he trembles and shakes, and is afraid. This technique, and Hodgson's cunning in keeping the reader guessing as to the final outcome, greatly strengthen the reader's identification with Carnacki, and whatever power resides in the tale resides in that identification.

Resetting his camera, Carnacki takes a flash picture of the chapel and then sits in a pew. As evening continues, various weird noises such as a metallic "clank" from near the altar, and what seem to be soft steps near him, keep him on his nerves' edge in the dark.

> "And suddenly I made a mighty effort and lowered my arms. I held my face up in the darkness. And, I tell you, I respect myself for the act, because I thought truly at that moment that I was going to die. But . . . by the slow revulsion of feeling which had assisted my effort. I was less sick, in that instant, at the thought of having to die, than at the knowledge of the utter weak cowardice that had so unexpectedly shaken me to bits, for a time."

Nothing untoward comes of these sounds, even when he shines his lantern after hearing a slithering noise. (These noises later prove to red herrings, which is perhaps a little unfair on the reader.) Investigating the chancel gate, he discovers that the dagger has disappeared from its scabbard above the altar. As he approaches the gate, afraid the dagger may be floating about, he opens the gate and the dagger strikes him in the chest, causing him to fall backwards. He loses his gun and the lantern smashes. He runs out of the chapel in a blind panic. Hodgson plays this scene ingeniously, suggesting that there may well be a malevolent supernatural force at play. Back in his room, Carnacki finds to his horror that the dagger point has pierced both chain mail and armor, leaving his chest scratched over his heart.

Returning to the chapel next morning, he finds his lantern shattered but the gun untouched. The camera is but slightly damaged, and the dagger lies in the aisle. He steps on it, as though to prevent its unnatural movement; though after a few minutes he picks it up and handles it: "'I am talking about the curiousness of learning in that moment a new shade of quality of fear that had hitherto been outside of my knowledge or imagination. Does it interest you?'" (The latter question is addressed to his friends in his Cheyne Walk drawing room where he is regaling them with his tale.)

Carnacki takes the camera plates to the photographer in town. The first plate developed shows nothing unusual in the chapel (it was the picture taken with the flash). The second plate shows some vague shapes that had been imprinted on the unexposed plate that was in the camera when he was attacked. But then Carnacki discovers something thrilling.

Sir Alfred Jarnock, who is unwell, has left instructions that no one is to enter the chapel without him. But Carnacki again disobeys, conducting some experiments in the chapel. With George, he then brings a dummy (dressed in armor plate) to the chapel, and they place it near the altar. Carnacki warns George away from the chancel gate. Carnacki then pushes the dummy forward so it leans on the gate. Immediately the dummy is thrown to the floor, struck by a massive blow and with the dagger buried in the armor. Carnacki now reveals the sleight-of-hand behind the trick, which he has uncovered due to a subtle difference between the "before" and "after" photographs of the altar's cast iron metalwork.

A section of the left-hand gatepost has a hinge that, when pressed down, opens a gap in the floor into which the post fits snugly. Carnacki replaces the dagger into the trap, resetting it. The ancient trap that guards the altar is a spring mechanism designed to hurl the dagger when the altar gate is opened.

Sir Alfred then confesses that he has set the trap every night, and had set it too early the day of the butler's wounding. Carnacki believes that in past ages the hole in the floor was used to hide valuables and it transpires that Sir Alfred has, in fact, concealed his wife's jewelry therein. The butler recovers, and the case is over. All the mysterious noises that Carnacki heard while in the chapel during the night are explained away as natural manifestations. The pentacle inscribed on the dagger appears to have had no particular supernatural significance; it was merely a touch of color that suggested possible occult forces behind the phenomenon.

Of course, this is mildly disappointing to the horror fan who prefers the supernatural as the root cause of the mysterious happenings. It must be said that the explanation of the mystery appears more than a little contrived. Carnacki managing to debunk the myth via his scientific equipment—effectively the Edwardian version of time-lapse photography—places him, in this story, firmly in the mold of the cogitating detective, rather like those Sherlock Holmes tales such as "The Sussex Vampire" in which Holmes reveals that despite apparently supernatural goings-on, human motives and causes are at the bottom of it all. Ellery Queen would have approved of "The Thing Invisible." However, the ending does not take away altogether from the atmosphere of the "abhuman" that Hodgson creates as Carnacki crouches in the chapel by night, his nerves strained to the limit.

"The Horse of the Invisible"

"The Horse [of the] Invisible" was the fourth story in the Carnacki series story to be published. It first appeared in the *Idler* (April 1910) and has been republished several times, notably in Hugh Greene's anthology *The Rivals of Sherlock Holmes* (1970). It was this appearance that led to Hodgson's tale being adapted for the Thames Television/ITV Network series *The Rivals of Sherlock Holmes*.[5] Two series of this show were made, the first screening in 1971 and the second in 1973. "The Horse of the Invisible" was featured as Episode 5 of Series One and starred Donald Pleasence as Carnacki. This is one of the few times Hodgson's work has been adapted for the visual medium.[6]

---

5. Not to be confused with similarly titled two-volume anthology edited by Alan K. Russell for Castle Books in 1978, which does not contain the Hodgson story. Hugh Greene edited three further volumes in his series: *Cosmopolitan Crimes: Foreign Rivals of Sherlock Holmes*. (Pantheon Books, 1971); *Further Rivals of Sherlock Holmes* (Pantheon Books, 1973); and *The American Rivals of Sherlock Holmes* (Pantheon Books, 1976).

6. "The Horse of the Invisible" is available on Acorn Media's DVD release of *The Rivals of Sherlock Holmes Series One*. At http://www.amazon.com/The-Rivals-Sherlock-Holmes-Set/ dp/ B001V7YZE8/ref=sr_1_7?ie=UTF8&qid=1369898965&sr=8-7&keywords=rivals+Sherlock+Holmes

This tale includes some of the occult paraphernalia that come to characterize the Carnacki series—his "electric pentacle," the Saaamaaa Ritual, and also the references to other, unrecorded cases (a device no doubt borrowed from Conan Doyle's Holmes stories). "The Black Veil" case is mentioned—a case in which young Aster is said to have died because he refused the protection of the electric pentacle. And an unnamed case is referred to—"I was inclined to parallel the case with that one of Harford's where the hand of the child kept materialising within the pentacle and patting the floor. As you will remember, that was a hideous business."

The plot of "The Horse of the Invisible," which contains an admixture of the "human" and the "ab-human," may be summarised as follows.

Carnacki exhibits some obvious bruising when his friends arrive at his home for the usual dinner invitation. Carnacki shows the narrator, who is first to arrive, some photographs of a young beautiful woman in various dark rooms. One shows her looking upward at what appears to be a large horse's hoof bearing down on her.

Carnacki explains he has just returned from East Lancashire, where a Captain Hisgins asked him to investigate a family curse. According to Hisgins family tradition, any first-born female will be haunted by a ghostly horse during her courtship. Five previous first-born girls had died tragically; each being engaged, they died by various means, there being an impression that the fifth girl had been kicked to death by a horse. This story has been long considered a legend, but now for the first time in seven generations there is a first-born female (Mary), and her fiancé, the young naval officer Beaumont, has just suffered a broken arm after an attack by a mysterious assailant in a darkened corridor. (Here again we note the fascination that Hodgson seems to have felt for the motif of the supernatural horse in the Carnacki stories. At least in this tale the theme is explored to a fuller extent than in "The Thing Invisible.")

On arrival at the Hisgins home, Carnacki, Mary, and her fiancé, Beaumont, hear hoofbeats in the night, but no horse is visible. Beaumont gives the story to Carnacki as they play billiards with Mary in the room. Carnacki cautions them that there may be natural explanations for the sounds, but when they leave the billiard room they all hear the sounds of a horse galloping around the room they have just left! No explanation presents itself, but Carnacki and Beaumont decide to investigate.

A further encounter with the ab-human horse follows: "'The great tread came right up to the door and then stopped and there was an instant of absolute silence, except that so far as I was concerned, the pulsing in my throat and temples almost deafened me.'" Here again we have Carnacki's very human (and understandable) reactions of fear and terror in the face of highly mysterious circumstances. After this the sound seems to vanish. Mary retires for the evening, and Carnacki sets up his electric pentacle as a protection around Mary's bed. He stations Mary's parents as guards in the room, and he and Beaumont guard the outside. Carnacki is positive that Beaumont is more in danger than his fiancée; he constructs a pentacle around Beaumont as well.

The hoofbeats are heard again during the night, but nothing else happens, and no hoofmarks can be found around the grounds next morning.

Next morning, Carnacki learns that Mary's cousin, Harry Parsket, is on the way from London to help fight the ghost. Carnacki admires the fellow's "tremendous pluck" and says he is "the particular kind of man I like to have with me in a bad case."

That evening, Carnacki advises the captain that the couple should marry immediately, as this may avert any supernatural danger; the captain agrees. Suddenly, hoofbeats and neighing are heard on the grounds and Mary is heard screaming from the darkened lawn. Shots are heard as everyone hurries to the lawn.

Carnacki rushes out and snaps a picture, but sees nothing, blinded by the flash. He finds Mary prone on the lawn, with Beaumont protecting her from some unseen evil. Beaumont has been struck in the head but is not badly injured save for a deep gash on his forehead; he claims that he has seen an enormous horse's head. Chased by the ghostly horse, he had fired at the sound. Carnacki and the other men search the grounds but find nothing. That night, Carnacki erects the same defenses, sure that the danger is imminent, but the night passes uneventfully.

Next morning, Carnacki finds the family has decided to accelerate the wedding plans, in the hopes that the haunting will vanish when Mary is no longer courting, but married. Beaumont goes to London for a special permit. During the day, Carnacki keeps close to Mary and uses the opportunity to photograph her in several rooms of the house. As he explains: "Sometimes the camera sees things that would seem very strange to normal human eyesight."

Carnacki takes his last pictures down in the basement, bringing Parsket and the captain with Mary for support. When Carnacki attempts another room, he hears neighing and galloping just as he snaps the picture and sees Mary looking upward. He senses danger and yells to the men to get clear, taking Mary to safety. Carnacki shuts and locks the door behind him, making the First and Eighth signs of the Saaamaaa Ritual—apparently a ritual of protection. After taking Mary upstairs, Parsket and the captain return with lanterns and guns, but find the room empty. Carnacki, equally frightened, locks the door and repeats the ritual signs of the Saaamaaa Ritual.

Later, when Carnacki and Parsket develop the photos, they observe that, in the photo taken in the last basement room, there is a spectral horse's hoof hanging above Mary's head. Carnacki warns Parsket not to tell Mary about this, but does tell the captain. That night, with Beaumont still in London, Carnacki again repeats his protective ritual precautions and he and Parsket guard Mary's door. But nothing untoward occurs and the house settles down to sleep.

Next morning, hoofbeats and neighing can be heard almost immediately, in what seems a direct assault by the abhuman being, the apparently invisible horse; Carnacki fires his weapon and Mary's father attacks with his sword. Meanwhile, Beaumont sends word that he will arrive by four, and that the rector will arrive to perform the wedding urgently. But Beaumont's train is delayed; he arrives late, and the rector, called away on more urgent business, will be unable to arrive until the next day.

Carnacki then rigs another trap—a cord to ring for the gamekeepers and butler, whom he warns to be on the alert. That same night, Parsket takes to walking nervously up and down the hall. Carnacki joins him but trips over his own rigged-up cord. Parsket points out that even though Carnacki tripped over the cord, the bell failed to ring; Parsket goes to check the wire. Just then, Beaumont hears galloping from the hall's far end.

An exciting scene follows in which the lamp is thrown, Carnacki fires his flashlight, the Captain shouts and women scream:

> "I had a sudden horrible fear that the monster had got into the bedroom, but in the same instant from up the corridor there came abruptly the vile, gobbling neighing that we had heard in the park and the cellar. I blew the whistle again and groped blindly for the bell-cord, shouting to Beaumont to stay in the Pentacle, whatever happened. I yelled again to the Captain to bring out a lamp and there came a smashing sound against the bedroom door. Then I had my matches in my hand, to get some light before that incredible, unseen Monster was upon us."

Carnacki strikes a match and whirls around to behold a monstrous horsehead close by Beaumont. The match is snuffed out as both Carnacki and Beaumont fire their pistols. Amidst the chaotic struggles and sounds, Carnacki can hear Beaumont fighting something in the darkness. Carnacki grabs what he thinks is an ear; then something falls on him, and he loses consciousness.

On awakening, Carnacki discovers that the captain has captured the "thing," which proves to be a man wearing a large horse-head, and wearing upon his hands hoof-like pads. When they remove the horsehead mask, they are shocked to discover it has been Parsket, the rejected suitor, all along.

But as they interrogate Parsket, hoofbeats are again heard in the house, and this time it is *no trick*. The hoofbeats approach Mary's door. Parsket bravely puts himself between the door and the abhuman horse, which seems to move away down the hall and off. Parsket collapses, dead of fright.

The marriage takes place as planned, and the abhuman manifestation is never heard from again. It is explained that Parsket had been madly in love with his cousin, and thus sought to scare Beaumont away via the use of the family "curse." After that proved ineffective, he tried more violent means.

It seems that both the natural and the supernatural have been at work in the scenario of this tale; for most of the manifestations were caused by Parsket (human)—but there is the matter of that photograph and the last spectral scene in the corridor, which appear to be genuinely *ab-human* manifestations.

While the ab-human in this case does not take on the truly cosmic and extramundane character of the ab-human forces in certain other Hodgson works, such as *The Night Land*, being confined merely to the suggestion that there is a genuinely spectral horse, there is enough of horror in Hodgson's descriptions of it as a Monster, and of its vile neighing and "gobbling," to suggest that it touches on the realm of the Outside things that represent the truly "ab-human."

Works Cited

Bell, Ian. "William Hope Hodgson: Voyager and Visionary." *Antiquarian Book Monthly Review* 12, No. 12 (December 1985): 460–65.

Cartmel, Andrew. *Foreign Devils (Doctor Who)*. Telos Publications (deluxe hardback, trade hardback, 2002; paperback, 2004). The volume includes a reprint of the Carnacki tale "The Whistling Room."

Corley, M. S. "Carnacki: Recorder of Things Strange." http://thomascarnacki.blogspot.com.au/.

Hurley, Kelly. *The Gothic Body: Sexuality, Materialism, and Degeneration at the Fin de Siècle*. Cambridge: Cambridge University Press, 2004.

Katz, Nathaniel. "William Hope Hodgson: Carnacki the Ghost-Finder." Online: http://evilhat.blogspot.com.au/2013/01/william-hope-hodgson-carnacki-ghost.html.

Rick Kennett, and A. F. Kidd. *No. 472 Cheyne Walk: Carnacki, the Untold Stories*. Ashcroft, BC: Ash-Tree Press, 2002.

Klein, T. E. D. "William Hope Hodgson." In *The Penguin Encyclopedia of Horror and the Supernatural*, ed. Jack Sullivan. New York: Viking, 1986.

Lovecraft, H. P. *The Annotated Supernatural Horror in Literature*. Edited by S. T. Joshi. 2nd ed. New York: Hippocampus Press, 2012.

———. *Selected Letters*. Edited by August Derleth, Donald Wandrei, and James Turner. Sauk City, WI: Arkham House, 1965–76. 5 vols.

Meikle, William. *Carnacki: Heaven or Hell*. Ghost House, 2011. Dark Regions Press, 2012.

Music for Thomas Carnacki (http://jonbrooks.bandcamp.com/album/music-for-thomas-carnacki).

Newman, Kim, ed. *The BFI Companion to Horror*. London: Cassell, 1996.

Queen, Ellery. "William Hope Hodgson and the Detective Story." *Reader and Collector* (June 1944). Available online: http://williamhopehodgson.wordpress.com/2012/08/10/william-hope-hodgson-and-the-detective-story-by-ellery-queen/.

Sinclair, Ian. "'Vibrations in a Vacuum': Carnacki: An Afterword." in *Carnacki the Ghost-Finder*. London: Grafton, 1991. 257-70.

Stableford, Brian. "William Hope Hodgson." In *St James Guide to Horror, Ghost and Gothic Writers*, ed. David Pringle. Detroit: St James Press, 1998.

———. "William Hope Hodgson." In *Supernatural Literature of the World: An Encyclopedia*, ed. S. T. Joshi and Stefan Dziemianowicz. Westport, CT: Greenwood Press, 2005.

Valentine, Mark. "Against the Abyss: Carnacki the Ghost-Finder." in *William Hope Hodgson: Voyages and Visions*, ed. Ian Bell. Oxford: A. Bell & Sons, 1987. 24-28.

Weinstein, Lee. "The First Literary Copernicus". *Nyctalops* No. 15 (January 1980). Available online: http://williamhopehodgson.wordpress.com/2012/07/23/the-first-literary-copernicus-2/.

YouTube/Librivox audio readings of Carnacki stories: http://www.youtube.com/watch?v=qEM8RdZkLp4.

Sexual Symbolism in W. H. Hodgson

Sid Birchby

The House on the Borderland was first published in 1908, and shows certain affinities with H. G. Wells's *Time Machine*. There is a time-travel episode, for instance, in which the hero notes the passage of day and night as "a sort of gigantic ponderous flicker," a convention familiar to most readers of time travel stories. "The Sun," he notes, "made one clean, clear sweep through the sky, . . . and the night came and went with a like haste."

There are pseudo-scientific footnotes to the text, which in a plonking way mirror those found in Wells, e.g., "I can only suppose that the time of the Earth's yearly journey had ceased to bear its present relative proportion to the period of the Sun's rotation." Such footnotes remained an accepted writer's device in science-fiction until well into the 1930s.

But behind the facade of straight science-fiction is a story told by Hodgson alone. Its hero, identified only as "The Recluse," lives in a lonely house in Western Ireland. This house, for no very clear reasons, is under siege by weird creatures which emerge from a nearby ravine. In mid-plot the Recluse finds himself making an apocalyptic trip into the future. From this he learns that the monsters have always existed underground, and always will until the remote age when the dead Earth falls into the Sun. He returns to the present and to his doom. The story ends as the creatures burst into his study.

The sense of nemesis brooding over the house is competently done, and looks backwards to Poe and forwards to Lovecraft. But where Poe's necrophily would have coloured the narrative, or Lovecraft's penchant for the degradation of Man, Hodgson lays on a wash of courtly romance. True to the idiom it is a Hopeless Romance; no more than two sketchy encounters with a Soul-mate while time-travelling, plus a certain amount of breast-beating and cries of "Shall we never meet again?" It could easily be discounted as standard literary practice at Hodgson's level and in his day, and of no special importance in understanding the work. Yet in the light of certain sexual symbols appearing in the story it is indeed, like the impassive iceberg, the only visible fraction of a submerged giant.

The besieging creatures are pallid swine-like things prowling through the bushes like the transformed lovers of Circe, yet as savage as those other symbols of erotic lust, the Gadarene swine. They are linked with images of carnality, foulness, and female genitalia: their home is "in the bowels of the world" and they pour out through a pit which mysteriously enlarges itself: "The side of the Pit appeared to have collapsed, forming a deep V-shaped cleft. In the angle of the V was a great hole, not unlike an arched doorway." We learn that through this hole the monsters emerge. Gradually the Pit fills with water and overflows into caverns under the House itself. The final end of the House is to collapse into the Pit.

Physical love is an animal thing, foul and all-engulfing. No good will come of sexual intercourse, only the savage lusts of the swine (whose speech is described as similar to human speech but "glutinous and sticky"). The True Love spurns physical contact: "She came over swiftly and touched me and it was as though Heaven had opened. Yet when I reached out my hands to her, she put me from her with tenderly stern hands, and I was abashed."

The Recluse meets her first as he stands upon the shore of an immense and silent sea, which she tells him is called "The Sea of Sleep." It is in fact the womb-image, from which she emerges in "a bubble of white foam floating up out of the depths." Overhead, reiterating the symbolism, was "a stupendous globe of pale fire, that swam a little above the far horizon, and shed a foam-like light above the quiet waters."

The true love is virginal as a new-born babe, and is glimpsed only in sleep. Or she is as impregnable as a Sleeping Princess.

Only once again does he meet her. It is after the end of the Solar System, and he sees "a boundless river of softly shimmering globes." He is impelled towards one of them: "Then I slid through into the interior without experiencing the least resistance." Would that the return to the womb were always so easy! Once inside the globe, he recognises his surroundings. He is again by the Sea of Sleep, and sure enough his loved one is there. With this wealth of imagery, can we any longer doubt her identity?

The distant future is also the main locale of *The Night Land*, published in 1912. At last the Sun has gone out and the human race is embattled in the Last Redoubt against various nyctaloptic beasts: "The Thing that Nods," "The Watcher in the South East," "The Night Hounds," and so on. The Redoubt is mostly underground; only a Pyramid shows on the surface. Outside all is darkness and terror, but once within we descend to lands of warmth and light, complete with pseudo-sun and pseudo sky. So might a mother's breast offer a haven against the dangers of the world, and rouse yearnings for the lost Eden of the womb.

As in *The House on the Borderland*, the hero tells the story but is not named. It is as if Hodgson identified himself so fully with his heroes that to name them would have broken the spell. The first half of the book sets the scene and tells how the hero makes telepathic contact with Naani, a girl in a far-off Redoubt. They fall in love and he sets out across the Night Land to rescue her from the monsters which are besieging her Redoubt.

Spiritual love, then, is more important than physical attributes. First there must be a meeting of minds. Having found the true love, the lover must at once rescue her from the temptations of the world.

He arrives at the Lesser Redoubt after an odyssey of superbly-written fantasy, only to find that it has fallen. Naani alone is saved, and the second half of the book describes their return to base. This is, on the surface, a simple Sir Galahad fantasy. He defends the girl against various monsters, he calls her "Mine Own Maid," and he even wears armour. To ensure that we do not miss the point, the entire story is written in a pseudo-mediaeval, and quite irritating, style, full of "verily's" and "Lo's." But from the very moment that he meets the girl, curious undertones become apparent. In the words of the old song, he seems to be fighting an impulse to use the traditional methods of protecting her from the foggy, foggy dew.

When they first meet, he has to strip off his cloak to cover her, for her clothes have been torn as she ran from the monsters. Later, while she sleeps, he does a far, far better thing by taking off his underclothes and laying them beside her, "for truly she was nigh unclothed." Egad!

Thenceforth the narrative abounds with instances of what I can only call sublimated stripping. She mends her torn garments, having first put on his underpants. She bathes in a pool, while he discreetly turns his back. She has her clothes ripped off by a savage. Naked fugitives from the sack of the Redoubt flit screaming through the night, hotly pursued by monsters. One of them, a girl, is ripped in half. And so forth.

Moreover, as the journey progresses, the hero develops foot-fetishism. It begins when she kisses him "thrice very passionate and warm upon the mouth." His reaction: "I made her to stand upon the rock, and I set free her hair over her shoulders, and I took then the boots from her, so that her little feet did show bare and pretty."

In another love-scene, he "kist her pretty toes," and in a third he openly admits his obsession: "She now to slip her footgear, that her feet be bare unto me, as I did love." It seems that Sir Galahad is sublimating madly.

But the fruits of sexual repression continue to ripen into new perversions. We learn that he is, as the advertisements discreetly say, interested in Discipline and the Whip. Only thus, it appears, can he make her realise that he is "surely her Master, and she mine own Baby-Slave." So, when food is short and she secretly gives him part of her rations, he whips her for being deceitful, "so hard that she had screamed if that she had been any coward." Fortunately, she derives an erotic stimulus from it, for "presently I knew that she kist the whipt hand secretly in the dark."

Perhaps for this reason, he is soon thinking of whipping her again for being fickle. In the middle of a love-scene, she suddenly tires of his advances! Two other whippings do take place, and each although justified with talk of "impudence" and "rebellion," is set in the context of a love-scene. The final episode begins with a new perversion—he ties a belt around her waist and leads her along by it. Soon she cuts herself free. He chases and catches her, "loosens her garment . . . and sets the belt thrice across her pretty shoulders." This incident is followed by a love-scene. It is with some relief that we watch them gain the safety of the Great Redoubt and so call a halt to this Poor Man's Kama Sutra.

Doubtless none of the above erotic nuances were intended to be displayed either by the characters or by the author. If the Galahad-theme constitutes the surface of the story, the eroticism is not the second, but the third layer, buried deep below the reach of all but our present post-Freudian generation. It is the middle layer of allegory that may have been meant to be excavated.

And now the meaning of the allegory is plain. In *The House on the Borderland* we are told to reject the bestial lust of physical passion—it is a pit dug under the human race from time immemorial. It will always be there until the world ends. The only love on which we can rely is that which demands nothing from us, and gives all; the unselfish love that only a mother can give. Nobody is more worthy of devotion. In a spiritual sense, of course.

Any fears lest such mother-fixation might arouse latent tendencies to homosexuality are dispelled as we interpret *The Night Land*'s message. With our mother's strength to back us, and armoured by her against the evils of the world, we find a young virgin and save her from worldly peril. Although she is wilful and disobedient at first, we force her, for her own good, to obey us in everything, because what we do is what our mother has taught us, and is Right. We take her home to mother, with whom we must live when we are married, for there is nowhere else left that is not overrun with evil things.

The last sentence of *The Night Land* reads: "For that which doth be truly Love doth mother Honour and Faithfulness; and they three to build the House of Joy."

No need for me to name the key-word.

The "Wonder Unlimited"—
The Tales of Captain Gault

Mark Valentine

It is understandable that William Hope Hodgson is most celebrated for his far-future fantasy *The Night Land* (1912), for the cosmic haunted-house story *The House on the Borderland* (1908), for the lively occult detective yarns in *Carnacki, the Ghost-Finder* (1913), and for his original and powerful contribution to the macabre with his tales of sea horrors such as *The Ghost Pirates* (1909) and "The Voice in the Night" (1907). That is quite enough accomplishment for one writer, surely? Indeed it is, but the survival of these works, now recognized as classics in the field, have cast a shadow over one other book by Hodgson, perhaps his least-regarded. In this essay, I want to look at *Captain Gault: Being the Exceedingly Private Log of a Sea-Captain* (Eveleigh Nash, 1917), the last book by Hodgson published in his lifetime. It was issued while Hodgson was on active front-line duty in the trenches.

For some reason, nautical tales generally have not survived so well as work in the genres of fantasy, crime, science fiction, and the supernatural. These each have ardent adherents who have celebrated and revived the work of the masters in their field, and even tracked down some of the obscurest authors and titles. Stories of the sea, by contrast, have nothing like the scholarly or enthusiast interest in them as these others. But at the time Hodgson was writing, this neglect would have seemed unlikely. There was a strong readership for nautical fiction, particularly of the swashbuckling and/or comic kind.

Two examples will suffice. One of the most popular characters of the Edwardian period was Captain Kettle, the freebooting, spade-bearded modern buccaneer, created by C. J. Cutcliffe Hyne, whose exploits were recounted in around a dozen volumes, such as *The Adventures of Captain Kettle* (1898) and the *Further Adventures* (1901). Kettle roves around the world, getting involved in colorful villainies and earning himself sundry fortunes, but always somehow coming out on the side of the angels. His ill-gotten proceeds are dutifully sent home to his family and friends, care of the Particular Baptist chapel in Wharfedale, a lovely valley in the Yorkshire Dales (indeed, Hyne himself retired there, appropriately enough to the village of Kettlewell, where he lies buried). Captain Kettle, it has been said, was once as popular as Sherlock Holmes, and just as great a mainstay of the periodicals. This may seem improbable to us now, but contemporary reports are clear: Kettle's adventures were awaited as impatiently, and devoured as avidly, as the tales of the Great Detective. And yet today Hyne, to the extent he is known at all, is remembered mostly as the author of the Atlantis fantasy *The Lost Continent* (1900). Captain Kettle and his shipmates have all been sunk without trace, or are marooned on a desert island of indifference.

Our second example is of a man Arthur Machen called a comic master, proclaiming that he would choose his stories above much ostensibly finer literature. He was referring to the humorous tales of ship's watchmen, old salts, and superannuated fishermen who gather at the Cauliflower Inn in London's eastern docks. They were the work of W. W. Jacobs and were gathered in collections such as *Many Cargoes* (1896) and *Sea Urchins* (1898). Once again, these were regular fare in the papers and magazines of the period and read with much relish. They usually involved his jolly reprobates' attempts to get more money for beer and 'baccy, often thwarted. And yet Jacobs is remembered today mostly for "The Monkey's Paw," a classic, much-reprinted macabre tale, and for one or two others in this vein: but not for the comic tales at all, which only have interest among Jacobs diehards.

There were plenty of other successful writers of sea fiction, such as W. Clark Russell, much admired by Conan Doyle's Dr. Watson; or H. M. Tomlinson, who wrote of melancholy, troubled young men on long voyages to the tropics. Hodgson himself praised one, now forgotten naval author, Edward Noble (1857-1941), a doctor's son who said he spent "twenty odd years wandering on the seven seas—in sailing and tramp and mail ship" as an engineer and in other jobs. Noble wrote eighteen books of fiction, many of them with a nautical theme, including *Waves of Fate* (1905), *The Lady Navigators and Incidentally the Man with the Nubbly Brow* (1905), and *Fisherman's Gat: A Story of the Thames Estuary* (1906) (it is "Gat," not "Cat," alas). Noble's breezy tone is quite like Hodgson's.

But the two prime examples, of Hyne and Jacobs, illustrate two things. Firstly, they help explain why Hodgson's Captain Gault stories have been neglected: not for anything intrinsically indifferent or unskilled in them, but simply as part of a general decline in the fortunes of this sort of light nautical fiction. When even those tales regarded in their time as the best in the field are no longer much read, we should not wonder that Hodgson's work here struggles to get a fresh readership. But secondly, the success of Cutcliffe Hyne and of W. W. Jacobs may suggest to us why Hodgson wrote the Captain

Gault stories. He was experienced in the world of ships, sailors, and the sea, he had shown he could depict these convincingly, and he could see that there was a ready market for good work here.

Hodgson's earlier books, despite the admiration of a few literary figures, had not earned the respect, nor the fortune, that the ebullient Hodgson probably thought was his due: R. Alain Everts reported that in 1915 Hodgson claimed neither *The Night Land* nor *Carnacki* had brought him "one farthing" (19). Instead, said Everts, Hodgson "stuck for the most part to light sea stories: which guaranteed an income instantly . . . trite for the most part, and boring little bits of fluff." The suggestion is that Hodgson consciously decided to try a different tack, in his quest to crack the better-paying popular fiction markets.

Indeed, if Hodgson is recognized today principally as a master of fantasy and horror fiction, it's worth reminding ourselves that this may not have been how contemporaries mainly saw him. As Jeremy Lassen has observed, in his introduction to *The Boats of the "Glen Carrig" and Other Nautical Adventures*:

> It was Hodgson's nautical fiction that first captured his contemporary readers' imaginations. His experiences of life at sea gave this nautical fiction a grounding in reality which, when combined with his weird and cosmic sensibilities, created balanced and remarkably effective narratives. Even his non-weird sea fiction benefited from this dynamic: his realistically detailed backgrounds served to make the overly dramatic flourishes of his adventure fiction seem less outlandish. His popular success encouraged editors to give him top billing in the popular fiction magazines of the day, and encouraged Hodgson to further develop his peculiar cosmic vision. (ix)

We can therefore understand why Hodgson wrote the Gault stories: they paid well and he was good at them. And we can see why they have not so far endured so well as his other work: they are in a genre that has not sustained such a strong readerly devotion. But is this comparative neglect entirely fair? What do we find when we take another look at them?

Twelve of the stories were published in the *London Magazine* during 1914–16. A few of the earliest stories were summarized in *Cargunka and Poems and Anecdotes* (1914), a volume principally aimed at protecting American copyright in Hodgson's work. The tactic was to provide enough of the plots to establish ownership and prevent the stories being stolen, but without printing the whole story.

However, the first real book publication was in *Captain Gault*, which gathered ten of the magazine stories (together with two rather oddly rollicking poems, somewhat like adult nursery rhymes). Hodgson was following the customary pattern of the working writer of the day: periodical appearance first, followed by reprinting in book form. The stories were presented as chapters in a novel, no doubt because of the perennial publishing assumption that novels sell better than gatherings of short stories. But little attempt was made to link the pieces together, and they still read as self-contained episodes.

The stories are very much on the model of Captain Kettle. Like Cutcliffe Hyne's bristling skipper, Gault is out for the main chance, intent on enriching himself, and he enjoys pitting his wits against customs officials, rival villains, indomitable ladies, and the enemy German navy. But, also like Kettle, he has his own code of conduct, which means as much to him as the plunder he so keenly seeks. For example, he always strictly adheres to agreements he has made, such as safe delivery of cargo or passengers, even though sometimes he sticks only to the barest literal letter, and not the spirit, of his agreement. But Hodgson departs further from the Kettle template when he gives his character some surprising accomplishments. Captain Gault is something more than a smuggler or trickster: in the stories he is revealed to be artistic, and rather a bon vivant, who enjoys taking discomfited customs men out to dinner for an off-the-record chinwag; and we also learn he plays the fiddle and the flute. He is also a romantic, his gallantry forever at the mercy of unscrupulous but charming women. Like Carnacki, he is also knowledgeable, as we learn in one story, in the occult: in fact, he is a member of a (Masonic-like) secret society with its own signs, which gives aid to brethren in distress. These flashes of colorful detail are often convenient for the plot, but they are clearly also meant to build Captain Gault up as a likeable rogue. Georges T. Dodds, in a 2003 review of *The Boats of the "Glen Carrig" and Other Nautical Adventures* on SF Site, has described Gault as "Raffles-at-sea," a very neat phrase that sums up the mixture of villainy and gentility in the character, even if the signs of Kettle's influence are rather stronger than those of Hornung's suave burglar.

The plot of most of the stories is in essence similar: how to smuggle contraband, mostly jewels, but in one case a cask of molasses and in another a large consignment of cigars, past custom officials without their discovering the goods. Captain Gault exhibits considerable ingenuity in the ways he achieves this: they include unusual places of concealment, sleights of hand, double-bluffing, and even apparent signs of outright honesty. The officials know that he is up to something; sometimes they have specific information; and they and Gault indulge in banter and pleasantries about the duel between them. One rumbustious customs official, MacAllister, the chief searcher, acknowledges the captain's supreme smartness by calling him "the Wonder Unlimited . . . *the* Classic," and of course this only sharpens his keenness to catch Gault out, and his adversary's zest to foil his official foes. And if the devious skipper somehow manages to figure out a ruse to stay ahead of his pursuers, he is sometimes almost worsted, not by the duty men, but by resourceful women, about whom he is always wary and rueful. Captain Gault, with all his cheery roguery, is an attractive character: as Sam Moskowitz commented, "he always accomplishes" his sly feats "in high style, good humour and a flourish". Moreover, he is "not without patriotism or conscience" (*Terrors of the Sea* 207).

The two stories published in the *London Magazine* but not included in the volume were "The Painted Lady" and "Trading with the Enemy." The first of these had already appeared in an earlier collection, *The Luck of the Strong*, with the character's name changed to "Captain Gumbolt Charity." It is one of the boldest pieces, concerning the smuggling of the *Mona Lisa*, in which the hero proves himself to have unsuspected artistic talents. The second was a war story that appeared in the October 1917 issue of the magazine, too late for inclusion in the book. It is hardly surprising to find Hodgson enlisting Gault for the war effort.

A thirteenth tale, "The Plans of the Reefing Bi-Plane," seems not to have been published in Hodgson's lifetime: it was discovered and published by Sam Moskowitz in *Terrors of the Sea* (1996). He explained that the story had been rejected by the *London Magazine*, probably because it was quite different from all the others. Whereas they are about a battle of wits, this is, as he says, "a tale of *action* and violence from end to end" and, moreover, an example of the frequent occurrence in Hodgson's tales of "the siege mentality"—the isolated heroes facing an implacable foe. "It will disorient those who have read the previous Captain Gault stories; it is as though Sherlock Holmes solved a case with a wrestling match instead of by brilliant deduction," Moskowitz adds (*Terrors of the Sea* 208). It is possible that Hodgson at first had in mind a different lead character for the story, or was simply trying to fit an unwieldy idea into what had proved to be a popular paying series.

How well do the stories stand up today? Hodgson himself described the novel version of them as "this simple, cheerful tale," in his dedication of the book to his brother-in-law Gilbert Farnsworth, who had been killed in action in May 1917: it had, he said, been "much to [his] liking." And a certain lightness and levity, a quality of the shaggy dog story, is certainly what first strikes the reader. The devious plots Gault concocts to conceal his contraband are often quite complex, but the motif of the stories—the outwitting of authority, and a snook-cocking subversion of society's rules—is ageless and uncomplicated.

Certainly, the reader who is most drawn to Hodgson's far-seeing visions and weird supernatural dimensions will not find these stories on the same plane at all. As mentioned, there are occult touches, for example, in "The Case of the Curio Dealer," which hinges on a mummy case, a hollow bronze goat-god idol, and the sinister Blood Monster, "carved from one lump of yellow amber; with every last detail of typified vileness, reproduced with an amazingly wonderful and horrible skill of workmanship." Indeed, this tale could, with suitable modifications, almost have been written as a Carnacki story, one of the rationalized cases of detection he tackles, and it would certainly not have been out of place as an episode in one of Sax Rohmer's later yarns of Dr. Fu Manchu. But this is the exception, and the satisfaction of the stories is mostly that of the logical puzzle, as in Carnacki's "The Find." They are rather like watching the work of a conjurer, where we know there is a trick coming, but cannot quite guess what it is.

Another distinctive feature in the stories is their gently cynical worldliness. Most of the characters are on the make; everyone has his own racket, or is living on his wits; they are none of them quite what they seem. Without becoming solemn or moralistic about it, Hodgson creates a little world full of hustling, hoaxing, and cunning, a thieves' den, where minor chicanery is always in the offing and wit, coolness, and audacity are valued.

Hope Hodgson always had a rather boisterous, schoolboyish sense of humor: a neighbor who knew him when she was a young girl in Borth remembered this most about him when she tried to recall him for me. That trait shimmers through the Captain Gault stories, perhaps more than in any of his other work. One feature of it is a fondness for very contrived word-play. In "The Problem of the Pearls," when the skipper admits to a customs snooper that he has handed over some pearls to a lady, his persecutor is unconvinced: from his spies he knows no woman has been on board the ship, and, he sarcastically remarks, "There are no ladies floating loose about the North Atlantic!" Ah, says Gault, perhaps she was no lady, but a "mere maid," adding that he believes it is "fashionable to omit the second 'e'!"

Gault can also be pungent with those who impugn him. We are several times assured that he is apt to employ "plain, healthy, vigorous words" or similar, in accordance with the popular notion that sailors are apt to be knowledgeable in oaths and epithets. In "From Information Received," he tells an abrupt customs man looking for the cache of prime Cuban cigars that the skipper is trying to run into Liverpool: "allow me to explain that I don't like your manners, your method of pronouncing your words, and your breath," adding saucily, given the subject under discussion, "The last is particularly objectionable. You should smoke better cigars!"

The stories are also sometimes seasoned with Captain Gault's salty wisdom. In "My Lady's Jewels," having outbluffed both the customs men and his wealthy lady client, he propounds: "I guess Life is either Training or Degeneration," which sounds like a maxim of the fitness-expert author himself. Gault draws a subtle distinction about the right route to successful smuggling: "It consists largely of *using* Circumstances," not *dodging* them, which is "plain Degeneration." This, too, reminds us of Hodgson's own bravado.

So, as well as the pleasant narrative satisfactions of these clever yarns, we may perhaps see in the Captain Gault stories an aspect of the author that does always not surface so clearly in the works of dark fantasy: the practical, capable, brisk man of affairs, resourceful and inventive—the traits in Hope Hodgson's character that undoubtedly made him a valuable lieutenant of field artillery. It is the same Hodgson that methodically worked out Houdini's escapology tricks, and how to contest them. The ingenuity and self-assurance, but also the breezy good humor and the personal and particular code of conduct of Captain Gault, are facets of his character that we may feel were shared by his creator.

Works Cited

Everts, R. Alain. *William Hope Hodgson: Night Pirate, Volume 2: Some Facts In The Case of William Hope Hodgson: Master of Phantasy*. Toronto: Soft Books, 1987.

Hodgson, William Hope. *The Boats of the "Glen Carrig" and Other Nautical Adventures*. The Collected Fiction of William Hope Hodgson, Volume 1. Edited by Jeremy Lassen. San Francisco: Night Shade Books, 2003.

———. *Terrors of the Sea*. Edited by Sam Moskowitz. Hampton Falls, NH: Donald M. Grant, 1996.

The House on the Borderland:
On Humanity and Love

Henrik Harksen

As China Miéville correctly asserts of Hodgson's stories, they work almost *in spite* of the style in which they are written. Despite their obvious failings, they continue to fascinate, and we forgive the awkward moments of the stories—"we get past them, because the books demand it; they hook us and haul us in and there is nothing we can do to resist them. We do not want to, and we do not try." As he says, they are "And yet"-stories (vii). Miéville is not alone with this critical view. In his essay "Supernatural Horror in Literature," H. P. Lovecraft remarks of Hodgson's style in general that he has "a tendency toward conventionally sentimental conceptions of the universe, and of man's relation to it and to his fellows" (114).

With Martha C. Nussbaum's theory on literature's usefulness in philosophy at hand, this strange puzzle can come a long way to be explained, I think. I will argue that there are good reasons to believe that Hodgson's stories fascinate so much *because* of the way they are written. Employing the style he works with, he conveys certain deeper layers of understanding of his themes—layers that are almost impossible to reach by other means. The story noted as "probably Hodgson's most finished work" by S. T. Joshi (*I Am Providence* 878), the novel *The House on the Borderland*, in particular seems to fit quite well within the framework provided by her theory.

The Hodgsonian subject-matter of my study will be his focus in the story on the house and the grounds on which it lies, and their relation to love and humanity. As Lovecraft says, *The House on the Borderland* "tells of a lonely and evilly regarded house in Ireland which forms a focus for hideous other-world forces and sustains a siege by blasphemous hybrid anomalies from a hidden abyss below" ("Supernatural Horror in Literature" 114). In a sentence somewhat overlooked in general, Lovecraft also remarks that few can rival Hodgson in "conveying feelings of the spectral and the abnormal in connexion with regions or buildings" (114). Almost without rivalry in Hodgson's complete oeuvre, the house in question and the weird incidents taking place around and in it demonstrate Lovecraft's remark that Hodgson is a master of conveying the spectral and strange in "connexion with regions or buildings"— or, to be precise, with regions *and* buildings. With Nussbaum's theory as my working tool, I will bring forth evidence that, more than telling a cosmic tale that "constitute[s] something almost unique in standard literature" ("Supernatural Horror in Literature" 114), *The House on the Borderland* is also a tale that revolves around just how important a sense of locality and home is for a person's imagination to truly work. Part of this is Hodgson's (on the surface) less successful passages—those dealing with love; what Lovecraft calls "commonplace sentimentality" (114) and Miéville "the egregious attempts at romance" (viii). Over-romantic and pathetic as those passages are, they are still an integral part of the story's sense of "grounding"; its sense of humanity. In her collection of essays *Love's Knowledge*, Nussbaum argues for what we can learn from literature about love. *The House on the Borderland* is an unexpected, yet quite powerful, text wherein one can find a strong, persistent view on love and romance as fundamental and important human traits—traits that are nevertheless powerless when corroded by the horrible truth of how vast the universe is, and how insignificant we humans really are.

It is Nussbaum's thesis that, contrary to traditional theories of literature, a text provides a particular insight by the way it is written. Traditionally, form and content have been delegated to their own separate fields of interest. That is why, for instance, one could maintain the belief that, e.g., philosophical texts are better at providing insight into their subject-matter than texts written in other styles. Content has always been the very goal for philosophical inquiry, and here, it was supposed, form was of no importance. This, argues Nussbaum, is plain wrong. Any given style conveys, in some sense, a certain view of life; a view whose contents cannot be separated from the form. As she says, "form and style are not incidental features. A view of life is *told*. [. . .] Life is never simply *presented* by a text; it is always *represented as* something" (5).

Nussbaum says that "any style makes, itself, a statement: [each style makes] a statement about what is important and what is not, about what faculties of the reader are important for knowing and what are not" (7). Her example makes this quite clear: a dry, academic text may be quite adequate and exact when it comes to dry, academic subject-matter, but it comes up short when it is time to adequately explain what love is. (She in fact refers, with a large dose of humor, to a specific essay entitled "A Conceptual Investigation of Love," by W. Newton-Smith; see Nussbaum 20.) This is where literary texts and their style come in handy. They can provide philosophical searches with sharpened pointers and, after a fashion, arguments.

Nussbaum's point is, as may be obvious, that our life and our world are much more diverse, much *richer*, than any precise, dry, academic text can ever hope to encompass. A dry text trying to grasp this very diversity and richness will, as a matter of fact, fall short of its mark—in reality being very imprecise in its eagerness to be precise. You cannot separate form and content. You can choose to look at each separately and independently; they remain two sides of the same thing: the text and the worldview(s) presented in it. To readers of this essay on Hodgson (whom I will get back to in a minute) and other fantastic authors, this may come as no big surprise, but it was quite an eye-opener in the academic milieus of the English-speaking world, when Nussbaum brought forth these views in the 1980s.

I will now highlight the features used to embrace the relevant elements in *The House on the Borderland*, in light of where they are important to the narrator. Following that, in order to better see *how* the story speaks about these subjects, I will look at the story's generality, precision, and explanations.

First and foremost, of course, is the home of the narrator telling the strange tale of the story. It is a house that is not only ancient but also, we learn, "a very strange house; a very awful house" (159). Also of note are the "huge, unkempt gardens" surrounding the house (117). Likewise, the narrator's two dogs must be noted—especially the first, Pepper—and Mary, his sister, who also acts as the sole housekeeper (117). Last, but certainly not least, is the woman (or girl?) he once loved, but whom he lost before the beginning of the story. More than anything else in the narrative, it is in the scenes including her and memories of her that we see what, at heart, characterizes humankind—love. Despite all the strangeness and the horrors, it is because of *her* that he stays till the bitter end, well knowing it may prove dangerous: "yet, after that which has happened, what need have I to care? For she has come to me out of the unknown. Strangely, she warned me; warned me passionately against this house; begged me to leave it; but admitted, when I questioned her, that she could not have come to me, had I been elsewhere" (160).

In fact, he thinks he made the best choice: "How well I was advised, in my heart—spite of those visions and sights of unknown and unexplainable things; for, had I not stayed, then I had not seen again the face of her I loved" (159-60). Elsewhere, nearing the end, he states: "I know that I shall stay on here, whatever happens" (195).

Now that it is clear what elements are important for the present study, I will look deeper into what the story tells about them—and what we can learn from the narrative. As I said, I will take a look at the story's generality, precision, and explanations. These tools are used according to Nussbaum's usage (cf. Nussbaum 34-35):

- *Generality:* To what extent are the subject-matters characterized in general terms and, thus, made objects of general claims? As the flip side of this generality: to what extent do particular people, places, and contexts figure in these claims, and how?

- *Precision:* How precise is the text concerning the subjects? How much vagueness and indeterminacy is in the text regarding the issue of precision? At the heels of that question comes—

- *Explanations:* What does the story offer to explain phenomena addressed, and what sort of explanation is employed? What kind of explanations about the subject matters is the focus of the story, and why?

If we examine first the house and the gardens, we are of course talking about the narrator's *home*. In itself this is on the one hand a general claim ('a home'), yet at the same time it is also a fairly particular claim—as it is, after all, *a home*, which is more specific than, e.g., something being merely 'a building.' Furthermore, we also learn something about the specific location of this home: see the very opening of the story: *"From the Manuscript, discovered in 1877 [. . .] in the ruins that lie to the South of the Village of Kraighten, in the West of Ireland"* (107). This is a fairly particular pointer to both place and date, yet open for uncertainty of specific location as well as time. We also learn that the house was ruined not only a couple of years ago, but many years before the date given: "in the 'ancient man's' youth—*and goodness knows how long back that was*—there had stood a great house in the center of the gardens, where now was left only that fragment of ruin" (201; my emphasis). One imagines that perhaps we are talking about at least a century back?

Even when it was still standing, the house was ancient—that much is certain. It is something else, however, that fascinates the narrator of the strange tale, and this brings him to focus our attention elsewhere: "its age strikes one less, perhaps, than the quaintness of its structure, which is curious and fantastic to the last degree. Little curved towers and pinnacles, with outlines suggestive of leaping flames, predominate; while the body of the building is in the form of a circle" (117). Moreover, it is surrounded not only by the unkempt gardens, but by superstition by the country people, who say that "the devil built the place" (117).

This description of the house immediately gives a clear picture in the reader's mind, as do other descriptions later in the story, detailing the interior and decor of the house. Even so, the house is always described in such general terms that, no matter how clearly one pictures the building from the outside, the narrator's study, or the cellars, it remains a kind of old, large building whose description matches just about any mansion that can be found scattered across the United Kingdom, or in the northern parts on the European continent, for that matter.

When we read about the gardens, they are even more fragmentarily described to us. The house is "surrounded by a huge estate, and wild and uncultivated gardens" and "at the back, distant some three hundred yards, is a dark, deep ravine–spoken of as the 'Pit,' by the peasantry" (126). There are shrubberies and trees as well (135), but that is just about all the information we get. It can hardly get more general than this. However, the few times something extra *is* added, it is something we note with mounting interest: "In the moonlight, it seemed as if the shrubberies were alive" (135). This is of course a classic Gothic narrative trick, one often employed in traditional weird tales. But it works.

The generality regarding the building, as well as the surroundings, in the story is no mere accident. In fact, it emphasizes the precision of the narrative. It is vague, yet precise enough to give a clear picture of where the narrator lives, and what kind of home he has. It is a generality that emphasizes the uncanny current of the narrative. His precise descriptions are laden with classic Gothic words: "quaint," "fantastic," "curved towers and pinnacles" (126); the cellars are "the hugest and weirdest," "great, gloomy caverns of places" with "different vaults" and "a huge, arched entrance, on which I observed strange, fantastic carvings" (143). The list goes on and on. Words that are all, historically, linked with an age when romantic notions and usage of superlatives in general were held in higher esteem than they were even at the time Hodgson published his stories. In some ways this approach is also, as we will see later, mirrored in his usage of words and situations describing love.

As can be seen, it is the very indeterminacy of the text that helps create the mood and the atmosphere around which the story evolves, especially around which the narrator lives his normal, 'down-to-earth' life. However, the house and the gardens do not simply help set the stage for what else transpires in the tale (even if, evidently, the main corpus does focus on something else–that of the wondrous visions he has); they are also utilized in a manner that helps to explain why and how the narrator gets to experience the dreadful and incredible things he experiences.

The important thing to remember here is that the usage of the Gothic style in itself is a certain point of view. The heavy usage of the words from that tradition immediately transports the reader into a world of semi-reality where supernatural events are possible. When we read words like the ones I cited earlier–and the story is truly loaded with them–the text is almost literally dripping with the fantastic. Here we must note with acute sensitivity that the story is told entirely from the narrator's perspective. Although from time to time he tries in vain to give a rational explanation to the more extravagant events, *the very way* he relates to us, the readers, how he perceives things around him—the fantastic as well as the mundane—reveals the world we are inevitably trapped in. It is a world where the house *is*, somehow, evil, and where the garden and the Pit below it *are* somehow filled with horrible creatures. The darkness and the horror *are* all too real. Whether we as readers believe him when he tells of his strange visions and what has befallen him is beside the point; the unrelenting point of truth is that the text's style *in itself* presents to us that that is how its world is. Form and content are one and the same.

This also goes for how those closest to the narrator are depicted in the text: his sister, Mary, his long-lost beloved, and the dogs (especially the first, Pepper). Reading about these, we learn something more, however: we learn about humanity and love.

It is early on obvious that even when Hodgson writes about specific persons—the narrator's sister or his beloved—on the whole they are presented quite *generally*; they are portrayed more as vaguely outlined characters than as specific, well-rounded individuals. Perhaps the only 'character' described most properly is Pepper, the first dog. It is also evident that there are two quite different kinds of love-relations in the story: the love between the narrator and the sister, which is a rather detached, distanced kind of love; and the more emotional kind of love, whether between a man and his dog or the romantic love between a man and woman. This we must keep in mind when analyzing the story.

The first thing we hear about Mary is that she is old, and she is the housekeeper (117). When the narrator says, shortly after, that he would "sooner have old Pepper than the rest of Creation together" (117), we are given the impression that she is not one who is especially close to him, nor does she understand him particularly well. She seems to be a quiet person who doesn't intrude into his privacy and need for frequent solitude: "My sister asked me no questions; for it is not, by any means, the first time that I have kept to my study for a whole day, and sometimes a couple of days, at a time, when I have been particularly engrossed in my books or work" (125-26). Like the narrator, Mary displays affection for Pepper, so when something seems to be wrong with the dog, she asks what has happened (see 127). So, clearly, while there is a formal kind of affection between brother and sister, it is a detached kind of love, without much strong emotion, something modern readers expect from love. Knowing how family ties have been regarded throughout history, and certainly in many upper-class circles, it is not an unlikely description of "normal love" in a family, but it is something that strikes a modern reader as quite cold, 'aloof.'

That said, she does care for her brother and she "seemed only half satisfied" and has "an expression of doubt upon her face" when the narrator demands that she return to the house while he tries to hunt out of the bushes "the wild cat that had wounded Pepper" (129) (in reality a swine-thing, of course). This scene shows us several important things: there *is* love (caring) between the siblings, and the narrator's love for his dog is so strong that he is willing to fight the unknown entity in the garden that hurt Pepper. He is willing to go against his "almost impersonal" fear, the "sensation of abhorrence" (128). Just as clearly the scene highlights the fact that it is a Gothic world and that the unknown is now starting to actively affect the life of those living in the house—through the Gothic garden.

It is less clear what Mary's expression and "half satisfaction" are meant to imply. They remain vague in nature, but this much seems likely: she is doubtful of the truth of what the narrator says to her, which seems to be the narrator's own thought (see the remark "I wondered if she had seen or guessed anything" [129]); and she is finding her brother's behavior stranger and stranger, and there is doubt regarding his sanity, a sentiment, then, shared by the peasantry mentioned in the beginning of the story (see 117). This fits well within a traditional approach to an I-narrator's behavior in Gothic tales, which always has an air of unreliability to it. A little later the narrator helps Mary, and here he realizes that she might be afraid of *him* (132), and she even tries to escape the house (see 140–41), resulting in his locking the door to her room, keeping her in effect a prisoner. Here he shows, in his own way, affection for his sister, concern for her safety. In all, the reader senses a genuine concern for her brother, and his concern for her, hence there is a strong sense of love between them, in spite of the estrangement. This estrangement is central to his musing late in the story: "My thoughts . . . continue to dwell upon her," he writes, "how little we have to do with one another. Is it because we have nothing in common; or only that, being old, we care less for society, than quietness?" (197).

The love for the dog Pepper is more obvious and, in terms of Nussbaum's theory, written more precisely, less ambiguously. "I would sooner have old Pepper than the rest of Creation together," says the narrator. "He, at least, understands me," he continues (117), at the same time giving us a clear explanation as to why this is. This is all, the narrator hints, in stark contrast to his relation with his sister and the peasantry who consider him mad. By extension, this probably encompasses humankind as a whole, in effect isolating him from the rest of the human world. It is no surprise that the first real sense of fear in the narrator happens when the dog shows fear: "It was this movement of the dog . . . that gave me the first twinge of *real* fear" (118). 'A dog is a man's best friend,' the old saying goes, and this is demonstrated throughout the story. It is the dog that helps him regain his senses after returning from the House in the Arena: "I seemed incapable of action or thought. Then, things came back to me, and I called 'Pepper,' faintly. I was answered by a joyous bark, and renewed and frantic caresses" (124). It is also the deep, emotional connection with Pepper that sparks anger and the willingness to fight the horrors: "Seeing Pepper thus mutilated, a furious feeling seized me, and . . . I sprang across, and into the bushes from which Pepper had emerged" (127). The dog always shows unconditional devotion and love for the narrator, no matter what has transpired: "Stooping, I spoke to him, and, in reply, he licked my hand, feebly. He was too ill to do more" (141), and it is also "the melancholy sound of Pepper's howling" (152) that gives the reader a sense of dread when the narrator descends the Pit, penetrating "further into the darkness" (152). The language here blurs the line between the Gothic landscape and the relation between man and dog, creating a unique sense of weirdness to move the reader in a way that would be impossible if this were another kind of text. It is a precise transferring of emotions and atmosphere from text to reader. Not surprisingly, it is the dog that helps the narrator escape the Pit: "faithful Pepper led me, dragged me, upward and onward, until, at last, ahead I saw a gleam of blessed light" (156).

One of the very few heart-rending scenes in *The House on the Borderland* is when the narrator discovers that Pepper has died. Returning from "that strange and terrible journey through space and time," he experiences "a blurred vista of visions, flaming before my sight" and is then "seated in my chair back again in this old study" (190). Pepper doesn't react when his name is called, and that, understandably, rises a fear in the narrator. "I reached the table, and stooped down to him, with a catching at my heart . . . There was no Pepper; instead, I was reaching towards an elongated little heap of grey, ash-like dust" (190).

This is at once sorrowful, filled with immense loss, and a scary scene of almost cosmic proportions, and is in many ways a culmination of all that has gone before. This in itself demonstrates, I propose, the importance of love in the story, as well as shows a sense of humanity in a story otherwise almost devoid of humanity and warmth. And it could not have been without the connection shown earlier in the tale, or without the extravagant, abstract imageries elsewhere filling the pages of the story. (In this light it can in some ways be said to resemble Lovecraft's tale "The Strange High House in the Mist," insofar as that tale, on a symbolic level, can be interpreted as combining more commonplace elements with abstract visions in the heavens—meeting in the strange house in the mist.) It also foreshadows the tale's direction from now on.

What do we know of the woman (girl?) the narrator has loved and lost? Not much. "How well I was advised, in my heart, when I stayed on here," he says, "for, had I not stayed, then I had not seen again the face of her I loved" (159-60). It is only in dreamlike sequences that we, the readers, encounter her, always in a fragmentary, elusive, and abstract manner. We are told that she is from the "sweet, old days," that she came to him "out of the unknown" and also warned him "passionately" against the house, as well as conceding, when he questioned her on the matter, that "she could not have come to me, had I been elsewhere" (160). A strange fragment also says a little but reveals less: "through tears . . . noise of eternity in my ears, we parted . . . She whom I love . . . O, my God . . . !" (161). Later they talk (see 184). The naturalness of this, as shown in the text, indicates that it reflects a quality in their relationship when she was alive. What is even more telling is that she seems, somehow (we are never enlightened on the matter), bound to the house or the grounds surrounding the house. This is only hinted at: "I just asked her, again, whether she would come to me elsewhere, *and she could only stand, silent*" (160; my italics). What does this mean, if not that she can only be where she is, in this particular Gothic landscape, this garden, always?

She may be elusive—to the narrator as well as the reader—but the text leaves no doubt that she stirs in the narrator a passion that is almost unparalleled, rivaled only by the fantastic vistas of his journeys through space and time. But where the latter stirs the imagination on an intellectual level, pointing beyond human existence, the former stirs a more earthbound element—that of love; indeed, one suspects, *a romantic* kind of love, a most human trait. As such, it reveals to us that there is humanity in the tale. It is, after all, a vital element of the narrative, a vital part of the narrator. That is why, when considering the option of leaving his home—"this house of mystery and terror" (195)—he can calmly state that he shall stay forever, "whatever happens" (195).

We now see that the "commonplace sentimentality" in *The House on the Borderland* is, indeed, necessary for the story. Love is what holds the narrator in the realm of humanity, despite everything else going on. And this love—exemplified most clearly by the elusive, romantic love, but certainly also by the love connecting him to the faithful dog and his sister—is deeply rooted in the Gothic landscape surrounding the house as well as in the house, the home, itself. Many of the failings seen in Hodgson's writing are vital to the story's power to fascinate even today.

Love is, in fact, the heart of the story.

Works Cited

Hodgson, William Hope. *The House on the Borderland.* In *The House on the Borderland and Other Novels.* London: Gollanz, 2002.

Joshi, S. T. *I Am Providence: The Life and Times of H. P. Lovecraft.* New York: Hippocampus Press, 2010. 2 vols.

Lovecraft, H. P. "Supernatural Horror in Literature." In *Collected Essays 2: Literary Criticism.* Edited by S. T. Joshi. New York: Hippocampus Press, 2004. 82–134.

———. "The Strange High House in the Mist." In *Dagon and Other Macabre Tales.* Sauk City, WI: Arkham House, 1986. 277–86.

Miéville, China. "'And Yet': The Antinomies of William Hope Hodgson." In *The House on the Borderland and Other Novels.* London: Gollancz, 2002. vii–ix.

Nussbaum, Martha C. *Love's Knowledge: Essays on Philosophy and Literature.* New York: Oxford University Press, 1990.

IV. Comparative Studies

Time Machines Go Both Ways: Past and Future in H. G. Wells and W. H. Hodgson

Andy Sawyer

To begin with, a synopsis: the novel in question was published within a few years of the turn of the nineteenth century. It is supposedly edited from the words of the person to whom it happened, and is a tale of time travel and disturbing threats from an underground, sub-human race. It shows a deep awareness of the scientific method, but coupled with this is a pessimistic vision that culminates in a dramatic description of the dying Earth.

Most people will probably assume that I am talking about *The Time Machine* (1895). In fact, I am thinking about William Hope Hodgson's *The House on the Borderland* (1908). My point, however, is not to suggest that Hodgson may have been indebted to Wells's masterpiece, but rather to underline areas of difference between the approaches of Wells, the science fiction writer, and Hodgson, the fantasist.

In *The House on the Borderland* and *The Night Land* (1912), Hodgson was attempting to communicate a vision that Wells had already articulated and which has remained central to much SF up to the present day. The nature of this vision will, I hope, become clearer as I continue, as will the nature of Hodgson's attempt to forge a narrative that would encompass it. Briefly, however, Hodgson looks to the past to frame his fictions, to the Gothic tradition of haunted houses and ghosts, ghouls and other supernatural horrors. This self-conscious archaism is as much a feature of his writing style as it is the subject of his stories. However, the paradox of the Gothic—which looks to the stories and modes of the past as subjects for fiction—is that it has often developed as a way of both commenting upon the writer's contemporary society and speculating on the future. Witness, for example, Edgar Allan Poe's position as a writer of both "Gothickry" and early SF.

William Hope Hodgson is known today as a writer of horror and ghost stories that were composed at the time of a great upsurge in British fantasy. The works of, among others, Lord Dunsany and Arthur Machen had their roots before the First World War, influenced perhaps by the *fin de siècle* Decadents and the sense that the uneasy peace that had settled over Europe was about to be torn apart. The distinguishing mark of such fantasy (which includes related writing such as the Jamesian or "English" ghost story) is a retreat from contemporary industrial society. Machen's fiction most certainly possesses a brooding quality, haunted by underground, supernatural races and monstrous occult forces, while Dunsany's lighter, more ironical works have a pervasive, feudal melancholy. Even M. R. James, the most "establishment" figure among major writers of the fantastic and supernatural, possesses an enigmatic sense of ennui as the Unknown erupts among his antiquarians and scholars (see Sullivan). Yet by the 1920s, Wells had already written some of the most significant SF in the English language, covering most of its major themes, and was being reprinted in the early American SF magazines.

If fantasy can be described as, in general, pessimistic and conservative, then SF is usually characterized as optimistic and radical, a hymn to the marvels of science. Although there is—particularly with regard to the American pulp SF tradition more or less founded by Hugo Gernsback—some truth in this division, it is for the most part an oversimplification. The type of SF crystallized by Wells and, after him, Olaf Stapledon is less concerned with reassurance and more with charting possibilities, which may well be the opposite of the cozy technical "fixes" popularized by Gernsback and his followers. Even in *The War of the Worlds* (1898), humanity is only saved from alien invasion by the evolutionary accident of the Martians having no resistance to Earthly disease.

The major difference, if there is one, between fantasy and SF is how writers adopting the two genres organise their fictions, and the use they make of the notion of change. Since Wells, SF has frequently been used—most notably by the writers associated with the Michael Moorcock-edited *New Worlds* magazine in the 1960s—as a metaphor for entropy and decline. It embraces the possibility of change rather than fearing it, following the lines of feasibility to their logical conclusions as opposed to rearing backwards from them, in the process using imagery with an often playful sense of exuberance, whereas fantasists such as Tolkien in the UK and Robert E. Howard in the US stop history some time before the Industrial Revolution and prefer magic to machinery. Returning to *The House on the Borderland* and *The Time Machine*, the essential difference is that, in thought and writing technique, Hodgson is looking backward while Wells is facing forward—even though, in both novels, a journey into the far future is the dramatic centre of events. The flow of time, in both these novels, is acceleration forward into the future. But time, as the quantum physicists tell us, can flow both ways. When Hodgson's protagonist moves forward in time his entire apparatus of imagery, ideology, and language is taking us back. Time machines are mental constructs, and they can point in both directions at once.

While Brian Stableford firmly places Hodgson as a writer of "scientific romances," he distinguishes him from Wells, M. P. Shiel, and J. D. Beresford precisely on the point that "they all built their metaphysical systems around ideas derived from evolutionary philosophy" while to Hodgson "the force that must ultimately win was the force of decay" (*Scientific Romance in Britain* 101). Yet both Wells and Hodgson share this image of the dying, desolate earth. I would like to suggest that if there is a fundamental difference, it lies in the road to this vision. In doing so, I will concentrate on Hodgson, though to set the scene I need to mention how Wells's Time Traveller views his future. As befits the rational, late Victorian scientific gentleman, it is through the method of observation, hypothesis, and testing the hypothesis against experience. His judgment is provisional—on observing the similarity between Eloi genders he concludes that it is due to social ease and tranquility: "This, I must remind you, was my speculation at the time. Later I was to appreciate how far it fell short of the reality" (*Time Machine* 26). Harmony has led to diminution of the *élan vital* and a fall in population. "That would account for the abandoned ruins. Very simple was my explanation and plausible enough—as most wrong theories are" (*Time Machine* 30). And the Eloi are, of course, the descendants of ruling capitalists as the Morlocks are of subjugated labor—"though, for myself, I very soon felt that it fell far from the truth" (*Time Machine* 43).

In apparent contrast to *The Time Machine*, the construction of *The House on the Borderland* is more complex. Although both novels are presented as "reported" texts, *The Time Machine* is related (by a narrator/editor) directly from the words of the Time Traveller, whereas *The House on the Borderland* is introduced by an account, signed by Hodgson, describing his reaction when the manuscript of the tale "was given into my care" (*House on the Borderland* 9). With the ms., there is an account (signed "Berreggnog") of how, while on a fishing trip in the remote west of Ireland, two companions discovered it in a weird ruin. Hodgson's characters, in so far as they have any social identification, are literary men and gentry; Wells's are intellectuals and practical men: the Psychologist; the editor, the skeptical Filby. Wells, moreover, is writing within a present shared by his narrator and his readers, one that is contemporaneous with the tale's composition. Hodgson, in contrast, describes events that—from the evidence that they happened in the youthful years of a now old man—are possibly eighteenth century. In both setting—the remotenesses of rural Ireland—and structural patterning the book recalls Charles Maturin's terror romance *Melmoth the Wanderer* (1820).

Once beyond the series of framing narratives, with the atmosphere of the uncanny already set by the "strange wailing noise" heard by Berreggnog and Tonnison (21), we have the story of an unnamed recluse, beginning with an initial out-of-body experience that takes him beyond space to a vast plain where stands an enormous green structure in the shape of the house from which he came. Among the mountains surrounding it are vast forms of mythological deities. A naked thing with swine-features attempts to enter the house. He is involuntarily drawn toward it, but the same force raises him up above it, leaving it "clutching upwards, with an expression of desire upon its face, such as I have never seen in this world," (*House on the Borderland* 31) and returns him home. Later, his dog disturbs something in a nearby ravine. This turns out to be another swine-thing, which sends him driving his sister back to the safety of the House. Much ambiguity arises from the fact that the sister sees nothing of the creatures, and his apparently insane behavior leads her to attempt to escape, while he sees in her a madwoman who cowers in terror at his touch.

Underground explorations reveal a huge Abyss beneath the house, and an apparent (the manuscript is here fragmentary and dreamlike) visit by the shade of a lost love warns the recluse to guard the house. Then follows another journey, but through time, not space. In an episode reminiscent of the time-traveling in Wells—though innocent of any mechanical contrivances—the narrator's perception of time speeds up, sunrise to sunset becoming first a matter of seconds and then to all intents and purposes instantaneous. His dog, sleeping by his side, falls to dust. His journey takes him beyond even the far future visited by Wells's Traveller, to a desolate Earth, one face to the sun, which, sputtering fitfully from the energies of the falling inner planets, is itself traveling through deserts of black space toward the vast Green Star, which it is suggested may be the cosmos's Central (binary) Sun. The House, together with the crew of swinefolk, collapses into the Abyss.

The Recluse first meets with, then parts from, his Lost Love on the shores of the Sea of Sleep and discerns human faces in the globes emanating from the Central Suns: images (so Hodgson himself suggests in his Introduction) of the world of "thought and emotion, working in conjunction with, and duly subject to, the scheme of material creation" (*House on the Borderland* 10). He finds himself on the Plain of his first experience, drifting into the huge House-analogue, and is back in his chair. Did it all happen? Beside him his dog is dead.

Strange happenings continue to take place. He is injured, and the wound becomes phosphorescent with corruption. The narrative closes with a final, disjointed confrontation, in the manner familiar to readers of so many first-person accounts of mounting supernatural terror, with something mounting the stairs to fumble at the door handle. Conveniently, instead of attempting to escape or prepare to defend himself, the narrator has continued writing to the end—his manuscript breaks off halfway through a word.

The Time Machine begins with mathematical and scientific speculation. The Time Traveller is, at least up until his actual arrival in the future, in control of his creation. *The House on the Borderland*, though, exhibits no such control or logic, the time traveling of its protagonist being entirely involuntary. Hodgson's traveler has no command over what happens to him in his visions and no explanation for the connection of the Swine-things who invade his house with the horrors he sees on the Plain where the giant green analogue of his house broods under a ring of fire. While the story is presented to the reader as dream or madness, Hodgson (as editor) is careful to note discrepancies with observed scientific fact, as when the narrator experiences hearing "the occasional, soft thud of falling matter" (*House on the Borderland* 102) in his journey through time. A footnote points out that sound could not have carried through the attenuated air, implying that some other sense must have been in operation. Additionally, possible astronomical anomalies are carefully noted.

While both novels present subterranean menaces and apocalyptic visions, there are important differences in their treatment of them. Wells's Morlocks arise from the structure of the story and, although they are explained, they remain horrific precisely because of their links to social conditions in contemporary England. Hodgson's swinefolk have no such overt connections and, in consequence, they remain Gothic horrors from some dark interior of the psyche. Wells's vision of a dying Earth concludes with the sun's eclipse revealing a black, starless sky and life remaining only (perhaps) in the form of a round, tentacled object "hopping fitfully about." So much for dreams and progress. Hodgson's annihilation of the solar system is, however, more complete and even more nihilistic: an endless progression of stars swallowed up by the galaxy's Central Suns. Human progress is an idea that is not even considered in Hodgson's universe, a cosmos of inexplicable horror where the physical world is only a shadow of more disturbing planes. *The Time Machine* ends with the stoical reflection that if human civilization is, in the long term, futile, then "it remains for us to live as though it were not so" (*Time Machine* 83), and its structure of observation/hypothesis/testing means that even this conclusion may not be based on full knowledge of the facts—as Stephen Baxter in *The Time Ships* cleverly reminds us. Much of Wells's subsequent writing was an attempt to suggest ways of living as though the ultimate decline "were not so." Hodgson remained fascinated by the Abyss and the dead Sun—the ultimate Nothingnesses at the end of time. *The House on the Borderland* concludes with the horrific death of a man whose name we do not even know.

The persuasiveness of Hodgson—and there is truth and a scientific approach in his work—is the truth of textual studies rather than scientific exploration. It is the creation of verisimilitude through footnotes dwelling on weak points in the argument, of mystery by unexplained references to events outside the story (such as the narrator's lost love) and the complex "editorial" situation. *The House on the Borderland*—which presents at least three cosmic journeys, one of which only exists as fragments—gives us an illusion of literary truth by creating an image of an old, half-obliterated manuscript, but by doing so makes the story less decipherable. Hodgson has dislocated his narrative and distanced the reader from it in several ways. Paradoxically, the very features that give a reality to the text by treating it exactly as a recently discovered manuscript that has been through several layers of exegesis—the anonymity of the narrator and the presentation of his manuscript within layers of editing, the lack of formal logic between parts of the story, the inclusion of scientific anomalies in the text and the attention drawn to them, and the fragmentation of the text itself when it reaches the point where the narrator is reunited with the soul of his lost love—are also the ones that proclaim its artificiality.

By the time we reach the actual story that Hodgson presents to us as the central part of the book we have passed through a dedicatory poem from Hodgson to his late father: in other words, a text that we can see as presented by the "real" author and in some way outside the following text (although the poem evokes precisely the images that are most central to the novel—of the incursion of something from out of space and time, of opening a door and listening to "the sorrowful cry / Of the wind in the dark . . . the sound that bids you to die") (*House on the Borderland* 5). Following this is the "Introduction" in which Hodgson is now in the persona of the editor of the manuscript that was "given into my care," suggesting that this "mutilated . . . simple, stiffly given account" may possess an "inner story" (9-10). Next is another poem, which we are meant to take as written by the manuscript's author. Entitled "Grief," it is a lament for loss, and presumably it is about the Lost Love of the succeeding text: a footnote tells us that it appears to have been written before the manuscript. Next a chapter describes the finding of the manuscript—and this is balanced by a concluding chapter describing the discoverers' responses on having read it.

The structure of the narrative itself has been analyzed by Brian Stableford, who finds convincing reason to suggest that the novel is built from an initial short story that is essentially chapters XXIV-XXVI of the novel (the concluding chapters of the Recluse's account), expanded as chapters V-XIII and linked by the visionary sequences one at least of which (the highly fragmentary Chapter XIV recording the reunion with the Lost Love and which is presented as a damaged portion of the manuscript) may have been an attempt by Hodgson to incorporate his own dream-experiences. Certainly the novel as it stands is a series of patterns that seem to weave in and out of each other: a more sophisticated version of the patterning in Maturin's *Melmoth the Wanderer*, which not only is constructed out of a series of framing narratives and stories-within-stories but also uses the device of the "broken narrative": "Here the manuscript was illegible for a few lines. . . . A long hiatus followed here, and the next passage that was legible, though its [sic] proved to be a continuation of the narrative, was but a fragment" (70).

Without doubt, though, the central image of the novel is the time-trip. At this point, *The House on the Borderland* becomes a work that fuses the Gothic novel tradition—the old house, hauntings, supernatural threats, and madness—with the newer, twentieth-century concern with knowing—even if also fearing—reality. We have the notion, unforgettably dramatized by Wells, that the earth will come to an end, increased and emphasized. The narrator observes the slowing down of the solar system, the dwindling of the very sun into ashes, with horrified and careful detail. Even the baleful Green Sun to which our dead star is attracted may be similar to the Black Hole that SF speculation has sometimes put at the center of our Galaxy, and while Hodgson's "swine-things" may be Monsters from the Id (the "desire" of the creature's gaze in the Recluse's first experience may be significant), they are reached through those dimensions that are fundamental to post-Wellsian science fiction: space and time.

If, in *The House on the Borderland*, the modern SF approach exists within a very traditional Gothic framework, then *The Night Land* has no such reservations, possessing unashamedly full-blooded SF elements. The remnants of humanity are huddled inside a fortress-pyramid, surrounded by monsters of all kinds, some of which are supernatural, others of which may be material beings from other parts of the cosmos, and still others (the Humped Men, the Giants) of which may be mutated descendants of humanity. It is a time perhaps glimpsed in The House: "And so, in that supremely future time, the world, dark and intensely silent, rode on its gloomy orbit around the ponderous mass of the dead sun" (103-4).

The Earth-Current (a relative of Bulwer-Lytton's "vril" or the ley-line energy beloved of New-Agers) supplies energy to the Pyramid, and among other concepts that have since become a part of science fiction are a form of telepathy called Night-Hearing, the Air Clog (a force field?), and the now-familiar idea of food tablets. *The Night Land* could well be one of the earliest fully fledged examples of the post-holocaust quest-narrative and, with its bleak images of a beleaguered humanity in a world grown totally hostile, still trying to understand the nature of phenomena such as the Seven Lights, the Road Where the Silent Ones Walk, or the Watcher of the South, it is still one of the most powerful.

Like *The House on the Borderland*, the story proper is framed by an introductory narration, in this case a preface that explains how the narrator met his Heart's Desire, the Lady Mirdath, courted and married her, and lost her in childbirth. Hodgson's language—of which more later—sets this in late medieval England, but of place we are given only the vaguest details. The real story begins when the narrator's dreams himself a youth in the Last Redoubt, where thanks to his "night-hearing" he senses the presence of another fortress in the unending darkness. The mind he is in most contact with is that of a young woman called Naani, who, it transpires, "remembers" his "earlier" self: in simpler terms, she is a reincarnation of his Lost Love. The title of the book, "The Night Land," of course refers to the fact that this is a realm of darkness far beyond even Wells's vision of a fading sun, but there is also a strong sense in which it refers to the fact that this epic quest takes place in the narrator's dreams:

> . . . for of late a wondrous hope has grown in me, in that I have, at night in my sleep, waked into the future of this world, and seen strange things and utter marvels . . . and have visited in my dreams those places where in the womb of Time, she and I shall again come together. . . . It was not as if I dreamed; but, as it were, that I waked there into the dark, in the future of this world. (33-34)

Perhaps we have, in this long and unwieldy book, an equally long and unwieldy pun on the term "Dark Ages."[1]

The mixture of science and spiritualism in *The Night Land* can be easily discerned by examining what we are told about how this world came into being: "A dim record there was of olden sciences (that are yet far off in our future) which, disturbing the unmeasurable Outward Powers, had allowed to pass the Barrier of Life some of these Monsters and Ab-human creatures, which are now so wondrously cushioned from us at this normal present" (44).There are forces of Good and Evil abroad in the Night Land which contend for the souls of humanity, as well as beings (such as the Silent Ones) who are mostly neutral but who will not allow interference without dire consequences. However, the scales are, it seems, tilted on the side of the horrors. For instance, shortly after the narrator hero rescues Naani/Mirdath—alone among the millions of the "peoples of the Lesser Redoubt"—a sinister spinning sound heralds the approach of "one of the great Evil Forces of the Land" (335), and the pair in their extremity are saved by "a clear burning Circle,

---

1. I am indebted to my colleague Peter Wright for drawing my attention to this pun.

above us in the night . . . one of those sweet Powers of Goodness, that did strive ever to stand between the Forces of Evil and the spirit of man" (337). The pair are saved, but the episode is preceded and followed by the horrific deaths of a nation. Why, we are perhaps entitled to ask, are only two saved and millions of others horribly killed? To provide a plot for the novel is the flippant answer, but out of the episode comes a pervasive sense of doubt and despair which is at odds with any message that "Good" may be superior to "Evil." Such labels are inapplicable in *The Night Land*, where Humanity is the victim of contending forces and the "sweet Powers of Goodness" are unaffected by human notions of morality. However advanced these humans are, their path is fixed. Wells has his Time Traveller deduce the nature of his future-world, and he offers us several possibilities as this body of evidence grows. Hodgson's narrator speculates, but the underlying nature of his world is the same at the beginning as at the end. There are no surprises once the scene is set. Static, the Night Land broods eternally around the Great Redoubt.

There seems to be a consensus that the vista of frightening cosmic loneliness envisioned in *The Night Land* is staggering in content, but that the style in which it is presented is sickly, verbose, over-sentimental, and grotesque.[2] Any discussion why Hodgson chose to write his novel in a particular way is really a matter for the literary biographer he so badly needs, but two things strike a careful reader. First, that there is clearly an attempt to create a sense of alienation and mystery, a depiction of a future so unutterably separated from our time that the very memory of our era has been lost. Second, that Hodgson was actually partially successful in this attempt.

Whereas Hodgson creates the alienation in *The House on the Borderland* by his organizing and fracturing of narrative, in *The Night Land* he does so by his employment of a series of sledgehammer blows at language itself. In an earlier version of this paper I described Hodgson's prose style as possibly based upon the archaic language of William Morris's attempts at medievalism and "excruciatingly awful" (Sawyer 49). Now I am less sure. Hodgson's archaism is obviously pastiche and, unlike the mock-seventeenth century prose of E. R. Eddison (author of *The Worm Ouroborous* and the "Zimiamvia" trilogy), it rarely progresses beyond pastiche. Eddison's archaic prose is capable of expressing high drama, tension, intrigue, wit, mystery, and eroticism; it is sinewy and flexible. Hodgson's is capable of expressing little but maudlin romanticism. Throughout *The Night Land* the reader is filled with suspicion that the writer has adopted a style that does not necessarily arise from the events of the story.

---

2. See Lin Carter's introduction to vol. 2 of the Pan/Ballantine (1973) edition and Stableford, *Scientific Romance* 99.

It may be argued that the language does spring from the introductory chapter, which describes the romance between the narrator and Mirdath the Beautiful, but unfortunately this "Gilbert and Sullivan" eroticism is precisely the weakest part of the novel. While Wells himself was not immune to the convention of presenting his protagonist with a flimsy and submissive Beauty to dominate (cf. Weena the Eloi in *The Time Machine*), the second half of *The Night Land* is full of passages that read like entries in "Bad Sex Writing" competitions: "And truly her knees did so tremble that she had not stood, let be to walk! And I caught her up again; and I kist her, and I told her that I did surely be her Master, in verity, and she mine own Baby-Slave." He does go immediately on to protest "And truly you shall not laugh upon me" (345), but the temptation in hindsight is too great. It is more instructive, however, to look at why Hodgson is writing in this manner.

No doubt there are biographical explanations. Hodgson spent some extremely physical years at sea in the Merchant Marine as a teenager, and some of his "realistic" stories suggest a brutal regime. When he returned to shore, he opened a School of Physical Culture. The narrator of *The Night Land* is fully aware of the attractions of his own body:

> But surely she denied me a moment of the vest, and stood before me, and had an admiring and wonder, very sweet and honest, because that my arms did be so great and hard with muscles. And indeed I did be very strong, as you have perceived; for I did be alway in affection of the Exercises that were taught in the Upringing of all the Peoples of the Mighty Pyramid; and by this explaining, you shall understand that I was like to be strong; but indeed, I owed the straightness and shaping of my body to the Mother that bore me. And afterward, in all my life, had I taken pride of my body to be of health and to have strength; and surely this is a matter very fit for pride; and to be told bravely and with honesty. (355)

Throughout his narrative—in this very distinctive breakdown of tenses to create what is in itself a tangling of time—Hodgson's language is on the verge of disintegration. To take a passage at random: "And she still to have no speech with me, but in a little to begin that she sing in a low voice; and to have her pretty body very upright and lithesome, and to go forward with a wondrous dainty swing, so that my heart told me that she did all be stirred with small thrillings of defiance unto me, and with thrillings of love . . ." (431).

Grammatically, this is like little ever dignified with the title of "the English Language"—at least, to modern ears—but does not its overt strangeness suggest that we are in a world where the normal laws of narrative language (not to mention sexuality) no longer apply? To gain some clue to Hodgson's touchstone here, we must remember that this is a story in which a young and pure hero sets out from a castle and battles Giants, Monsters, and Spiritual Danger to rescue a Maiden in Distress. We must remember the armor that protects him, and his weapon, the Diskos, which he wields like a whirling sword or axe. We must remember that despite the "wondrous dainty swing," the cuddlings and kissings and frequent occasions of nudity, the relations between the narrator and Naani are thoroughly chaste. We must remember the English of Malory, with its "wit you well," "that should little need," and "Then the king, at the queen's request, made him to alight and to unlace his helm."[3] This is a tale of chivalry, reminiscent of tales of medieval knighthood, told by a gentleman of (perhaps) the seventeenth century (Malory, *Le Morte d'Arthur* 2.201, 1.79, 2.247).[4] The rescue party that vainly sets out to save the Lesser Redoubt has to undergo a spiritual and physical preparation before it proceeds, to ensure that it is "as it might be, holy" (93).

Even so, however, the self-conscious archaism of the language is at odds with the world Hodgson is describing. He is creating a picture of the far future, of a world in terminal decay, but the language and (to some extent) the coy flirtatiousness and rather nasty chauvinism of his love interest drags him back to the past. This is a story that incorporates what was to become science fiction in its concern for the future, its assumption of scientific and technological development, even in its late Victorian concern to present a rigorously scientific paradigm for the realms dabbled in by spiritualists (Hodgson also wrote stories featuring that interesting fusion of genres, the "psychic detective"). Yet our mental journey into the far future is pulled back by the fact that what we are reading is a dream or series of dreams by someone who in our terms is a dweller in the past, yet who is constantly addressing us, the readers: "for as you may know from my past tellings" (144) . . . "Further, as you may have perceived" (170) . . . "but yet I to have no certainty in this matter, as you do perceive . . ." (374). Just as the narrator can only share his confusion, we are unable to create a stable location for the voice by which Hodgson tells his tale.

"In writing it down I feel with only too much keenness the inadequacy of pen and ink," writes Wells's narrator of *The Time Machine* (15) . ". . . and truly you to know how I mean; only that I have no skill of such matters," stammers

---

3. I must point out that the writer, editor and critic Darrell Schweitzer, in an email communication with me, disagreed with my finding echoes of Malory in Hodgson.

4. Lin Carter, drawing perhaps upon the discussion of Hodgson in H. P. Lovecraft's "Supernatural Horror in Literature" essay of 1927, calls the narrator of *The Night Land* "a seventeenth-century gentleman" in his introduction to vol. 2 of the 1972 Pan/Ballantine *The Night Land*.

Hodgson's narrator of *The Night Land* (441). In one disclaimer we have a conventional underpinning to what we know will be a skillful narrative; in the other we have—what, an ironic admission of failure? Not quite, I think, because somehow Hodgson has created literature that is worth the attention. Faced with a vision embracing the end of the Victorian era—the dashing of its ideas of progress and the culmination of its spiritual and social doubt—Wells and Hodgson crystallized this in the motif of a dying Earth. Wells, in keeping with his rational, modern approach, expressed it in straightforward prose, the clear scientific narrative of the twentieth century. Hodgson, on the other hand, took the more audacious step of attempting to manipulate the language and structure of his novels in order to create a verbal analogue of the spiritual dislocation embodied within them. I cannot say that I think he succeeded, in his mock-medievalism and Victorian sentimentality, but then again perhaps he did not altogether fail.

William Hope Hodgson stands at the head of a more fractured approach to language and narrative, an approach designed to create atmosphere and underline what is said rather than to describe accurately and in scientific detail. William Burroughs's "cut-ups," Michael Moorcock's ironic, oblique 1970s "Jerry Cornelius" stories, Brian Aldiss's occasional Joycean word-play and *nouveau roman* approach, and J. G. Ballard's iconic imagery are all examples of this technique employed by later writers whose trajectories bring them within the boundaries of science fiction. While I do not think that Hodgson was as successful as these writers in realizing this method in his work, I do believe that he can be most rewardingly read not as a minor dabbler in "Gothickry" but rather as a writer on the borderland of speculative fiction and genre SF—one who developed some of their concerns with a vision that looked toward the future, but a literary technique that was refined from the past.

Both the apparent ascendancy of the Morlocks (emphasized with the final dramatic scene on the beach below a dying Sun) in Wells and the threat of evil supernatural forces in Hodgson suggest that humanity's place in the universe is necessarily beleaguered and weak. Wells explores an immediately modern, collective future. Hodgson's futures are individual, despairing. Both fictions suggest that models of both physical reality and social constructs are only provisional. Human consciousness itself seems only contingent on the kind of life an educated Englishman would live. Hodgson's is the Englishman of the past: literary, chivalric, sentimental and the light of civilization in the darkness of uncouth races and spiritual desolation. Wells's is the Englishman of the future extrapolated from him; curious, arrogantly confident, and culturally determined by the discovery that the universe was not created for the English ruling class to play with, but might still serve as recreation for its technocratic successors. Both seemed to find unease in those stereotypes. Wells, however, was more congenial to an audience that could accept his final conclusion that, even if civilization is doomed to failure in the long run, "it remains for us to live as though it were not so": an ambiguous stoicism that is perhaps the nearest the succeeding history of the twentieth century can look to for optimism.

Works Cited

Coveney, Peter, and Roger Highfield. *The Arrow of Time*. London: Flamingo, 1991.

Eddison, E. R. *The Worm Ouroboros*. Introduced and edited by Paul Edmund Thomas. New York: Dell, 1991.

———. *Zimiamvia: A Trilogy*. Introduced and edited by Paul Edmund Thomas. New York: Dell, 1992.

Gribbin, John. *In Search of Schrodinger's Cat*. London: Black Swan, 1991.

Hodgson, William Hope. *The House on the Borderland*. 1908. St. Albans, UK: Panther 1969.

———. *The Night Land*. London: Eveleigh Nash, 1912.

———. *The Night Land*. Abridged ed., introduced by Lin Carter. London: Pan/Ballantine, 1973.

Malory, Thomas. *Le Morte d'Arthur*. Harmondsworth, UK: Penguin 1986. 2 vols.

Maturin, Charles Robert. *Melmoth the Wanderer*. Harmondsworth, UK: Penguin, 1971.

Sawyer, Andy. "A Writer on the Borderland." In *William Hope Hodgson: Voyages and Visions*, ed. Ian Bell. Oxford: I. Bell & Sons, 1987. 44-51.

Stableford, Brian. "The Composition of *The House on the Borderland*." In *William Hope Hodgson: Voyages and Visions*, ed. Ian Bell. Oxford: I Bell & Sons, 1987. 29-36.

———. *Scientific Romance in Britain 1890-1950*. London: Fourth Estate, 1985.

Sullivan, Jack. *Elegant Nightmares: The English Ghost Story from Le Fanu to Blackwood*. Athens: Ohio University Press 1978.

Wells, H. G. *The Time Machine*. 1895. London: Pan, 1973.

———. *The War of the Worlds*. 1898. London: Penguin, 2005.

The Long Apocalypse:
The Experimental Eschatologies of
H. G. Wells and William Hope Hodgson

Brett Davidson

Science fiction occupied an explicitly ambiguous position in late Victorian literature in that the original term for the genre, "scientific romance," denoted speculative essays as well as speculative or fantastic fiction. This ambiguity, rather than indicating vagueness, highlights the peculiar status of a genre that has placed itself as a mediator between science and culture. As defined by Brian Aldiss (in what is admittedly a contentious description): "Science fiction is the search for a definition of mankind and his status in the universe which will stand in our advanced but confused state of knowledge (science), and is characteristically cast in the Gothic or post-Gothic mode" (25).

Science fiction could not resist the impulse to imbue supposedly objective natural phenomena with human meaning—and, indeed, that is arguably its point. As Joanna Russ put it in her essay, "Towards an Aesthetic of Science Fiction":

> Even the human devolution pictured in the story is only a special case of the iron physical law that constitutes the true center of the book and the true agony of Wells's vision. . . . *The Time Machine* is not about a lost Eden; it is—passionately and tragically—about the Three Laws of Thermodynamics, especially the second. (7-8)

If you do not *passionately* feel that the knowledge presented by science matters, she writes, you have no business with science fiction (8). This is as crucial as Aldiss's insistence that the science fiction's definition of mankind must stand in the light of science, and indeed the two critics complement each other.

The second law of thermodynamics—that in a closed system, entropy tends to the maximum over time—suggests that eventually the universe would suffer what was called a "heat death" wherein all light would eventually be extinguished and all matter would cool to near absolute zero (recent cosmology is more complicated, to put it mildly). Not only was this an astronomical phenomenon, it was a basic fact of the world; the law that caused stars to dim was also the one that could be observed to make tea go cold. Lacking knowledge of nuclear reactions, the physicists Herman von Helmholtz and William Thomson (later Lord Kelvin) put varying limits on the age of the sun itself and its likely life expectancy according to the mechanisms of gravitational contraction or combustion, which suggested that it had shone for only a few million years and in only thousands or at most a few million years, it would be dark and the earth doomed. This put the natural end of the world within the potential scope of human history, and thus the end of the world, previously understood as an externally imposed event, was built into its very fabric and in the process of working itself out from the beginning. In terms of cultural significance and the anxiety it engendered, entropy surpasses modern concerns with global climate change, not least because it is universal and apparently inexorable.

(The New Wave of the sixties took entropy as a metaphor—J. G. Ballard, M. John Harrison, Pamela Zoline, and Michael Moorcock dealt with it as an aesthetic and existential theme—but in the late nineteenth and early twentieth centuries, it was entropy itself as a thermodynamic phenomenon in itself that was of interest.)

Another major discovery of the century was the mechanism of evolution of natural selection. Darwin's theory eventually won out over Lamarck's rival mechanism of evolution by the acquisition of new characteristics. It must be said that Darwinian evolution by natural selection was by no means a proven case; selection might well operate, but the actual mechanisms of acquisition and inheritance were still obscure through much of the nineteenth century. Only Gregor Mendel's research into genetics at the turn of the century was really able to tilt the balance in favor of Darwin by showing how inheritance could operate in a scientifically definable manner.

However, there was still the obstacle of time. The facts as they appeared simply did not allow enough time for evolution to occur. On one hand, Darwinian evolution and the geological record showed that the earth was millions of years old and that that amount of time was necessary for the development of higher organisms; but according to the only known mechanisms for the incandescence of the sun—combustion or gravitational contraction—the allowed timescale was far briefer. Darwin admitted himself that the studies of solar luminosity by Thomson caused him the greatest disquiet (Beer 163). As we know now, the fusion of hydrogen is more than sufficient, and though this was not fully described until 1939 by Hans Bethe, the discovery of radioactivity was enough to hold out the possibility of a reconciliation or congruence by 1904 (Beer 175).

Despite this conflict, both evolution and entropy became linked in public discourse. This conflation may seem an exercise in grim narcissism, but nineteenth-century imperial theory supported this with the supposed duty to impose order on other, "lesser" races and was coupled with a rise in eugenics movements, "anthropological" definitions of racial hierarchy, and the call to maintain "purity." The vulgar understanding of evolution might inspire triumphalism, and it is at its most gratifying in the ideology of Social Darwinism, but it seems that inevitably triumphalism invites overt skepticism at least and is accompanied by fear of contamination, general anxiety and doubt that themselves become articulated as a pervading cultural force. The publication of Max Nordau's *Degeneration* in 1893 (translated into English in 1895) expressed this anxiety acutely, warning that the "highest" races must constantly struggle to maintain their superiority against external contamination and internal decadence.

Thus, to put it in simplistic terms, in the nineteenth century we have an imperialist European culture that is on one hand unchallenged in its mundane power, but deeply troubled by the reminder that pride goeth before the fall. What force then might cause the empires to topple? Degeneration? The influx of lesser bloodlines? Revolution? Lukewarm tea?

The invisible worm of despair can be found boring its way through much of the literature of the Romantic age, from Mary Shelley's *The Last Man* through Matthew Arnold's poem "Dover Beach," lamenting the ebb of faith. A sense of ending found its most sensual literary expression in the Decadents who were inspired by Edgar Allan Poe, the author of some end-of-the-world stories such as "The Colloquy of Monos and Una" (1841), which gave an overtly erotic cast to the dissolution wrought by time. Poe of course was not *just* a Gothic writer, but also a keen speculator on matters scientific and metaphysical, as is shown in much of his fiction and nonfiction. "Monos and Una" is an armature supporting earnest discussions on these matters, and there is the example of his cosmological speculation, *Eureka* (1848). More mainstream writers such as the eminent astronomer Camille Flammarion were not averse to exercises in spiritualism mingled with straight scientific extrapolation about the scope of the cosmos and the nature of the end times. Certainly Flammarion's works such as *Lumen* (1872; translated into English in 1897), *Uranie*, and *La Fin du Monde* (1894; translated into English as *Omega* that year) have inspired authors in the twentieth century such as David Lindsay, who wrote *A Voyage to Arcturus*, and Olaf Stapledon, whose *Star Maker* owes much to *Lumen*. One can follow this line still further through the more metaphysical speculations of Arthur C. Clarke in *Childhood's End*.

Both entropy and biological degeneration are central to the narratives of novels by H. G. Wells and William Hope Hodgson: *The Time Machine*, by Wells, first serialized in 1894, and Hodgson's *The House on the Borderland*, published in 1908, and *The Night Land,* published in 1912. Both of these authors are remarkable for the great intensity of the literary scenarios that they created in response to these phenomena and for the fact that their sight was unflinching; many contemporary and later authors exploring the degeneration and end of the world turned back from the absolute end of all things and cast their narratives as preludes to renewal; but neither Wells nor Hodgson took that easy option. Nonetheless, they are still very different.

The Time Machine's basic plot is well known: an unnamed inventor undertakes a journey into the distant future where he finds an Edenic landscape populated by the elfin Eloi, but they are mere cattle for the brutish (but nonetheless of human stock) Morlocks. He falls in love with an Eloi, Weena, but is unable to save her from the Morlocks and barely escapes himself. Venturing much farther into the future, he witnesses a terminal beach under a dim, dying sun in which cycles of mindless predation and flight will be repeated until the final night falls.

In Hodgson's *The House on the Borderland,* a recluse (also unnamed) living sometime in the early nineteenth century finds his house flung into the future at an ever-accelerating pace and is besieged by Morlock-like "swine-things." In fragmentary visionary segments, his spirit leaves his mortal body as it decays and perceives a great convergence about two suns at the center of the universe, one black and one green. Eventually all matter will be consumed by these suns and all souls gathered in a "Sea of Sleep" about the green sun.

Written as a separate novel, but with a narrative that can be seen as being nested within the cosmology described in *The House on the Borderland, The Night Land* is the tale of a hero—again, nameless, but conventionally referred to as "X"—who sets out from a great fortress called the Last Redoubt across a monster-infested earth under a sunless sky to rescue a maiden and bring her back into his refuge. Where Wells was ironic, Hodgson was earnest, as is demonstrated by his deliberate use of mock-antique prose; the story is meant to imitate a medieval romance of chivalric love and triumph in the face of the oncoming end.

What is marked about these apocalypses is that they are apocalypses by degrees: nothing is revealed all at once; rather, they are worked out through the accumulation of knowledge over time. I use the specific term "Long Apocalypse" as opposed to "millennial apocalypse" to describe the exact nature of the entropic catastrophe because there are quite clear, fundamental differences with significant ramifications.

In its original Greek, "apocalypse" denotes an unveiling. Implicit with that is the belief that the world as we see it is secondary to a transcendent reality and that, therefore, when the most basic elemental forces of good and evil are brought into their ultimate conflict, the apparent world will be stripped away to reveal this conflict, its resolution and the new order that shall follow.

The Long Apocalypse is of an entirely different nature from that of the millennial apocalypse. The miracles portending a millennial apocalypse are by their nature extraordinary, but there are no miracles in the world of the Long Apocalypse, because entropy is not an unveiling. The Long Apocalypse is more than immanent, it is intrinsic, and the second law of thermodynamics could be observed first-hand by any tea drinker.

Simply showing an incrementally dimming sun would be less effective in conveying immense passages of time involved than linking visions dramatically altered from our familiar image of the sun (and it would have resulted in a very much thicker book as well). Wells shows a vertiginous acceleration of time as the Time Traveller undertakes his journey, and this is indicated by the slow, familiar movement of the sun across the sky becoming a rapid flickering alternation of day and night, and then as the Time Machine further accelerates, becoming a wavering band of fire. By the time he arrives in the era of the Eloi and the Morlocks in the eight hundred and second century, the sun is superficially unaltered, but when he travels still thirty million years further into the future he sees at last the sun stilled, bloated, and red. Wells places it on the horizon, linking the decline of the sun's energy with the accessible image of the sunset, and as an evolutionist who believed that life initially emerged from the sea, he ironically follows the corrupt Eden of the previous age with a tableau of the last remnants of life flopping about on the shore.

Hodsgon uses a similar means of depicting the initial fall into deep time by the sun's transformation into a band of light for his time traveler, though as it is due to some unexplained supernatural means, his narrator is more hapless observer than cautious experimenter. However, his destination lies at a far greater remove, beyond even the destruction of the solar system. Even the sun and the earth are made cosmically subordinate as the vast green and black "Central Suns" of the cosmos appear. They are orders of magnitude greater than the sun of earth in magnitude and in greater and stranger in quality as well: they are not merely sources of the physical forces of light and gravitation, they are *metaphysical* suns.

The Central Suns preside over versions of Heaven and Hell, as construed by Hodgson's eccentric imagination, integrating previous glimpses of these realms that the Recluse has already seen. Each sun is accompanied by clouds of orbs, which, it transpires, are kinds of "pocket universes": within an orb attending the Green Sun, the Recluse sees it as a white sun and finds himself standing on the shore of a "Sea of Sleep" wherein is preserved the soul and memory of a lost beloved and with whom he might be joined in an eternity of perpetual and conclusive fulfillment. However, by the Dark Sun the view within one of its attendant orbs shows it as a ring of red fire over a "Plain of Silence," a horrible, forbidding desert dominated by vast stone effigies and a twin of his strange house. Unfortunately in one case and fortunately in the other, these visions are temporary, and his floating viewpoint withdraws, experiencing an unguided tour rather than finding its proper end.

The symmetry is quite striking. They are opposites in that one is oceanic and the other dry, but they are both places of quiet and stillness, and these common attributes are then given their positive or negative qualities according to the deeper natures of their Suns: the life-principle of the Green Sun produces fulfillment in its stillness, the death-principle of the Dark Sun produces desolation and dread.

Certainly one can see these realms as attempts to create analogues of Heaven and Hell, but they do have their own peculiar quality that sets them apart from those overtly created by supernatural intelligence. During an eclipse of the Green Sun by its dark companion, Hodgson's narrator perceives a corona of violet rays projecting out from it, along each of which there run corpuscles of light, which he believes to be messengers of some kind, though explicitly he holds back from committing himself absolutely to declaring that either Central Sun is the abode of any intelligence (117). Neither the Sea of Sleep nor the Plain of Silence need to be made as such according to the decree of a conscious agency any more than the presence of light and warmth on earth is dependent on our sun being sentient. This is an interesting metaphysical image and a thoroughly post-Newtonian concept of heavenly influence. Rather than there being ordering entities or "resonances" of some unexplained mechanism between the scales of the macrocosm and the microcosm in "conventional" magical thought ("as above, so below," as a proverb has it), Hodgson proposes that life and death, fulfillment and desolation, are analogues of radiative force operating exactly like light or gravitation.

The eschatological scenarios of Wells and Hodgson are different in scale and also in intention. Wells sees evolutionary processes working themselves out according to the laws of thermodynamics in space and time because that is what space and time permit and compel, while Hodgson sees the driving principles of those processes permeating space and time as light fills a void. There is a distinct difference in the two viewpoints, but there is a similarity in that both characterize what might be taken as moral states as natural phenomena, not miracles.

Wells's red sun looming over the terminal beach of *The Time Machine* is a representation of the consequences of natural law, the abstract's effect on the tangible and amenable to interpretation as a symbol of romantic despair as well as a symptom of the unwinding of the cosmos. The Central Suns of *The*

House on the Borderland are of a different nature. They are meaning made visible, quasi-Manichean order manifested in the cosmos, radiating motive throughout the universe as they radiate light and gravitational force. The fact that all objects orbit them is not merely a consequence of their great mass; it is because they are the moral foci of the universe itself as well as marking gravitational and temporal center. Hodgson's universe is utterly permeated with motive, and therefore his characters—and the human race for which his characters are exemplars—are driven to find their place through finding and fulfilling their purpose, however symbolic. Despite the fact that X's heroics seem to the cynical reader to be ultimately futile—the Last Redoubt is still doomed in the long run as it exhausts its power source—he is in fact successful even in the long run because history cannot be completed without purpose. His good fortune is that he has millions of living witnesses as well as his own conscience, whereas the unnamed tentacled thing on Wells's drear beach had only the woeful regard of the Time Traveller. In Wells's physics, there are photons, but no quanta of purpose, no "telons," as they might be called. When his sun gives no more light, it gives nothing else either. Maybe Hodgson's suns will eventually cease to emit their telons.

As we can see, there are similarities and there are differences not only in the literary imagery used, but in the fundamental conceptions that produce those images. A central issue that arises here is the truth-value of a brand of rhetoric. Wells draws his authority as an extrapolator from his fidelity to the newly dominant force of science as a definer of truth, but in relation to Wells, Hodgson occupies a somewhat ambiguous position. Certainly he owes much to Wells, and the visions of *The House on the Borderland* and *The Night Land* fit too closely as direct repudiations of the polemic of *The Time Machine* to be usefully considered otherwise, but he has other sources that he draws upon in his battle with Wells's scientism.

Ironically, one of these sources might be Wells himself: his short story "The Plattner Story" (1896), which is an intellectual exercise that probably takes its own inspiration from Plato's "Vision of Er." "The Plattner Story" has a number of elements that might now be considered typically "Hodgsonian": there is, for example, a shadowy land under a vast green sun, haunted (apparently) by the souls of the dead. In order to maintain a tone of unease, all descriptions are literal rather than interpretative and are likely to be undermined by the skeptical second-hand narrator; the sheer uncertainty exists in tension with a compelling possibility of an interpretation and thus conjures up in the mind of the reader a much richer map of possibilities than is overtly described. This is a technique often used by Hodgson.

Again, though, where Wells is ironic, Hodgson is earnest. Digging deeper into cultural history, Hodgson tries to do what Wells definitively refuses to do in his longer serious works. Science explicitly rejects the authority of tradition—the motto of the Royal Society is, after all, *Nullis in Verbia* ("Take No One's Word")—but Hodgson is attempting a seamless evolution of esoteric tradition so that it might still prosper in the light of science (as he wishes it to be). In his own short stories, while secular explanations might be offered for phenomena that at first seem supernatural, the balance clearly tilts toward the supernatural: his psychic detective, Carnacki, might find the odd hoax, but he definitely lives in a universe in which supernatural forces are real and present in other realms and seek to break through into our own. Indeed, this breaking through a siege-line is a dominant motif in most of his writing.

Hodsgon was clearly inspired by visionary and esoteric tradition (as Wells was in his reading of Plato) and the Central Suns trope old esoteric traditions, but he is also deeply respectful of science and *The Night Land* advocates a well-functioning technology wielded by a secular technocracy. His way out of this dilemma is to suggest a more complex, non-homogeneous system of meaning; that is, to invoke a system of a natural and a supernatural realms complementing each other. This is not anti-scientific; rather, it is related to the system that Dante called "polysemy" in a letter to his patron, Can Grande. According to Dante, a thing will have layers of meaning: at one level accessible to the senses, it will have a literal meaning, but on progressively ascending levels it will have allegorical, analogical and anagogic meaning (Phillips 285). Crucially, in Hodgson's conception, the supernatural is assumed to be at least partly explicable and controllable on the terms of science and technology: Carnacki uses an electrified pentacle and the Last Redoubt is protected by a force field powered by the Vril-like "Earth Current."

Another difference between Dante and Hodgson lies in their concepts of time and space, and this reveals the fundamental epistemological differences of the eras in which they lived. *The House on the Borderland* and *The Night Land* have episodic structures, suggesting the transition between realms, as one progresses in comprehension between layers of meaning as Dante does in his layers of symbolic level and eschatological realm. However, the episodic structure is a mixture of literary device and contingency in Hodgson's case, serving to compress time and to connect periods in resonance. Brian Stableford, in his study of the novel, argues strongly that *The House on the Borderland* was assembled out of the fragments of separate stories, embedding a homeless cosmological romance in a more conventional haunted house story (30). If this is so, it is interesting to imagine what a more "pure" cosmological romance would have been like, and if it would have even more clearly anticipated the work of Olaf Stapledon. In any case, the Recluse's journeys through time and space and their effects are explicitly *continuous* and can be read today on their own terms, with or without the framing narrative of the sinister house.

Modern Western culture has tended to homogenize its conceptions of space and time, or at least to draw a sharp line between differing kinds. The Cartesian concept of space and linear chronological time as measurable and explicable became a dominant paradigm in scientific culture, a position challenged only by the emergence of Einstein's special and general theories of relativity. However, with variations, non-Western and pre-Modern cultures have had a more varied and integrated set of temporal and spatial concepts. For example, Frank Kermode, in *The Sense of an Ending*, contrasts the different kinds of time in mythic and mundane experience: linear time, measured by clocks, is *chronos* time; then there is *kairos* time, the critical moment where the event of a revelation or crucial cliffhanger moment connects with its eternal context; there is *eternity*, which is not linear time extended infinitely, but a time in which all is present forever; and there is the *pleroma*, or "fullness" of time completed (35-64). Sometimes these differentiations are artefacts of theological hair-splitting and the ambiguities of translation, but the point remains that space and time are not always continuous, unbounded and homogeneous in many cultures—and in fact those influences have persisted into the modern and postmodern period in the West.

What we see in the literature of Hodgson and many of his contemporaries is an attempt to reconcile the ancient with the modern on harmonious terms where each may illuminate the other. *The House on the Borderland* and *The Night Land* present scenarios in which this is achieved. Hodgson does not create distinct demarcations of time. His use—following Wells—of depicting continuous chronological time travel to lead to the ultimate shows quantitative change generating a qualitative change in a kind of supra-chronos time and allied supra-Cartesian space, *not* strictly segmented or layered time and space. Overall, however, his stance and technique can be described as ambiguous or hybrid. On one hand he accepts the authority of science in describing phenomena and is inspired by it, and he accepts also the use of technology as an arm of science, but on the other hand he has tried to retain the existence of spiritual realms and concepts. As a result, his spatio-temporal architecture is a compromise with elements of ancient and modern, and the narrative structure of *The House on the Borderland* is severely disjointed, mixing the slow working out of entropy with an unveiling. *The Night Land*, published later, is much smoother in its construction, but does not have the scope of the former novel.

While Wells introduced the fourth dimension of time as being analogous to space, he tied it closely to the workings of space as intimately as any relativistic physicist who talks of "spacetime." The Time Traveller enjoys no elevated transcendental view, but rather occupies his own relativistic "frame of reference" when traveling. In imagining this continuum, he eliminated entirely from his vision any requirement for transcendental planes and proposed a new architectonics. This is allied with his intention to comment on the separation of the working and leisured classes in his own day by extrapolating its evolutionary effect through time; continuity rather than demarcation of spacetime was fundamental to his rhetoric. They are separated by the lines of species and ecological role, he tells us, but the path from the Industrial Revolution to their world is one that is direct and unobstructed.

While "obviously" there is no visible spiritual dimension to the Long Apocalypse of *The Time Machine*, what is less obvious is Wells's extraordinary mental courage in refusing to admit one when his contemporaries and even his successors such as Stapledon tried so hard to find one.

Works Cited

Aldiss, Brian W., with David Wingrove. *Trillion Year Spree: The History of Science Fiction*. London: Victor Gollancz, 1986.

Beer, Gillian. "The Death of the Sun: Victorian Solar Physics and Solar Myth." In *The Sun Is God: Painting, Literature, and Mythology in the Nineteenth Century*, ed. J. B. Bullen. Oxford: Oxford University Press, 1989. 159-80.

Flammarion, Camille. *Lumen*. Trans. Brian Stableford. Middletown, CT: Wesleyan University Press, 2002.

Flammarion, Camille. *Omega: The Last Days of the World*. Lincoln: University of Nebraska Press, 1999.

Gafford, Sam. "Writing Backwards: The Novels of William Hope Hodgson." *Studies in Weird Fiction* No. 11 (Spring 1992): 12-15.

Hodgson, William Hope. *The Night Land*. Doylestown, PA: Wildside Press, 2001.

———. *The House on the Borderland*. London: Robinson Publishing, 1988.

Kermode, Frank. *The Sense of an Ending: Studies in the Theory of Fiction*. New York: Oxford University Press, 1967.

Phillips, Tom, trans. and illus. *Dante's Inferno*. London: Thames & Hudson, 1985.

Russ, Joanna. *To Write Like a Woman: Essays in Feminism and Science Fiction*. Bloomington: Indiana University Press, 1995.

Stableford, Brian. "The Composition of *The House on the Borderland*." In *William Hope Hodgson: Voyages and Visions*, ed. Ian Bell. Oxford: I. Bell & Sons, 1987. 29-36.

Wells, H. G. "The Plattner Story." In *The Short Stories of H. G. Wells*. London: Ernest Benn, 1934. 367–90.

———. *The Time Machine*. In *The Short Stories of H. G. Wells*. London: Ernest Benn, 1934. 9–103.

Shadow out of Hodgson

John D. Haefele

A recent flurry—perhaps full-fledged revival—of scholarly interest in British author William Hope Hodgson goads me again into wondering why his work is not acknowledged for being a major influence on H. P. Lovecraft's masterpiece, "The Shadow out of Time." Whenever the two authors are compared, any similarities are framed as merely coincidental, products of kindred spirits. That is because conventional wisdom, based solidly upon surviving correspondence, divulges that Lovecraft's earliest encounter with the Hodgson novels (midway through 1934) occurred too late to have influenced his writing, especially because in the period following that encounter and lasting until the end of his life Lovecraft managed only to produce one "major" tale. But that "one" was the momentous "Shadow out of Time," which renowned scholars S. T. Joshi and David E. Schultz estimate one of only *two* in Lovecraft's oeuvre (the other being the short novel *At the Mountains of Madness*) celebrated for evoking "infinitely vast gulfs of space and time and the consequent insignificance of the human race within them" (8); together they comprise "Lovecraft's most distinctive contribution to literature." That being said, it seems to me exceedingly important that the possibility of Lovecraft's reading of Hodgson informing this seminal piece be satisfactorily addressed. Hodgson's name is nowhere to be found in Joshi and Schultz's otherwise definitive, thoroughly annotated, and fully explicated edition of *The Shadow out of Time* (Hippocampus, 2001), where they analyze the genesis of this story. My objective is either to open the door to this possibility or else to incite a convincing rebuttal. Cursory delving suggests the former.

I begin with *The Shadow out of Time*, the section titled "Literary and Other Influences" (18–31), where Joshi and Schultz list the novels of H. G. Wells, another handful of less obvious novels including *The Shadowy Thing* by H. B. Drake, and the 1933 Hollywood film *Berkeley Square*, all elements inspiring Lovecraft to write his story, any of them the possible impetus. The latter in particular is emphasized ("both the play and the film are worth studying" [20]), especially for its treatment of time-travel. Only this begs the question how Hodgson's novels, which suggest connections far *less* tenuous than any of these, are overlooked or ignored. Perhaps because the scholars prove undeniably that Lovecraft's tale had been fermenting since 1930, and how many of its distinctive plot devices (in particular, the discovery of the impossibly ancient document written in the finder's own hand) were Lovecraft's own. They remind us that Lovecraft recorded precisely when he wrote the final draft of "The Shadow out of Time": it was between November 10, 1934, and February 22, 1935 (SOT 10). But as thorough and convincing a picture as these marshaled facts make, this bare depiction does not consider a true linchpin development in the genesis: Lovecraft's first-time reading of *all* Hodgson's novels in the preceding months—preceding *weeks* in the case of *The Night Land*—before completing "The Shadow out of Time." Moreover, the fact that Hodgson's impact upon Lovecraft was dramatic—so much so that for me it is incomprehensible Lovecraft would not carry it into the writing—is plain to see when we look chronologically at contemporary remarks Lovecraft made to a variety of correspondents:

[3?–6 August 1934]: Those Koenig books—3 of W. H. Hodgson's—have come from Klarkash-Ton [Clark Ashton Smith]. Hope I'll like 'em . . . (*FF* 158)

[8 August 1934]: Got Aug. WT, but haven't had time to read it. Hodgson books also unread. (*FF* 160)

[after 6 August 1934]: Have . . . read 3 weird books by William Hope Hodgson—"The Boats of the Glen Carrig", "The House on the Borderland", & "The Ghost Pirates". . . . In some respects they have a peculiar & magnificent power—an ability to suggest realms & dimensions just out of reach, & sieges by hellish legions of the nameless from unsuspected, fathomless abysses of night. (*ES* 656)

[14 August 1934]: *The Boats of the Glen Carrig* is really magnificent . . . horrors are only vaguely adumbrated & subtly manifested—in a way strongly suggesting Blackwood's "Willows". . . . I'm now reading *The House on the Borderland*–& it looks as if it were going to be great. (*FF* 163-64)

[22 August 1934]: Have read all three Hodgson books—& sink me if they aren't *magnificent!* The second one—*The House on the Borderland*–had some cosmic stuff that got Grandpa up on his hind legs yelling! (*FF* 168)

31 August 1934: This is the season for me to *absorb* impressions—not put them forth. I'm still reveling in the discovery of William Hope Hodgson. (*SL* 26)

30 September 1934: Well—as you see, I surely have become a premier Hodgson fan! . . . the masterpiece, so far as I can see, is *The House on the Borderland.* Boy—that dim, brooding air of menace! And that stupefying cosmic sweep! I am all on edge to read *The Night Land.* (*SL* 41)

6 November [1934]: Well—I'm a couple of hundred pages into *The Night Land*—but it's damned hard going. . . . And yet the chronological-geographical idea & some of the macabre concepts are *magnificent!* (ES 666)

To be sure, architectural megapolises, vast interdimensional entities, and cosmic sweeps of time were already hallmarks of Lovecraft, and already to be found to various degrees in works by Algernon Blackwood and others; but it seems dubious, given Lovecraft's demonstrated fervor over *The House on the Borderland*, to preclude this novel as *special* influence. We might debate if as a result of reading Hodgson Lovecraft accordingly *heightened* cosmicism in his story, but other unsettled similarities abound. Do not the mighty cities of the Great Race (in the midst of shunned black towers and trapdoors, once guarded for fear of Elder Things characterized by "monstrous *plasticity*" and "temporary *lapses of visibility*" [SOT 62]) conjure on a different scale (using Lovecraft's own words) the "house in Ireland which forms a focus for hideous other-world forces and sustains a siege by blasphemous hybrid anomalies from a hidden abyss below" (SHIL 59)? In fact, Hodgson's *The House on the Borderland* provides for readers one of the most astonishing and bizarre moments ever set down as prose fiction, as (using Lovecraft's words again) "the dead writer of the diary—his mind projected forward in time—witnesses the destruction of the solar system!" (FF 168). Compare (or contrast) this concept with Joshi's description of a similar moment in "The Shadow out of Time," the "spectacular concluding tableau [of] a man finding a document he must have written 150,000,000 years ago," which Joshi concedes "one of the most *outré* moments in all literature" (SOT 24).

In my opinion, however, it is correspondences between "The Shadow out of Time" and *The Night Land* that show Hodgson's influence best—to begin with, Hodgson's setting, where we find the surviving remnant of the human race (Lovecraft again) "besieged by monstrous, hybrid, and altogether unknown forces of the darkness . . . shapes and entities of an altogether non-human and inconceivable sort—the prowlers of the black, man-forsaken, and unexplored world outside . . . *suggested* and *partly* described with ineffable potency" [SHIL 59-60]), all of which is strikingly similar to what befell the Great Race. And from here the comparisons grow only more specific. In Hodgson, the first chapter is used to recount the unnamed seventeenth-century medium's relationship with Lady Mirdath; in Lovecraft, an early section relates Peaslee's period of amnesia, which in actuality circumscribes the machinations of the occupying member of the Great Race in the twentieth century—and in neither of these does this "character," early incarnation or occupying alien, factor into the rest of the tale. Then there is Hodgson's protagonist, a future incarnation of the narrator, who little by little reveals the earth he occupies billions of years in the future by means of a series of occasionally incomplete and often incomprehensible dream-visions, and Lovecraft's narrator, who in similar fashion pieces together the earth he visited 150,000,000 years in the remote past from fragments of hitherto suppressed memory surviving his actual visit to these prehistoric days, which resurface as a series of increasingly detailed dreams—both recount worlds swathed in horror. And there are the comparable "siege" concepts, which I will wager must linger the longest in readers' minds after reading these stories: Lovecraft's Elder Things, which the Great Race manages to wall out temporarily, and Hodgson's Watcher (and other transdimensional entities) that humanity in the future "let in" inadvertently. Eventually both of these protagonists perceive (as do readers) more about their respective worlds—and even with this codifying there are parallels, not least of which are two imposing libraries housed in megalithic stone structures containing books that are cased in metal—to act and finally bring about events leading to the climax of their tales.

But if all this is not sufficient to convince, my trump card asks how anyone can possibly fail to see narrative similarities between the *Night Land* protagonist's painstaking descent downward, into the Gorge, then his fearful retracing of steps past the House of Silence when regaining the surface and normalcy, and, in Lovecraft, Peaslee's descent into the depths of buried ruins beneath the desert sands and unnerved flight back and over the open trapdoors to the surface in "The Shadow out of Time." Do Lovecraft's words (describing *The Night Land*) not fit both tales perfectly? "Midway in the book the central figure ventures . . . through death-haunted realms untrod by man for millions of years—and in his slow, minutely described, day-by-day progress over unthinkable leagues of immemorial blackness there is a sense of cosmic alienage, breathless mystery, and terrified expectancy" (*SHIL* 59)? In Lovecraft the progress would be "hour-by-hour," but the rest, by George, is all Peaslee.

If the use of such similar plot devices turned out to be nothing more than coincidence, there would still remain the likelihood that Lovecraft's mere reading of Hodgson served to inspire, motivate, and perhaps re-energize him at a crucial time when he struggled to find his author's voice (this difficult genesis of "The Shadow out of Time" is not only covered succinctly by Joshi and Schultz, but is a frequent topic in Lovecraft's letters of the period), that without Hodgson there might not be "The Shadow out of Time." This diminishes Lovecraft's achievement not a jot—we need only recall Lovecraft's words of September 28, 1935, referring to Blackwood, Robert W. Chambers, and Hodgson: "These writers create a sort of distinctive awe of their own and manage to say something fresh despite all that has been said before" (*SL* 198). Indeed! So too Lovecraft in his masterwork, "The Shadow out of Time."

Works Cited

Lovecraft, H. P. *The Annotated Supernatural Horror in Literature*. Edited by S. T. Joshi. New York: Hippocampus Press, 2000. [SHIL]

———. *O Fortunate Floridian: H. P. Lovecraft's Letters to R. H. Barlow*. Edited by S. T. Joshi and David E. Schultz. Tampa, FL: University of Tampa Press, 2007. [FF]

———. *Selected Letters: 1934–1937*. Edited by August Derleth and James Turner. Sauk City, WI: Arkham House, 1976. [SL]

———. *The Shadow out of Time: The Corrected Text*. Edited by S. T. Joshi and David E. Schultz. New York: Hippocampus Press, 2001. [SOT]

Lovecraft, H. P., and August Derleth. *Essential Solitude: The Letters of H. P. Lovecraft and August Derleth*. Edited by David E. Schultz and S. T. Joshi. New York: Hippocampus Press, 2008. [ES]

R. H. Barlow's "A Memory" in William Hope Hodgson's *The Night Land*

Marcos Legaria

> Glad you appreciate the Hodgson material, which is really extremely distinctive. Some day, perhaps, "The Night Land" (which so resembles your Californian story) will get back into circulation.
> —H. P. Lovecraft to R. H. Barlow, 29 January 1936 (OFF 317)[1]

When one reads R. H. Barlow's dreamlike "A Memory" and his last man tale, "'Till A' the Seas,'" one cannot help but think of William Hope Hodgson's epic novel *The Night Land*. Massimo Berruti, in his study *Dim-Remembered Stories: A Critical Study of R. H. Barlow*, states:

> "A Memory" presents a version of the future of the human race, choosing the viewpoint of the memory of a character in the far future—a narrative structure reminiscent of that of William Hope Hodgson's *The Night Land* (1912), although Barlow did not probably read this novel before writing "A Memory." (229)

Without further evidence, it is fruitless to attempt an analysis of the influence of Hodgson's novel on Barlow's tales, but we can attempt to discern if Barlow discovered Hodgson's stories before Lovecraft himself came upon them and

---

1. As in Massimo Berruti's chapter dealing with "Vagueness" in *Dim-Remembered Stories: A Critical Study of R.H. Barlow*, we are left to wonder if Barlow had already read *The Night Land* and perhaps wished to borrow the copy H. P. Lovecraft had which H. C. Koenig started circulating to the Lovecraft Circle. Lovecraft first felt a tinge of déjà-vu while reading Hodgson's *Night Land*, which reminded him of Barlow's short tale "'Till A' the Seas,'" which first appeared in the *Californian* (Summer 1935). Both "A Memory," which also appeared in the *Californian* (Winter 1935), and "'Till A' the Seas'" (which Lovecraft revised) are collected in *Eyes of the God: The Weird Fiction and Poetry of R. H. Barlow*. S. T. Joshi has observed that the "*Californian* offered unprecedented space for lengthy prose contributions" (975).

championed them among the Lovecraft Circle. First let us savor Berruti's spectacular comparison of both tales:

> This rich and substantial tale shows that Barlow's concern for the future of mankind is not necessarily and exclusively revealed in his cosmic visions, but of the race's—and the planet's—dreadful end discussed in the paragraph on cosmic time. Barlow is not, mainly or solely, a "catastrophist." "A Memory" is a tale that provides glimpses of the (far) future of the race; but these future visions are discussed as the remembrances of a person of the future itself. The tale is not concerned with the representation of the final doom, but with a previous stage of the process—placed, however, in the far future with respect to the reader's present. Scientifically accurate is Barlow's depiction of the way, for instance, in which humanity shall develop and modify its city architecture into a distinctly "centered" model—reminiscent of Hodgson's "Great Redoubt." (229)

Lovecraft visited Barlow for the first time in person in Cassia, Florida, on 2 May 1934, in a trip that would last almost two months. Robert Hayward Barlow (1918-1951) became an active correspondent of Lovecraft at the age of thirteen, a student of Thomas Hart Benton in Kansas City, Missouri, and also Lovecraft's literary executor at eighteen, an activist poet in San Francisco at twenty-one, coeditor of the Mesoamerican journal *Tlalocan* at twenty-three, Carl Sauer's teaching assistant at twenty-four, a leading Aztec scholar at the age of twenty-seven, head of the anthropology department at Mexico City College at thirty, and just formally entered the field of Mayan studies before his death by suicide at the age of thirty-two. The period of Lovecraft's first visit to the Barlow family, covered by Kenneth W. Faig Jr. in his essay "R. H. Barlow" and by Massimo Berruti in the introduction to *Dim-Remembered Stories*,[2] likely marks Lovecraft's introduction to the works of William Hope Hodgson. In a letter to August Derleth sometime after 6 August 1934, Lovecraft writes:

> Have also read 3 books by William Hope Hodgson—"The Boats of the Glen Carrig", "The House on the Borderland", and "The Ghost Pirates"—lent me by Koenig. Do you know these? In some respects they have a peculiar and magnificent power—an ability to suggest realms and dimensions just out of reach and sieges by hellish legions of the nameless from unsuspected, fathomless abysses of night. "The House on the Borderland" has a breathtaking cosmic reach. No comparison is possible between these fine works and Hodgson's later feeble attempt—"Carnacki the Ghost Finder"[3]—which I read

---

2. For more on Lovecraft's first visit to Barlow, see OFF, which contains Barlow's sincere memoir of Lovecraft's visit, "The Wind That Is in the Grass" (1944).

3. A catalog of the weird fiction library Barlow had in Mexico City, made by his

in Florida. I have prepared a note on Hodgson to be slipped into my Sup. Horror article in the *Fantasy Fan*. (*ES* 656)

In his biography of Lovecraft, S. T. Joshi says of Lovecraft's first meeting with Koenig:

> Herman C. Koenig (1893-1959) was, like Searight,[4] well beyond his teen years when he wrote to Lovecraft in the fall of 1933. An employee of the Electrical Testing Laboratories in New York City, Koenig had an impressive private collection of rare books, and he had asked Lovecraft about the *Necronomicon* and how it could be procured. Lovecraft, disillusioning Koenig about the reality of the volume, nevertheless continued to stay in touch with him, and Koenig would lend him a significant number of weird books that would affect Lovecraft strongly over the next several years. (668)

In early August 1934, upon his return to Providence from Florida, Lovecraft received the first batch of Hodgson's books from Koenig, which included the novels *The Boats of the "Glen Carrig," The House on the Borderland*, and *The Ghost Pirates*. In a letter dated 3 August 1934, Lovecraft writes to Barlow:[5]

> Those Koenig books—3 of W. H. Hodgson's—have come from Klarkash-Ton.[6] Hope I'll like 'em—though Carnacki didn't raise the wildest expectations. One is laid in my beloved 18th century . . . what happened to the survivors of a ship wrecked in 1757. Haven't had time to read 'em yet. (*OFF* 158)

Clark Ashton Smith seems to have received five Hodgson books from Koenig. Aside from the three mentioned, he received *Carnacki, the Ghost-Finder* and *The Night Land* sometime around June 1934. The next mention of Hodgson's books is in Lovecraft's letter to Derleth of 8 September 1934, wherein Lovecraft sent the Hodgson books to Derleth:

> These books are Koenig's property, but in his generosity he is offering to lend them to anybody in the gang who cares to read them. Accordingly I'd suggest that you send them on—when fully through with them—to the next logical

---

friend and literary executor George T. Smisor, can be found at the John Hay library of Brown University. Barlow possessed Henry S. Whitehead's own copy of *Carnacki, the Ghost-Finder*.

4. Richard F. Searight, correspondent of Lovecraft from 1933 to 1937 and known for his tale "The Sealed Casket," published in *Weird Tales*. Eugene J. Biancheri's biographical sketch, *H. C. Koenig: Reader and Collector*, contains more information on Koenig.

5. As noted, Lovecraft read Barlow's copy of *Carnacki, the Ghost-Finder*, but did Barlow already have a copy of Hodgson's *The Night Land*?

6. Lovecraft's sobriquet for Clark Ashton Smith.

candidate for perusal . . . DUANE W. RIMEL,[7] BOX 100, ASOTIN, WASHINGTON. Dwyer is next on the list after him. (*ES* 660)

Lovecraft thought highly of the books, as he remarked to Barlow on 14 August 1934:

> Well—I've gotten around at last to the William Hope Hodgson books and & am very pleasantly disappointed. "The Boats of the Glen Carrig" is really magnificent except for a slight letdown & petering out (adventure & romance gaining the ascendancy) in the last quarter. It concerns the survivors of a wrecked ship & the strange unknown realms of horror to which they drift in small boats. In most cases these horrors are only vaguely adumbrated & subtly manifested—in a way strongly suggesting Blackwood's "Willows". Clearly, "Carnacki" was no real test of Hodgson—& I fancy that good old Canevin's [i.e., Henry S. Whitehead] praise must have been based on a perusal of the other items. I'm now reading "The House on the Borderland"—& it looks as if it were going to be great. The boy has atmosphere—& his characters react to abnormal phenomena in the right way. If you like, I'll sub-sub lend (they belong to Koenig & come to me from Klarkash-Ton) you these volumes. They're certainly worth reading—& I believe Hodgson really ought to go into my supernatural horror article. The one main fault about the Glen Carrig is the sort of pseudo-archaic 18th century English employed. Actually, it is not the English of the 18th century at all—being stilted & romantic, & full of expressions out of keeping with the period. This novel was published in 1907—seven years before "Carnacki", if I recall aright. The one I'm now reading is dated 1908, & deals with phenomena in a fearsomely situated & evilly regarded house on the edge of a sinister chasm in the west of Ireland. The third book—"The Ghost Pirates"—has an ominous frontispiece by Sime which you'd enjoy. (*OFF* 163-64)

Then, having read the books, Lovecraft enthusiastically writes Barlow on 22 August 1934:

> Have read all three Hodgson books—& sink me if they aren't magnificent! The second one—"The House on the Borderland"—had some cosmic stuff that got Grandpa up on his hind legs yelling! The dead writer of the diary—his mind projected forward in time—witnesses the destruction of the solar system! I've prepared a note to insert in my article at the proper point (near the end of Ch. IX) & sent it to Hornig[8] Hodgson simply can't be left out of any

---

7. Duane W. Rimel began corresponding with Lovecraft January 1934 and is known for his poetry cycle "The Dreams of Yith."

8. S. T. Joshi and David Schultz in *OFF* (170n6), speaking of Charles D. Hornig, publisher of the *Fantasy Fan*, point out that "the note did not see print in *FF* because

historical survey of this sort—& he certainly deserves to be brought to notice. Without question, "Carnacki" must be his very poorest work. (OFF 168)

Koenig had sent *Carnacki* and *The Night Land* to Smith sometime in June 1934. The books came to Lovecraft by way of August Derleth. On 3 October 1934 Lovecraft writes to Derleth: "CAS informs me that—also at Koenig's request—he is now forwarding to you two more Hodgsoniania . . . 'Carnacki, the Ghost Finder' & 'The Night Land' . . . which you are in turn to forward me" (ES 661).

In the fall of 1934, while the Hodgson books were being circulated, Barlow moved to Washington, D.C., to seek eye treatment. He may around that time have written "A Memory" and "'Till A' the Seas,'"[9] meaning Barlow had written the bulk of the stories around September 1934. As noted, elements of *The Night Land* seem to appear in "A Memory" and "'Till A' the Seas,'" but did Barlow read *The Night Land* before Lovecraft? It is difficult to say, since few of Barlow's letters to Lovecraft exist, but Lovecraft's letters to Derleth and Barlow provide clues. By November 1934, Lovecraft received *Carnacki* and *The Night Land* from Derleth. Lovecraft wrote to Derleth on 6 November 1934:

> Well—I'm a couple of hundred pages into "The Night Land"—but it's damned hard going. God, what a verbose mess. And yet the chronological-geographical idea & some of the macabre concepts are *magnificent!* Don't know whether I'm going to side with you or with Klarkash-Ton in the end. The pseudo-archaic English is an acute agony—a cursed hybrid jargon belonging to no age at all! That's Hodgson's weakness—you'll note a sort of burlesque Elizabethan speech supposed to be of the 18th century in "Glen Carrig". (ES 666)

---

the magazine folded before it reached that point in the serialization of *SHL*. Lovecraft later published it as a separate article, 'The Weird Work of William Hope Hodgson,' and it eventually did become incorporated into Ch. IX of *SHL*."

9. I have in my possession an unpublished short story sketch by Barlow called "Chant," which deals with Lovecraft's god "Nyarlathotep"; the sketch appeared in an unknown journal of the National Amateur Press Association for September 1934. What is interesting about this sketch is that the back page contains Barlow's hand-penciled notations for a projected booklet with the title "Fragments" to be issued in a private edition of 25 copies. The contents would have included the following stories: "The Summons"; "A Memory"; "'Till A' the Seas'"; "The Fugitive"; "Marionette"; "# 13 Garoth"; "The Traveller"; "The Dreamer"; "The Prophet"[?]; "The Window"[?]; "The Watcher" (tail-piece). It seems such a small edition did not appear, but the three above tales were published in the *Californian*.

By way of a postscript, Lovecraft asked Derleth to send *The Boats of the "Glen Carrig," The House on the Borderland,* and *The Ghost Pirates* to Duane W. Rimel, and when Lovecraft was done he would send *Carnacki* and *The Night Land* to Bernard Austin Dwyer.[10] By June 1935, Derleth still had not sent the books to Rimel. Lovecraft reminded him on 4 June 1935: "Don't forget that young Duane W. Rimel ... stands next on the list" (*ES* 697). We hear little concerning the books until Lovecraft writes Barlow on 17 December 1935: "The first batch of Hodgson stuff is now moving along, & will come to you from Mrs. Wooley" (*OFF* 307).[11] Barlow received *The Boats of the "Glen Carrig," The House on the Borderland,* and *The Ghost Pirates* from Wooley by the end of December 1935. Lovecraft wrote to Barlow on 27 December 1935: "I thought you'd appreciate that Hodgson stuff, & imagine you'll agree anent the superiority of 'The House on the Borderland'" (*OFF* 309).

By 26 January 1936, Lovecraft was lamenting to Barlow that Dwyer had still not sent Hodgson's *The Night Land* to the next recipient on the waiting list. He wrote: "Glad you appreciate the Hodgson material, which is really extremely distinctive. Some day, perhaps, 'The Night Land' (which so resembles your Californian story) will get back into circulation" (*OFF* 317). The trail then grows cold. Until further letters by Lovecraft are available, we will not know if Barlow received *The Night Land,* and which of Lovecraft's correspondents may have read the remaining Hodgson books. Barlow certainly ended up with a couple of volumes by Hodgson after Lovecraft's death on 15 March 1937, as they were listed as part of his Mexico City collection:

Carnacki, the Ghost-Finder. London: Eveleigh Nash, 1914. (Henry S. Whitehead's copy).
The House on the Borderland. London: Chapman & Hall, 1908.
The House on the Borderland and Other Novels. Sauk City, WI: Arkham House, 1946.
The Night Land: A Love Tale. London: Eveleigh Nash, 1912.

We may never know if R. H. Barlow read *The Night Land* before Lovecraft did. Regardless, elements of *The Night Land* are manifest in Barlow's "A Memory" and "'Till A' the Seas.'" Thanks to H. C. Koenig and H. P. Lovecraft, William Hope Hodgson's novels spread far beyond the Lovecraft Circle, and to this day continue to attract new admirers.

---

10. Little is known about Bernard Austin Dwyer, but his interest seemed to be centered on weird art. Dwyer began corresponding with Lovecraft in early 1927 (Joshi 682–83).
11. Natalie H. Wooley, a poet and late correspondent of Lovecraft (*OFF* 308n3).

Works Cited

Barlow, Robert H. *Eyes of the God: The Weird Fiction and Poetry of R. H. Barlow*. Edited by S. T. Joshi, Douglas A. Anderson, and David E. Schultz. New York: Hippocampus Press, 2002.

Berruti, Massimo. *Dim-Remembered Stories: A Critical Study of Robert H. Barlow*. New York: Hippocampus Press. 2011.

Biancheri, Eugene J. *H. C. Koenig: Reader and Collector. A Biographical Sketch with Annotated Bibiography*. Privately printed, 2004.

Faig, Kenneth W., Jr. *The Unknown Lovecraft*. New York: Hippocampus Press. 2009. [Contains "R. H. Barlow" and "Robert H. Barlow as H. P. Lovecraft's Literary Executor: An Appreciation."]

Joshi, S. T. *I Am Providence: The Life and Times of H. P. Lovecraft*. New York: Hippopcampus Press. 2010. 2 vols.

Lovecraft, H. P. *O Fortunate Floridian: H. P. Lovecraft's Letters to R. H. Barlow*. Edited by S. T. Joshi and David E. Schultz. Tampa, FL: University of Tampa Press. 2007. [Abbreviated in the text as OFF.]

———. *The Annotated Supernatural Horror in Literature*. Edited by S. T. Joshi. New York: Hippocampus Press, 2000 (rev. ed. 2012).

Lovecraft, H. P., and August Derleth. *Essential Solitude: The Letters of H. P. Lovecraft and August Derleth*. Edited by David E. Schultz and S. T. Joshi. New York: Hippocampus Press. 2008. 2 vols. [Abbreviated in the text as ES.]

William Hope Hodgson: A Bibliography

S. T. Joshi and Sam Gafford, with Mike Ashley

This is the first comprehensive bibliography of the publications of William Hope Hodgson, and to some degree it remains provisional. The compilers have attempted to examine every item personally, but in some instances this proved impossible. Any items marked with an asterisk indicate those items that have not been seen.

In Section I.A (Books and Pamphlets), we have recorded every separate publication by Hodgson during and after his lifetime. Several early items are difficult to locate, especially the so-called "copyright volumes"—small pamphlets containing plot synopses of Hodgson's novels and tales, apparently published in the United States (and deposited in the Library of Congress) to protect his copyrights at a time when American publishers were issuing unauthorised editions of works published in Great Britain. In recent years, many print-on-demand editions of Hodgson's works have appeared, and many of these are difficult to locate or verify. We have listed only those editions whose existence we have confirmed.

Section I.B (Contributions to Books and Periodicals) lists periodical publications of Hodgson's shorter work, with cross-references to appearances of these works in anthologies and books by Hodgson. A small section (I.C) of "Media Adaptations" lists the few known adaptations of Hodgson's work for film and television. Section II (Hodgson in Translation) is the most provisional section, since (aside from a few French, German, Italian, and all Swedish publications) *many of these* publications have not been seen; instead, information on them has been derived from online catalogues such as WorldCat and other such reference sources. The listing of Hodgson criticism (Section III) is divided into books about Hodgson, bibliographies, criticism in books and periodicals, book reviews, and other subsections. There are probably many more reviews of Hodgson's books during his lifetime than what we have listed, as the article in this book by A. Langley Searles suggests that Hodgson's works were widely reviewed in British newspapers of the period; but these publications are difficult of access and are not generally indexed, so locating reviews is a challenge. Selected items in this translation have been annotated to give an idea of their content and focus.

The bibliography concludes with an index of names, titles by Hodgson, and periodicals.

We are grateful to numerous individuals for their assistance in the preparation of this work: Douglas A. Anderson; Martin Andersson; Robert N. Bloch; Marco Frenschkowski; Philippe Gindre; Pietro Guarriello; Rickard Berghorn; Ola Hultin; Jan Reimer; Alexander Öström; and Henrick Pålsson.

Abbreviations used in the bibliography are as follows:

  hc hardcover
  p pamphlet
  pb paperback
  tpb trade paperback
  pod print on demand

I. Works by Hodgson in English

A. Books and Pamphlets

1. *The Boats of the "Glen Carrig."*
   a. London: Chapman & Hall, 1907. [hc]
   b. London: Holden & Hardingham, 1920. [hc]
   c. New York: Ballantine, 1971. [pb]
   d. Westport, CT: Hyperion Press, 1976. [tpb]
   e. London: Sphere, 1982. [pb]
   f. London: Grafton, 1991. [pb]
   g. Grand Rapids, MI: Bargain Book Stores, 2001. [hc, pod]
   h. San Bernardino, CA: Borgo Press, 2001. [hc]
   i. Holicong, PA: Wildside Press, 2001. [tpb]
   j. London: Gollancz, 2002. [tpb]
   k. n.p.: Spirit Lake Press, 2002. [tpb]
   l. Teddington, UK: Echo Library, 2006. [?]
   m. Lenox, MA: Hard Press, 2006. [tpb, pod]
   n. n.p.: IndyPublish, 2006. [tpb]
   o. Paddington, Australia: Readhowyouwant.com, 2006. [?]
   p. Charleston, SC: BiblioBazaar, 2007. [hc, tpb, pod]
   q. Lowfield Heath, UK: ABC Books, 2008 [hc, pod]
   r. Toronto: Bastian, 2008. [hc, pod]
   s. n.p.: Tredition, 2011. [tpb]

t. n.p.: BiblioLife, 2012. [hc]
u. n.p.: General Books, 2012. [tpb, pod]
v. Raleigh, NC: Lulu Press, 2012. [tpb, pod]

Notes. Hodgson's first published novel, although it was his fourth in order of composition, completed in September 1905 (see Gafford [III.D.41]). The first edition has a lengthy subtitle: "Being an account of their Adventures in the Strange Places of the Earth, after the foundering of the good ship GLEN CARRIG through striking upon a hidden rock in the unknown seas to the Southward. As told by John Winterstraw, Gent., to his Son James Winterstraw, in the year 1757, and by him committed very properly and legibly to manuscript."

2. *The House on the Borderland.*
   a. London: Chapman & Hall, 1908. [hc]
   b. London: Holden & Hardingham, 1921. [hc]
   c. New York: Ace, 1962. [pb]
   d. New York: Freeway Press, 1974. [?]
   e. Westport, CT: Hyperion Press, 1976. [tpb]
   f. Laurel, NY: Lightyear Press, 1976. [?]
   g. New York: Manor, 1978. [pb]
   h. London: Sphere, 1980. [pb]
   i.1. New York: Carroll & Graf, 1983. [pb]
   i.2. New York: Carroll & Graf, 1996. [pb]
   j. London: Robinson, 1988. [tpb?]
   k. London: Grafton, 1990. [pb]
   l. London: New English Library, 1996. [pb]
   m. Cutchogue, NY: Buccaneer, 2000. [hc]
   n. n.p.: North, 2000. [?]
   o. San Bernardino, CA: Borgo Press, 2001. [hc]
   p. Holicong, PA: Wildside Press, 2001. [tpb]
   q. Amsterdam: Coppens & Frenks, 2001. [hc]
   s. London: Gollancz, 2002. [tpb]
   t. London: Orion, 2002. [pb]
   u. n.p.: Spirit Lake Press, 2002. [tpb]
   v. Gullane, UK: Soft Editions, 2002. [?]
   w. Amsterdam: Coppens & Frenks, 2003. [hc]
   x. Grand Rapids, MI: Bargain Book Stores, 2005. [hc, pod]
   y. n.p.: BiblioBazaar, 2006. [?]
   z. Teddington, UK: Echo Library, 2006. [?]
   aa. n.p.: IndyPublish, 2006. [tpb, pod]
   bb. Paddington, Australia: Readhowyouwant.com, 2006. [?]
   cc. Lowfield Heath, UK: ABC Books, 2008. [hc, pod]
   dd. Toronto: Bastian, 2008. [hc, pod]
   ee. Mineola, NY: Dover Publications, 2008. [tpb]
   ff. London: Penguin Classics, 2008. [tpb]

gg. n.p.: Tutis Digital Publishing, 2008. [tpb]
hh. n.p.: Postern Press, 2009. [tpb]
ii. n.p.: Jackson Mahr, 2010. [tpb]
jj. Whitefish, MT: Kessinger Publishing, 2010. [hc, pod]
kk. Seattle: CreateSpace, 2011. [tpb, pod]
ll. n.p.: Tredition, 2011. [tpb]
mm. London: Bibliolis Books Ltd., 2012. [tpb, pod]
nn. n.p.: Book Jungle, 2012. [tpb, pod]
oo. n.p.: Cornford Press, 2012. [tpb, pod]
pp. n.p.: Perfect Crime Books, 2012. [tpb, pod]
qq. Richmond Hill, ON: Prohyptikon, 2012. [tpb, pod]
rr. n.p. (UK): Read, 2012. [tpb, pod]
ss. Gullane, UK: Soft Editions Ltd., 2012. [tpb, pod]

Notes. Hodgson's second published novel, and the second in order of composition, written in 1904. Hodgson notes that "*The House of Mysteries* has been refused twenty-one times" (letter to Coulson Kernahan, 25 September 1905).

3. *The Ghost Pirates.*
   a. London: Stanley Paul & Co., 1909. [hc]
   b. London: Holden & Hardingham, 1920. [hc]
   c.1. London: Sphere, 1975. [pb]
   c.2. London: Sphere, 1981. [pb]
   d. Westport, CT: Hyperion Press, 1976. [tpb]
   e. Laurel, NY: Lightyear Press, 1976. [?]
   f. London: Grafton, 1991. [pb]
   g. Cutchogue, NY: Buccaneer, 2000. [?]
   h. Holicong, PA: Wildside Press, 2001. [tpb]
   i. London: Gollancz, 2002. [tpb]
   j. n.p.: Spirit Lake Press, 2002. [tpb]
   k. Ashcroft, BC: Ash-Tree Press, 2003. [hc]
   l. Grand Rapids, MI: Bargain Book Stores, 2005. [hc, pod]
   m. n.p.: IndyPublish.com, 2005. [?]
   n. n.p.: BiblioBazaar, 2006. [tpb]
   o. Teddington, UK: Echo Library, 2006. [?]
   p. Paddington, Australia: Readhowyouwant.com, 2006. [?]
   q. Lowfield Heath, UK: ABC Books, 2008. [hc, pod]
   r. n.p.: Book Jungle, 2008. [tpb]
   s. Toronto: Bastian, 2008. [hc, pod]
   t. London: Dodo Press, 2008. [tpb, pod]
   u. n.p.: HardPress Publishing, 2010. [tpb]
   v. Whitefish, MT: Kessinger Publishing, 2010. [hc]
   w. n.p.: ValdeBooks, 2010. [tpb, pod]
   x. n.p.: Tredition, 2011. [tpb]
   y. Charleston, NC: BiblioBazaar, 2012. [hc, pod]

    z.   Seattle: CreateSpace, 2012. [tpb, pod]
    aa.   n.p.: General Books, 2012. [tpb, pod]
    bb.   n.p.: Assistedreadingbooks.com, n.d. [?]

> *Notes.* Hodgson's third published novel, and third in order of composition, written in 1904-05. In his letter to Coulson Kernahan (25 September 1905), Hodgson notes that the novel had been rejected fourteen times. The Ash-Tree Press edition includes, in an appendix, the original ending of *The Ghost Pirates*, "The Silent Ship 'Tells How Jessop Was Picked Up.'"

4. *The Ghost Pirates, A Chaunty, and Another Story.*
    a.   New York: R. H. Paget, 1909. [pb?]

> *Contents:* "The Ghost Pirates" [abridgment]; "The Hell! Oo! Chaunty" [poem]; "The Thing Invisible" [story].
>   *Notes.* An abridgment of *The Ghost Pirates*, evidently to protect Hodgson's copyright in the U.S.

5. *Carnacki, the Ghost Finder and a Poem.*
    a.   New York: P. R. Reynolds, 1910. [pb]
    b.   London: [No publisher given], 1910. [pb?]

> *Contents:* Abridgement of "The Gateway of the Monster," "The House among the Laurels," "The Whistling Room," and "The Horse of the Invisible" into one story plus "Lost" [poem].
>   *Notes.* An abridged version of four Carnacki stories, evidently to protect Hodgson's copyright in the U.S.

6. *The Captain of the Onion Boat.*
    a.   New York: R. H. Paget, 1911. [pb?]

> *Notes.* First separate publication of the story (see B.i.13).

7. *The Night Land: A Love Tale.*
    a.   London: Eveleigh Nash, 1912. [hc]
    b.   London: George Bell & Sons, 1912. [hc]
    c.   London: Holden & Hardingham, 1921 (abridged). [hc]
    d.   New York: Ace, 1962. [pb]
    e.   New York: Ballantine, 1972. 2 vols. [pb]
    f.   New York: Freeway Press, 1974. [?]
    g.   Westport, CT: Hyperion Press, 1976. [tpb]
    h.   Laurel, NY: Lightyear Press, 1976. [?]
    i.   New York: Manor, 1978. [pb]
    j.1. London: Sphere, 1979. [pb]
    j.2. London: Sphere, 1981. [pb]
    k.   London: Pan, 1989. 2 vols. [pb]
    l.   London: Grafton, 1990. [pb]
    m. Lilburn, GA: Purple Mouth Press, 1995. [?]
    n.   Cutchogue, NY: Buccaneer, 2000. [?]

o. Grand Rapids, MI: Bargain Book Stores, 2001. [hc, pod]
p. London: Gollancz, 2002. [tpb]
q. Holicong, PA: Wildside Press, 2003 (as *Night Lands*). 2 vols. [tpb]
r. Lenox, MA: Hard Press, 2006. [?]
s. Teddington, UK: Echo Library, 2006. [?]
t. Charleston, SC: BiblioBazaar, 2007 [tpb, pod]
u. n.p.: IndyPublish, 2007. [hc, pod]
v. U. K.: ABC Books, 2008. [hc, pod]
w. Toronto: Bastian, 2008. [hc, tpb, pod]
x. n.p.: Book Jungle, 2008. [tpb]
y. London: Dodo Press, 2008. [tpb]
z. n.p.: Standard Publications, 2008. [tpb]
aa. Richmond Hill, ON: Prohyptikon Publishing, 2009. [tpb]
bb. Seattle: CreateSpace, 2010. [tpb, pod]
cc. Whitefish, MT: Kessinger Publishing, 2010. [hc]
dd. n.p.: Valdebooks, 2010. [tpb]
ee. Winchester, UK: Ransom Publishing, 2011. [tpb]
ff. n.p.: Alan Rodgers Books, 2012. [tpb, pod]
gg. n.p.: General Books, 2012. [hc, tpb, pod]
hh. n.p.: Nabu Press, 2012. [tpb, pod]
ii. Provo, UT: Repressed Publishing, 2012. [tpb, pod]
jj. n.p.: Tredition, 2012. [tpb]
kk. n.p.: HiLoBooks, 2012. [tpb] Afterword by Erik Davis.

Notes. Hodgson's fourth published novel, although (incredibly) the first in order of composition, probably written in 1903.

8. *"Poems" and "The Dream of X."*
   a. New York: R. H. Paget, 1912. [pb?]
   b. London: A. P. Watt & Son, 1912.

   Contents: "I Have Borne My Lord a Son"; "Bring Out Your Dead"; "I Come Again": "The Song of the Great Bull Whale"; "Speak Well of the Dead"; "Little Garments"; "The Sobbing of the Freshwater"; "O Parent Sea!"; "Listening"; "My Babe, My Babe"; "The Night Wind"; "Grey Seas Are Dreaming of My Death"; "The Dream of X"; "Mutiny" [abridgement of "The 'Prentices' Mutiny"].

   Notes. A slim collection of poems and a radical abridgment of *The Night Land*, evidently to protect Hodgson's copyright in the U.S.

9. *Carnacki, the Ghost-Finder.*
   a. London: Eveleigh Nash, 1913. [hc]
   b. London: Holden & Hardingham, 1921. [hc]
   c. Sauk City, WI: Mycroft & Moran, 1947. [hc]
   d. London: Tom Stacey, 1972. [hc]
   e. St. Albans: Panther, 1974. [pb]
   f. London: Tandem, 1974. [pb]

g.1. London: Sphere, 1974. [pb]
g.2. London: Sphere, 1980. [pb]
g.3. London: Sphere, 1981. [pb]
h. London: White Lion, 1975. [?]
i. London: Grafton, 1991. [pb]
j. San Bernardino, CA: Borgo Press, 2001. [hc]
k. Holicong, PA: Wildside Press, 2003. [hc, tpb]
l. n.p.: IndyPublish, 2004. [tpb]
m. Lenox, MA: Hard Press, 2006. [?]
n. Paddington, Australia: Readhowyouwant.com, 2006. [?]
o. Ware, UK: Wordsworth Editions, 2006. [tpb]
p. Charleston, SC: BiblioBazaar, 2007. [tpb, pod]
1. Lowfield Heath, UK: ABC Books, 2008. [hc, pod]
r. Toronto: Bastian, 2008. [hc, pod]
s. n.p.: Book Jungle, 2008. [tpb, pod]
t. n.p.: Standard Publications, 2008. [tpb, pod]
u. Whitefish, MT: Kessinger Publishing, 2010. [hc, pod]
v. n.p.: Tredition, 2011. [tpb]
w. n.p.: General Books, 2012. [tpb]
x. Raleigh, NC: Lulu Press, 2012. [2012, pod]

Contents: "The Thing Invisible"; "The Gateway of the Monster"; "The House among the Laurels"; "The Whistling Room"; "The Searcher of the End House"; "The Horse of the Invisible."

Notes. Hodgson's first collection of stories, revolving around the "psychic detective" Thomas Carnacki. The Mycroft & Moran edition adds "The Haunted *Jarvee*," "The Find," and "The Hog." Later editions include all nine stories.

10. *Impressionistic Sketches.*
    a. New York: R. Harold Paget, 1913.

    Notes. Contents unknown. Possibly lost.

11. *Men of the Deep Waters.*
    a. London: Eveleigh Nash, 1914. [hc]
    b. London: Holden & Hardingham, 1921. [hc]
    c.1. North Hollywood, CA: Aegypan, 2006. [hc, pod]
    c.2. North Hollywood, CA: Aegypan, 2012. [hc, pod]
    d. n.p.: Alan Rodgers, 2006. [tpb]
    e. n.p.: Nabu Press, 2012. [tpb, pod]
    f. Provo, UT: Repressed Publishing, 2012. [hc, pod]

    Contents: "The Song of the Great Bull Whale" [poem]; "On the Bridge" [foreword]; "The Sea Horses"; "The Derelict"; "My House Shall Be Called the House of Prayer"; "From the Tideless Sea"; "The Captain of the Onion Boat"; "The Voice in the Night"; "Through the Vortex of a Cyclone"; "The Mystery of the Derelict"; "The *Shamraken* Homeward-Bounder."

Notes. Hodgson's second collection of stories, a gathering of his tales of horror and the supernatural with nautical settings.

12. *Cargunka and Poems and Anecdotes.*
    a. New York: R. Harold Paget; London: A. P. Watt & Son, 1914.

    Contents: [Contents not entirely known. It is known to contain "D.C.O. Cargunka—The Bells of the *Laughing Sally*," "The Dumpley Acrostics," "The Last Word in Mysteries," "The Psychology of Species," "Senator Sandy MacGhee," and ten poems and short two- to four-page summaries of twenty five short stories.]

    Notes. Possibly another publication done to maintain Hodgson's copyrights.

13. *The Luck of the Strong.*
    a. London: Eveleigh Nash, 1916. [hc]
    b. London: Holden & Hardingham, 1920. [hc]

    Contents: "The Pirates"; "Capt. Gumbolt Charity and the Painted Lady"; "Capt. Jat—The Island of the Ud"; "Capt. Jat—The Adventure of the Headland"; "The Getting Even of 'Parson' Guyles"; "D.C.O. Cargunka—The Adventure with the Claim Jumpers"; "D.C.O. Cargunka—The Bells of the *Laughing Sally*"; "We Two and Bully Dunkan"; "The Stone Ship"; "The Ship."
    Notes. Hodgson's third collection of stories.

14. *Captain Gault: Being the Exceedingly Private Log of a Sea-Captain.*
    a. London: Eveleigh Nash, 1917. [hc]
    b. New York: McBride & Sons, 1918. [hc]
    c. London: Holden & Hardingham, 1921. [hc]
    d. Lowfield Heath, UK: ABC Books, 2009. [hc, pod]
    e. Whitefish, MT: Kessinger Publishing, 2009. [tpb, pod]
    f. Holicong, PA: Wildside Press, 2009. [tpb, pod]
    g. n.p.: General Books, 2012. [tpb, pod]
    h. n.p.: Nabu Press, 2012. [tpb, pod]

    Contents: "Amanda Panda"; "My Lady's Jewels"; "The Diamond Spy"; "The Case of the Chinese Curio Dealer"; "The Red Herring"; "The Drum of Saccharine"; "The Problem of the Pearls"; "'From Information Received'"; "Contraband of War"; "The German Spy"; "The Adventure of the Garter"; "Billy Ben." In b., the poems are omitted.
    Notes. Hodgson's collected tales of Captain Gault, an engaging smuggler. Two stories that appeared in magazines were not included (see B.i.68 and 97); they have been collected in A.46 and 54 below.

15. *The Calling of the Sea.*
    a. London: Selwyn & Blount, 1920. [hc]

    Contents: "Introduction" by A[rthur] St. John Adcock; "Beyond the Dawning"; "The Calling of the Sea"; "Down the Long Coast"; "Eight Bells"; "Grey Seas Are Dreaming of My Death"; "Lost"; "The Morning Lands"; "The Pirates"; "The Place of Storms"; "Rest"; "The Ship"; "The Sobbing of the Freshwater"; "The Song of the Great Bull Whale"; "Song of the Ship"; "Storm"; "Thou Living Sea."

Notes. A posthumous collection of Hodgson's poetry, mostly concerning the sea.

16. *The Voice of the Ocean.*
    a. London: Selwyn & Blount, 1921. [hc]
    b. Holicong, PA: Wildside Press, 2009. [tpb, pod]
    c. n.p.: Nabu Press, 2012. [tpb, pod]
    d. Provo, UT: Repressed Publishing, 2012. [tpb, pod]

    Notes. A long poem about the sea.

17. *The House on the Borderland and Other Novels.*
    a. Sauk City, WI: Arkham House, 1946. [hc]

    Contents: "William Hope Hodgson: Master of the Weird and Fantastic," by H. C. Koenig; *The Boats of the "Glen Carrig"*; *The House on the Borderland*; *The Ghost Pirates*; *The Night Land*; "Bibliography of the Published Books of William Hope Hodgson," by A. Langley Searles.

    Notes. An omnibus of Hodgson's four novels—the end result of a long campaign by H. C. Koenig to resurrect Hodgson's reputation. An oversize volume similar to the Arkham House edition of Lovecraft's *The Outsider and Others* (1939).

18. *Deep Waters.*
    a. Sauk City, WI: Arkham House, 1967. [hc]

    Contents: "Foreword," by August Derleth; "Sea-Horses"; "The Mystery of the Derelict"; "From the Tideless Sea"; "The Voice in the Night"; "The Thing in the Weeds"; "The Island of the Ud"; "The Adventure of the Headland"; "The *Shamraken* Homeward-Bounder"; "The Stone Ship"; "The Crew of the *Lancing*";" The Habitants of Middle Islet"; The Call in the Dawn."

    Notes. A collection of Hodgson's supernatural sea stories, culled (by August Derleth) from *Men of the Deep Waters* (A.11) as well as from uncollected or unpublished sources.

19. *Out of the Storm: Uncollected Fantasies.* Edited by Sam Moskowitz.
    a. West Kingston, RI: Donald M. Grant, 1975. [hc]
    b. New York: Centaur Books, 1980. [pb]

    Contents: "William Hope Hodgson," by Sam Moskowitz; "A Tropical Horror"; "Out of the Storm"; "The Finding of the *Graiken*"; "Eloi Eloi Lama Sabachthani"; "The Terror of the Water-Tank"; "The Albatross"; "The Haunting of the *Lady Shannon*."

    Notes. The first of Moskowitz's editions of rare and unreprinted texts by Hodgson, with a long introduction (omitted in the Centaur Books edition). Fourteen copies of the Grant edition were signed by Moskowitz for special British distribution.

20. *The Dream of X.*
    a. West Kingston, RI: Donald M. Grant, 1977. [hc]
        Notes. Reprint of the abridgment of *The Night Land* (see A.8 above).

21. *Masters of Terror, Volume 1–William Hope Hodgson.*
    a. London: Corgi, 1977. [pb]
        Contents: "William Hope Hodgson: His Life and Work," by Peter Tremayne; "The Voice in the Night"; "A Tropical Horror"; "The Mystery of the Derelict"; "The Terror of the Water-Tank"; "The Finding of the Graiken"; "The Stone Ship"; "The Derelict."
        Notes. Miscellaneous collection of short horror tales.

22. *Poems of the Sea.*
    a. London: Ferret Fantasy, 1977.
        Contents: "Introduction," by George Locke; "Beyond the Dawning"; "The Calling of the Sea"; "Down the Long Coast"; "Eight Bells"; "Grey Seas Are Dreaming of My Death"; "Lost"; "The Morning Lands"; "The Pirates"; "The Place of Storms"; "Rest"; "The Ship"; "The Sobbing of the Freshwater"; "The Song of the Great Bull Whale"; "Song of the Ship"; "Storm"; "Thou Living Sea"; *The Voice of the Ocean.*
        Notes. Combined publication of *The Calling of the Sea* (A.15) and *The Voice of the Ocean* (A.16).

23. *William Hope Hodgson: A Centenary Tribute.*
    a. Birmingham: The British Fantasy Society, 1977. [p]
        Contents: "The Riven Night"; "The Phantom Ship"; "W. Hope Hodgson: His Life and Work," by Peter Tremayne.
        Notes. Reprint of two rare stories.

24. *The Haunted 'Pampero.'*
    a. London: Ferret Fantasy, 1980. [p]
    b. n.p. (UK): Read, 2012. [tpb]
        Notes. First reprint of an uncollected tale.

25. *Spectral Manifestations.* Edited by Ian Bell.
    a. Oxford: Bellknapp Books, 1984. [p]
        Contains: "Introduction," by Ian Bell; "The Ghost Pirates: Abridged by the author"; "Carnacki, the Ghost Finder: Condensed by the author"; "Bibliography," by Ian Bell.
        Notes. Small-press publication gathering Hodgson's abridgments of *The Ghost Pirates* (A.4) and *Carnacki, the Ghost-Finder* (A.5).

26. *Tales of Land and Sea.*
    a. London: Ferret Fantasy, 1984. [?]
        Contents: "Preface," by George Locke; "The Getting Even of Tommy Dodd"; "The Regeneration of Captain Bully Keller"; "The Inn of the

Black Crow"; "What Happened in the Thunderbolt"; "The Friendship of Monsieur Jeynois"; "Jem Binney and the Safe at Lockwood Hall"; "How Sir Jerrold Treyn Dealt with the Dutch in Caunston Cove"; "The Second Mate of *The Buster.*"

Notes. Collection of unreprinted stories, mostly from the *Red Magazine*. Only 10 copies printed, all signed by Locke.

27. *The Baumoff Explosive.*
    a. Madison, WI: The Strange Company, 1988. [p]

    Notes. The first of 15 pamphlets reprinting rare or uncollected stories unearthed by R. Alain Everts.

28. *Fifty Dead Chinamen All in a Row.*
    a. Madison, WI: The Strange Company, 1988. [p]

29. *From the Tideless Sea.*
    a. Madison, WI: The Strange Company, 1988. [p]

30. *The Goddess of Death.*
    a. Madison, WI: The Strange Company, 1988. [p]

31. *The Heaving of the Log.*
    a. Madison, WI: The Strange Company, 1988. [p]

32. *Homeward Bound.*
    a. Madison, WI: The Strange Company, 1988. [p]

33. *The Mystery of the Ship in the Night.*
    a. Madison, WI: The Strange Company, 1988. [p]

34. *Old Golly.*
    a. Madison, WI: The Strange Company, 1988. [p]

35. *The Phantom Ship.*
    a. Madison, WI: The Strange Company, 1988. [p]

36. *The Riven Night.*
    a. Madison, WI: The Strange Company, 1988. [p]

37. *The Room of Fear.*
    a. Madison, WI: The Strange Company, 1988. [p]

38. *Sea-Horses.*
    a. Madison, WI: The Strange Company, 1988. [p]

39. *The Terrible Derelict.*
    a. Madison, WI: The Strange Company, 1988. [p]

40. *The Valley of Lost Children.*
    a1. Madison, WI: The Strange Company, 1988. [p]
    a2. London: Magpie Books, 2005. [tpb]

41. *The Ways of the Heathens.*
    a. Madison, WI: The Strange Company, 1988. [p]

42. *The Room of Fear and Other Grues.* Edited by R. Alain Everts.
    a. Madison, WI: The Strange Company, 1988. [hc]

    Contents: "Introduction," by H. P. Lovecraft; "The Storm"; "The Dreaded Derelict"; "The Mystery of the Ship in the Night"; "The Phantom Ship"; "The Ways of the Heathens"; "Old Golly"; "The Goddess of Death"; "The Baumoff Explosive"; "The Valley of Lost Children"; "Fifty Dead Chinamen All in a Row"; "The Heaving of the Log"; "Homeward Bound"; "The Riven Night"; "The Terrible Derelict"; "The Room of Fear"; "From the Tideless Sea"; "Sea-Horses."

    Notes. Collected edition of the 15 pamphlets issued by Everts, along with two additional stories.

43. *The Haunted Pampero.* Edited by Sam Moskowitz.
    a.1. Hampton Falls, NH: Donald M. Grant, 1991. [hc]
    a.2. Hampton Falls, NH: Donald M. Grant, 1996. [hc]

    Contents: "The Posthumous Acceptance of William Hope Hodgson 1918–1943," by Sam Moskowitz; "The Haunted *Pampero*"; "The Ghosts of the Glen Doon"; "The Valley of Lost Children"; "Carnacki, the Ghost Finder" (abridgment); "The Silent Ship"; "The Goddess of Death"; "A Timely Escape"; "The Wild Man of the Sea"; "Date 1965: Modern Warfare"; "Bullion"; "Old Golly"; "The Storm."

    Notes. Moskowitz's second volume of rare and unreprinted Hodgsoniana, with another lengthy introduction.

44. *Demons of the Sea.* Edited by Sam Gafford.
    a. West Warwick, RI: Necronomicon Press, 1992. [p]

    Contents: "Unearthing the Forgotten," by Sam Gafford; "Demons of the Sea"; "The Goddess of Death"; "The Valley of Lost Children"; "The Haunted *Pampero*"; "The Painted Lady"; "The Storm"; "The Bells of the Laughing Sally"; "Date 1965: Modern Warfare"; "Is the Mercantile Navy Worth Joining?"; "Through the Vortex of a Cyclone"; "Bibliography."

    Notes. Collection of rare and largely unreprinted stories and essays.

45. *At Sea.* Edited by Sam Gafford.
    a. West Warwick, RI: Necronomicon Press, 1993. [p]

    Contents: "The Road to Adventure," by Sam Gafford; "The 'Prentices' Mutiny"; "The Island of the Crossbones"; "On the Bridge"; "The Waterloo of a Hard-Case Skipper."

    Notes. Another collection of rare and unreprinted stories.

46. *The Exploits of Captain Gault.* Edited by Sam Gafford.
   a. Bristol, RI: Hobgoblin Press, 1993. 2 vols. [p]

   Contents:
   Volume 1: "The Smuggling Life," by Sam Gafford; "Contraband of War"; "The Diamond Spy"; "The Red Herring"; "The Case of the Chinese Curio Dealer"; "The Drum of Saccharine"; "From Information Received"; "Bibliography."
   Volume 2: "He 'Assists' the Enemy"; "The Problem of the Pearls"; "The Painted Lady"; "The Adventure of the Garter"; "My Lady's Jewels"; "Trading with the Enemy."
   Notes. Reprints of the original magazine appearances, not the 1917 book publication.

47. *The Uncollected William Hope Hodgson.* Edited by Sam Gafford.
   a. Bristol, RI: Hobgoblin Press, 1995. 2 vols. [p]

   Contents:
   Volume 1 (*Non-Fiction*): "Introduction," by Sam Gafford; "Dr. Thomas's Vibration Method vs. Sandow's"; "Health from Scientific Exercise"; "Physical Culture: A Talk with an Expert"; "Physical Culture vs. Recreative Exercise"; "The Poet vs. the Stonemason"; "Regarding Similar Names"; "A Review of the Totem Question"; "9 Letters to Coulson Kernahan"; "The Magic of Kipling"; "Maarten Maarten's New Novel"; "The Trade in Sea Apprentices"; "The Peril of the Mine."
   Volume 2 (*Fiction*): "Introduction," by Sam Gafford; "Judge Barclay's Wife"; "Jack Grey, Second Mate"; "The Albatross."
   Notes. Substantial collection of rare stories and essays.

48. *Beyond the Dawning: The Poems of William Hope Hodgson.* Edited by Sam Gafford.
   a. Bristol, RI: Hobgoblin Press, 1995. [p]

   Contents: ["Introduction"], by Sam Gafford; "Beyond the Dawning"; "The Calling of the Sea"; "Down the Long Coast"; "Eight Bells"; "Grey Seas Are Dreaming of My Death"; "Grief"; "The Hell! Oo! Chaunty"; "Lost"; "Madre Mia"; "Mimosa"; "The Morning Lands"; "Nevermore"; "The Pirates"; "The Place of Storms"; "Rest"; "The Ship"; "Shoon of the Dead"; "The Sobbing of the Freshwater"; "The Song of the Great Bull Whale"; "The Song of the Ship"; "Speak Well of the Dead"; "Storm"; "Thou Living Sea"; *The Voice of the Ocean.*
   Notes. Combined edition of *The Calling of the Sea* (A.15) and *The Voice of the Ocean* (A.16), with additional poems.

49. *Terrors of the Sea.* Edited by Sam Moskowitz.
   a. Hampton Falls, NH: Donald M. Grant, 1996. [hc]

   Contents: "The Sharks of the *St. Elmo*"; "Demons of the Sea"; "Captain Dang"; "The Heathen's Revenge"; "The Promise"; "The Room of Fear"; "The Riven Night"; "The Island of the Crossbones"; "R. M. S. *Empress of Australia*" [not by Hodgson]; "The Plans of the Reefing Bi-plane"; "By the Lee"; "'Sailormen'"; "Ten Months at Sea"; "Writers of Ghost Stories"; "William Hope Hodgson's Sister: Roadblock to Recognition," by Sam Moskowitz. *Notes.* Moskowitz's third and final collection of rare Hodgsoniana.

50. *Down in the Weeds.* Edited by Sam Gafford.
   a.   Bristol, RI: Hobgoblin Press, 1997. [p]

   Contents: "Sinking in the Sargasso," by Sam Gafford; "From the Tideless Sea"; "More News from the *Homebird*"; "The Mystery of the Derelict"; "The Weed Men"; "The Finding of the *Graiken*."
   Notes. Collection of Hodgson's supernatural sea stories.

51. *All Gothic*
   a.   n.p.: Xlibris, 2001. 2 vols. [tpb?, pod]

   Contents:
   Volume 1: *The Boats of the "Glen Carrig"*; *The House on the Borderland*.
   Volume 2: *The Ghost Pirates* (with "The Silent Ship"); "The Thing Invisible"; "The Gateway of the Monster"; "The House among the Laurels"; "The Whistling Room"; "The Searcher of the End House"; "The Horse of the Invisible"; "The Haunted *Jarvee*"; "The Find"; "The Hog."
   Notes. Print-on-demand edition of three of Hodgson's novels and a selection of tales.

52. *Borderlands: Four Horror Fantasies*
   a.   n.p.: Xlibris, 2001. [tpb]

   Contents: "Foreword," by Robert Raven; *The House on the Borderland*; *The Boats of the "Glen Carrig"*; "The Voice in the Night"; "The Derelict."
   Notes. Litrix Edition No. 2. Print-on-demand edition.

53. *The House on the Borderland and Other Stories*
   a.   London: Orion/Gollancz, 2002. [tpb]

   Contents: "'And Yet': The Antinomies of William Hope Hodgson," by China Miéville; *The Boats of the "Glen Carrig"*; *The House on the Borderland*; *The Ghost Pirates*; *The Night Land*.
   Notes. Omnibus of Hodgson's four novels.

54. *The Boats of the "Glen Carrig" and Other Nautical Adventures.* Edited by Jeremy Lassen.
   a.   San Francisco: Night Shade Books, 2003. [hc]

   Contents: "Editor's Introduction," by Jeremy Lassen; *The Boats of the "Glen Carrig"*; "From the Tideless Sea" (parts one and two); "The Mystery of the Derelict"; "The Thing in the Weeds"; "The Finding of the *Graiken*"; "The Call in the Dawn"; "Contraband of War"; "The Diamond Spy"; "The Red Herring"; "The Case of the Chinese Curio Dealer"; "The Drum of Saccharine"; "From Information Received"; "The German Spy"; "The Problem of the Pearls"; "The Painted Lady"; "The Adventure of the Garter"; "My Lady's Jewels"; "Trading with the Enemy"; "The Plans of the Reefing Bi-plane"; "The Island of the Ud"; "The Adventure of the Headland";

"The Bells of the *Laughing Sally*"; "The Adventure with the Claim Jumpers"; "A Note on the Texts" [by Lassen].
    Notes. The Collected Fiction of William Hope Hodgson, Volume 1. No dust jacket, but with cover and interior art by Jason Van Hollander.

55. *The House on the Borderland and Other Mysterious Places.* Edited by Jeremy Lassen.
    a. San Francisco: Night Shade Books, 2004. [hc]

    Contents: "Editor's Introduction," by Jeremy Lassen; *The House on the Borderland*; "The Thing Invisible"; "The Gateway of the Monster"; "The House among the Laurels"; "The Whistling Room"; "The Searcher of the End House"; "The Horse of the Invisible"; "The Haunted *Jarvee*"; "The Find"; "The Hog"; "The Goddess of Death"; "Terror of the Water-Tank"; "Bullion"; "The Mystery of the Water-Logged Ship"; "The Ghosts of the *Glen Doon*"; "Mr. Jock Danplank"; "The Mystery of Captain Chappel"; "The Home-coming of Captain Dan"; "Merciful Plunder"; "The Haunting of the *Lady Shannon*"; "The Heathen's Revenge"; "A Note on the Texts" [by Lassen].
    Notes. The Collected Fiction of William Hope Hodgson, Volume 2. No dust jacket, but with cover and interior art by Jason Van Hollander.

56. *From the Tideless Sea*
    a.1. [Whitefish, MT:] Kessinger Publishing, 2004. [tpb, pod]
    a.2. [Whitefish, MT:] Kessinger Publishing, 2012. [hc, pod]
    b.   Lowfield Heath, UK: ABC Books, 2010. [hc, pod]

57. *The Derelict*
    a.1. [Whitefish, MT:] Kessinger Publishing, 2004. [tpb, pod]
    a.2. [Whitefish, MT:] Kessinger Publishing, 2012. [hc, pod]
    b.   Lowfield Heath, UK: ABC Books, 2010. [hc, pod]

58. *The Sea Horses*
    a. New York: Kessinger Publishing, 2004. [tpb, pod]
    b. Lowfield Heath, UK: ABC Books, 2010. [hc, pod]

59. *The Ghost Pirates and Other Revenants of the Sea.* Edited by Jeremy Lassen.
    a. San Francisco: Night Shade Books, 2005. [hc]

    Contents: "Editor's Introduction," by Jeremy Lassen; *The Ghost Pirates*; "The Silent Ship"; "A Tropical Horror"; "The Voice in the Night"; "The *Shamraken* Homeward-Bounder"; "Out of the Storm"; "The Albatross"; "The 'Prentices' Mutiny"; "On the Bridge"; "The Derelict"; "The Island of the Crossbones"; "The Stone Ship"; "The Regeneration of Captain Bully Keller"; "The Mystery of Missing Ships"; "We Two and Bully Dunkan"; "The Haunted *Pampero*"; "The Real Thing: 'S. O. S.'"; "Jack Grey, Second Mate"; "A Fight with a Submarine"; "In the Danger Zone"; "Old Golly"; "Demons of the Sea"; "The Wild Man of the Sea"; "The Habitants of Middle Islet"; "The Riven Night"; "The Heaving of the Log"; "The Sharks of the *St. Elmo*"; "'Sailormen'"; "By the Lee"; "A Note on the Texts" [by Lassen].

Notes. The Collected Fiction of William Hope Hodgson, Volume 3. No dust jacket, but with cover and interior art by Jason Van Hollander.

60. *The Lost Poetry of William Hope Hodgson.* Edited by Jane Frank.
    a. Harrogate, UK: PS Publishing/Tartarus Press, 2005. [hc]
        Contents: "To God"; "Death"; "I Come Again"; "Ballade"; "Speak Well of the Dead"; "My Babe, My Babe"; "Listening"; "Bring Out Your Dead"; "The World of Dreams"; "Madre Mia"; "Mors Deorum"; "Beyond the Dawning"; "If I Were Dead"; "Over There"; "Night"; "Night and Day"; "The Mystery of Life"; "The Bridge of Melody"; "Passing"; "Shoon of the Dead"; "Ode to a Vase"; "The Thresher"; "The Cynic in Hell"; "Thou, Who Art Jesus' Mother!"; "The Death Cry of Young Genius"; "The Night Wind"; "The Sobbing of the Freshwater"; "The Morning Lands"; "Fame"; "Inspiration"; "Grief"; "Scent"; "Old-Time Hands"; "Little Garments"; "My Son! My Son!"; "Foot Falls"; "Gone"; "How It Happened"; "(Untitled)"; "Love"; "Love Song to the Dead"; "Lost Years"; "In Eternity"; "I Have Borne My Lord a Son"; "The Hunger Land"; "O Parent Sea!"; "Thou Living Sea"; "The Place of Storms"; "The Smoke of the Blast"; "Rest"; "Wrecked"; "Song of the Ship"; "The Sea of Silence"; "Thou and I"; "Storm"; "Conquest"; "The Shore of Desolation"; "Thy Wandering Soul"; "Lost"; "Southern Lights"; "The Voice of One Crying in the Wilderness"; "Dying"; "After the Years"; "The Calling of the Sea"; "Drowned"; "Grey Seas Are Dreaming of My Death"; "Farewell."
        Notes. Collected edition of Hodgson's poetry, including much unpublished verse. Limited to 150 copies.

61. *The Wandering Soul: Glimpses of a Life: A Compendium of Rare and Unpublished Works by William Hope Hodgson.* Edited by Jane Frank.
    a. Harrogate, UK: PS Publishing/Tartarus Press, 2005. [hc]
        Contents: "Foreword: The Last Redoubt," by Mike Ashley; "Introduction: The Wandering Soul," by Jane Frank; "Physical Culture: A Talk with an Expert"; "From the *Blackburn Evening Telegraph*"; "Physical Culture vs. Recreative Exercise"; "Health from Scientific Exercise"; "Ship's Log"; "A Sailor and His Camera"; "Through the Heart of a Cyclone"; "When the Sea Gets Cross"; "A Cyclonic Storm"; "Through the Vortex of a Cyclone"; "Portfolio of Photographs"; "Is the Mercantile Navy Worth Joining—Certainly Not!"; "The Poet vs. the Stonemason"; "The Trade in Sea Apprentices"; "The Peril of the Mine"; "How the French Soldier Deals with Spies"; "A Pen Picture of How Frenchmen Fight"; "The 'Emergency Door' of the Sea: 'Out Boats'"; "An Old French Woman and Her Chickens"; "Boy Billy Boo-Hoo"; "Little Feet of Maggie Lee"; "The Heart Cry"; "Monsieur les Vidoques"; "Tramp! Tramp!"; "Nevermore"; "The Ocean of Eternity"; "Sea Revelry"; "One Nation Are We"; "Pillars of the Empire"; "Gun Drill"; "The Conqueror"; "The Fruit of the Tree of Life"; "Scraps! Scraps!! Scraps!!!"; "Down the Long Coast"; "S.O.S.: The Real Thing"; "The Regeneration of Captain Bully Keller"; "The Island of the Crossbones"; "The Inn of the Black Crow"; "Jack Grey, Second Mate";

"The Friendship of Monsieur Jeynois"; "Judge Barclay's Wife"; "Captain Dan Danblasten"; "A Literary Letter" (III.D.68).

Notes. Collection of rare (including some unpublished) stories and essays. Limited to 500 copies.

62. *Adrift on the Haunted Seas: The Best Short Stories of William Hope Hodgson.* Edited by Douglas Anderson.
   a. Cold Spring Harbor, NY: Cold Spring Press, 2005. [pb]

   Contents: "Introduction," by Douglas Anderson; "On the Bridge"; "The Voice in the Night"; "Grey Seas Are Dreaming of My Death"; "Out of the Storm"; "The Voice in the Dawn"; "The Haunted *Jarvee*"; "From the Tideless Sea (First Part)"; "From the Tideless Sea (Second Part)"; "The Derelict"; "The Wild Man of the Sea"; "The Place of Storms"; "The Haunted *Pampero*"; "An Adventure of the Deep Waters"; "Demons of the Sea"; "Through the Vortex of a Cyclone"; "The Finding of the *Graiken*"; "A Tropical Horror"; "Thou Living Sea"; "The Mystery of the Derelict"; "The Stone Ship"; "The *Shamraken* Homeward-Bounder"; "Farewell"; "Source Notes" [by Anderson].

   Notes. New selection of Hodgson's stories.

63. *The Night Land and Other Romances.* Edited by Jeremy Lassen.
   a. San Francisco: Night Shade Books, 2005. [hc]

   Contents: "Editor's Introduction," by Jeremy Lassen; *The Night Land*; "The Captain of the Onion Boat"; "The Smugglers"; "In the Wailing Gully"; "The Girl with the Grey Eyes"; "Kind, Kind and Gentle Is She"; "A Timely Escape"; "A Note on the Texts" [by Lassen].

   Notes. The Collected Fiction of William Hope Hodgson, Volume 4. No dust jacket, but cover and interior art by Jason Van Hollander.

64. *The Dream of X and Other Fantastic Visions.* Edited by Douglas A. Anderson.
   a. San Francisco: Night Shade Books, 2007. [hc]

   Contents: "Introduction," by Ross E. Lockhart; *Fantastic Visions:* "The Valley of Lost Children"; "Date 1965: Modern Warfare"; "My House Shall Be Called the House of Prayer"; "Judge Barclay's Wife"; "The Getting Even of Tommy Dodd"; "Sea Horses"; "How the Honourable Billy Darrell Raised the Wind"; "The Getting Even of 'Parson' Guyles"; "The Friendship of Monsieur Jeynois"; "The Inn of the Black Crow"; "What Happened in the Thunderbolt"; "How Sir Jerrold Treyn Dealt with the Dutch in Caunston Cove"; "Jem Binny and the Safe at Lockwood Hall"; "Diamond Cut Diamond with a Vengeance"; "Eloi, Eloi, Lama Sabachthani"; "The Room of Fear"; "The Promise"; "Captain Dang"; "Captain Dan Danblasten"; *Copyright Versions:* "The Ghost Pirates"; "Carnacki, the Ghost Finder"; "The Dream of X"; "Senator Sandy MacGhee"; "The Last Word in Mysteries"; "The Dumpley Acrostics"; *Alternate Versions:* "An Adventure of the Deep Waters"; "Captain Gumbolt Charity and the Painted Lady"; "The Storm"; "The Crew of the *Lancing*"; *Counterfeits:* "The Raft"; "R.M.S. 'Empress of Australia'"; "A Note on the Texts" [by Anderson].

Notes. The Collected Fiction of William Hope Hodgson, Volume 5. No dust jacket, but cover and interior art by Jason Van Hollander.

65. [*Selected Works.*]
   a. Lakewood, CO: Centipede Press, 2009. [hc]

   Contents: "Introduction," by Sam Moskowitz; *The Boats of the "Glen Carrig"*; *The House on the Borderland*; *The Ghost Pirates*; *The Night Land*; "The Gateway of the Monster"; "The House among the Laurels"; "The Whistling Room"; "The Horse of the Invisible"; "The Searcher of the End House"; "The Haunted *Jarvee*"; "The Thing Invisible"; "Eloi Eloi Lama Sabachthani"; "The Hog"; "From the Tideless Sea" (parts one and two); "A Tropical Horror"; "The Voice in the Night"; "The Derelict"; "The Stone Ship"; "Out of the Storm"; "The Albatross"; "The Finding of the *Graiken*"; "The Terror of the Water-Tank"; "The Haunting of the *Lady Shannon*."

   Notes. Part of the publisher's Masters of the Weird Tale series. Limited to 200 copies. Interior illustrations by Stephen E. Fabian, Hannes Bok, and Ian Miller. No dust jacket, but the book is enclosed in a slipcase with ribbon marker.

66. *Bordercrossings: The Fantasy Novels of William Hope Hodgson.*
   a. n.p.: Coachwhip Publications, 2009. [tpb]

   Contents: The Boats of the "Glen Carrig"; The House on the Borderland; The Ghost Pirates; The Night Land.

67. *Three Gothic Horror Tales.*
   a. Seattle: CreateSpace, 2009. [tpb]

   Contents: The Ghost Pirates; The Boats of the "Glen Carrig"; "The Voice in the Night."

68. *The Finding of the Graiken.*
   a. Lowfield Heath, UK: ABC Books, 2010. [hc, pod]
   b. Whitefish, MT: Kessinger, 2012. [hc, pod]

69. *The House among the Laurels.*
   a. n.p. (UK): Read, 2011. [tpb]

70. *The Ghost Pirates and Others: The Best of William Hope Hodgson.* Edited by Jeremy Lassen.
   a. San Francisco: Night Shade Books, 2012. [tpb]

   Contents: "Haunted Ships and Broken Men," by Jeremy Lassen; *The Ghost Pirates*; "A Tropical Horror"; "The Sea Horses"; "The Searcher of the End House"; "The Stone Ship"; "The Voice in the Night"; "Eloi Eloi Lama Sabachthani"; "The Mystery of the Derelict"; "We Two and Bully Dunkan"; "The *Shamraken* Homeward-Bounder"; "Demons of the Sea"; "Out of the Storm."

   Notes. A selection of works derived from Night Shade's five-volume edition of the Collected Fiction.

B. Contributions to Books and Periodicals

i. *Fiction*

1. "The Adventure of the Garter." [Captain Gault]
    a. *London Magazine* 37, No. 1 (September 1916): 107-16.
    b. In A.14.
    c. In A.46.
    d. In A.54.

2. "The Adventure with the Claim Jumpers."
    a. *Red Magazine* No. 134 (15 January 1915): 125-40.
    b. *Short Stories* 84, No. 5 (November 1915): 147-60 (as "Jumping the Claim Jumpers").
    c. In A.13 (as "D.C.O. Cargunka—The Adventure with the Claim Jumpers").
    d. In A.54.

3. "The Albatross."
    a. *Adventure* 2 No. 3 (July 1911): 437-43.
    b. *New Magazine* No. 43 (October 1912): 69-77.
    c. In A.19.
    d. In Alden H. Norton, ed. *Hauntings and Horrors: Ten Grisly Tales*. New York: Berkley Medallion, 1969, pp. 111-25.
    e. In A.47.
    f. In A.59.
    g. In A.65.

4. "The Apprentices' Mutiny."
    a. *Sea Stories Magazine* 6, No. 6 (20 October 1923): 24-34.

5. "The Baumoff Explosive."
    a. *Nash's Weekly* 2, No. 2 (20 September 1919): 3-5, 34, 37.
    b. *Weird Tales* 47, No. 2 (Fall 1973): 2-12.
    c. In A.19 (as "Eloi, Eloi Lama Sabachthani").
    d. In A.27.
    e. In A.42.
    f. In Douglas A. Anderson, ed. *Tales Before Tolkien*. New York: Ballantine/Del Rey, 2003, pp. 238-52.
    g. In A.64 (as "Eloi, Eloi, Lama Sabachthani").
    h. In Mike Ashley, ed. *The Mammoth Book of Extreme Fantasy*. London: Robinson, 2008; Philadelphia: Running Press, 2008, pp. 237-56 (as "Eloi Eloi Lama Sabachthani").
    i. In A.65 (as "Eloi Eloi Lama Sabachthani").
    j. In A.70 (as "Eloi Eloi Lama Sabachthani").

6. "The Bells of the *Laughing Sally.*"
   a. *Red Magazine* No. 121 (15 April 1914): 29–44.
   b. *Short Stories* 82, No. 3 (September 1914): 125–37.
   c. In A.12.
   d. In A.13 (as "D.C.O. Cargunka—The Bells of the *Laughing Sally*").
   e. In A.44.
   f. In A.54.

7. *The Boats of the "Glen Carrig."*
   a. A.1.
   b. *Famous Fantastic Mysteries* 6, No. 5 (June 1945): 10–76 (abridged).
   c. In A.17.
   d. In Hugh Lamb, ed. *The Thrill of Horror.* London: W. H. Allen, 1975; New York: Taplinger, 1975, pp. 95–103 (extract; as "The Weed Men").
   e. In Roger Elwood and Howard Goldsmith, ed. *Spine-Chillers: Unforgettable Tales of Terror.* Garden City, NY: Doubleday, 1978, pp. 258–96 (extract; as "The Weed Men").
   f. In T. Liam McDonald, Stefan Dziemianowicz, and Martin H. Greenberg, ed. *Sea-Cursed.* New York: Barnes & Noble, 1994, pp. 70–180.
   g. In A.50 (extract; as "The Weed Men").
   h. In A.51.
   i. In A.53.
   j. In A.65.
   k. In A.66.
   l. In A.67.

8. "Bullion."
   *a. *Everybody's Weekly* (11 March 1911): ?–?.
   b. In Jack Adrian and Robert Adey, ed. *The Art of the Impossible.* London: Xanadu, 1990; New York: Carroll & Graf, 1990 (as *Murder Impossible*), pp. 48–57.
   c. In A.43.
   d. In A.55.

9. "Captain Dan Danblasten."
   a. *People's Favorite Magazine* 28, No. 4 (10 November 1918): 85–94 (as "The Buccaneer Comes Back").
   b. In A.61.
   c. In A.64.

10. "Captain Dang."
    a. In A.49.
    b. In A.64.
       Unpublished novel fragment.

11. "Captain Jat—Adventure of the Headland."
    a. *Red Magazine* No. 86 (1 November 1912): 197-209.
    b. In A.13.
    c. In A.18 (as "The Adventure of the Headland").
    d. In A.54 (as "Adventure of the Headland").

12. "Captain Jat—The Island of the Ud."
    a. *Red Magazine* No. 75 (15 May 1912): 361-74.
    b. *Short Stories* 78, No. 4 (October 1912): 41-55 (as "Captain Jat: An Account of Certain Adventures: The Island of the Ud").
    c. In A.13.
    d. In Dennis Wheatley, ed. *A Century of Horror Stories*. London: Hutchinson, 1935, pp. 939-60 (as "The Island of the Ud").
    e. *Argosy* (UK) 1, No. 4 (May 1940): 121-39 (as "The Island of the Ud").
    f. In Christina Stead, ed. *Great Stories of the South-Sea Islands*. London: F. Muller, 1955, pp. 105-29.
    g. In A.18 (as "The Island of the Ud").
    h. In Dennis Wheatley, ed. *Shafts of Fear*. London: Arrow Books, 1964; London: Hutchinson, 1968 (as *Dennis Wheatley's Book of Horror Stories: 1*), pp. 48-70 (as "The Island of the Ud").
    i. In Tim Haydock, ed. *The Mammoth Book of Classic Chillers*. London: Robinson, 1986, pp. 188-209 (as "The Island of the Ud").
    j. In A.54 (as "The Island of the Ud").

13. "The Captain of the Onion Boat."
    a. *Nash's Magazine* No. 21 (December 1910): 233-42.
    b. A.6.
    c. In A.11.
    d. In A.63.

14. "Carnacki, the Ghost-Finder." [abridgment]
    a. In A.5.
    b. In A.43.
    c. In A.64.

15. "The Crew of the *Lancing*."
    a. In August Derleth, ed. *Over the Edge*. Sauk City, WI: Arkham House, 1964, pp. 3-14.
    b. In A.18.
    c. In Vic Ghidalia and Roger Elwood, ed. *Beware More Beasts*. NY: Manor, 1975, pp. 140-51.
    d. In A.64.

16. "Demons of the Sea."
    a. *Sea Stories Magazine* 6, No. 5 (5 October 1923): 109-15.

  b. In A.44.
  c. In Stefan Dziemianowicz, Robert Weinberg, and Martin H. Greenberg, ed. *100 Creepy Little Creature Stories*. New York: Barnes & Noble, 1994, pp. 111-19.
  d. In A.49.
  e. In A.59.
  f. In A.62.
  g. In A.70.

17. "The Derelict."
  a. *Red Magazine* No. 88 (1 December 1912): 490-504.
  b. In A.11.
  c. *All Around Magazine* 11, No. 4 (February 1916): 79-95.
  d. In Dennis Wheatley, ed. *A Century of Horror Stories*. London: Hutchinson, 1935, pp. 983-1007.
  e. *Famous Fantastic Mysteries* 5, No. 5 (December 1943): 94-107.
  f. *Super Science and Fantasy Stories* (Canadian) No. 17 (April 1945): 44-58.
  g. In Groff Conklin, ed. *The Science Fiction Galaxy*. New York: Permabooks, 1950, pp. 73-103.
  h. In Donald A. Wollheim, ed. *Avon Fantasy Reader No. 4*. New York: Avon, 1947, pp. 202-23.
  i. In R. C. Bull, ed. *Perturbed Spirits: A Book of Ghost and Terror Stories*. London: Arthur Barker, 1954, 1958, pp. 143-69.
  j. In Dennis Wheatley, ed. *Shafts of Fear*. London: Arrow Books, 1964; London: Hutchinson, 1968 (as *Dennis Wheatley's Book of Horror Stories: 1*), pp. 71-96.
  k. In John Keir Cross, ed. *Best Horror Stories 2*. London: Faber & Faber, 1965, pp. 220-49.
  l. In A.18.
  m. In Robert Arthur, ed. *Monster Mix: 13 Chilling Tales*. New York: Dell, 1968, pp. 204-34.
  n. In Bryan A. Netherwood, ed. *Terror!* London: Blackie, 1970, pp. 68-101.
  o. In A.21.a.
  p. In J. A. Cuddon, ed. *The Penguin Book of Horror Stories*. Harmondsworth: Penguin, 1984; New York: Viking, 1985, pp. 202-23.
  q. In [Unsigned, ed.] *Chamber of Horrors*. London: Octopus Books, 1984, pp. 210-29.
  r. In Tim Haydock, ed. *The Mammoth Book of Classic Chillers*. London: Robinson, 1986, pp. 60-84.
  s. In Charles G. Waugh and Frank D. McSherry, ed. *Spooky Sea Stories*. Camden, ME: Yankee, 1991, pp. 147-70.
  t. In Stefan Dziemianowicz, Robert E. Weinberg, and Martin H. Greenberg, ed. *Famous Fantastic Mysteries*. New York: Gramercy, 1991, pp. 177-97.

*u.   In [Unsigned, ed.] *Truly Scary Stories for Fearless Kids*. Toronto: Key Porter, 1998, pp. ?–?.
   v.   In A.52.
   w.   A.57.
   x.   In A.59.
   y.   In A.62.
   z.   In John Grafton, ed. *Great Horror Stories*. Mineola, NY: Dover, 2008, pp. 28–49.
   aa.   In A.65.

18. "Diamond Cut Diamond with a Vengeance."
    a.   *Red Magazine* No. 210 (1 January 1918): 566–73.
    b.   In A.64.

19. "The Dream of X."
    a.   In A.8.
    b.   A.20.
    c.   In A.64.

20. "The Dumpley Acrostics."
    a.   In A.12.
    b.   In A.64.

21. "The Exploits of Captain Gault: 1. Contraband of War."
    a.   *London Magazine* 32, No. 5 (July 1914): 577–85.
    b.   In A.14 (as "Contraband of War").
    c.   In A.46 (as "Contraband of War").
    d.   In A.54 (as "Contraband of War").

22. "The Exploits of Captain Gault: 2. The Diamond Spy."
    a.   *London Magazine* 32, No. 6 (August 1914): 733–41.
    b.   In A.14 (as "The Diamond Spy").
    c.   In A.46 (as "The Diamond Spy").
    d.   In A.54 (as "The Diamond Spy").

23. "The Exploits of Captain Gault: 3. The Red Herring."
    a.   *London Magazine* 33, No. 1 (September 1914): 21–28.
    b.   In A.14 (as "The Red Herring").
    c.   In Ellery Queen, ed. *Rogues' Gallery: The Great Criminals of Modern Fiction*. Boston: Little, Brown, 1945, pp. 124–31.
    d.   *Argosy* (UK) 7, No. 2 (February 1946): 31–39 (as "The Red Herring").
    *e.   In Phyllis R. Fenner, ed. *Contraband: Stories of Smuggling the World Over*. New York: William Morrow, 1967, pp. ?–?.
    f.   In A.46 (as "The Red Herring").
    g.   In A.54 (as "The Red Herring").

24. "The Exploits of Captain Gault: 4. The Case of the Chinese Curio Dealer."
    a. *London Magazine* 33, No. 2 (October 1914): 179–90.
    b. In A.14 (as "The Case of the Chinese Curio Dealer").
    c. In A.46 (as "The Case of the Chinese Curio Dealer").
    d. In A.54 (as "The Case of the Chinese Curio Dealer").

25. "The Exploits of Captain Gault: 5. The Drum of Saccharine."
    a. *London Magazine* 33, No. 3 (November 1914): 366–70.
    b. In A.14 (as "The Drum of Saccharine").
    c. In A.46 (as "The Drum of Saccharine").
    d. In A.54 (as "The Drum of Saccharine").

26. "The Exploits of Captain Gault: 6. 'From Information Received.'"
    a. *London Magazine* 33, No. 4 (December 1914): 509–17.
    b. In A.14 (as "'From Information Received'").
    c. In A.46 (as "'From Information Received'").
    d. In A.54 (as "'From Information Received'").

27. "The Exploits of Captain Gault: 7. He 'Assists' the Enemy."
    a. *London Magazine* 33, No. 5 (January 1915): 601–10.
    b. In A.14 (as "The German Spy").
    c. In A.46 as "He 'Assists' the Enemy").
    d. In A.54 (as "The German Spy").

28. "The Exploits of Captain Gault: 8. The Problem of the Pearls."
    a. *London Magazine* 34, No. 3 (May 1915): 287–96.
    b. In A.14 (as "The Problem of the Pearls").
    c. In A.46 (as "The Problem of the Pearls").
    d. In A.54 (as "The Problem of the Pearls").

29. "The Exploits of Captain Gault: 9. The Painted Lady."
    a. *London Magazine* 35, No. 3 (November 1915): 367–78.
    b. In A.13 (as "Captain Gumbolt Charity and the Painted Lady").
    c. In A.44 (as "The Painted Lady").
    d. In A.46 (as "The Painted Lady").
    e. In A.54 (as "The Painted Lady").
    f. In A.64 (as "Captain Gumbolt Charity and the Painted Lady").

30. "A Fight with a Submarine."
    a. *Canada in Khaki* 2 (25 January 1918): 92–101.
    b. In A.59.

31. "Fifty Dead Chinamen All in a Row."
    a. A.28.
    b. In A.42.
    c. In A.49 (as "The Sharks of the *St. Elmo*").

32. "The Find." [Carnacki]
    a. In A.9.b-h.
    b. In A.51.
    c. In A.55.

33. "The Finding of the *Graiken*."
    a. *Red Magazine* No. 93 (15 February 1913): 287-98.
    b. *Weird Tales* 47, No. 4 (Summer 1974): 18-29.
    c. In A.19.
    d. In A.21.
    e. In William Pattrick, ed. *Mysterious Sea Stories*. London: W. H. Allen, 1985; Boston: Salem House, 1986; London: Star, 1986; New York: Dell, 1987, pp. 171-92.
    f. In John Betancourt and Robert Weinberg, ed. *Weird Tales: Seven Decades of Terror*. New York: Barnes & Noble, 1997, pp. 307-30.
    g. In A.50.
    g. In A.54.
    h. In A.62.
    i. In A.65.
    j. A.68.

34. "The Friendship of Monsieur Jeynois."
    a. *Red Magazine* No. 152 (1 August 1915): 157-68.
    b. In A.26.
    c. In Mike Ashley, ed. *The Mammoth Book of Hearts of Oak*. London: Robinson, 2001; New York: Carroll & Graf, 2001 (as *The Mammoth Book of Sea Battles*); London: Magpie, 2005 (as *The World's Greatest Master and Commander Stories*), pp. 137-59.
    d. In A.61.
    e. In A.64.

35. "From the Tideless Sea."
    a. *Monthly Story Magazine* 2, No. 6 (April 1906): 1198-208.
    b. *London Magazine* No. 105 (May 1907): 264-74.
    c. In A.11 (as "From the Tideless Sea (First Part)").
    d. In A.18 (includes "More News from the Homebird").
    e. In Michel Parry, ed. *Waves of Terror: Weird Stories about the Sea*. London: Victor Gollancz, 1976, pp. 18-37.
    f. In Hugh Lamb, ed. *The Taste of Fear*. London: W. H. Allen, 1976; New York: Taplinger, 1976; London: Coronet, 1977, pp. 40-82 (includes "More News from the Homebird").
    g. A.29.
    h. In A.42.

i. In Hugh Lamb, ed. *Terror by Gaslight.* London: Constable, 1992, pp. 205–42 (includes "More News from the Homebird").
j. In A.50.
k. In A.54 (includes "More News from the Homebird" as "From the Tideless Sea, Part Two").
l. A.56 (includes "More News from the Homebird").
m. In A.62 (includes "More News from the Homebird" as "From the Tideless Sea (Second Part)").
n. In A.65.

36. "The Gateway of the Monster." [Carnacki]
    a. *Idler* No. 88 (January 1910): 403–16.
    b. In A.9.
    c. In Roger Elwood and Vic Ghidalia, ed. *Horror Hunters.* New York: Macfadden Bartell, 1971; New York: Manor, 1972, pp. 59–81.
    d. In Michel Parry, ed. *The Supernatural Solution: Chilling Stories of Spooks and Sleuths.* New York: Taplinger, 1976; St. Albans: Panther Books, 1976, pp. 70–92.
    e. In Michel Parry, ed. *Ghostbreakers.* London: Granada, 1985, pp. 11–32.
    f. In Richard Dalby, ed. *The Mammoth Book of Victorian and Edwardian Ghost Stories.* London: Robinson, 1995, pp. 555–73.
    g. In Charles G. Waugh and Martin H. Greenberg, ed. *Supernatural Sleuths.* New York: Penguin/Roc, 1996, pp. 71–94.
    h. In [Unsigned, ed.] *Great Ghost Stories.* London: Readers Digest Association, 1997, pp. 242–57.
    i. In A.51.
    j. In A.55.
    k. In Mark Valentine, ed. *The Black Veil and Other Tales of Supernatural Sleuths.* Ware, UK: Wordsworth Editions, 2008, pp. 31–38.
    l. In A.65.
    m. In Michael Kelahan [i.e. Stefan Dziemianowicz], ed. *M Is for Monster.* New York: Fall River Press, 2011, pp. 294–312.
    n. In Gary Gianni, ed. *Gary Gianni's Monstermen and Other Scary Stories.* Milwaukie, OR: Dark Horse, 2012, pp. 131–41. Includes illustrations by Gary Gianni.

37. "The Getting Even of 'Parson' Guyles."
    a. *Red Magazine* No. 134 (1 November 1914): 237–51.
    *b. *Popular Magazine* 39, No. 4 (7 February 1916): ?–?.
    c. In A.13.
    d. In A.64.

38. "The Getting Even of Tommy Dodd."
    a. *Red Magazine* No. 81 (15 August 1912): 358–66.
    b. In A.26.

c. In A.64.

39. *The Ghost Pirates.*
    a. A.3.
    b. In A.17.
    c. *Famous Fantastic Mysteries* 5, No. 6 (March, 1944): 88-130 (abridged).
    d. *Super Science Stories* (Canadian) No. 13 (August 1944): 4-48 (abridged).
    e. In Sam Moskowitz, ed. *Horrors Unseen.* New York: Berkley Medallion, 1974, pp. 11-130.
    f. In A.51.
    g. In A.52.
    h. In A.53.
    i. In A.59.
    j. In A.65.
    k. In A.66.
    l. In A.67.
    m. In A.70.

40. "The Ghost Pirates" (abridgment).
    a. In A.4.
    b. In A.25.
    c. In A.64.

41. "The Ghosts of the *Glen Doon.*"
    a. *Red Magazine* No. 64 (1 December 1911): 479-87.
    b. *Sea Stories Magazine* 7, No. 1 (5 November 1923): 38-47 (as "The Old Glen Doon").
    c. In A.55.

42. "The Girl with the Grey Eyes."
    a. *Red Magazine* No. 91 (15 January 1913): 9-13.
    b. In A.63.

43. "The Goddess of Death."
    a. *Royal Magazine* 11, No. 6 (April 1904): 564-70.
    b. In Gene Marshall and C. F. Waedt, ed. *Incredible Adventures No. 1.* Chicago: Robert Weinberg, 1977, pp. 37-44.
    c. A.30.
    d. In A.42.
    e. In A.43.
    f. In A.44.
    g. In A.55.

44. "The Habitants of Middle Islet."
   a. In August Derleth, ed. *Dark Mind, Dark Heart*. Sauk City, WI: Arkham House, 1962, pp. 79-94.
   b. In A.18.
   c. In Robert H. Boyer and Kenneth J. Zahorski, ed. *Dark Imaginings*. New York: Dell (Delta), 1978, pp. 199-212.
   d. In A.59.

45. "The Haunted *Jarvee*." [Carnacki]
   *a. *Empire Magazine* (March 1929): ?-?.
   b. *Premier Magazine* NS No. 30 (March 1929): 539-48.
   c. In A.9.b-h.
   d. In Donald A. Wollheim, ed. *Avon Fantasy Reader No. 18*. New York: Avon, 1952, pp. 116-28.
   e. In Peter Haining, ed. *The Ghost Ship: Stories of the Phantom Flying Dutchman*. London: William Kimber, 1985, pp. 109-26.
   f. In George Locke, ed. *Mostly Ghostly*. London: Murqi Press, 1999, pp. 9-16.
   f. In A.51.
   h. In A.55.
   i. In A.62.
   j. In A.65.
   k. In Michael Kelahan [i.e. Stefan Dziemianowicz], ed. *The Body Snatcher and Other Classic Ghost Stories*. New York: Fall River Press, 2011, pp. 424-38.

46. "The Haunted *Pampero*."
   a. *Short Stories* 89, No. 2 (February 1918): 95-103.
   b. *Premier Magazine* No. 59 (March 1919): 106-12.
   c. A.24.
   d. In Peter Haining, ed. *Tales of Dungeons and Dragons*. London: Century, 1986, pp. 183-99.
   e. In A.43.
   f. In A.44.
   g. In George Locke, ed. *Mostly Ghostly*. London: Murqi Press, 1999, pp. 1-8.
   h. In A.59.
   i. In A.62.

47. "The Haunting of the *Lady Shannon*."
   a. In A.19.
   b. In A.55.
   c. In A.65.

48. "The Heaving of the Log."
   a. A.31.
   b. In A.42.
   c. In A.59.

49. "The Hog." [Carnacki]
   a. *Weird Tales* 39, No. 9 (January 1947): 6-28.
   b. *Weird Tales* (Canadian) 38, No. 4 (March 1947): 2-30.
   c. In A.9.b-h.
   d. In Stephen Jones and Dave Carson, ed. *H. P. Lovecraft's Book of Horror*. London: BCA/Robinson, 1993; New York: Barnes & Noble, 1993, pp. 347-84.
   e. In A.51.
   f. In A.55.
   *g. In Stephen Jones and Dave Carson, ed. *The World's Greatest Horror Stories*. London: Magpie, 2004; New York: Barnes & Noble, 2004, pp. 346-68.
   h. In A.65.

50. "The Home-coming of Captain Dan."
   a. *Red Magazine* No. 217 (1 May 1918): 13-22.
   b. In A.55.

51. "The Horse of the Invisible." [Carnacki]
   a. *Idler* No. 91 (April 1910): 696-713.
   b. In A.9.
   c. In Hugh Greene, ed. *The Rivals of Sherlock Holmes: Early Detective Stories*. New York: Pantheon, 1970, 1983; London: The Bodley Head, 1970, pp. 294-324. Harmondsworth: Penguin, 1971, 1973, 1974, 1975, 1976, 1978, 1979, pp. 278-305. *Secaucus, NJ: Castle Books, 1978, pp. ?-?.
   d. In Seon Manley and Gogo Lewis, ed. *Baleful Beasts: Great Supernatural Stories of the Animal Kingdom*. New York: Lothrop, Lee & Shepard, 1974, pp. 70-103.
   e. In Helen Hoke, ed. *Ghostly, Grim and Gruesome*. London: J. M. Dent, 1976; Nashville: Thomas Nelson, 1977, pp. 68-91.
   f. In Roger Elwood and Howard Goldsmith, ed. *Spine-Chillers: Unforgettable Tales of Terror*. Garden City, NY: Doubleday, 1978, pp. 258-96.
   g. In Michel Parry, ed. *Ghostbreakers*. London: Granada, 1985, pp. 101-28.
   h. In Stephen Jones, ed. *Dark Detectives*. Minneapolis, MN: Fedogan & Bremer, 1999, pp. 60-82.
   i. In A.51.
   j. In A.55.
   k. In A.65.

52. "The House among the Laurels." [Carnacki]
    a. *Idler* No. 89 (February 1910): 515-28.
    b. In A.9.
    c. In Peter Haining, ed. *The Wild Night Company: Irish Stories of Fantasy and Horror.* London: Victor Gollancz, 1970; London: Sphere, 1971; New York: Bonanza, 1988, pp. 247-69. New York: Taplinger, 1970, pp. 225-45.
    d. In A.51.
    e. In A.55.
    f. In A.65.
    g. A.69.

53. *The House on the Borderland.*
    a. A.2.
    b. In A.17.
    c. In August Derleth, ed. *Beyond Time & Space.* New York: Pellegrini & Cudahy, 1950, pp. 287-304 (extract; as "The Noise in the Night").
    d. In A.51.
    e. In A.52.
    f. In A.53.
    g. In A.55.
    h. In A.65.
    i. In A.66.

54. "How Sir Jerrold Treyn Dealt with the Dutch in Caunston Cove."
    a. *Red Magazine* No. 170 (1 May 1916): 139-51.
    b. In A.26.
    c. In A.64.

55. "How the Honourable Billy Darrell Raised the Wind."
    a. *Red Magazine* No. 95 (15 March 1913): 636-54.
    b. In A.64.

56. "In the Danger Zone."
    a. *Canada in Khaki* 3(1 June 1919): 86, 89-92, 95-98, 103-5.
    b. In A.59.

57. "In the Wailing Gully."
    a. *Grand Magazine* No. 79 (September 1911): 15-26.
    b. In A.63.

58. "The Inn of the Black Crow."
    a. *Red Magazine* No. 156 (1 October 1915): 777-86.
    b. In A.26.

     c.   In Mike Ashley, ed. *The Mammoth Book of Historical Detectives*. London: Robinson, 1995; New York: Carroll & Graf, 1995; Edison, NJ: Castle, 2002 (as *Historical Detectives*), pp. 358-71.
     d.   In A.61.
     e.   In A.64.

59. "The Island of the Crossbones."
     a.   *Short Stories* 80, No. 4 (October 1913): 113-25.
     b.   *Red Magazine* No. 114 (1 January 1914): 752-63.
     c.   In A.45.
     d.   In A.49.
     e.   In A.59.
     f.   In A.61.

60. "Jack Grey, Second Mate."
     a.   *Adventure* 14, No. 3 (July 1917): 159-77.
     b.   In A.47.
     c.   In A.59.
     d.   In A.61.

61. "Jem Binney and the Safe at Lockwood Hall."
     a.   *Red Magazine* No. 181 (16 October 1916): 9-16.
     b.   In A.26.
     c.   In A.64.

62. "Judge Barclay's Wife."
     a.   *London Magazine* 28, No. 4 (July 1912): 641-48.
     b.   *Adventure*, 4, No. 6 (October 1912): 97-104.
     c.   *Argosy* (UK) No. 72 (May 1932): 67-72.
     d.   In A.47.
     e.   In A.61.
     f.   In A.64.

63. "Kind, Kind and Gentle Is She."
     a.   *Red Magazine* No. 96 (1 April 1913): 775-84.
     b.   In A.63.

64. "The Last Word in Mysteries."
     a.   In A.12.
     a.   In A.64.

65. "Merciful Plunder."
     a.   *Argosy All-Story Weekly* 170, No. 4 (25 July 1925): 634-40.
     b.   In A.55.

66. "More News from the *Homebird.*"
   a. *Blue Book Magazine* 5, No. 4 (August 1907): 758-69.
   b. *London Magazine* 26, No. 7 (May 1911): 389-400 (as "The Fifth Message from the Tideless Sea").
   c. In A.11 (as "From the Tideless Sea (Second Part)").
   d. In A.18 (incorporated into "From the Tideless Sea").
   e. In Michael Parry, ed. *Waves of Terror: Weird Stories about the Sea.* London: Victor Gollancz, 1976, pp. 179-201.
   f. In Hugh Lamb, ed. *The Taste of Fear.* London: W. H. Allen, 1976; New York: Taplinger, 1976; London: Coronet, 1977, pp. 40-82 (incorporated into "From the Tideless Sea").
   g. In Hugh Lamb, ed. *Terror by Gaslight.* London: Constable, 1992, pp. 205-42 (incorporated into "From the Tideless Sea").
   h. In A.50.
   i. In A.54 (incorporated into "From the Tideless Sea" as "From the Tideless Sea, Part Two").
   j. A.56 (incorporated into "From the Tideless Sea").
   k. In A.62 (as "From the Tideless Sea (Second Part)").

67. "Mr. Jock Danplank."
   a. *Red Magazine* No. 72 (1 April 1912): 829-41.
   b. In A.55.

68. "My House Shall Be Called the House of Prayer."
   a. *Cornhill Magazine* 3rd Series, No. 179 (May 1911): 664-71.
   b. *To-day's Magazine* 7, No. 5 (1 June 1911): 198-200.
   c. In A.11.
   d. *Argosy* (UK) No. 44 (January 1930): 59-62.
   e. In A.64.

69. "My Lady's Jewels." [Captain Gault]
   a. *London Magazine* 37, No. 4 (December 1916): 438-47.
   b. In A.14.
   c. In A.46.
   d. In A.54.

70. "The Mystery of Captain Chappel."
   a. *Red Magazine* No. 193 (15 April 1917): 11-20.
   b. In A.55.

71. "The Mystery of Missing Ships."
   a. *All Around Magazine* 11, No. 2 (December 1915): 167-83.
   b. *Premier Magazine* No. 82 (February 1920): 33-46 (as "Ships That Go Missing").

      c.   In George Locke, ed. *Mostly Ghostly*. London: Murqi Press, 1999, pp. 17–30 (as "Ships That Go Missing").
      d.   In A.59.

72.   "The Mystery of the Derelict."
      a.   *Story-teller* No. 4 (July 1907): 557–64.
      b.   In A.11.
      c.   *Blue Book Magazine* 25, No. 5 (September 1918): 144–49 (as "The Terrible Derelict").
      d.   *Argosy* (UK) No. 37 (June 1929): 91–96.
      e.   In Donald A. Wollheim, ed. *Avon Fantasy Reader No. 17*. New York: Avon, 1951, pp. 119–28 (as "The Mystery of the Sargasso").
      f.   In A.18.
      g.   In A.21.
      h.   In Hugh Lamb, ed. *Forgotten Tales of Terror*. London: Magnum/Eyre Methuen, 1978, pp. 147–59.
      i.   A.39 (as "The Terrible Derelict").
      j.   In A.42 (as "The Terrible Derelict").
      k.   In A.50.
      l.   In A.54.
      m.   In A.62.

73.   "The Mystery of the Water-Logged Ship."
      a.   *Grand Magazine* No. 75 (May 1911): 307–18.
      b.   *Short Stories* 76, No. 4 (October 1911): 11–22.
      c.   In A.55.

74.   *The Night Land: A Love Tale*.
      a.   A.7.
      b.   In A.17.
      c.   In A.53.
      d.   In A.63.
      e.   In A.65.
      f.   In A.66.

75.   "Old Golly."
      a.   *Short Stories* 92, No. 6 (December 1919): 171–75.
      b.   A.34.
      c.   In A.42.
      d.   In A.43.
      e.   In A.59.

76.   "Out of the Storm."
      a.   *Putnam's Monthly* 5, No. 5 (February 1909): 554–57.
      b.   In A.19.

c. In Al Sarrantonio and Martin H. Greenberg, ed. *100 Hair-Raising Little Horror Stories*. New York: Barnes & Noble, 1993, pp. 351–55.
d. *Terror Tales* No. 1 (1997): 2–6.
e. In A.59.
f. In A.62.
g. In A.65.
h. In A.70.

77. "The Phantom Ship."
a. *Shadow* No. 20 (October 1973): 14–18.
b. In Sam Moskowitz, ed. *Horrors Unseen*. New York: Berkley Medallion, 1974, pp. 131–38 (as "The Silent Ship Tells How Jessop Was Picked Up").
c. In A.23.
d. A.35.
e. In A.42.
f. In A.43 (as "The Silent Ship").
g. In A.59 (as "The Silent Ship").
h. In A.3.k (as "The Silent Ship Tells 'How Jessup Was Picked Up'").

78. "The Plans of the Reefing Bi-plane."
a. In A.49.
b. In A.54.

79. "The Promise."
a. In A.49.
b. In A.64.

79A. "R. M. S. *Empress of Australia*." [not by Hodgson]
a. In A.49.
b. In A.64.

79B. "The Raft." [not by Hodgson]
a. In A.64.

80. "The Real Thing: On the Bridge."
a. *Saturday Westminster Gazette* No. 5899 (20 April 1912): 9.
b. In A.11 (as "On the Bridge").
*c. *All Around Magazine* 12, No. 5 (September 1916): ?–?.
d. In A.45 (as "On the Bridge").
e. In A.59 (as "On the Bridge").
f. In A.62 (as "On the Bridge").

81. "The Real Thing; 'S.O.S.'"
a. *Cornhill Magazine* 3rd Series, No. 247 (January 1917): 107–12.
*b. *Adventure* 20, No. 1 (1 January 1919): ?–? (as "The Real Thing").
c. In A.59.

d. In A.61 (as "S.O.S.: The Real Thing").

82. "The Regeneration of Captain Bully Keller."
  a. *Red Magazine* No. 143 (15 March 1915): 613-24.
  b. In A.20.
  c. In A.59.
  d. In A.61.

83. "The Riven Night."
  a. *Shadow* No. 19 (April 1973): 22-25.
  b. *New Dimensions* 1, No. 3 (May-June 1973): 4-8.
  c. In A.23.
  d. *Etchings & Odysseys* No. 3 (1983): 99-102.
  e. A.36.
  f. In A.42.
  g. In A.49.
  h. In A.59.

84. "The Room of Fear."
  a. *Etchings & Odysseys* No. 2 (1983): 21-25.
  b. A.37.
  c. In A.42.
  d. In A.49.
  e. In A.64.

85. "Sea-Horses."
  a. *London Magazine* 30, No. 1 (March 1913): 41-53.
  b. In A.11 (as "The Sea Horses").
  c. In A.18.
  d. A.38.
  e. In A.42.
  f. A.58 (as *The Sea Horses*).
  g. In A.64.
  h. In A.70 (as "The Sea Horses").

86. "The Searcher of the End House." [Carnacki]
  a. *Idler* No. 92 (May 1910): 996-1012.
  b. In A.9.
  c. In A.55.
  d. In A.65.
  e. In A.70.

87. "The Second Mate of *The Buster*."
  a. *Red Magazine* No. 98 (1 May 1913): 143-63.
  b. In A.26.

88. "Senator Sandy MacGhee."
    a. In A.12.
    b. In A.64.

89. "The *Shamraken* Homeward-Bounder."
    a. *Putnam's Monthly* 4, No. 1 (April 1908): 33–39.
    b. *Windsor Magazine* No. 215 (November 1912): 657–63 (as "Homeward Bound").
    c. In A.11.
    d. In A.18.
    e. *Argosy* (UK) No. 143 (April 1938): 43–48 (as "Homeward Bound").
    f. A.32 (as "Homeward Bound").
    g. In A.42 (as "Homeward Bound").
    h. In A.59.
    i. In A.62.
    j. In A.70.

90. "The Smugglers."
    a. *Grand Magazine* No. 73 (March 1911): 1–10.
    b. In A.63.

91. "The Stone Ship."
    a. *Red Magazine* No. 126 (1 July 1914): 735–46 (as "The Mystery of the Ship in the Night").
    b. *Short Stories* 90, No. 6 (December 1918): 133–47.
    c. In A.13.
    d. In Donald A. Wollheim, ed. *Avon Fantasy Reader No. 9*. New York: Avon, 1949, pp. 87–109.
    e. In Robert Arthur, ed. *Davy Jones' Haunted Locker: Great Ghost Stories of the Sea*. New York: Random House, 1965, pp. 93–125.
    f. In A.18.
    g. In Richard Dalby, ed. *The Sorceress in Stained Glass*. London: Tom Stacey, 1971, pp. 169–97.
    h. In Gahan Wilson, ed. *Gahan Wilson's Favorite Tales of Horror*. New York: Tempo Books, 1976, pp. 53–86.
    i. In A.21.
    j. A.33 (as The Mystery of the Ship in the Night).
    k. In A.42 (as "The Mystery of the Ship in the Night").
    l. In A.59.
    m. In A.62.
    n. In A.65.
    o. In A.70.

92. "The Storm."
    a. *Short Stories* 92, No. 6 (December 1919): 175–76.

    b.   In A.42.
    c.   In A.43.
    d.   In A.44.
    e.   In A.64.

93. "The Terror of the Water-Tank."
    a.   *Blue Book Magazine* 5, No. 5 (September 1907): 987-94.
    b.   *Weird Tales* 47, No. 3 (Winter 1973): 11-18.
    c.   In A.19.
    d.   In A.21.
    e.   In Marvin Kaye, ed. *Weird Tales: The Magazine That Never Dies*. Garden City, NY: Science Fiction Book Club/Doubleday, 1988, pp. 164-78.
    f.   In A.55.
    g.   In A.65.

94. "The Thing in the Weeds."
    a.   *Story-teller* No. 60 (January 1913): 637-45.
    b.   *Short Stories* 85, No. 2 (February 1916): 141-48 (as "An Adventure of the Deep Waters").
    c.   In A.18.
    d.   In Alexander Enfield [pseud. of Peter Haining], ed. *Sea Captain's Tales*. London: Century, 1986; North Pomfret, VT: David & Charles, 1986, pp. 263-77.
    e.   In A.54.
    f.   In A.62 (as "An Adventure of the Deep Waters").
    g.   In A.64 (as "An Adventure of the Deep Waters").

95. "The Thing Invisible." [Carnacki]
    a.   *New Magazine* No. 34 (January 1912): 511-20.
    b.   In A.4.
    c.   In A.9.
    d.   *Mike Shayne Mystery Magazine* 33, No. 1 (June 1973): 116-42.
    e.   In A.51.
    f.   In A.55.
    g.   In A.65.

96. "A Timely Escape."
    a.   *Blue Magazine* No. 36 (June 1922): 50-56.
    b.   In A.43.
    c.   In A.63.

97. "Trading with the Enemy." [Captain Gault]
    a.   *London Magazine* 39, No. 2 (October 1917): 167-75.
    b.   In A.46.

c. In A.54.

98. "The Trimming of Captain Dunkan."
   a. *Red Magazine* No. 128 (1 August 1914): 246–60.

99. "A Tropical Horror."
   a. *Grand Magazine* 1, No. 5 (June 1905): 844–50.
   b. *Weird Tales* 47, No. 1 (Summer 1973): 66–71.
   c. In A.19.
   d. In A.21.
   e. In Bill Pronzini, ed. *Creature! A Chrestomathy of "Monstery."* New York: Arbor House, 1981, pp. 158–70.
   f. In Hugh Lamb, ed. *Gaslight Nightmares 2*. London: Futura, 1991, pp. 17–29.
   g. In A.59.
   h. In A.62.
   i. In Scott Allie, ed. *The Dark Horse Book of Monsters*. Milwaukie, OR: Dark Horse, 2006, pp. 27–38. Includes illustrations by Gary Gianni.
   j. In Hugh Lamb, ed. *Gaslit Horror*. Mineola, NY: Dover Publications, 2008, pp. 203–14.
   k. In A.65.
   l. In Gary Gianni, ed. *Gary Gianni's Monstermen and Other Scary Stories*. Milwaukie, OR: Dark Horse, 2012, pp. 142–46. Includes illustrations by Gary Gianni.
   m. In A.70.

100. "The Valley of Lost Children."
   a. *Cornhill Magazine* 3rd Series, No. 116 (February 1906): 214–24.
   b. A.40.
   c. In A.42.
   d. In Richard Dalby, ed. *The Mammoth Book of Ghost Stories*. London: Robinson, 1990; New York: Carroll & Graf, 1990; London: Tiger, 1994 (as *The Anthology of Ghost Stories*), pp. 267–77.
   e. In A.43.
   f. In A.44.
   g. In A.64.

101. "The Voice in the Dawn."
   a. *Premier Magazine* (5 November 1920): 55–62.
   b. In A.18 (as "The Call in the Dawn").
   c. In George Locke, ed. *Mostly Ghostly*. London: Murqi Press, 1999, pp. 31–38.
   d. In A.54 (as "The Call in the Dawn").
   e. In A.62.

102. "The Voice in the Night."
- a. *Blue Book Magazine* 6, No. 1 (November 1907): 136-42
- b. *Nash's Magazine* No. 10 (January 1910): 237-45.
- c. In A.11.
- d. In Colin de la Mare, ed. *They Walk Again*. London: Faber & Faber, 1931; New York: E. P. Dutton, 1931, 1942, pp. 236-51.
- e. In J. M. Parrish, ed. *The Mammoth Book of Thrillers, Ghosts, and Mysteries*. London: Odhams Press, 1936, pp. 705-16. London: Bracken, 1994 (abridged; as *Mysteries*), pp. 545-56.
- f. *Argosy* (UK) 10, No. 6 (June 1949): 99-109.
- g. In Bernadine Kielty, ed. *A Treasury of Short Stories*. New York: Simon & Schuster, 1947, pp. 589-97.
- h. In Donald A. Wollheim, ed. *Avon Fantasy Reader No. 1*. New York: Avon, 1947, pp. 57-67.
- i. *Suspense* [1, No. 1] (Spring 1951): 21-29.
- j. *Playboy* 1, No. 7 (July 1954): 21, 24, 28, 48, 50.
- k. In Alfred Hitchcock, ed. *Alfred Hitchcock Presents: Stories They Wouldn't Let Me Do on TV*. New York: Simon & Schuster, 1957, pp. 130-42; New York: Dell, 1959, pp. 158-73.
- l. In R. C. Bull, ed. *Upon the Midnight: An Anthology of Ghost and Horror Stories*. London: Macdonald, 1957, pp. 13-27.
- m. In Elizabeth Lee, ed. *Spine Chillers: An Anthology of Mystery and Horror*. London: Elek, 1961, pp. 356-67.
- n. In Robert Aickman, ed. *The Fontana Book of Great Ghost Stories*. London: Fontana, 1964; New York: Beagle, 1971, pp 70-81.
- o. In Edmund Crispin, ed. *Best Tales of Terror 2*. London: Faber & Faber, 1965, pp. 40-53
- p. In Robert Arthur, ed. *Davy Jones' Haunted Locker: Great Ghost Stories of the Sea*. New York: Random House, 1965, pp. 133-47.
- r. In A.18.a.
- s. In Sam Moskowitz, ed. *Science Fiction by Gaslight*. Cleveland: World Publishing Company, 1968, pp. 190-200.
- t. In Stephen P. Sutton, ed. *More Tales to Tremble By*. Racine, WI: Whitman Books, 1968, pp. 119-38.
- u. In Donald A. Wollheim and George Ernsberger, ed. *The Avon Fantasy Reader*. New York: Avon, 1968, pp. 131-44.
- v. In Peter C. Smith, ed. *The Haunted Sea*. London: William Kimber, 1975, pp. 177-89.
- w. In Les Daniels, ed. *Dying of Fright: Masterpieces of the Macabre*. New York: Scribner's, 1976, pp. 138-46.
- x. In Helen Hoke, ed. *Creepies, Creepies, Creepies*. New York: Franklin Watts, 1977, pp. 136-52.
- y. In Malcolm Blacklin, ed. *Ghosts Four*. London: Macmillan, 1978, pp. 92-108.

z. In Mark Ronson, ed. *The Beaver Book of Horror Stories*. London: Hamlyn, 1981, pp. 23-37.
aa. In Leslie Shepard, ed. *The Dracula Book of Great Horror Stories*. Secaucus, NJ: Citadel Press, 1981; New York: Outlet, 1991 (as *The Book of Dracula*); London: Robert Hale, 1992 (as *The Dracula Book of Classic Horror Stories*), pp. 173-85.
bb. Rod Serling's "The Twilight Zone" Magazine 2, No. 1 (April 1982): 73-79.
cc. In [Unsigned, ed.] *Great Short Tales of Mystery and Terror*. Pleasantville, NY: Reader's Digest, 1982, pp. 505-17 [abridged].
dd. In Mary Danby, ed. *65 Great Spine Chillers*. London: Octopus, 1982, pp. 352-62.
ee. In Jack Sullivan, ed. *Lost Souls: A Collection of English Ghost Stories*. Athens: Ohio University Press, 1983, pp. 267-78.
ff. In Lincoln Child, ed. *Dark Company: The Ten Greatest Ghost Stories*. New York: St. Martin's Press, 1984, pp. 260-72.
gg. Rod Serling's "The Twilight Zone" Magazine Special No. 1 (1984): 149-60.
hh. In Lincoln Child, ed. *Tales of the Dark*. New York: St. Martin's Press, 1987, pp. 172-84.
ii. *Alfred Hitchcock's Mystery Magazine* 34, No. 7 (July 1989): 135-47.
jj. *Damned Thing* No. 1 (Spring 1991): 19-28, 9, 18.
kk. In Greg Ioannou, ed. *Truly Scary Stories for Fearless Kids*. Toronto: Key Porter Books, 1998, pp. 239-54.
ll. In S. T. Joshi, ed. *Great Weird Tales*. Mineola, NY: Dover, 1999, pp. 34-45.
mm. In A.52.
nn. *Pulpdom* No. 29 (March 2002): 9-16.
oo. In A.59.
pp. In A.62.
qq. In Stephen Jones, ed. *H. P. Lovecraft's Book of the Supernatural*. New York: Pegasus, 2006, pp. 443-60.
rr. In A.65.
ss. In A.67.
tt. In A.70.

103. "The Waterloo of a Hard-Case Skipper."
    a. *Everybody's Magazine* 41, No. 1 (July 1919): 42-46, 99-100.
    b. In A.45.

104. "The Ways of the Heathens."
    a. A.41.
    b. In A.42.
    c. In A.49 (as "The Heathen's Revenge").

d. In A.55 (as "The Heathen's Revenge").

105. "We Two and Bully Dunkan."
   a. In A.13.
   b. In A.59.
   c. In A.70.

106. "What Happened in the Thunderbolt."
   a. *Red Magazine* No. 163 (15 January 1916): 25-33.
   b. In A.26.
   c. In A.64.

107. "The Whistling Room." [Carnacki]
   a. *Idler* No. 90 (March 1910): 599-611.
   b. In A.9.
   c. In Dennis Wheatley, ed. *A Century of Horror Stories*. London: Hutchinson, 1935, pp. 963-79.
   d. *Argosy* (UK) 2, No. 14 (March 1941): 135-46.
   e. *Mysterious Traveler Mystery Reader* No. 5 (1952): 103-17.
   f. In Alfred Hitchcock, ed. *Alfred Hitchcock Presents: Stories for Late at Night*. New York: Random House, 1961, pp. 154-69.
   g. In Alfred Hitchcock, ed. *Alfred Hitchcock Presents: More Stories for Late at Night*. New York: Dell, 1962, pp. 85-106.
   h. In Herbert Van Thal, ed. *The Third Pan Book of Horror Stories*. London: Pan, 1962, 1963, 1964, pp. 182-99.
   i. In Alfred Hitchcock, ed. *Alfred Hitchcock Presents: Stories for Late at Night, Part 1*. London: Pan, 1964, pp. 170-87.
   j. In Dennis Wheatley, ed. *Quiver of Horror*. London: Arrow, 1964, 1965, pp. 249-66; London: Hutchinson, 1968 (as *Dennis Wheatley's Second Book of Horror Stories*), pp. 249-66.
   k. *Magazine of Horror* 2, No. 3 (June 1965): 105-20.
   l. In Henry Mazzeo, ed. *Hauntings: Tales of the Supernatural*. Garden City, NY: Doubleday, 1968, pp. 217-33.
   m. In Herbert Van Thal, ed. *Selections from Pan Horror #3*. New York: Berkley Medallion, 1970, pp. 125-43.
   n. In Ross R. Olney, ed. *Shudders*. Racine, WI: Golden Press, 1972, pp. 102-31.
   o. In Anthony Masters, ed. *Cries of Terror*. London: Arrow, 1976, pp. 62-81.
   p. In Helen Hoke, ed. *Haunts, Haunts, Haunts*. New York: Franklin Watts, 1977; New York: Franklin Watts, 1977 (as *Spectres, Spooks and Shuddery Shades*), pp. 140-59.
   q. In Les Daniels and Diane Thompson, ed. *Thirteen Tales of Terror*. New York: Scribner's, 1977, pp. 76-95.
   r. In Mary Danby, ed. *65 Great Tales of the Supernatural*. New York: Octopus Books, 1979, pp. 343-56.

s. In Peter C. Smith, ed. *Uninvited Guests*. London: William Kimber, 1984, pp. 138-55.
t. In [Unsigned, ed.] *Great Vampires and Other Horrors*. London: Chancellor Press, 1992, pp. 347-60.
u. *Alfred Hitchcock's Mystery Magazine* 39, No. 9 (September 1994): 136-51.
v. In Peter Haining, ed. *The Mammoth Book of Haunted House Stories*. London: Robinson; New York: Carroll & Graf, 2000, pp. 513-32.
w. In A.51.
x. In A.55.
y. In A.65.

108. "The Wild Man of the Sea."
a. *Sea Stories Magazine* 12, No. 3 (May 1926): 78-87.
b. In August Derleth, ed. *Travellers by Night*. Sauk City, WI: Arkham House, 1967, pp. 95-119.
c. In A.59.
d. In A.62.

ii. Nonfiction

1. "By the Lee."
   a. In A.49.
   b. In A.59.

2. "Chair Exercises."
   *a. *Penny Pictorial Weekly* (25 June 1904): ?.

3. "Challenge to the 'Handcuff King' at Blackburn."
   a. *Northern Daily Telegraph* (24 October 1902): 1.

   Hodgson challenges Harry Houdini to escape from handcuffs.

4. "A Cyclonic Storm."
   a. In A.61.

5. "Date 1965: Modern Warfare."
   a. *New Age* 4, No. 9 (24 December 1908): 183-84.
   b. In A.43.
   c. In A.44.
   d. In A.64.

   A conjecture as to the nature of warfare in the future, placed in the words of "Mr. John Russell, M.P."

6. "Downstairs on a Bicycle: A Daring Feat at Blackburn."
   a. *Blackburn Weekly Telegraph* (30 August 1902): 7 (as by "The Vagabond").

b. *Shadow* No. 19 (April 1973): 9-10.
   c. In A.61 (as "From the Blackburn Evening [sic] Telegraph").

   Brief essay, written in the third person, about Hodgson's riding a bicycle down the steps of the Capitol in Washington, D.C.

7. "Dr. Thomas's Vibration Method *versus* Sandow's."
   a. *Sandow's Magazine* No. 38 (August 1901): 121-22.
   b. In A.47.

   Brief essay on the effects of a muscle-developing exercise as developed by a Dr. Thomas as compared to that by Sandow. Contains one photograph of "Mr. Hodgson's arm."

8. "The Dreaded Derelict."
   a. In A.42.

   Brief account of several shipwrecks, including that of the *Golden Gate* and that of the *Marie Celeste*.

9. "The 'Emergency Door' of the Sea: 'Out Boats.'"
   a. *Westminster Gazette* (6 April 1914).
   b. In A.61.

10. "Health from Scientific Exercise."
    a. *Cassell's Magazine* 36, No. 6 (November 1903): 603-7.
    b. In A.47.
    c. In A.61.

    On the benefits of exercise to physical and mental health. Includes 14 photos of Hodgson performing various exercises.

11. "Hints on Physical Culture."
    a. *Sandow's Magazine* No. 62 (August 1903): 198-99.

    Brief essay on the benefits of exercise.

12. "The Houdini Exhibition."
    a. *Northern Daily Telegraph* (27 October 1902): 6.
    b. *Blackburn Times* (1 November 1902): 10.

13. "How the French Soldier Deals with Spies."
    a. *Westminster Gazette* (10 October 1914).
    b. In A.61.

14. "Is the Mercantile Navy Worth Joining?"
    a. *Grand Magazine* No. 7 (September 1905): 30-34.
    b. In A.44.
    c. In A.61.

Pungent essay on the hardships of being a sailor. Followed by an essay by "A Marine Superintendent" espousing the opposite view (pp. 34-36).

15. "Maarten Maartens' New Novel."
    a. *Bookman* (London) No. 229 (October 1910): 49.
    b. In A.47.

    Review of *Harmen Pols* by Maarten Maartens, about a peasant farmer.

16. "The Magic of Kipling."
    a. *Bookman* (London) No. 218 (November 1909): 99-100.
    b. In A.47.

    Review of *Actions and Reactions*, a short story collection by Rudyard Kipling. Hodgson singles out the story "With the Night Mail."

17. "9 Letters to Coulson Kernahan."
    a. In A.47.

    Letters from 1905 and 1906 in which Hodgson discusses his work and his attempts to secure its publication.

18. "An Old French Woman and Her Chickens."
    *a. *Westminster Gazette* (10 October 1914).
    b. In A.61.

19. "A Pen Picture of How Frenchmen Fight."
    *a. *Westminster Gazette* (12 October 1914).
    b. In A.61.

20. "The Peril of the Mine."
    a. *Ideas* (6 April 1910): 9.
    b. In A.47.
    c. In A.61.

    On the dangers of coal mining and the inadequate safeguards to protect the lives of miners.

21. "Physical Culture: A Talk with an Expert."
    a. *Blackburn Weekly Telegraph* (7 September 1901): 3.
    b. In A.47.
    c. In A.61.

    A self-interview stressing the benefits of exercise. Contains a sketch of Hodgson and a photograph of "Mr. Hodgson's good right arm.'"

22. "Physical Culture versus Recreative Exercise."
    a. *Sandow's Magazine* No. 56 (February 1903): 122-24.
    b. In A.47.
    c. In A.61.

Stresses the importance of exercise in the maintenance of health and the curing of illness. Contains a sketch of Hodgson.

23. "The Poet v. the Stonemason; or, Why Not a New Market for Poetry?"
    a. *Author* 16, No. 6 (March 1906): 182-83.
    b. In A.47.
    c. In A.61.

    Argues that there is a market for poetry, but only as written by genuine poets.

24. "Portfolio of Photographs."
    a. In A.61.

25. "The 'Prentices' Mutiny."
    a. *Wide World Magazine* 28, No. 5 (February 1912): 424-30; 28, No. 6 (March 1912): 580-86; 29, No. 1 (April 1912): 57-62.
    b. In A.8 (as "Mutiny").
    c. In A.45.
    d. In A.59.

    Often assumed to be a work of fiction (and confused with "The Apprentices' Mutiny" [i.4]), this is an essay dealing with a mutiny on the "full-rigged ship *Lady Morgan*—a thoroughly serious affair that occurred on the voyage home round Cape Horn." It is, however, narrated in the manner of a short story.

26. "The Psychology of Species."
    a. In A.12 (untitled).
    b. *Wormwood* No. 6 (Spring 2006): 43-46.

27. "Regarding Similar Names."
    a. *Author* 16, No. 4 (January 1906): 110-11.
    b. In A.47.

    Whimsical essay recommending that authors with common names attach a symbol next to their names in print so as to distinguish themselves from others.

28. "A Review of the Totem Question."
    a. *Author* 16, No. 7 (April 1906): 215-17.
    b. In A.47.

    A follow-up to "Regarding Similar Names," suggesting various objects that could serve as "totems" for authors to distinguish themselves.

29. "A Sailor and His Camera."
    a. In A.61.

    One of Hodgson's earliest lectures. Frank lists it as once containing "thirteen photographs" which are now lost. A view of life on the sea.

30. "'Sailormen.'"
    a. In A.49.

b. In A.59.

31. "Ship's Log."
    a. In A.61.

    Hodgson's personal log from his trip on the *Canterbury*.

32. "Ten Months at Sea."
    a. In A.49.

    Text of an autobiographical slide lecture.

33. "Through the Heart of a Cyclone."
    a. In A.61.

34. "Through the Vortex of a Cyclone."
    a. *Cornhill Magazine* 3rd Series, No. 137 (November 1907): 643-63.
    b. *Putnam's Monthly* 3, No. 2 (November 1907): 193-204.
    c. In A.11.
    d. *Strand Magazine* No. 351 (March 1920): 282-83 (as "A Cyclonic Storm: The Dreaded 'Tiger of the Oceans'"; abridged).
    e. In A.44.
    f. In A.61.
    g. In A.62.

    Dramatic account of the passing of the "four-masted bark *Golconda*" through a cyclone. Often believed to be a work of fiction. It contains 7 photos of the ship and of the cyclone itself, taken by Hodgson.

35. "Totems for Authors."
    a. *Author* 16, No. 5 (February 1906): 160.

36. "Totems for Authors."
    a. *Author* 16, No. 9 (June 1906): 276.

37. "The Trade in Sea Apprentices."
    a. *Nautical Magazine* 76, No. 3 (September 1906): 233-37 (unsigned).
    b. In A.47.
    c. In A.61.

    A fictitious dialogue stressing the poor pay for ships' apprentices and their hard life.

38. "Two Letters."
    a. *Arkham Sampler* 1, No. 2 (September 1983): 12-14.

    Letters to Arthur St. John Adcock, 14 March 1917 and 2 August 1916.

39. "When the Sea Gets Cross."
    a. In A.61.

40. "Writers of Ghost Stories."
    a. In A.49.
       Fragment of an essay on supernatural fiction.

iii. *Poetry*

1. "After the Years."
   a. In A.60.

2. "Amanda Panda."
   a. In A.14.

3. "Ballade."
   a. In A.60.

4. "Beyond the Dawning."
   a. In A.15.
   b. In A.22.
   c. In A.48.
   d. In A.60.

5. "Billy Ben."
   a. In A.14.a, c.

6. "Boy Billy Boo-Hoo."
   a. In A.61.

7. "The Bridge of Melody."
   a. In A.60.

8. "Bring Out Your Dead."
   a. In A.8.
   b. In A.60.

9. "The Calling of the Sea."
   a. In A.15.
   b. In A.22.
   c. In A.48.
   d. In A.60.

10. "The Conqueror."
    a. In A.61.

11. "Conquest."
    a. In A.60.

12. "The Cynic in Hell."
    a. In A.60.

13. "Death."
    a. In A.60.

14. "The Death Cry of Young Genius."
    a. In A.60.

15. "Down the Long Coast."
    a. In A.15.
    b. In A.22.
    c. In A.48.
    d. In A.61.

16. "Drowned."
    a. In A.60.

17. "Dying."
    a. In A.60.

18. "Eight Bells."
    a. In A.15.
    b. In A.22.
    c. In A.48.

19. "Fame."
    a. In A.60.

20. "Farewell."
    a. In A.60.
    b. In A.62.

21. "Foot Falls."
    a. In A.60.

22. "The Fruit of the Tree of Life."
    a. In A.61.

23. "Gone."
    a. In A.60.

24. "Grey Seas Are Dreaming of My Death."
    a. In A.8.
    b. In A.11.
    c. In A.15.
    d. In A.22.

      e. In A.48.
      f. In A.60.
      g. In A.62.

25. "Grief."
    a. In A.2.
    b. In A.48.
    c. In A.60.

26. "Gun Drill."
    a. In A.61.

27. "The Heart Cry."
    a. In A.61.

28. "The Hell! Oo! Chaunty."
    a. In A.3.
    b. In A.17.
    c. In A.48.

29. "How It Happened."
    a. In A.60.

30. "The Hunger Land."
    a. In A.60.

31. "I Come Again."
    a. In A.8.
    b. In A.60.

32. "I Have Borne My Lord a Son."
    a. In A.8.
    b. In A.60.

33. "If I Were Dead."
    a. In A.60.

34. "In Eternity."
    a. In A.60.

35. "Inspiration."
    a. In A.60.

36. "Listening."
    a. In A.8.
    b. In A.60.

37. "Little Feet of Maggie Lee."
    a. In A.61.

38. "Little Garments."
    a. In A.8.
    b. In A.60.

39. "Lost."
    a. In A.5.
    b. In A.15.
    c. In A.22.
    d. *Arkham Collector* No. 5 (Summer 1969): 134.
    e. In A.48.
    f. In A.60.
    *g. In Jo Fletcher, ed. *Off the Coastal Path: Dark Poems of the Seaside.* Hornsea, UK: PS Publishing, 2010, p. ?.

40. "Love."
    a. In A.60.

41. "Love Song to the Dead."
    a. In A.60.

42. "Madre Mia."
    a. In A.1.
    b. In A.48.
    c. In A.60.

43. "Mimosa."
    a. In Jonathan Bacon and Steve Troyanovich, ed. *Omniumgathum: An Anthology of Verse by Top Authors in the Field of Fantasy.* Lamoni, IA: Stygian Isle Press, 1976, p. 35.
    b. In A.48.

44. "Monsieur les Vidoques."
    a. In A.61.

45. "The Morning Lands."
    a. In A.15.
    b. In A.22.
    c. In A.48.
    d. In A.60.

46. "Mors Deorum."
    a. In A.60.

47. "My Babe, My Babe."
   a. In A.8.
   b. In A.60.

48. "My Son! My Son!"
   a. In A.60.

49. "The Mystery of Life."
   a. In A.60.

50. "Nevermore."
   a. In Jonathan Bacon and Steve Troyanovich, ed. *Omniumgathum: An Anthology of Verse by Top Authors in the Field of Fantasy.* Lamoni, IA: Stygian Isle Press, 1976, p. 57.
   b. In A.48.
   c. In A.61.

51. "Night."
   a. In A.60.

52. "Night and Day."
   a. In A.60.

53. "The Night Wind."
   a. In A.8.
   b. In A.60.

54. "O Parent Sea!"
   a. In A.8.
   b. In A.60.

55. "The Ocean of Eternity."
   a. In A.61.

56. "Ode to a Vase."
   a. In A.60.

57. "Old-Time Hands."
   a. In A.60.

58. "One Nation Are We."
   a. In A.61.

59. "Over There."
   a. In A.60.

60. "Passing."
    a. In A.60.

61. "Pillars of the Empire."
    a. In A.61.

62. "The Pirates."
    a. In A.13.
    b. In A.15.
    c. In A.22.
    d. In A.48.

63. "The Place of Storms."
    a. In A.15.
    b. In A.22.
    c. In A.48.
    d. In A.60.
    e. In A.62.

64. "Rest."
    a. In A.15.
    b. In A.22.
    c. In A.48.
    d. In A.60.

65. "Scent."
    a. In A.60.

66. "Scraps! Scraps!! Scraps!!!"
    a. In A.61.

67. "The Sea of Silence."
    a. In A.60.

68. "Sea Revelry."
    a. In A.61.

69. "The Ship."
    a. In A.13.
    b. In A.15.
    c. In A.22.
    d. In A.48.

70. "The Shore of Desolation."
    a. In A.60.

71. "The Smoke of the Blast."
    a. In A.60.

72. "The Sobbing of the Freshwater."
    a. In A.8.
    b. *London Magazine* 28, No. 3 (May 1912): 374.
    c. In A.15.
    d. In A.22.
    e. In A.48.
    f. In A.60.

73. "The Song of the Great Bull Whale."
    a. In A.8.
    b. *Grand Magazine* No. 85 (March 1912): 57.
    c. In A.11.
    d. In A.15.
    e. In A.22.
    f. In A.48.

74. "Song of the Ship."
    a. In A.15.
    b. In A.22.
    c. In A.48.
    d. In A.60.

75. "Southern Lights."
    a. In A.60.

76. "Speak Well of the Dead."
    a. In A.8.
    b. In Jonathan Bacon and Steve Troyanovich, ed. *Omniumgathum: An Anthology of Verse by Top Authors in the Field of Fantasy.* Lamoni, IA: Stygian Isle Press, 1976, p. 33.
    c. In A.48.
    d. In A.60.

77. "Storm."
    a. In A.15.
    b. In A.22.
    c. In A.18.
    d. In A.60.

78. "Thou and I."
    a. In A.60.

79. "Thou Living Sea."
   a. In A.15.
   b. In A.22.
   c. In A.48.
   d. In A.60.
   e. In A.62.

80. "Thou, Who Art Jesus' Mother!"
   a. In A.60.

81. "The Thresher."
   a. In A.60.

82. "Thy Wandering Soul."
   a. In A.60.

83. "To God."
   a. In A.60.

84. "To My Father."
   a. In A.2.
   b. *Arkham Collector* No. 5 (Summer 1969): 136.
   c. In A.48 (as "Shoon of the Dead").
   d. In A.60 (as "The Shoon of the Dead").

85. "Tramp! Tramp!"
   a. In A.61.

86. "The Voice of One Crying in the Wilderness."
   a. In A.60.

87. *The Voice of the Ocean.*
   a. In A.16.
   b. In A.22.
   c. In A.48.

88. "Who Make Their Bed in Deep Waters."
   *a. *Fantasy Crossroads* No. 12 (November 1977): ?.

89. "The World of Dreams."
   a. In A.60.

90. "Wrecked."
   a. In A.60.

91. [Untitled.]
   a. In A.60.

C. Media Adaptations

1. "The Whistling Room."
   a. In *The Pepsi-Cola Playhouse*. Revue Productions, 18 July 1954. ABC-TV. Adapted by Howard J. Green. Directed by Axel Gruenberg. Starring Alan Napier, Barbara Bestar, and Edmund Purdom.

2. "The Voice in the Night."
   a. In *Suspicion*. Shamley Productions, 24 March 1958. NBC-TV. Adapted by Stirling Silliphant. Directed by Arthur Hiller. Starring James Coburn, James Donald, and Patrick Macnee.

3. *Matango*.
   a. Japan: Toho Company, 1963. Color, 89 minutes. Adapted by Takeshi Kimura and Shinichi Hoshi. Directed by Ishiro Honda. Starring Akira Kubo, Kumi Mizuno, and Hiroshi Hoizumi.

   Adaptation of "The Voice in the Night." Released in the United States under the title *Attack of the Mushroom People*.

4. "The Horse of the Invisible."
   a. In *The Rivals of Sherlock Holmes*. Pearson Television International, 18 October 1971. Thames TV. Adapted by Philip Mackie. Directed by Alan Cooke. Starring Donald Pleasence, Tony Steedman, and Michele Dotrice.

5. "The Case of the Whistling Room."
   a. In *Dark Ventures Presents Two Thrilling Radio Dramas*. Minneapolis, MN: Fedogan & Bremer/Equinox Productions, 1979. (Audio cassette)

   Adaptation of "The Whistling Room."

6. *The House on the Borderland*.
   a. West Warwick, RI: Necronomicon Press/A-Typical Productions, [c. 1994]. Audiobook. Read by Vince Ceglie. Produced by Wayne Haigh. Liner notes by S. T. Joshi. Cover art by Jason Eckhardt. 4 cassettes (5 hours).

7. *The House on the Borderland*.
   a. New York: DC Comics, 2000. Graphic Novel. Adapted by Richard Corben and Simon Revelstroke. Illustrated by Richard Corben. Introduction by Alan Moore.

II. Hodgson in Translation

A. Breton

i. Books

1. *Ar morgezeg.*
   a. n.p.: Preder, 2012. Tr. Ronan An Deroff.
       Contents: Preface, by Peter Tremayne; "Ar morgezeg" ("Sea Horses").
       Notes. Illustrations by Jennifer Day.

B. Czech

i. Books

1. *Dům na rozhraní.*
   a. Brno: AF 167, 1997. Tr. Jan Jam Oščádal and Jana Oščádalová.
       Translation of *The House on the Borderland.*

ii. Short Stories

1. "The Baumoff Explosive."
   a. In Douglas A. Anderson, ed. *Otcové prstenu: Kořeny moderní fantasy před Tolkienem.* Prague: Baronet, 2004, pp. ?–? (as"Výbušnina Baumoff"; tr. Michael David). [Translation of *Tales Before Tolkien* (I.B.i.5.f).]

2. "The Haunted *Pampero.*"
   a. In Peter Haining, ed. *Krypty a draci.* Prague: Talpress, 2004, pp. ?–? (as"Smolné Pampero"; tr. Jan Kantůrek). [Translation of *Tales of Dungeons and Dragons* (I.B.i.46.d).]

3. "The Voice in the Night."
   a. In Patricia Vandenberg, ed. *Hlas krve.* Prague: IŽ, 1996, pp. ?–? (as"Hlas ve tmě"; tr. ?).

4. "The Whistling Room."
   a. In Alfred Hitchcock, ed. *Strašidla na dobrou noc.* Prague: ABR, 1995, pp. ?–? (as"Hlas z temnot"; tr. Ivana Peroutková). [Translation of *Alfred Hitchcock Presents: Stories for Late at Night* (I.B.i.107.f).]
   b. In Ondřej Müller, ed. *Přízraky, zázraky & spol.* Prague: Albatros, 2007, pp. ?–? (as"Hvízdavý pokoj"; tr. Jan Čermák).

C. Danish

i. Books

1. *Et fund.*
   a. Næstved: Tryk Central Trykkeriet, 1983. Tr. Bjarne Nielsen.
      Translation of "The Find."

D. Dutch

i. Books

1. *De Stem in de nacht: Griezelverhalen.*
   a. Utrecht: A. W. Bruna & Zoon, 1969. Tr. L. Winick and R. Germeraad.
      Contents: "Het Verlaten Schip" ("The Derelict") and "De Stem in de nacht" ("The Voice in the Night") (tr. L. Winick); *Het huis op de drempel can de oneindigheid (The House on the Borderland)* (tr. R. Germeraad).

2. *Carnacki, de spokenjager.*
   a. Breda: Brabantia Nostra, 1977. Tr. Jef Panken.
      Contents: "De onzichtbare dader" ("The Thing Invisible"); "De poort van het monster" ("The Gateway of the Monster"); "Het huis tussen de laurierheesters" ("The House among the Laurels"); "De gierende kamer" ("The Whistling Room"); "Het geheim van de raadselachtige bezoeker" ("The Searcher of the End House"); "Het paard van de onzichtbare" ("The Horse of the Invisible"); "Het spookschip Jarvee" ("The Haunted *Jarvee*"); "De vondst" ("The Find"); "Het vreselijke varken" ("The Hog").
      Notes. Translation of *Carnacki, the Ghost-Finder*.

ii. *Short Stories*

1 "The Derelict."
   a. In Tonke Dracht, ed. *Water is gevaarlijk*. The Hague: Leopold, 1977, pp. ?-? (as "Het wrak"; tr. anon.).
   b. In Erik Lankester, ed. *De griezeligste verhalen*. Amsterdam: Loeb, 1981, pp. ?-? (as "Het scheepswrak"; tr. anon.).

2. "The Voice in the Night."
   a. In [Unsigned, ed.] *Verhalen die Hitchcock koos*. Utrecht: Spectrum, 1959, pp. ?-? (as "De stem in de nacht"; tr. anon.).
   b. *Humo* No. 1558 (16 July 1970): ?-? (as "De stem in de nacht"; tr. ?).
   c. In Erik Lankester, ed. *Van E. A. Poe tot Roald Dahl: De 50 beste griezelverhalen*. n.p.: Publiboek-Baart, 1980, pp. ?-? (as "De stem in de nacht"; tr. ?).

    d. In Erik Lankester and Peter Loeb, ed. *De beste griezelverhalen*. n.p.: The Golden Label (K-Tel), 1982, pp. ?-? (as "De stem in de nacht"; tr. ?).
    e. In Alfred Hitchcock, ed. *Verhalen die ik niet durde te verfilmen*. Amsterdam: Loeb, 1984, pp. ?-? (as "De stem in de nacht"; tr. Tilly Schell). [Translation of *Alfred Hitchcock Presents: Stories They Wouldn't Let Me Do on TV* (I.B.i.102.k).]
3. "The Whistling Room."
    a. In Aart C. Prins, ed. *Het monster in de lift en andere griezelverhalen*. Utrecht: A. W. Bruna & Zoon, 1966, pp. 19-42 (as "De fluitende kamer"; tr. C. A. G. van den Broek).
    b. In Erik Lankester, ed. *Van E. A. Poe tot D. Hammett*. Amsterdam: Loeb, 1981, pp. ?-? (as "De fluitende kamer"; tr. ?).

E. Estonian

i. Books

1. *Viirastuspiraadid.*
    a. Tartu: Fantaasia, 2004. Tr. Tarmo Vaarpuu.
        Translation of *The Ghost Pirates*.

F. Finnish

i. Books

1. *Kauhujen talo.*
    a. Helsinki: Jalava, 1989. Tr. Kari Nenonen.
        Translation of *The House on the Borderland*.

ii. Shorter Works

1. "The Derelict."
    a. In Markku Sadalahto, ed. *Amerikkalaiset aaveet*. Helsinki: WSOY, 1994, pp. ?-? (as "Hylky"; tr. unknown).
2. "The Goddess of Death."
    a. *Aamulehti* (6 July 1910): ?-?.
3. "The Valley of Lost Children."
    a. In Richard Dalby, ed. *Suuri kummituskirja*. Hyvinkää: Book Studio, 1993, pp. ?-? (as "Menetettyjen lasten laakso"; tr. Pertti Koskela). [Translation of *The Mammoth Book of Ghost Stories* (I.B.i.100.d).]

4. "The Voice in the Night."
   a. In Markku Sadalahto, ed. *Haudantakaisia*. Helsinki: Jalava, 1994, pp. 228-41 (as "Ääni yössä"; tr. Osmo Saarinen).

G. French

i. Books

1. *La Chose dans les algues.*
   a. Paris: Editions Planète, 1968. Tr. Jacques Baron.

   Translation of *Deep Waters*.

2. *La Maison au bord du monde; Les Canots de "Glen Carrig"; Les Pirates fantômes.*
   a. Paris: Editions Opta, 1971. Tr. Jacques Parsons.

   Contents: *The House on the Borderland, The Boats of the "Glen Carrig"*, and *The Ghost Pirates*.

3. *Carnacki et les fantômes.*
   a. Paris: Librairie de Champs-Elysées, 1977. Tr. François Truchaud.
   b. Paris: Nouvelles Editions Oswald, 1982.
   c. Paris: Union Générale d'Editions (10/18), 1995.

   Contents: "Hodgson ou la quête du surnaturel," by François Truchaud; "La Porte" ("The Gateway of the Monster"); "La Maison parmi les lauriers" ("The House among the Laurels"); "La Chambre qui sifflait" ("The Whistling Room"); "Le Mystère de la maison hantée" ("The Searcher of the End House"); "Le Cheval de l'invisible" ("The Horse of the Invisible"); "Le Jarvee" ("The Haunted *Jarvee*"); "Le Verrat" ("The Hog").
   Translations of seven stories from *Carnacki, the Ghost-Finder*.

4. *La Maison au bord du monde.*
   a. Paris: Livre de Poche, 1977. Tr. Jacques Parsons.
   b. Paris: Nouvelles Editions Oswald, 1988.
   c. Rennes: Terre de Brume, 1999.
   d. n.p.: Couverture Rigide, 2010.

   Translation of *The House on the Borderland*.

5. *Le Pays de la nuit.*
   a. Paris: Editions Opta, 1977. Tr. Jean-Pierre Pugi.
   b. Paris: Nouvelles Editions Oswald, 1982. 2 vols.
   c. Rennes: Terre de Brume, 2005.

   Translation of *The Night Land*.

6. *Les Pirates fantômes.*
   a. Paris: Livre de Poche, 1978. Tr. Jacques Parsons.
   b. Paris: Nouvelles Editions Oswald, 1986.

    c.   Rennes: Terre de Brume, 2002. [Translation revised by Patrick Marcel.]

    Translation of *The Ghost Pirates*. The 2004 edition has a preface by Brian Stableford.

7. *Les Canots du "Glen Carrig."*
   a. Paris: Nouvelles Editions Oswald, 1979. Tr. Jacques Parsons.
   b. Saint-Pierre-lès Nemours: Eurédif/Playboy, 1984.
   c. Rennes: Terre de Brume, 2004.

   Translation of *The Ghost Pirates*. With introduction, "Hodgson ou la voix de l'océan," by François Truchaud.

8. *La Chose dans les algues; Deux Adventures de Carnacki.*
   a. Paris: Nouvelles Editions Oswald, 1979. Tr. Jacques Baron, François Truchaud, and Habby Sahl.
   b. Dinan: Terre de Brume, 2007.

   Contents: "W. H. Hodgson, celui qui venait de la mer," by François Truchaud; "Préface," by Jacques Baron; "Les Chevaux marins" ("Sea-Horses"); "L'Épave" ("The Derelict"); "La 'Chose' dans les algues" ("The Thing in the Weeds"); "De la mer immobile" ("From the Tideless Sea"); "Le Cinquième Message" ("More News from the Homebird"); "L'Île de Ud" ("The Island of the Ud"); "La Voix dans la nuit" ("The Voice in the Night"); "L'Aventure du promontoire" ("Captain Jat—The Adventure of the Headland"); "Le Mystère de l'épave" ("The Mystery of the Derelict"); "Le Dernier Voyage du Shamraken" ("The *Shamraken* Homeward-Bounder"); "Le Bateau de pierre" ("The Stone Ship"); "L'Équipage du Lancing" ("The Crew of the *Lansing*"); "Les Habitants de l'îlot du milieu" ("The Habitants of Middle Islet"); "Le Monstre de l'île aux algues" ("The Voice in the Dawn"); "La Chose invisible" ("The Thing Invisible"); "Bibliophilie" ("The Find").
       Translation of *Deep Waters* plus two stories from *Carnacki, the Ghost-Finder*. The first thirteen stories are translated by Baron; "La Chose invisible" and "Bibliophilie" are translated by Truchaud; "Le Monstre de l'île aux algues" is translated by Sahl.

9. *L'Horreur tropicale: Nouvelles.*
   a. Paris: Nouvelles Editions Oswald, 1983. Tr. François Truchaud.
   b. Rennes: Terre de Brume, 2010.

   Contents: "L'Horreur tropicale" ("A Tropical Horror"); "Une Voix dans la tempête" ("Out of the Storm"); "A la recherche du *Graiken*" ("The Finding of the *Graiken*"); "Eloi eloi lama sabachthani" ("The Baumoff Explosive"); "Le Réservoir de la peur" ("The Terror of the Water-Tank"); "L'Albatross" ("The Albatross"); "Le Fantôme du Lady Shannon" ("The Haunting of the *Lady Shannon*").
       Translation of *Out of the Storm*.

10. *Les Spectres Pirates et six autres récits fantastiques.*
   a. Amiens: Encrage, 1988.

   Contents: "Chronologie" (chronology of Hodgson's life); "Les Espaces inquets de William Hope Hodgson" by Max Duperray; "Introduction" (unsigned); "Le Passager du 'Pampero'" ("The Haunted 'Pampero'"); "Carnacki, le chasseur de fantômes" ("Carnacki, the Ghost-Finder" [abridgement]); "Les Spectres Pirates" ("The Ghost Pirates" [abridgment]); "Le Vaisseau fantôme" ("The Phantom Ship"); "Le Rêve de X" ("The Dream of X"); "La Chambre d'épouvante" ("The Room of Fear"); "Quand s'entrouvre la nuit" ("The Riven Night" [tr. Maurice Lévy]); "Bibliographie" (bibliography of Hodgson works in English and French). All texts, save where indicated, translated by Patrick Marcel.

11. *Carnacki, le chasseur de fantomes.*
   a. Dinan: Terre de Brume, 2008. Tr. Émile Chardome et al.

   Translation of *Carnacki, the Ghost-Finder.*

ii. Shorter Works

1. "The Baumoff Explosive."
   a. *Opta* No. 285 (1977): ?-? (as "Eloi eloi lama sabachthani"; tr. ?).

2. "The Derelict."
   a. In Roland Lacourbe, ed. *Eaux mystérieuses et mers infernales.* Nantes: L'Atalante, 2000, pp. ?-? (as "L'Épave"; tr. ?).

3. "The Gateway of the Monster."
   a. *Revue Belge* 2, No. 5 (1 June 1924): 401-22 (as "La Porte du monstre"'; tr. Emile Chardome).
   b. In Roland Stragliati, ed. *Les Miroirs de la peur.* Paris: Casterman, 1969, pp. ?-? (as "Par là entrait le monstre . . ."; tr. ?).

4. "The Habitants of Middle Islet."
   a. In Jacques Goimard and Roland Stragliati, ed. *Histoires de maléfices.* Paris: Presses Pocket, 1981, pp. ?-? (as "Les Habitants de l'îlot du milieu"; tr. ?).
   b. In Jacques Goimard and Roland Stragliati, ed. *La Grande Anthologie du fantastique.* Paris: Presses de la Cité, 1997, Vol. 3, pp. ?-? (as "Les Habitants de l'îlot du milieu"; tr. ?).

5. "The Hog."
   a. In [Unsigned, ed.] *Histoires d'horreur: Une Anthologie de la revue Weird Tales.* Paris: Opta, 1966, pp. ?-? (as "Le Verrat"; tr. ?).

6. "The Terror of the Water-Tank."
   a. *Fantastik* No. 10 (1982): ?-? (as "Le Réservoir de la peur"; tr. ?).

7. "A Tropical Horror."
   a. *Opta* No. 285 (1977): ?–? ("Horreur tropicale"; tr. ?).
   b. In Christian Grenier, ed. *L'Horreur tropicale et autres récits sur l'océan*. Paris: Gallimard, 1983, pp. ?–? (as "L'Horreur tropicale"; tr. ?).
8. "The Voice in the Night."
   a. In Alfred Hitchcock, ed. *Histoires abominables*. Paris: Presses Pocket, 1979, 1983, 1988, pp. ?–? (as "La Voix dans la nuit"; tr. ?). [Translation of *Alfred Hithcock Presents: Stories They Wouldn't Let Me Do on TV* (I.B.i.102.k).]
9. "The Whistling Room."
   a. In Jean Marc Lofficier, ed. *Weird Tales by Great Masters/Les Grands Maîtres du fantastique*. Paris: Presses Pocket, 2000, 2003, pp. ?–? (as "La Chambre qui sifflait"; tr. ?). [Bilingual edition.]

H. Galician

i. Books

1. *A casa no confín.*
   a. Santiago de Compostela: Urco, 2009. Tr. Tomás González Ahola.
   Translation of *The House on the Borderland*.

I. German

i. Books

1. *Stimme in der Nacht: Unheimliche Geschichten.*
   a. Frankfurt am Main: Insel-Verlag, 1970. Tr. Wulf Teichmann.
   b.1. Frankfurt am Main: Suhrkamp, 1982.
   b.2. Frankfurt am Main: Suhrkamp, 1997.

   Contents: *Die Boote der "Glen Carrig"* (*The Boats of the "Glen Carrig"*); "Die Herrenlose" ("The Derelict"); "Stimme in der Nacht" ("The Voice in the Night"); "Die Crew der Lancing" ("The Crew of the *Lancing*").

2. *Das Haus an der Grenze und andere phantastischen Erzählungen.*
   a. 1. Frankfurt am Main: Insel-Verlag, 1973. Tr. Traude Dienel.
   a. 2. Frankfurt am Main: Suhrkamp, 1985.

   Contents: *Das Haus an der Grenze* (*The House on the Borderland*); "Das pfeifende Zimmer" ("The Whistling Room"); "Der Schicksalsring der Anderson-Familie" ("The Gateway of the Monster"); "Der grunzende Mann" ("The Hog").

3. *Das Nachtland.*
   a. Bergisch Gladbach: Bastei-Verlag Lübbe, 1982. Tr. Annette von Charpentier.
   b. Bergisch Gladbach: Lübbe Verlagsgruppe, 1987.
   Notes. Translation of *The Night Land.*

4. *Geisterpiraten und andere schauerliche Seegeschicten.*
   a. Frankfurt am Main: Suhrkamp, 1987. Tr. Friedrich Polakovics.
   Contents: *Geisterpiraten* (*The Ghost Pirates*); "Das Ding im Seetang" ("The Thing in the Weeds"); "Das steinerne Schiff" ("The Stone Ship").

5. *Das Haus an der Grenze.*
   a. Leipzig: Festa, 2004. Tr. Michael Siefener.
   Notes. Translation of *The House on the Borderland*. Contains a foreword by Brian Stableford.

6. *Das Rufen des Meeres: Gedichte.*
   a. Hamburg: rough art, 2004. Tr. Denis Vidinski.
   Contents: "Das Rufen des Meeres" ("The Calling of the Sea"); "Die Stimme des Ozeans" (*The Voice of the Ocean*); "Graue Meere träumen von meinem Tode" ("Grey Seas Are Dreaming of My Death").
   Notes. Limited to 100 numbered copies.

7. *Carnacki, der Geisterfinder.*
   a. Norderstedt: Books on Demand, 2007. Tr. Martin Clauss.
   Translation of *Carnacki, the Ghost-Finder.*

ii. Shorter Works

1. *The Boats of the "Glen Carrig."*
   a. In [Hans Joachim Alpers, ed.] *Dämonen an Bord*. Erfstadt: Area, 2005, pp. 394-586 (as *Die Boote der "Glen Carrig"*; tr. Wulf Teichmann).

2. "The Crew of the *Lancing*."
   a. In Klaus Seehafer, ed. *Im Mahlstrom des Grauens*. Leer: Leda, 2001, pp. 203-14 (as "Die Crew der 'Lancing'"; tr. Wulf Teichmann).
   b. In [Hans Joachim Alpers, ed.] *Dämonen an Board*. Erfstadt: Area, 2005, pp. 601-11 (as "Die Crew der 'Lancing'"; tr. Friedrich Polakovics).

3. "Demons of the Sea."
   a. *daedalos* No. 8 (Autumn 1999): 52-67 (as "Dämonen des Meeres"; tr. Hubert Katzmarz).

4. "The Derelict."
    a. In [Hans Joachim Alpers, ed.] *Dämonen an Bord*. Erfstadt: Area, 2005, pp. 555-85 (as "Die Herrenlose"; tr. Wulf Teichmann).

5. "The Gateway of the Monster."
    a. In Roger Elwood and Vic Ghidalia, ed. *Zwischen Mitternacht und Jenseits*. Rastatt: Erich Pabel Verlag, 1978, pp. 88-112 (as "Das graue Zimmer"; tr. Annegret Gross-Hermanns). [Translation of *Horror Hunters* (I.B.i.36.c).]

6. *The Ghost Pirates*.
    a. In [Hans Joachim Alpers, ed.] *Dämonen an Bord*. Erfstadt: Area, 2005, pp. 231-377 (as *Geisterpiraten*; tr. Friedrich Polakovics).

7. "The Habitants of Middle Islet."
    a. In August Derleth, ed. *Rendezvous mit dem Würgeengel*. Rastatt: Erich Pabel Verlag, 1976, pp. 7-25 (as "Das Wrack am Höllengrund"; tr. Werner Gronwald). [Translation of *Dark Mind, Dark Heart* (I.B.i.44.a).]

8. "The Haunted *Jarvee*."
    a. In Frank Festa, ed. *Die Pflanzen des Dr. Cinderella*. Leipzig: Festa, 2007, pp. ?-? (as "Der Spuk auf der Jarvee"; tr. ?).

9. "The Horse of the Invisible."
    a. In Hugh Greene, ed. *Die Rivalen des Sherlock Holmes*. Düsseldorf: Marion von Schröder, 1971, pp. 318-50 (as "Das Geisterpferd"; tr. ?). [Translation of *The Rivals of Sherlock Holmes* (I.B.i.51.e).]
    b. In Hugh Greene, ed. *Die Rivalen des Sherlock Holmes 2*. Frankfurt am Main: Fischer, 1974, pp. 118-44 (as "Das Geisterpferd"; tr. ?). [Abridged translation of *The Rivals of Sherlock Holmes* (I.B.i.51.e).]
    c. In [Unsigned, ed.] *Die unheimlichsten Gespenstergeschichten*. Vienna: Tosa, 1978, pp. 12-39 (as "Das Geisterpferd"; tr. ?).
    d. In Hugh Greene, ed. *Der rote Seidenschal und andere spannende Detektivgeschichten des 19. Jahrhunderts*. Eltville: Rheingauer Verlagsgesellschaft, 1980, pp. 327-59 (as "Das Geisterpferd"; tr. ?). [Translation of *The Rivals of Sherlock Holmes* (I.B.i.51.e).]
    e. In [Unsigned, ed.] *Haus im Schilf und andere Gespenstergeschichten*. Vienna: Carl Ueberreuter, 1988, pp. 12-39 (as "Das Geisterpferd"; tr. ?).

10. "The Inn of the Black Crow."
    a. In Mike Ashley, ed. *Räuber, Schurken, Lumpenpack*. Bergisch Gladbach: Bastei-Lübbe, 1998; Erfstadt: Area, 2004, pp. 509-25 (as "Das Wirtshaus zur schwarzen Krähe"; tr. Bettina Albrod). [Translation of *The Mammoth Book of Historical Detectives* (I.B.i.58.c).]

11. "The Island of the Ud."
    a. *Omen* No. 2 (2005): 192-214 (as "Die Insel des Ud"; tr. Andreas Diesel).

12. "The Searcher of the End House."
    a. In [Michael Görden, ed.] *Die besten englischen Schauergeschichten*. Bergisch Gladbach: Bastei-Lübbe, 1981, pp. 259-86 (tr. Rudolf Mühlstrasser).

13. "The Thing in the Weeds."
    a. In [Hans Joachim Alpers, ed.] *Dämonen an Bord*. Erfstadt: Area, 2005, pp. 377-93 (as "Das Ding im Seetang"; tr. Friedrich Polakovics).

14. "A Tropical Horror."
    a. In Joachim Körber, ed. *Das dritte Buch des Horrors*. Munich: Wilhelm Heyne, 1992, pp. 59-72 (as "Tropischer Schrecken"; tr. Joachim Körber).
    b. In Joachim Körber, ed. *Abgründe*. Bern: Scherz, 1996, pp. 51-74 (as "Tropischer Schrecken"; tr. Joachim Körber).

15. "The Voice in the Night."
    a. In Ingrid and Walter Spiegel, ed. *Ullstein Kriminalmagazin 15*. Frankfurt am Main: Ullstein, 1969, pp. 43-51 (as "Die Stimme aus der Nacht"; tr. ?).
    b. In Lothar Sauer, ed. *Die Geisterkogge*. Freiburg: Herder, 1970, pp. 217-37 (as "Der Pilzwald"; tr. Lothar Sauer).
    c. In [Unsigned, ed.] *Die phantastischen Fantasy-Geschichten*. Vienna: Tosa, 1985, pp. 204-19 (as "Stimme in der Nacht"; tr. Wulf Teichmann).
    d. In Barbara Zoschke, ed. *Gruselgeschichten*. Bindlach: Loewes, 1996, pp. 54-75 (as "Der Pilzwald"; tr. Lothar Sauer).
    e. In Angelika Feilhauer, ed. *Grusel-Omnibus*. Munich: Bertelsmann Jugendbuchverlag, 1998, pp. 47-64 (as "Die Stimme in der Nacht"; tr. Angelika Feilhauer).
    f. In Frank Festa, ed. *Necrophobia–Meister der Angst*. Leipzig: Festa, 2005, pp. 17-33 (as "Die Stimme in der Nacht"; tr. Andreas Diesel).
    g. In [Hans Joachim Alpers, ed.] *Dämonen an Bord*. Erfstadt: Area, 2005, pp. 586-600 (as "Stimme in der Nacht"; tr. Wulf Teichmann).

16. "The Whistling Room."
    a. In Manfred Kluge, ed. *Gespenstergeschichten aus England*. Muncih: Wilhelm Heyne, 1978, pp. 86-105 (as "Das pfeifende Zimmer"; tr. Traude Dienel).

J. Greek

i. Books

1. *To spiti tīs avyssou.*
   a. Athens: Ōrora, 1988. Tr. Giorgos Balanos.
      Translation of *The House on the Borderland*.

2. *To spiti sta synora tou kosmou.*
   a. Athens: Portokali, 2007. Tr. Tetī Sōlou.
      Translation of *The House on the Borderland*.

K. Italian

i. Books

1. *La casa sull'abisso.*
   a. Milan: Mondadori, 1963. Tr. Carlo Fruttero and Franco Lucentini.
      Notes. Translation of *The House on the Borderland*.

2. *Naufragio nell'ignoto.*
   a. Rome: Fanucci, 1974. Tr. Alfredo Pollini.
   b. Rome: Fanucci, 1989.
   c. Milan: Magenes Editoriale, 2011.

      Contents: "Introduzione: Il mare e i suoi simboli nella letteratura fantastica," by Gianfranco de Turris and Sebastiano Fusco; *Naufragio nell'ignoto* (*The Boats of the "Glen Carrig"*).

      Notes. Futuro: Biblioteca di Fantascienza 6. Cover art for the 1974 edition by Giauco Cartocci.

3. *Carnacki, cacciatore di spettri.*
   a. Milan: SIAD, 1978. Tr. Paolo Busnelli.

      Contents: "La cosa invisibile" ("The Thing Invisible"); "Il varco del mostro" ("The Gateway of the Monster"); "La casa tra i lauri" ("The House among the Laurels"); "La stanza che fischiava" ("The Whistling Room"); "L'inquilino dell'ultima casa" ("The Searcher of the End House"); "Il cavallo invisibile" ("The Horse of the Invisible"); "Il 'Jarvee' infestato" ("The Haunted *Jarvee*"); "Il ritrovamento" ("The Find"); "Il maiale" ("The Hog").

      Notes. Translation of *Carnacki, the Ghost-Finder*.

4. *La casa sull'abisso e altri racconti.*
   a. Rome: Fanucci, 1985. Tr. Riccardo Valla and Gianni Pilo.

      Contents: *La casa sull'abisso* (*The House on the Borderland*); "Middle Islet" ("The Habitants of Middle Islet"); "Il ritrovamento della *Graiken*" ("The Finding of

the *Graiken*"); "La tempesta" ("Out of the Storm"); "Terrore ai tropici" ("A Tropical Horror"); Domenico Cammarota, "Gli abissi di Hodgson."

Notes. I miti di Cthulhu 2. Cover art by Tim White.

5. *I pirati fantasma.*
    a. Rome: Fanucci, 1986. Tr. Daniela Galdo and Gianni Pilo.
    b. Rome: Campagnia del Fantastico (Newton), 1994.
    c. Milan: Magenes Editoriale, 2012.

    Contents: "William Hope Hodgson: Vita e opere," by Gianni Pilo; *I pirati fantasma* (*The Ghost Pirates*); "Il terrore della cisterna" ("The Terror of the Water-Tank"); "Un incubo in letteratura: *The House on the Borderland*," by Giorgio Giorgi.

    Notes. I miti di Cthulhu 8. Cover art for the 1986 edition by Boris Vallejo (uncredited).

6. *L'orrore del mare.*
    a. Rome: Newton Compton, 1993. Tr. Gianni Pilo.

    Contents: "Gli incubi marini di Hodgson," by Gianni Pilo; "Il mostro" ("A Tropical Horror"); "Lamie" ("The Habitants of Middle Islet"); "Il mare" ("Out of the Storm"); "La bestia orribile" ("The Terror of the Water-Tank"); "Dio, dio, perché non mi aiuti?" ("The Baumoff Explosive"); "Il mare di Sargassi" ("The Finding of the *Graiken*").

7. *La casa sull'abisso.*
    a. Rome: Campagnia del Fantastico (Newton), January 1994. Tr. Gianni Pilo.
    b. Rome: Gruppo Editoriale Newton, September 2003.

    Notes. Translation of *The House on the Borderland*. The 2003 edition contains Pilo's "Gli incubi marini di Hodgson" (from item 6) as an introduction. Cover art for the 2003 edition by Alessandro Tiburtini.

8. *La terra dell'eterna notte.*
    a. Rome: Fanucci, 1996. Tr. Ornella Ranieri Davide.

    Notes. Translation of *The Night Land*. I Maestri dell'Orrore IX. The novel appears to be abridged.

9. *La casa sull'abisso a eltri storie del terrore.*
    a. Milan: Arnoldo Mondadori Editore, December 1996. Tr. Maria Barbara Piccioli.

    Contents: "Nota editoriale," by Giuseppi Lippi; "Presentazione," by H. P. Lovecraft; "Vita eroica di William Hope Hodgson," by Alex Voglino; "Nota bibliografica," by Pietro Guarriello; *La casa sull'abisso* (*The House on the Borderland*); "Il terrore della cisterna" ("The Terror of the Water-Tank"); "La tempesta" ("Out of the Storm"); "Eloi, Eloi lama sabachthani" ("The Baumoff Explosive"); "L'assedio e il viaggio," by Gianfranco De Turris.

Notes. Classici Urania 237. Cover art by Jacopo Bruno.

10. *Carnacki, l'indagatore dell'occulto*. Ed. Gabriele Scalessa. Tr. ?.
    a. S. Cesario di Lecce: Manni, 2013. {needs to be indexed}
    Notes. Translation of *Carnacki the Ghost-Finder*.

ii. Shorter Works

1. "The Albatross."
    a. In Gianni Pilo, ed. *La saga di Cthulhu*. Rome: Fanucci, 1986, pp. 45–62 (as "L'albatro"; tr. Daniela Galdo and Gianni Pilo).
    b. In Antonio Bellomi, ed. *Horror Story n. 4*. Milan: Garden, 1990, pp. 83–99 (as "L'albatros"; tr. Mida).
    c. In Gianni Pilo and Sebastiano Fusco, ed. *Storie dell'orrore*. Rome: Newton, July 1999, pp. 164–73 (as "L'albatro"; tr. Gianni Pilo).

2. "The Baumoff Explosive."
    a. In Gianni Pilo, ed. *Il segno di Cthulhu*. Rome: Fanucci, 1986, pp. 73–91 (as "Eloi eloi lama sabachthani"; tr. Maria Teresa Tirone).
    b. In Antonio Bellomi, ed. *Horror Story n. 4*. Milan: Garden, 1990, pp. 47–65 (as "Eloi eloi lama sabachthani"; tr. Mida).
    c. In Gianni Pilo and Sebastiano Fusco, ed. *Storie di diavoli*. Rome: Newton, June 1997, pp. 49–59 (as "Dio, dio, perché non mi aiuti?"; tr. Gianni Pilo).

3. "Bullion."
    a. In Antonio Bellomi, ed. *Delitti impossibili*. Milan: Garden, 1993, pp. 81–95 (as "Verghe d'oro!"; tr. Stefania Carimati).

4. "Captain Jat—The Adventure of the Headland."
    a. In Antonio Bellomi, ed. *Horror Story n. 9*. Milan: Garden, 1991, pp. 3–27 (as "L'avventura del promontorio"; tr. Patrizia Tosi).

5. "The Crew of the *Lancing*."
    a. In Antonio Bellomi, ed. *Horror Story n. 9*. Milan: Garden, 1991, pp. 91–101 (as "L'equipaggio del *Lancing*"; tr. Patrizia Tosi).

6. "The Derelict."
    a. In Antonio Bellomi, ed. *Horror Story n. 7*. Milan: Garden, 1991, pp. 25–51 (as "Il relitto"; tr. Stefania Carimati).

7. "The Exploits of Captain Gault."
    a. In Pico Tamburini, ed. *La polizia indaga: Racconti polizieschi*. Florence: Fallechi, 1958, pp. ?–? (as "L'esca di Captain Gault"; tr. ?).
    It is not clear which story has been translated.

8. "The Finding of the *Graiken*."
   a. In Antonio Bellomi, ed. *Horror Story* n. 4. Milan: Garden, 1990, pp. 21–46 (as "Alla ricerca della *Graiken*"; tr. Mida).
   b. In Gianni Pilo, ed. *I più raccapriccianti racconti dell'orrore*. Rome: Newton, 2006, pp. 46–59 (as "Il Mar di Sargassi"; tr. Gianni Pilo).

9. "From the Tideless Sea."
   a. In Antonio Bellomi, ed. *Horror Story* n. 7. Milan: Garden, 1991, pp. 66–86 ("Il mare immobile"; tr. Stefania Carimati).

10. "The Gateway of the Monster."
    a. In Gianni Pilo and Sebastiano Fusco, ed. *Gli indagatori dell'incubo*. Rome: Newton & Compton, 1993, pp. 54–72 (as "L'anello"; tr. Gianni Pilo and Sebastiano Fusco).
    b. In Gianni Pilo, ed. *Storie di streghe*. Rome: Newton & Compton, 1996, pp. 200–214 (as "L'anello"; tr. Gianni Pilo).

11. *The Ghost Pirates*.
    a. In Antonio Bellomi, ed. *Horror Story* n. 12. Milan: Garden, 1992, pp. 3–132 (as *Orrore dagli abissi*; tr. Patrizia Tosi).
    b. In Gianni Pilo and Sebastiano Fusco, ed. *Storie di fantasmi*. Rome: Newton & Compton, October 1995, pp. 533–613 (as *I pirati fantasma*; tr. Daniela Galdo and Gianni Pilo).

12. "The Habitants of Middle Islet."
    a. In Bruno Tasso, ed. *Horror I*. Milan: Sugar, 1965, pp. 469–84 ("Gli abitanti di Middle Islet"; tr. Lia Volpatti).
    b. In Bruno Tasso, ed. *Creature dell'altro mondo*. Milan: Sugar, 1984, pp. 71–86 (as "Gli abitanti di Middle Islet"; tr. Lia Volpatti).
    c. *Speciale Weird Tales* No. 2 (1985): 5–8 (as "Middle Islet"; tr. anon.).
    d. In Antonio Bellomi, ed. *Horror Story* n. 9. Milan: Garden, 1991, pp. 102–16 (as "Gli abitanti dell'isolotto di mezzo"; tr. Patrizia Tosi).
    e. In Gianni Pilo and Sebastiano Fusco, ed. *Storie di fantasmi*. Rome: Newton, October 1995, pp. 521–28 (as "Gli abitanti di Middle Islet"; tr. anon.).

13. "The Haunting of the *Lady Shannon*."
    a. In Gianni Pilo, ed. *La saga di Cthulhu*. Rome: Fanucci, 1986, pp. 169–87 (as "La Lady Shannon"; tr. Daniela Galdo and Gianni Pilo).
    b. In Antonio Bellomi, ed. *Horror Story* n. 4. Milan: Garden, 1990, pp. 100–117 (as "Il fantasma della *Lady Shannon*"; tr. Mida).
    c. In Gianni Pilo and Sebastiano Fusco, ed. *Storie di vampiri*. Rome: Newton, May 1994, 2005, pp. 394–402 (as "La vendetta"; tr. Gianni Pilo and Sebastiano Fusco).

14. "The Hog."
    a. In Gianni Montanari, ed. *Investigatori dell'occulto*. Milan: Rizzoli, 1990, pp. 169–220 (as "Il verro"; tr. Gaetano Staffilano).
    b. In Stephen Jones, ed. *L'orrore secondo Lovecraft*. Milan: Mondadori, 1995, pp. 487–538 (as "Il maiale"; tr. Diego Pastorino). [Translation of *H. P. Lovecraft's Book of Horror* (I.B.i.49.d).]

15. "The Horse of the Invisible."
    a. In Hugh Greene, ed. *I rivali di Sherlock Holmes*. Milan: Bompiani, 1979, 1990, pp. ?–? (as "Il cavallo fantasma"; tr. anon.). [Translation of *The Rivals of Sherlock Holmes* (I.B.i.51.e).]
    b. In [Unsigned, ed.] *Incubo di cristallo*. Milan: Il Romanzo Giallo 8 (Garden), May 1986, pp. ?–? (as "Il cavallo dell'invisibile"; tr. Abramo Luraschi).
    c. In Antonio Bellomi, ed. *Horror Story n. 6*. Milan: Garden, 1991, pp. 244–73 (as "Il cavallo dell'invisibile"; tr. Abramo Luraschi).

16. *The House on the Borderland*.
    a. *Urania* No. 8 (1 June 1953): 77–88 (abridged; as "Oltre il futuro"; tr. anon.).
    b. In Juan Debra [et al.]. *Il sepolcro nel castello*. Rome: Editrice P.E.N., 1961, pp. ?–? (abridged; as "La polvere del tempo"; tr. unknown).
    c. In R. Notking [et al.]. *Lo schleletro sogghigna*. Rome: Editrice P.E.N., 1961, pp. 106–22 (abridged; as "La polvere del tempo"; tr. unknown).
    d. In Carlo Fruttero and Franco Lucentini, ed. *Universo a sette incognite*. Milan: Mondadori, 1963, pp. 837–916 (as *La casa sull'abisso*; tr. Giuliana De Carlo; abridged).
    e. In Gianni Pilo, ed. *I grandi romanzi dell'orrore*. Rome: Grandi Tascabili Economici Newton, 1996, pp. 474–548 (as *La casa sull'abisso*; tr. Gianni Pilo).
    f. In Gianni Pilo and Sebastiano Fusco, ed. *H. P. Lovecraft: I miei orrori preferiti*. Rome: Newton Compton, 1994, pp. 123–200 (as *La casa sull'abisso*; abridged; tr. anon.).

17. "The Island of the Ud."
    a. In Antonio Bellomi, ed. *Horror Story n. 7*. Milan: Garden, 1991, pp. 106–27 (as "L'isola di Ud"; tr. Stefania Carimati).

18. "More News from the *Homebird*."
    a. In Antonio Bellomi, ed. *Horror Story n. 7*. Milan: Garden, 1991, pp. 87–105 (as "Il quinto messaggio"; tr. Stefania Carimati).

19. "The Mystery of the Derelict."
   a. *Millemon di Estate* (June 1990): 160–72 (as "Il mistero del mar dei Sargassi"; tr. Lydia Di Marco).
   b. In Antonio Bellomi, ed. *Horror Story* n. 9. Milan: Garden, 1991, pp. 28–42 (as "Il mistero del relitto"; tr. Patrizia Tosi).

20. "Out of the Storm."
   a. In Antonio Bellomi, ed. *Horror Story* n. 4. Milan: Garden, 1990, pp. 15–20 (as "Una voce nella tempesta"; tr. Mida).

21. "The Real Thing: On the Bridge."
   a. *Orient Express* No. 2 (November 2006): ?–? (as "Sul ponte"; tr. Bernardo Cicchetti).

22. "The Riven Night."
   a. In August Derleth, ed. *I miti di Cthulhu*. Rome: Fanucci, 1975, pp. 87–94 (as "La notte squarciata"; tr. Alfredo Pollini and Sebastiano Fusco).

23. "Sea-Horses."
   a. In Antonio Bellomi, ed. *Horror Story* n. 7. Milan: Garden, 1991, pp. 3–24 (as "I cavallucci marini"; tr. Stefania Carimati).

24. "The *Shamraken* Homeward-Bounder."
   a. In Antonio Bellomi, ed. *Horror Story* n. 9. Milan: Garden, 1991, pp. 43–56 (as "L'ultimo viaggio dello Shamraken"; tr. Patrizia Tosi).

25. "The Stone Ship."
   a. In Antonio Bellomi, ed. *Horror Story* n. 9. Milan: Garden, 1991, pp. 57–90 (as "La nave di pietra"; tr. Patrizia Tosi).

26. "The Terror of the Water-Tank."
   a. In Antonio Bellomi, ed. *Horror Story* n. 4. Milan: Garden, 1990, pp. 66–82 (as "Il serbatoio della paura"; tr. Mida).

27. "The Thing in the Weeds."
   a. In Antonio Bellomi, ed. *Horror Story* n. 7. Milan: Garden, 1991, pp. 52–65 (as "La 'cosa' nelle alghe"; tr. Stefania Carimati).

28. "A Tropical Horror."
   a. *L'Eternauta* No. 64b (July 1988): 70–74 (as "Orrore tropicale"; tr. Maria Barbara Piccioli).
   b. In Antonio Bellomi, ed. *Horror Story* n. 4. Milan: Garden, 1990, pp. 3–14 (as "Orrore ai tropici"; tr. Mida).

29. "The Voice in the Dawn."
   a. In Antonio Bellomi, ed. *Horror Story n. 9*. Milan: Garden, 1991, pp. 117-31 (as "Il mostro dell'isola delle alghe"; tr. Patrizia Tosi).

30. "The Voice in the Night."
   a. In Alfred Hitchcock, ed. *25 racconti del terrore vietati alla TV*. Milan: Feltrinelli, 1959, pp. 174-88; Milan: Garzanti, 1970, pp. 156-69 (as "Una voce nella notte"; tr. Tilde Arcelli). [Translation of *Alfred Hitchcock Presents: Stories They Wouldn't Let Me Do on TV* (I.B.i.102.k).]
   b. In Alfred Hitchcock, ed. *Altri 13 racconti del terrore*. Milan: Feltrinelli, 1964, pp. 111-22 (as "Una voce nella notte"; tr. Tilde Arcelli). [Abridged translation of *Alfred Hitchcock Presents: Stories They Wouldn't Let Me Do on TV* (I.B.i.102.k).]
   c. In [Unsigned, ed.] *Horroriana*. Milan: Mondadori, 1979, pp. 177-94 (as "Al largo"; tr. Giuseppe Lippi).
   d. *Giallo d'Epoca* No. 7 (1990): 107-20 (as "Una voce nella notte"; tr. Roberta Formenti).
   e. In Sam Moskowitz, ed. *Il futuro era gia'cominciato*. Milan: Mondadori, 1991, pp. 298-315 (as "La voce nella notte"; tr. G. Cossato and S. Sandrelli). [Translation of *Science Fiction by Gaslight* (I.B.i.102.s).]
   f. In Antonio Bellomi, ed. *Horror Story n. 7*. Milan: Garden, 1991, pp. 128-40 (as "Una voce nella notte"; tr. Stefania Carimati).

31. "The Whistling Room."
   a. In Alfred Hitchcock, ed. *Racconti per le ore piccole*. Milan: Garzanti, 1962, pp. 219-37 (as "La stanza col fischio"; tr. Rita Fanoli). [Translation of *Alfred Hitchcock Presents: Stories for Late at Night* (I.B.i.107.f).]
   b. In Alfred Hitchcock, ed. *Racconti per le ore piccole 1*. Milan: Garzanti, 1973, pp. 219-37 (as "La stanza col fischio"; tr. Rita Fanoli). [Abridged translation of *Alfred Hitchcock Presents: Stories for Late at Night* (I.B.i.107.f).]

32. "The Wild Man of the Sea."
   a. *Psycho* No. 1 (1978): 19-39 (as "Il selvaggio del mare"; tr. Paolo Busnelli).
   b. In [Unsigned, ed.] *I Classici del terrore: Raccolta Psyco 1*. Milan: Armenia Editore, 1979, pp. 19-39 (Part 1) (as "Il selvaggio del mare"; tr. Paolo Busnelli).

L. Japanese

i. *Books*

1. *Ijigen o nosoku ie*.
   a. Tokyo: Hayakawa, 1972. Tr. Seiji Dan.
      Translation of *The House on the Borderland*.

2. *Yûrei karyûdo Carnacki.*
   a. Tokyo: Kokusho Kankôkai, 1977. Tr. Yukio Tazawa.
   Translation of *Carnacki the Ghost-Finder.*

3. *Naito rando.*
   a. Tokyo: Gekkan Pensha, 1980-81. 3 vols. Tr. Hiroshi Aramata.
   b. Tokyo: Hara Syobou, 2002.
   Translation of *The Night Land.*

4. *Yuro no koe.*
   a.1. Tokyo: Sogensha, 1985. Tr. Akemi Itsuji.
   a.2. Tokyo: Sogensha, 1995.
   Translation of "The Voice in the Night" and other stories.

5. *Umi fukaku.*
   a. Tokyo: Kokusho Kankôkai, 1986. Tr. Takashi Ogura.
   Translation of ?.

6. *Yûrei karyûdo Carnacki no zikenbo.*
   a. Tokyo: Sogensha, 2008. Tr. Kenzi Natuki.
   Translation of *Carnacki, the Ghost-Finder.*

ii. Shorter Works

1. "The Voice in the Night."
   a. In ?, ed. *Ansoroji: Kyofu to genso (2).* Tokyo: Gekkan Pensha, 1971, pp. ?-? (as "?"; tr. Kozaburo Yano?).

M. Norwegian

i. Short Stories

1. "?"
   a. In ?, ed. *Stemmen i natten og andre grøsserhistorier.* Oslo: Gyldendal, 2004, 2006, pp. ?-? (as "?"; tr. ?).
   Issued as an audiobook (Oslo: Lydbokforl, 2006).

N. Polish

i. Books

1. *Dom na granicy Światów.*
   a. Warsaw: Czytelnik, 1985. Tr. Małgorzata Targowska-Grabińska.
   Translation of *The House on the Borderland.*

2. *Widmowi piraci.*
   a. Katowice: PIK, 1992. Tr. Andrzej Keyha.
      Translation of *The Ghost Pirates.*

O. Romanian

i. *Books*

1. *Carnacki, vânătorul de fantome.*
   a. Bucharest: Aldo Press, 2003. Tr. Nicu Gecse.
      Translation of *Carnacki, the Ghost-Finder.*

2. *Pirații fantomă.*
   a. Bucharest: Aldo Press, 2004. Tr. Emilia Oanță.
      Translation of *The Ghost Pirates.*

P. Russian

i. *Shorter Works*

1. "The Whistling Room."
   a. In A. Serdjukova and N. M. Latyseva, ed. *Reanimator.* Moscow: EskKIZ, 1992, pp. 260-76 (as "Sphistyashchaya kamnata"; tr. A. Moroz and G. Kot).

Q. Spanish

i. *Books*

1. *La casa en el limite.*
   a. Buenos Aires: Ediciones Andromeda, 1976. Tr. Héctor R. Pessina and Jorge A. Sánchez.
   b. Barcelona: Ediciones Abraxas, 2004.
      Translation of *The House on the Borderland.*

2. *La casa en el confín de la tierra.*
   a.1. Barcelona: Bruguera, 1978. Tr. Francisco Torres Oliver.
   a.2. Barcelona: Bruguera, 1983.
   b. Mexico City: Bolsilibro, 1986.
   c. Madrid: Valdemar, 1998.
      Translation of *The House on the Borderland.*

3. *El reino de la noche.*
   a. Madrid: Francisco Arellano, 1978. Tr. Francisco Cusó.
   b. Barcelona: Forum, 1985. 2 vols.
   c. Guadalajara, Mexico: Río Henares Producciones Gráficas, 2004 (as *El pais de la noche*).

   Translation of *The Night Land*.

4. *Aquas profundas (seis relatos de horror).* Ed. Jorge A. Sánchez.
   a. Buenos Aires: El Cid, 1979. Tr. Elvio E. Gandolfo.

   Contents: "The Derelict"; "From the Tideless Sea"; "The Voice in the Night"; "The *Shamraken* Homeward-Bounder"; "The Stone Ship"; "The Habitants of Middle Islet."

5. *Los piratas fantasmas.*
   a. Barcelona: Fontamara, 1980. Tr. Francisco Cusó.
   b. Barcelona: Forum, 1985.
   c. n.p.: Ediciones Coyoach, 1985.

   Translation of *The Ghost Pirates*.

6. *Los espectros del mar.*
   a. Argentina: Ediciones de la Urraca, 1980. Tr. ?

   Contents: ?.

7. *El casa en el confín del mundo.*
   a.1. Barcelona: Fontamara, 1981. Tr. Rufo G. Salcedo.
   a.2. Barcelona: Forum, 1984.
   b. n.p.: Ediciones Coyoach, n.d.

   Translation of *The House on the Borderland*.

8. *Los náufragos de las tinieblas.*
   a.1. Barcelona: Martinez Roca, 1983. Tr. Mariano Casas.
   a.2. Barcelona: Martinez Roca, 1986.

   Translation of *The Boats of the "Glen Carrig."*

9. *Cuentos de alta mar.*
   a. Barcelona: Forum, 1985. Tr. Iria Brendán.

   Contents: "The Derelict" and other stories.

10. *Carnacki, el cazafantasmas.*
    a.1. Madrid: Anaya, 1992. Tr. Javier Martin Lalanda.
    a.2. Madrid: Anaya, 1993.

    Translation of *Carnacki, the Ghost-Finder*.

11. *La nave abandonada y otros relatos de horror en el mar.*
    a.1. Madrid: Valdemar, 1997. Tr. Esperanza Castro.
    a.2. Madrid: Valdemar, 2000.
    b.   Barcelona: RBA Coleccionables, 2002.

    Translation of "The Derelict," "The *Shamraken* Homeward-Bounder," "The Voice in the Night," "From the Tideless Sea," "The Stone Ship," and "The Habitants of Middle Islet."

12. *Los piratas fantasmas.*
    a. Madrid: Valdemar, 1999. Tr. José Maria Nebreda.
    b. Barcelona: RBA Coleccionables, 2002.

    Translation of *The Ghost Pirates.*

13. *Un horror tropical y otros relatos.*
    a.1. Madrid: Valdemar, 1999. Tr. José Maria Nebreda.
    a.2. Madrid: Valdemar, n.d.
    a.3. Madrid: Valdemar, 2006.

    Translation of "A Tropical Horror" and other stories.

14. *Los botes del "Glen Carrig."*
    a. Madrid: Valdemar, 2002. Tr. José Maria Nebreda.

    Translation of *The Boats of the "Glen Carrig."*

15. *Los piratas fantasmas y otros cuentos de fantasmas.*
    a. Mexico City: Editores Mexicanos Unidos, 2004. Tr. ?.

    Translation of *The Ghost Pirates* and other stories.

16. *La casa en confín del mundo.*
    a. Guadalajara, Mexico: Río Henares Producciones Gráficas, 2004. Tr. Francisco Javier Arellano.

    Translation of *The House on the Borderland.*

17. *Trilogía del abismo.*
    a. Madrid: Valdemar, 2005. Tr. José Maria Nebreda and Francisco Torres Oliver.

    Translation of *The Boats of the "Glen Carrig," The House on the Borderland,* and *The Ghost Pirates.*

18. *Los mares grises sueñan con mi muerte: Cuentos completos de terror en el mar.*
    a. Madrid: Valdemar, 2010. Tr. José Maria Nebreda.
    b. Madrid: Valdemar, 2014.

    A large volume (776 pp.) containing 35 of Hodgson's stories.

19. *Carnacki, el cazador de fantasmas.*
    a. Madrid: Valdemar, 2011. Tr. Lorenzo Díaz.
    Translation of *Carnacki, the Ghost-Finder*.

ii. *Short Stories*

1. "The Habitants of Middle Islet."
    a. In Andrea Boronzini, ed. *Cuentos con espectros, sombras y vampiros.* Buenos Aires: Ediciones Colihue, 2001, pp. ?-? (as "Los habitantes de la Isleta Central"; tr. ?).

2. "The Phantom Ship."
    a. In Alaric Balam, ed. *Cuentos clásicos de fantasmas.* Mexico City: Editores Mexicanos Unidos, 2006, pp. ?-? (as "El navío silencioso"; tr. Alaric Balam).

3. "The Voice in the Night."
    a. In [Unsigned, ed.] *Felices pesadillas: Los mejores relatos de terror aparecidos en Valdemar (1987–2003).* Madrid: Valdemar, 2003, pp. ?-? (as "Una voz en la noche"; tr. anon.).

4. "?"
    a. In Diego Bigongiari, ed. *Los mejores relatos marinos.* Rosario, Argentina: Ameghino, 1998, pp. ?-? (as "El mar de los sargazos"; tr. Diego Bigongiari).

R. Swedish

i. *Books*

1. *Huset vid avgrunden.*
    a. Stockholm: B. Wahlström, 1982. Tr. Gunnar Redmalm.
    Notes. Translation of *The House on the Borderland*.

2. *Huset vid avgrunden.*
    a. Bromma: Sam J. Lundwall Fakta & Fantasi, 1990. Tr. Sam J. Lundwall.
    Translation of *The House on the Borderland*.

3. *Rösten i mörkret och andra skräckfyllda berättelser.* Ed. Rickard Berghorn.
    a. Saltsjö-Boo: Aleph, 2003.
    Contents: "Vraket" ("The Derelict"; tr. Birgitta Hylin); "Eloi eloi lama sabachthani" ("The Baumoff Explosive"); "Havet utan ebb och flod" ("From the Tideless Sea" and "More News from the *Homebird*"); "Hemsökelsen i

slutet av gatan" ("The Searcher of the End House"; tr. Maria Hansson and Rickard Berghorn); "Rösten i morkret" ("The Voice in the Night"; tr. Maria Hansson); "Hemsökelsen på Lady Shannon" ("The Haunting of the *Lady Shannon*"; tr. Maria Hansson and Rickard Berghorn); "William Hope Hodgson—En presentation," by Rickard Berghorn.
Translated by Rickard Berghorn save where indicated.

ii. *Shorter Works*

1. "The Crew of the *Lancing*."
   a. In [Unsigned, ed.] *Fem ruggiga rysare*. Stockholm: B. Wahlström, 1976, pp. 123-32 (as "Skräkens skepp"; tr. Hans Flintzberg).
   b. In [Unsigned, ed.] *Spindlarna*. Stockholm: B. Wahlström, 1978, pp. 143-56 (as "Havets monster"; tr. Peter Schinkler).

2. "Demons of the Sea."
   a. *Eskapix* No. 4 (2007): 41-45 (as "Skräcken ur djupet"; tr. Mikael Fransson).

3. "The Derelict."
   a. In Olof Strandberg, ed. *Kalla kårar: Sällsamma historier*. Stockholm: Rabén & Sjögren, 1944, pp. 199-224 (as "Vraket"; tr. Birgitta Hylin).
   b. *Allt i fickformat* No. 7 (1945): 83, 85-86, 88-92, 94-96, 98-101 (as "Vraket"; tr. anon.).
   c. In Olof Strandberg, ed. *Kalla kårar: En antologi*. Stockholm: Rabén & Sjögren, 1956, pp. 182-212 (as "Vraket"; tr. Birgitta Hylin).
   d. *Veckorevyn* No. 38 (1956): 49-50, 52 (as "Vraket"; abridged; tr. anon.).
   e. In [Unsigned, ed.] *Vraket*. Stockholm: B. Wahlström, 1973, 1980, pp. 124-60 (as "Vraket"; tr. Birgitta Hylin).

4. "The Dream of X."
   a. *Jules Verne-Magasinet* No. 403 (1984): 2-31 (as "Nattlandet"; tr. Sam J. Lundwall).
   b. In Sam J. Lundwall, ed. *Den eviga grodan*. Bromma: Sam J. Lundwall Fakta & Fantasi, 1986, pp. 30-67 (as "Nattlandet"; tr. Sam J. Lundwall).
   c. In Sam J. Lundwall, ed. *Första stora monsterboken*. Bromma: Sam J. Lundwall Fakta & Fantasi, 1991, pp. 79-113 (as "Nattlandet"; tr. Sam J. Lundwall).

5. "The Find."
   a. *Jury: Tidskrift för deckarvänner* No. 2 (1984): 38-43 (as "Fyndet"; tr. Karl G. & Lilian Frederiksson).

6. "From the Tideless Sea."
   a. In [Michel Parry, ed.] *Havsmonster*. Stockholm: B. Wahlström, 1978, pp. 5-26 (as "Havets fånge"; tr. Solveig Rasmussen). [Translation of *Waves of Terror* (I.B.i.35.e).]

7. "The Gateway of the Monster."
   a. In [Unsigned, ed.] *I den ondes makt*. Stockholm: B. Wahlström, 1977, pp. 134-60 (as "I den ondes makt"; tr. Gösta Zetterlund).

8. "The Goddess of Death."
   a. *Lektyr* 1, No. 12 (1904): 178-80; 1, No. 13 (1904): 194-97 (as "Dödens gudinna"; tr. anon.).
   b. *Mellan fantasi och verklighet* (supplement to *Allers Familj-Journal*) No. 21 (1906): 1-2 (as "Dödens gudinna"; tr. anon.).
   c. *Kring aftonlampan* No. 1 (2002): 2-17 (as "Dödens gudinna"; tr. anon.). [Reprint of b.]

9. "The Hog."
   a. *Minotauren* Nos. 26-28 (December 2005): 151-82 (as "Svinvarelsen"; tr. Martin Andersson).

10. "The Horse of the Invisible."
    a. *DAST-Magazine* 37, No. 2 (2004): 68-87 (as "Det osynligas häst"; tr. Bertil Falk).

11. "The House among the Laurels."
    a. In Sven Christer Swahn, ed. *Sällsamma berättelser i mästarklass*. Stockholm: Klassikerförlaget, 1997, pp. 67-83 (as "Huset bland lagerträden"; tr. Sven Christer Swahn).

12. *The House on the Borderland.*
    a. In Steven Ekholm, ed. *Skräck: Antologi*. Stockholm: Natur & Kultur, 2001, pp. 29-39 (extract; as "Ur *Huset vid avgrunden*"; tr. Sam J. Lundwall).

13. "More News from the *Homebird*."
    a. In [Michel Parry, ed.] *Havsmonster*. Stockholm: B. Wahlström, 1978, pp. 137-59 (as "Skräcknatt ombord"; tr. Solveig Rasmussen). [Translation of *Waves of Terror* (I.B.i.66.e).]

14. "The Mystery of the Derelict."
    a. In Hugh Lamb, ed. *Spökspegeln*. Stockholm: B. Wahlström, 1979, pp. 111-34 (as "Vrakets hemlighet"; tr. Solveig Rasmussen). [Translation of *Forgotten Tales of Terror* (I.B.i.72.h).]

15. *The Night Land.*
    a. In Sam J. Lundwall, ed. *Den fantastiska romanen 2: Gotisk skräckromantik från Horace Walpole till H. P. Lovecraft.* Stockholm: Gummesson, 1973, pp. 318-29 (extract; as "Nattlandet"; tr. Sam J. Lundwall).

16. "A Tropical Horror."
    a. In Rickard Berghorn, ed. *Berättelser i svart.* Saltsjö-Boo: Aleph Bokförlag, 2000, pp. 95-106 (as "En tropisk skräck"; tr. Hanna Svensson).

17. "The Weed Men" [I.B.7.d].
    a. In [Unsigned, ed.] *Fem öppna gravar.* Stockholm: B. Wahlström, 1976, pp. 145-59 (as "Sjögräsfolket"; tr. Peter Gissy).
    b. In Hugh Lamb, ed. *Vaxkabinettet.* Stockholm: B. Wahlström, 1980, pp. 145-56 (as "Sjögräsmonstren"; tr. Knut Rosén). [Translation of *The Thrill of Horror* (I.B.i.7.d).]

18. "The Whistling Room."
    a. *Min värld* No. 1 (1964): 45, 47 (abridged; as "Det visslande rummet"; tr. anon.).
    b. *Minotauren* No. 20 (December 2003): 36-49 (as "Det visslande rummet"; tr. Maria Hansson).
    c. In Rickard Berghorn, ed. *Syner i natten del 2.* Saltsjö-Boo: Aleph Bokförlag, 2004, pp. 33-45 (as "Det visslande rummet"; tr. Maria Hansson).

III. Works about Hodgson

A. Bibliographies

1. Ashley, Mike. "The Fiction of William Hope Hodgson: A Working Bibliography." *Science Fiction Collector* No. 15 (July 1981): 15-18.

2. Bell, Ian. "Bibliography." In A.25, pp. 49-51.

3. Bell, Joseph. *William Hope Hodgson: Night Pirate Volume One: An Annotated Bibliography of Published Works 1902-1987.* Toronto: Soft Books, 1987.

4. Currey, L. W. "William Hope Hodgson." In *Science Fiction and Fantasy Authors: A Bibliography of First Printings of Their Fiction and Selected Nonfiction.* Boston: G. K. Hall, 1979, pp. 242-44.

5. Guarriello, Pietro. "Nota bibliografica." In II.K.i.9, pp. 29-36.

6. Locke, George. *A Spectrum of Fantasy: The Bibliography and Biography of a Collection of Fantastic Literature.* London: Ferret Fantasy, 1980, pp. 113-15.

7. Searles, A. Langley. "Bibliography of William Hope Hodgson." *Fantasy Commentator* 1, No. 3 (Fall 1944): 35, 42. In I.A.17, pp. 638-39 (as "Bibliography of the Published Books of William Hope Hodgson").

8. Tuck, Donald H. *The Encyclopedia of Science Fiction and Fantasy through 1968*. Chicago: Advent, 1974, Vol. 1, pp. 224-25.

B. Books about Hodgson

1. Bell, Ian, ed. *William Hope Hodgson: Voyages and Visions*. Oxford: A. Bell & Sons, 1987. viii, 64 pp.

    Contents: "Notes on Contributors" [by Ian Bell] (iv); "A WHH Chronology" [by Ian Bell] (v-vi); "Introduction," by Ian Bell (vii-viii); "WHH and Blackburn," by Ian Bell (1-3); "WHH in *Sandow's Magazine*," by Richard Dalby (4-9) [includes "Dr. Thomas's Vibration Method versus Sandow's," 4-5; "Physical Culture versus Recreative Exercise," 5-8; "Hints on Physical Culture," 8-9]; "WHH and Borth," by Mark Valentine (10); "Child of All the Sea: The Sea-Horror Fiction," by Peter Tremayne (11-18); "Alone on a Wide Wide Sea: *The Ghost Pirates*," by Michael Goss (19-23); "Against the Abyss: Carnacki the Ghost-Finder," by Mark Valentine (24-28); "The Composition of *The Night Land*," by Brian Stableford (29-36); "The Restoration of *The Night Land*," by Ian Bell (37-43); "A Writer on the Borderland," by Andy Sawyer (44-51); "Tales of Remote Futures," by Roger Dobson (52-56); "WHH: In the Wake of Disaster," introduced by Mike Ashley (57-61) [includes "The Real Thing: On the Bridge," 59-61]; "WNH: Another Hodgson," introduced by Ian Bell (62) [includes "Before Action" by W. N. Hodgson, 62]; "Bibliography" [by Ian Bell] (63-64).

    Reviews:
    a. Joshi, S. T. *Studies in Weird Fiction* No. 2 (Summer 1987): 40-41.

    Substantial small-press collection of original essays on Hodgson. For discussion of individual items, see Section D.

2. Everts, R. Alain. *Some Facts in the Case of William Hope Hodgson: Master of Phantasy*. Madison, WI: Strange Co., 1974. Rev. ed. Toronto: Soft Books, 1987 (as *William Hope Hodgson: Night Pirate Volume 2*).

    Reprint of D.17.

3. Gafford, Sam. *Hodgson: A Collection of Essays*. Warren, RI: Ulthar Press, 2013.

    Contents: "A William Hope Hodgson Chronology" (4-9); "A WHH Publishing Chronology" (10-14); "A Life on the Borderland" (15-18); "Hodgson's First Story" (19-20); "Writing Backwards: The Novels of William Hope Hodgson" (21-26); "A Brief History of Hodgson Studies" (27-32); "Meet Mrs. Hodgson" (33-34); "MATANGO!" (35-37); "A Hodgson Mystery" (38-40); "On 'The Baumoff Explosive'" (41-42); "WHH in WWI" (43-44); "The Non-Fiction Hodgson" (45-46); "The Copyright

Volumes" (47-49); "Hodgson's Serial Characters" (40-52); "Houdini v Hodgson: The Challenge at Blackburn" (53-70).

Interesting collection of mostly unpublished articles and notes about Hodgson's life and work.

C. Dictionary and Encyclopedia Articles

1. Ash, Brian. "W. H. Hodgson." In *Who's Who in Science Fiction*. New York: Taplinger, 1976, pp. 118-19.

2. Ashley, Mike. "William Hope Hodgson." In *Who's Who in Horror and Fantasy Fiction*. New York: Taplinger, 1977, pp. 94-95.

3. Bleiler, E. F. *The Guide to Supernatural Fiction*. Kent, OH: Kent State University Press, 1983, pp. 245-48.

    Plot summaries and brief critical evaluations of Hodgson's major works.

4. ———. "Hodgson, William Hope." In *Twentieth Century Crime and Mystery Writers*, ed. John M. Reilly. New York: St. Martin's Press, 1985, p. 462.

5. ———. "William Hope Hodgson." In *Supernatural Fiction Writers*, ed. E. F. Bleiler. New York: Scribner's, 1985, Vol. 1, pp. 421-48.

    Substantial discussion of Hodgson's four novels, *Carnacki*, and other short stories.

6. Bloom, Harold, ed. "William Hope Hodgson." In *Modern Horror Writers*. New York: Chelsea House, 1995, pp. 93-107.

    Contains: Extracts from criticism by [Unsigned] (F.3.b), C. K. S. (D.68), Arthur St. John Adcock (D.1), H. P. Lovecraft (D.56), [Unsigned] (F.10.c), Peter Christensen (D.21), Gary K. Wolfe (C.29), Brian Stableford (D.74), Mark Valentine (D.83), Ian Bell (D.9), and Sam Gafford (D.41). With biographical sketch and primary bibliography.

7. Borowitz, Albert. "William Hope Hodgson." In *British Mystery Writers, 1860-1919*, ed. Bernard Benstock and Thomas Staley. (Dictionary of Literary Biography, Volume 70.) Detroit: Gale Research Co., 1988, pp. 166-68.

    Brief biocritical discussion, with bibliography.

8. Borselli, Mauro. "Hodgson, William Hope." In *Enciclopedia della paura*. Milan: Bonelli Editore, 1991, pp. ?-?.

9. Cawthorn, James, and Michael Moorcock. "*The House on the Borderland*." In *Fantasy: The 100 Best Books*. London: Xanadu, 1988; New York: Carroll & Graf, 1988, pp. 53-54.

10. ———. "The Night Land." In *Fantasy: The 100 Best Books*. London: Xanadu, 1988; New York: Carroll & Graf, 1988, pp. 65-66.

11. De Turris, Gianfranco, and Sebastiano Fusco. "Hodgson." In *Arcana*. Milan: Sugar, 1969.

12. H[eje], J[ohan]. "Hodgson, William Hope (1877-1918)." In *The New Encyclopedia of Science Fiction*, ed. James Gunn. New York: Viking Penguin, 1988, pp. 225-26.

13. Herron, Don. "Carnacki the Ghost-Finder." In *Survey of Modern Fantasy Literature*, ed. Frank N. Magill. Englewood Cliffs, NJ: Salem Press, 1983, pp. 193-96 (Vol. 1).

    Survey of the Carnacki stories, concluding that "when the occult manifestations are proven to be rigged, the reader is disappointed. . . . Another factor working against the artistic impact of the Carnacki tales is the series format."

14. Klein, T. E. D. "Hodgson, William Hope." In *The Penguin Encyclopedia of Horror and the Supernatural*, ed. Jack Sullivan. New York: Viking, 1986, pp. 203-4.

15. Neilson, Keith. "The Boats of the 'Glen Carrig.'" In *Survey of Modern Fantasy Literature*, ed. Frank N. Magill. Englewood Cliffs, NJ: Salem Press, 1983, pp. 143-45 (Vol. 1).

    Brief summary of the novel, concluding that it is "an exciting, powerful, scary book, probably the best extended introduction to Hodgson's writing."

16. ———. "The Night Land." In *Survey of Modern Fantasy Literature*, ed. Frank N. Magill. Englewood Cliffs, NJ: Salem Press, 1983, pp. 1105-10 (Vol. 3).

    Summary of the novel, with some critical commentary.

17. Pratchett, Terry. "The House on the Borderland." In *Horror: 100 Best Books*, ed. Stephen Jones and Kim Newman. London: Xanadu, 1988; New York: Carroll & Graf, 1988, pp. 71-73.

18. Searles, Baird; Last, Martin; Meachum, Beth; and Franklin, Michael. *A Reader's Guide to Science Fiction*. New York: Avon, 1979, pp. 84-85.

19. Searles, Baird; Meachum, Beth; and Franklin, Michael. *A Reader's Guide to Fantasy*. New York: Avon, 1982, pp. 74-75.

20. Stableford, Brian. "Deep Waters." In *Survey of Science Fiction Literature*, ed. Frank N. Magill. Englewood Cliffs, NJ: Salem Press, 1979, pp. 524-28 (Vol. 2).

    Survey of the story collection, stating that the stories are "tales of superstitious dread, filled with fogs and strange noises, each climaxing in some kind of monstrous visitation."

21. ———. "Early Modern Horror Fiction." In *Horror Literature: A Reader's Guide*, ed. Neil Barron. New York: Garland, 1990, pp. 126-27. Rev. ed. as *Fantasy and Horror*. Lanham, MD: Scarecrow Press, 1999, pp. 120-21.

22. ———. "Hodgson, William Hope." In *The Encyclopedia of Science Fiction: An Illustrated A to Z*, ed. Peter Nicholls. St Albans: Granada, 1979, pp. 288-89. Garden City, NY: Doubleday, 1979, p. 288.

23. ———. "Hodgson, William Hope." In *Horror, Ghost & Gothic Writers*, ed. David Pringle. Detroit: St. James Press, 1998, pp. 273-75.

    Brief biocritical survey, with bibliography.

24. ———. "Hodgson, William Hope." In *Supernatural Literature of the World: An Encyclopedia*, ed. S. T. Joshi and Stefan Dziemianowicz. Westport, CT: Greenwood Press, 2005, pp. 551-55 (Vol. 2).

    Brief biocritical survey, with secondary bibliography.

25. Steinbrunner, Chris, and Otto Penzler. "Carnacki." In *Encyclopedia of Mystery and Detection*. New York: McGraw-Hill, 1976, p. 62.

26. ———. "Hodgson, William Hope." In *Encyclopedia of Mystery and Detection*. New York: McGraw-Hill, 1976, p. 205.

27. Sullivan, Jack. "Psychological, Antiquarian, and Cosmic Horror: 1872-1919." In *Horror Literature: A Core Collection and Reference Guide*, ed. Marshall B. Tymn. New York: R. R. Bowker, 1981, pp. 247-48.

28. Wingrove, David. "Hodgson, William Hope (1877-1918)." In *The Science Fiction Source Book*. New York: Van Nostrand Reinhold Co., 1984, p. 164.

29. Wolfe, Gary K. "*The House on the Borderland*." In *Survey of Modern Fantasy Literature*, ed. Frank Magill. Englewood Cliffs, NJ: Salem Press, 1983, pp. 744-48 (Vol. 2).

    Survey of the novel, finding in it an exemplification of Hodgson's theme of the "central opposition . . . between flesh and spirit."

30. ———. "Hodgson, William Hope." In *Twentieth-Century Science-Fiction Writers*, ed. Curtis C. Smith. New York: St. Martin's Press, 1981, pp. 264-65. 2nd ed. Chicago: St. James Press, 1986, pp. 342-43. 3rd ed., ed. Noelle Watson and Paul E. Schellinger. Chicago: St. James Press, 1991, pp. 379-80. 4th ed. (as *St. James Guide to Science Fiction Writers*), ed. Jay P. Pederson. Detroit: St. James Press, 1996, pp. ?-?.

31. [Unsigned.] "Hodgson, William Hope." In *Contemporary Authors*, ed. Hal May. Detroit: Gale Research Co., 1984, Vol. 111, p. 230.

32. [Unsigned, ed.] "William Hope Hodgson." In *Twentieth Century Literary Criticism*, ed. Dennis Poupard and James E. Person, Jr. Detroit: Gale Research Co., 1984, Vol. 13, pp. 228-38.

> Contains: Extracts from review of *The Boats of the "Glen Carrig"* (F.1.c); review of *The Ghost Pirates* (F.3.b); review of *The Night Land* (F.4.c); review of *Carnacki the Ghost-Finder* (F.5.e); review of *The Calling of the Sea* (F.9.b); H. P. Lovecraft, "Supernatural Horror in Literature" (D.55); Clark Ashton Smith, "In Appreciation of William Hope Hodgson" (D.71); B. V. Winebaum, "Four Decker Horror Special" (F.10.b); Sid Birchby, "Sexual Symbolism in W. H. Hodgson" (D.14); Lin Carter, Introduction to *The Boats of the "Glen Carrig"* (D.20); Lin Carter, Introduction to *The Night Land, Volume 1* (D.19); Sam Moskowitz, Introduction to *Out of the Storm* (D.60); Dennis Wheatley, Introduction to *The Ghost Pirates* (D.92).

D. Criticism in Books or Periodicals

1. Adcock, A[rthur] St. John. "Introduction." In A.15, pp. 3-6.
    Brief memoir, emphasizing Hodgson's character traits and his poetry.

2. Alder, Emily. "'Always Sea and Sea': *The Night Land* as Sea-scape." *Sargasso* 1, No. 1 (Fall 2013): 89-101.
    Studies how Hodgson's sea experiences shaped the weird atmosphere of *The Night Land*.

3. ———. "'Buildings of the New Age': Dwellings and the Natural Environment in the Futuristic Fiction of H. G. Wells and William Hope Hodgson." In *H. G. Wells: Interdisciplinary Essays*, ed. Steven McLean. Newcastle, UK: Cambridge Scholars Publishing, 2008, pp. 114-29.

4. ———. "Doorways in the Night." *The Gothic Imagination*, 27 September 2011 (http://www.gothic.stir.ac/uk/guestblog/doorways-in-the-night-william-hope-hodgson/).

5. ———. "'Passing the Barrier of Life': Spiritualism, Psychical Research and Boundaries in William Hope Hodgson's *The Night Land*." In *Boundaries*, ed. Jenni Ramone and Gemma Twitchen. Newcastle, UK: Cambridge Scholars Publishing, 2006, pp. 120-39.

6. Aldiss, Brian W. *Billion Year Spree: The True History of Science Fiction*. Garden City, NY: Doubleday, 1973, pp. 171-74. Rev. ed. as *Trillion Year Spree: The History of Science Fiction* (with David Wingrove). New York: Atheneum, 1986, pp. 167-69.
    Summary of *The House on the Borderland* and *The Night Land*, presenting lengthy quotations from them and supplying brief critical evaluations.

7. Anderson, Douglas A. "Introduction." In I.A.62.

8. Anderson, Douglas A. "Introduction to William Hope Hodgson's 'The Psychology of Species.'" *Wormwood* No. 6 (Spring 2006): 41–42.

9. ———. "Some Notes on *The Ghost Pirates*." In I.A.3.k.

10. Ashley, Mike. "The Essential Writers: William Hope Hodgson." *Rod Serling's "The Twilight Zone" Magazine* 7, No. 1 (April 1982): 69–72.

    Overview of Hodgson's life and work.

11. ———. "Foreword: The Last Redoubt." In I.A.61.

12. ———. "WHH: In the Wake of Disaster." In B.1, pp. 57–58.

    Introductory note to "The Real Thing: On the Bridge," discussing Hodgson's reaction to the sinking of the *Titanic*.

13. Behrends, Steve. "Spinning in the Night Land: A Footnote to William Hope Hodgson." *Studies in Weird Fiction* No. 13 (Summer 1993): 35–36.

    Relates an image in *The Night Land* to a waterspout as described in "Through the Vortex of a Cyclone."

14. Bell, Ian. "A Dream of Darkness: William Hope Hodgson's *The Night Land*." *Studies in Weird Fiction* No. 1 (Summer 1986): 13–18. Rev. ed. in B.1, pp. 37–43 (as "The Restoration of *The Night Land*").

    Discussion of the novel, defending the "central importance" of the love story and the prose style of the work.

15. ———. "Introduction." In A.25, pp. v–vii.

16. ———. "WHH and Blackburn." In B.1, pp. 1–3.

    Study of Hodgson's writings in Blackburn newspapers.

17. ———. "WNH: Another Hodgson." In B.1, p. 62.

    Brief note on William Noel Hodgson (d. 1916); includes one of his poems, "Before Action."

18. ———. "William Hope Hodgson: Voyager and Visionary." *Antiquarian Book Monthly Review* 12, No. 12 (December 1985): 460–65.

    General study of Hodgson's work.

19. Birchby, Sid. "Sexual Symbolism in W. H. Hodgson." *Riverside Quarterly* 1, No. 2 (November 1964): 70–74.

    Finds sexual imagery in *The House on the Borderland* and *The Night Land*.

20. Blackmore, Leigh. "Things Invisible: 'Human' and 'Ab-human' in Two of Hodgson's Carnacki Stories." *Sargasso* 1, No. 1 (Fall 2013): 176–97.

21. Boulter, Amanda. "*The House on the Borderland*: The Sexual Politics of Fear." In *Creepers: British Horror and Fantasy in the Twentieth Century*, ed. Clive Bloom. London: Pluto Press, 1993, pp. 24-34.

    Analysis of the novel that finds sexual undertones in many of its features and incidents.

22. Cammarota, Domenico. "Gli abissi di Hodgson." In II.J.i.4.

23. Campbell, Lori. "Confronting Chaos at the In-Between: William Hope Hodgson's *The House on the Borderland*." In Campbell's *Portals of Power: Magical Agency and Transformation in Literary Fantasy*. Jefferson, NC: McFarland, 2010, pp. 103-19.

24. Carter, Lin. "Across the Shadowy Land." In A.7.e, Vol. 2, pp. vii-xii.

25. ———. *Imaginary Worlds: The Art of Fantasy*. New York: Ballantine, 1973, pp. 88-91.

26. ———. "The Last Redoubt." In A.7.e, Vol. 1, pp. vii-xii.

27. ———. "Strange Odyssey." In A.1.c, pp. vii-xii.

28. Christensen, Peter. "William Hope Hodgson: *Carnacki the Ghost-Finder*." *Armchair Detective* 12, No. 2 (Spring 1979): 122-24.

    Brief survey of the Carnacki stories, finding that they "acknowledge the possibility that supernatural appearances may be explained rationally."

29. Dalby, Richard. "WHH in *Sandow's Magazine*." In B.1, p. 4.

    Brief survey of Hodgson's writings on physical culture in *Sandow's Magazine*.

30. ———. "William Hope Hodgson." *Book and Magazine Collector* No. 35 (February 1987): 30-38.

31. Davidson, Brett. "The Long Apocalypse: The Experimental Eschatalogies of H. G. Wells and William Hope Hodgson." *Sargasso* 1, No. 1 (Fall 2013): 102-16.

    Studies the influence of Wells's *Time Machine* on *The House on the Borderland*.

32. Derleth, August. "Foreword." In A.18, pp. ix-x.

    Brief discussion of the compilation of *Deep Waters*.

33. ———. "William Hope Hodgson." *Reader and Collector* 3, No. 3 (June 1944): 8.

    One-paragraph discussion of Hodgson's works.

34. De Turris, Gianfranco. "L'assedio e il viaggio." In II.J.i.9, pp. 241-68.

    Extensive treatment of Hodgson's work in the context of the supernatural literature of his time.

35. De Turris, Gianfranco, and Sebastiano Fusco. "Il mare e i suoi simboli nella letteratura fantastica." In II.J.i.2, pp. 7-17.

36. Dobson, Roger. "Tales of Remote Futures." In B.1, pp. 52-56.

    Study of the cosmic elements in *The House on the Borderland* and *The Night Land*.

37. Duperray, Max. "Les Espaces inquiets de William Hope Hodgson." In II.F.i.10, pp. 19-28.

    Biographical and critical overview.

38. ———. "*La Maison au bord du monde* du William Hope Hodgson." *Horizons du fantastique* No. 22 (1972): 4-17.

    Detailed analysis of *The House on the Borderland*, stressing its place in the history of supernatural fiction.

39. Edkins, E. A. "The Poetry of William Hope Hodgson." *Reader and Collector* 3, No. 3 (June 1944): 9.

    Brief discussion of Hodgson's poetry, concluding that he "lacks the poetic gift, principally because he is technically unskilled in poetic forms."

40. Ellis, Phillip A. "A Reassessment of William Hope Hodgson's Poetry." *Sargasso* 1, No. 1 (Fall 2013): 14-39.

    Exhaustive discussion of a wide range of Hodgson's poems and an assessment of their effectiveness.

41. Everts, R. Alain. "Some Facts in the Case of William Hope Hodgson: Master of Phantasy." *Shadow* No. 19 (April 1973): 4-11; No. 20 (October 1973): 7-13. Rev. ed. as B.2.

    Extensive biographical study of Hodgson, emphasizing his involvement with Houdini and his military service.

42. Frank, Jane. "Introduction: The Wandering Soul." In I.A.61, pp. 1-51.

43. ———. "William Hope Hodgson's Sales Log: The Pleasures and Consequences of Collecting." *Sargasso* 1, No. 1 (Fall 2013): 40-54.

    Tells of what can be learned of the progression of Hodgson's work from a study of his sales log.

44. Gafford, Sam. "HPL and WHH: Ships in the Night." *Weird Fiction Review* No. 4 (2013): 36-47.

    Overview of Hodgson's influence on Lovecraft.

45. ———. "Houdini vs. Hodgson: The Blackburn Challenge." *Weird Fiction Review* No. 3 (2012): 29-50. In B.3.

    Detailed account of Hodgson's celebrated meeting with Houdini in 1902.

46. ———. "Introduction." In I.A.48, Vol. 1, p. 4.

    Brief survey of Hodgson's essays and reviews.

47. ———. "Introduction." In I.A.48, Vol. 2, p. 3.

    Brief study of the stories contained in the volume.

48. ———. ["Introduction."] In I.A.49, p. 3.

    Brief account of Hodgson's poetry.

49. ———. "The Road to Adventure." In A.45, pp. 5-6.

    Analysis of Hodgson's adventure writings.

50. ———. "The Smuggling Life." In A.46, Vol. 1, pp. 5-9.

    Overview of the Captain Gault stories.

51. ———. "Unearthing the Forgotten." In I.A.44, pp. 5-6.

    Discussion of Hodgson's uncollected writings.

52. ———. "William Hope Hodgson: Master of the Sea." *Damned Thing* 1, No. 1 (Spring 1991): 10-18.

    General survey of Hodgson's fiction, stressing his deliberate lack of characterization and his cosmicism.

53. ———. "Writing Backwards: The Novels of William Hope Hodgson." *Studies in Weird Fiction* No. 11 (Spring 1992): 12-15. In B.3.

    Using primary documents (mostly letters), Gafford establishes that Hodgson's novels were written in nearly opposite order from their order of publication.

54. Giorgi, Giorgio. "Un incubo in letteratura: *The House on the Borderland*." *Fantasycon* No. 4 (23-25 April 1983): 67-80. In II.J.i.5. In Giorgi's *Percorsi nel fantastico*. Rimini: Il Cherchio Editore, 1997, pp. 139-54 (as "Gli incubi di W. H. Hodgson").

55. Goss, Michael. "Alone on a Wide Wide Sea: *The Ghost Pirates*." In B.1, pp. 19-23.

    Analysis of the novel, concluding that it "is arguably the most mature of Hodgson's essays upon the isolation theme."

56. Haefele, John D. "Shadow out of Hodgson." *Sargasso* 1, No. 1 (Fall 2013): 7–13.

    Makes a compelling case for the influence of *The Night Land* on H. P. Lovecraft's "The Shadow out of Time."

57. Hurley, Kelly. *The Gothic Body: Sexuality, Materialism, and Degeneration at the Fin de Siècle*. Cambridge: Cambridge University Press, 1996, pp. 3, 12, 23–25, 28, 29–31, 36–38, 39, 40, 41, 42, 45–46, 59, 62, 90, 94, 103, 147–48, 149, 154–55, 157–59, 160, 168, 171, 188–89.

    In a book that discusses the "ruination of the human subject" in late 19th-century weird fiction, Hurley studies several of Hodgson's tales and novels, mostly those involving the sea, and utilizes his concept of the "abhuman."

58. ———. "The Modernist Abominations of William Hope Hodgson." In *Gothic Modernisms*, eds. Andrew Smith and Jeff Wallace. Basingstoke, UK: Palgrave, 2001, pp. 129–49.

59. Jones, Darryl. "Borderlands: Spiritualism and the Occult in Fin de Siècle and Edwardian Welsh and Irish Horror." *Irish Studies Review* 17, No. 1 (February 2009). 31–44.

60. Joshi, S. T. "Things in the Weeds: William Hope Hodgson." In Joshi's *Unutterable Horror: A History of Supernatural Fiction*. Hornsea, UK: PS Publishing, 2012, Vol. 2, pp. 445–51.

    Overview of Hodgson's career, with an emphasis on supernaturalism in the short stories.

61. Kidd, A. F. "The Realism of the Unreal: *The Ghost Pirates*, Hodgson's Little Masterpiece." In I.A.3.j, pp. vii–ix.

62. Koenig, H. C. "William Hope Hodgson." *Fantasy Fan* 2, No. 4 (December 1934): 56, 64.

63. ———. "On the Trail of the Weird and Phantastic: More Notes on William Hope Hodgson." *Phantagraph* 5, No. 4 (January 1937): 4–6.

64. ———. "William Hope Hodgson: Master of the Weird and Fantastic." *Reader and Collector* 3, No. 3 (June 1944): 1–4. In A.17, pp. vii–xi.

    Survey of Hodgson's life and work by the leading figure in Hodgson's posthumous recognition.

65. Lassen, Jeremy. "Editor's Introduction." In I.A.54, pp. ix–xi.

    Brief survey of *The Ghost Pirates*, the Captain Gault stories, and other works in the volume.

66. ———. "Editor's Introduction." In I.A.55, pp. ix-xi.

   Overview of *The House on the Borderland*, *Carnacki the Ghost-Finder*, and other works in the volume.

67. ———. "Editor's Introduction." In I.A.59, pp. ix-xiv.

   Survey of Hodgson's sea stories.

68. ———. "Editor's Introduction." In I.A.63, pp. ix-x.

   Brief overview of *The Night Land*.

69. Leiber, Fritz, Jr. "William Hope Hodgson: Writer of Supernatural Horror." *Reader and Collector* 3, No. 3 (June 1944): 11-12.

   Brief essay on Hodson's supernatural work, concluding that "the chief reason for his success in this field is the extreme, even naive, seriousness with which he went to work."

70. Lewis, C. S. "On Science Fiction." In *Of Other Worlds: Essays and Stories*. Ed. Walter Hooper. London: Geoffrey Bles, 1966; New York: Harcourt, Brace & World, 1967, p. 71.

   Lecture delivered to the Cambridge English Club, 24 November 1955. Contains a portion of a paragraph on *The Night Land*.

71. Lippi, Giuseppe. "Hodgson: La voce dell'abisso." In *Almanacco della paura*. Milan: Bonelli Editore, 2001, pp. 159-68.

72. Locke, George. "Introduction." In A.22, p. 6.

73. Lovecraft, H. P. "Supernatural Horror in Literature." In *The Outsider and Others*. Ed. August Derleth and Donald Wandrei. Sauk City, WI: Arkham House, 1939, pp. 541-43. New York: Ben Abramson, 1945; New York: Dover, 1973, pp. 82-85. Pawtucket, RI: Montilla Publications, 1992, pp. 85-86, 91. Chislehurst, UK: Gothic Society/Chatham House, 1994, pp. ?-?. Toronto: Bloodstone Press, 2002, pp. ?-?. New Kent, VA: Dead Letter Press, 2005, pp. ?-?. In *Dagon and Other Macabre Tales*, ed. August Derleth. Sauk City, WI: Arkham House, 1965, pp. 395-97; rev. ed. 1986 (ed. S. T. Joshi), pp. 417-19. As *The Annotated Supernatural Horror in Literature*. Ed. S. T. Joshi. New York: Hippocampus Press, 2000, pp. 58-60; rev. ed. 2012, pp. 77-79.

   Slightly altered version of below.

74. ———. "The Weird Work of William Hope Hodgson." *Phantagraph* 5, No. 5 (February 1937): 5-7. *Reader and Collector* 3, No. 3 (June 1944): 5-6. In A.42 (as "Introduction"). Tr. by Gianni Pilo as "I romanzi fantastici di William Hope Hodgson." In Lovecraft's *In difesa di Dagon e altri saggi sul fantastico*. Milan: SugarCo, 1995, pp. 173-78. In II.J.i.9, pp. 9-13 (as "Presentazione").

Tr. by Claudio De Nardi as "I romanzi fantastici di William Hope Hodgson." In Lovecraft's *Teoria dell'orrore*. Rome: Castelvecchi, 2001, pp. 142-46.

> Pioneering essay on Hodgson's four novels and the Carnacki stories, based on books lent to Lovecraft by H. C. Koenig. Later incorporated into "Supernatural Horror in Literature" (above), ch. 9.

75. Miéville, China. "'And Yet': The Antinomies of William Hope Hodgson." In I.A.53, pp. vii–ix.

76. ———. "Weird Fiction." In *The Routledge Companion to Science Fiction*, ed. Mark Bould, Andrew Butler, Adam Roberts, and Sherryl Vint. London & New York: Routledge, 2009, pp. 510-15.

77. Moskowitz, Sam. "The Posthumous Acceptance of William Hope Hodgson, 1918-1943." In I.A.43, pp. 11-79.

> Essay detailing the growth of Hodgson's reputation after his death and the handling of Hodgson's literary estate by his wife until her death.

78. ———. "Return to the Night Land: An Introduction," In I.A.20, pp. 9-12.

79. ———. "William Hope Hodgson." *Weird Tales* 47, No. 1 (Summer 1973): 38-49; 47, No. 2 (Fall 1973): 62-73; 47, No. 3 (Winter 1973): 35-48. Rpt. as the introduction to I.A.19, pp. 9-117.

> Exhaustive account of Hodgson's life and work.

80. ———. "William Hope Hodgson's Sister: Roadblock to Recognition." In I.A.47, pp. 11-52.

81. Pilo, Gianni. "Gli orrori marini di Hodgson." In II.J.i.6 (pp. 7-13), 7.

> Overview of Hodgson's horror tales of the sea.

82. ———. "Gli orrori di Hodgson." In Pilo's *I grandi romanzi dell'orrore*. Rome: Newton Compton, 1996, pp. 469-73.

83. ———. "William Hope Hodgson: Vita e opere." In II.J.i.5.

84. Queen, Ellery. "William Hope Hodgson and the Detective Story." *Reader and Collector* 3, No. 3 (June 1944): 10.

> Brief study of the Carnacki stories and their importance in the history of detective fiction.

85. Sawyer, Andy. "A Writer on the Borderland." In B.1, pp. 44-51.

> Study of *The House on the Borderland* and *The Night Land*, comparing these works to the science fiction novels of H. G. Wells.

86. [Searles, A. Langley.] "William Hope Hodgson: In His Own Day." *Fantasy Commentator* 1, No. 3 (Fall 1944): 43–48.

    Survey of the early reviews of Hodgson's books.

87. S[horter], C[lement] K. "A Literary Letter: The Loneliness of Eastbourne." *Sphere* (8 June 1918): 184.

    Part of the column announces the death of Hodgson, supplies an overview of his work, and quotes from one of his letters.

88. Sinclair, Iain. "An Aberrant Afterword: Blowing Dust in the House of Incest." In I.A.2.k, pp. 179–88.

    Eccentric analysis of *The House on the Borderland*, seeing it as "a spread tarot of dark possibilities. A challenge to our sanity and our courage."

89. ———. "'Vibrations in a Vacuum': Carnacki: An Afterword." In I.A.9.i, pp. 257–70.

    Idiosyncratic survey of the Carnacki stories.

90. Smith, Clark Ashton. "In Appreciation of William Hope Hodgson." *Phantagraph* (March–April 1937): ?–? (abridged; in H. C. Koenig's column "On the Trail of the Weird and Fantastic"). *Reader and Collector* 3, No. 3 (June 1944): 7. In *Planets and Dimensions: Collected Essays of Clark Ashton Smith*, ed. Charles K. Wolfe. Baltimore: Mirage Press, 1973, pp. 46–47.

    Praises Hodgson's imaginative vision and hopes for a wider readership for his work.

91. Spurlock, Neal Alan. "Ab-reality: The Metaphysical Vision of William Hope Hodgson." *Sargasso* 1, No. 1 (Fall 2013): 117–37.

    Discusses metaphysical, epistemological, and other philosophical issues in Hodgson's works.

92. Stableford, Brian. "The Composition of *The House on the Borderland*." In B.1, pp. 29–36.

    Examines the structure of the novel and conjectures that chapters 24–26 were written first.

93. ———. "Introduction." In I.A.2.o.

94. ———. "William Hope Hodgson." In *Scientific Romance in Britain 1890–1950*. London: Fourth Estate, 1985; New York: St. Martin's Press, 1985, pp. 91–102.

    Substantial discussion of Hodgson's novels and short stories, concluding that "there is nothing in his work which is authentically supernatural; his metaphysics is just as thoroughly dis-enchanted as Wells's, though it is certainly baroque."

95. Suster, Gerald. "Introduction." In I.A.9.g.3, pp. 7-10.
    Overview of Hodgson's life and work in the context of the Carnacki stories.

96. ———. "Introduction." In I.A.2.h, pp. ix-xiii.
    Brief and superficial survey of *The House on the Borderland*.

97. ———. "Introduction." In I.A.3.c.2, pp. ix-xi.

98. Szumskyj, Benjamin. "Outer Monstrosities: William Hope Hodgson's 'The Hog.'" *Wormwood* No. 12 (Spring 2009): 32-38.
    Briefly discusses the authorship controversy surrounding the story and then studies the possible sources for the theme of demonic swine in the story and in *The House on the Borderland*.

99. Tearle, Oliver. "Dustopian Fictions: William Hope Hodgson and the Thing to Do." *Interdisciplinary Humanities* 27, No. 2 (Fall 2010): 121-31.

100. Tremayne, Peter. "Child of All the Sea: The Sea-Horror Fiction." In B.1, pp. 11-18.
    General survey of Hodgson's sea horror tales, notably "The Voice in the Night."

101. ———. "High Priest of Horror: W. Hope Hodgson." *Lancashire Life* (January 1977): 30-31. Rev. ed. in I.A.21, pp. 7-14, and A.23, pp. 7-10, 15 (as "W. Hope Hodgson: His Life and Work").

102. Truchaud, François. "Hodgson ou la quête du surnaturel." In II.F.i.3.

103. ———. "Hodgson ou La voix de l'océan." In II.F.i.7, n.p.

104. ———. "W. H. Hodgson, celui qui venait de la mer." *Planète* (April-May 1972): ?-?. In II.F.i.8. Tr. by Fabio Calabrese as "William Hope Hodgson." *Il Re in Giallo* No. 6 (1979): 6-10.

105. Valentine, Mark. "Against the Abyss: *Carnacki the Ghost-Finder*." In B.1, pp. 24-28.
    Examination of the Carnacki tales, concluding that Carnacki's "encounters with the raw supernatural are amongst the most compellingly authentic in weird fiction."

106. ———. "WHH and Borth." In B.1, p. 10.
    Brief discussion of Hodgson's residence at Borth, in Wales.

107. ———. "The 'Wonder Unlimited'—The Tales of Captain Gault." *Sargasso* 1, No. 1 (Fall 2013): 79-88.
    Argues for the entertainment value of the Captain Gault stories.

108. Van Herp, Jacques. "Lovecraft, Jean Ray, Hodgson." *L'Herne* No. 12 (1969): 157-62.

109. Voglino, Alex. "Vita eroica di William Hope Hodgson." In II.J.i.9, pp. 14-28.

    Overview of Hodgson's life and work.

110. Wagar, W. Warren. *Terminal Visions: The Literature of Last Things*. Bloomington: Indiana University Press, 1982, pp. 21, 72, 94.

    Scattered discussion of *The Night Land*.

111. Warren, Alan. "Full Fathom Five: The Supernatural Fiction of William Hope Hodgson." In Darrell Schweitzer, ed. *Discovering Classic Horror Fiction I*. Mercer Island, WA: Starmont House, 1992, pp. 41-52.

    Wide-ranging survey of Hodgson's supernatural short stories, novels, and Carnacki stories.

112. Waugh, Arthur. *A Hundred Years of Publishing: Being the Story of Chapman & Hall, Ltd*. London: Chapman & Hall, 1930, pp. 217-18.

    Relates an anecdote in which Hodgson suggested a novel publicity campaign for *The Boats of the "Glen Carrig."*

113. Weinstein, Lee. "The First Literary Copernicus." *Nyctalops* 3, No. 1 (January 1980): 17-19.

    Maintains that Hodgson anticipated Lovecraft in the use of cosmicism as the basis for terror in his fiction. Several short stories and novels are studied in detail.

114. Wheatley, Dennis. "Introduction." In I.A.9.f.1, pp. ?-?.

115. ———. "Introduction." In I.A.3.c.1, pp. 9-10.

116. [Unsigned.] "William Hope Hodgson: Master of the Weird and Terrible." *Bookman's Journal & Print Collector* 2, No. 40 (30 July 1920): 215.

    Brief biocritical survey, with an analysis of Hodgson's methodology of supernatural writing.

E. Academic Papers

1. Alder, Emily Ruth. "William Hope Hodgson's Borderlands: Monstrosity, Other Worlds, and the Future at the Fin de Siècle." Ph.D. diss.: Edinburgh Napier University, 2009. 300 pp.

    Comprehensive analysis of Hodgson's life and works, focusing on the four novels and their relations to spiritualism, the occult, entropy, and other issues.

F. Book Reviews

1. *The Boats of the "Glen Carrig"* (1907)
   a. Koger, Grove. "All at Sea: The Best Novels, Stories, and Poems of the Sea." *Wilson Library Bulletin* 69, No. 4 (December 1994): 36–38 (esp. 37).
   b. Moslander, C. *Luna Monthly* Nos. 38/39 (July–August 1972): 47.
   c. [Unsigned.] *Bookman* (London) No. 196 (January 1908): 181.
   d. [Unsigned.] *Times Literary Supplement* No. 301 (17 October 1907): 319.

2. *The House on the Borderland* (1908)
   a. Carnell, John. *Science Fantasy* No. 55 (October 1969): 112.
   b. Cawthorn, James. *New Worlds* No. 189 (April 1969): 64.
   c. D'Ammassa, Don. *Science Fiction Chronicle* 5, No. 7 (April 1984): 34.
   d. Stableford, Brian. "Beneath the Bottom of the Barrel." *Necrofile* No. 22 (Fall 1996): 18–20.
   e. Sutton, David. *British Fantasy Society Newsletter* 11, No. 6 (Winter 1984–85): 77.
   f. [Unsigned.] *Books and Bookmen* 18, No. 7 (April 1973): 141.
   g. [Unsigned.] *Fantasy Review* 7, No. 6 (June 1984): 28.
   h. [Unsigned.] *Library Journal* 114, No. 6 (15 October 1989): 47.
   i. [Unsigned.] *New York Times Book Review* (10 June 1984): 36.
   j. [Unsigned.] *Spectator* No. 7576 (8 September 1973): 317.
   k. [Unsigned.] *Times Literary Supplement* No. 330 (7 May 1908): 151.
   l. [Unsigned.] *Washington Post Book World* (8 July 1984): 12.

3. *The Ghost Pirates* (1909)
   a. Barr, Robert. "A Creepy Ghost Book." *Idler* No. 87 (December 1909): ?–?.
   b. [Unsigned.] *Bookman* (London) No. 217 (October 1909): 54.
   c. [Unsigned.] "Hope Hodgson's Stories." *Bookman* (London) No. 348 (September 1920): 209.

4. *The Night Land* (1912)
   a. Chesson, W. H. *Occult Review* 15, No. 6 (June 1912): 376.
   b. Frederick, J. *Son of WSFA Journal* No. 100 (July 1973): 6.
   c. Pendennis [pseud.]. *Pall Mall Gazette* (4 May 1912): 9.
   d. [Unsigned.] *Bookman* (London) No. 249 (June 1912): 137.
   e. [Unsigned.] *Choice* 24, No. 4 (December 1986): 597.
   f. [Unsigned.] *Times Literary Supplement* No. 535 (11 April 1912): 147.
   g. [Unsigned.] *Vanity Fair* (London) No. 2273 (22 May 1912): 652–53.

   Other reviews are known to have appeared in the *Manchester Courier, Morning Leader, Country Life,* and *Morning Post.*

5. *Carnacki, the Ghost-Finder* (1913)
    a. Hays, R. W. *Armchair Detective* 5, No. 2 (January 1972): 99.
    b. Moskowitz, Sam. *Fantastic Novels Magazine* 3, No. 5 (January 1949): 115.
    c. [Pirie-Gordon, Harry (13th Laird of Buthlaw).] *Times Literary Supplement* No. 585 (27 March 1913): 131.
    d. Sandoe, James. *Chicago Sun Book Week* (6 February 1948): 72.
    e. [Unsigned.] *Bookman* (London) No. 261 (June 1913): 142.
    f. [Unsigned.] "Hope Hodgson's Stories." *Bookman* (London) No. 348 (September 1920): 209.
    g. [Unsigned.] *Saturday Review of Literature* 31, No. 7 (14 February 1948): 34.
    h. [Unsigned.] *Spectator* No. 7576 (8 September 1973): 317.

    Other reviews are known to have appeared in the *Westminster Gazette*, *British Weekly*, *Globe*, *Daily Express*, and *Liverpool Courier*.

6. *Men of the Deep Waters* (1914)
    a. [Capper, John Brainerd.] "Short Stories of the Sea." *Times Literary Supplement* No. 664 (8 October 1914): 448.
    b. [Unsigned.] *Bookman* (London) No. 278 (November 1914): 54.

    Other reviews are known to have appeared in the *London Times*, *Glasgow Herald*, and *Liverpool Courier*.

7. *The Luck of the Strong* (1916)
    a. [Unsigned.] *Bookman* (London) No. 299 (August 1916): 142.

    Another review is known to have appeared in the *Daily Telegraph*.

8. *Captain Gault* (1917)
    a. [Unsigned.] *Boston Transcript* (11 September 1918): 6.
    b. [Unsigned.] *Nation* No. 2768 (20 July 1918): 74.
    c. [Unsigned.] *New York Times Book Review* (4 April 1918): 167.
    d. [Unsigned.] *Springfield Republican* (26 May 1918): 15.

9. *The Calling of the Sea* (1920)
    a. [Dalton, Frederick Thomas.] *Times Literary Supplement* No. 948 (18 March 1920): 191.
    b. [Unsigned.] "Hope Hodgson's Poems." *Bookman* (London) No. 344 (May 1920): 81.

10. *The House on the Borderland and Other Novels* (1946)
    a. Boucher, Anthony. "Recent Books on Horror and Fantasy." *San Francisco Chronicle* (22 September 1946), *This Week* section, p. 18.
    b. Winebaum, B. V. "Four-Decker Horror Special." *New York Times Book Review* (15 September 1946): 20.
    c. [Unsigned.] New York Herald Tribune Weekly Book Review (29 September 1946): 12.

11. *Deep Waters* (1967)
    a. Lowndes, Robert A. W. *Startling Mystery Stories* 1, No. 5 (Summer 1967): 117.
12. *Spectral Manifestations* (1984)
    a. Stableford, Brian. *Fantasy Review* 8, No. 2 (February 1985): 16.
13. *The Haunted Pampero* (1991)
    a. Bush, Laurence C. "The White Rat among the Grey." *Necrofile* No. 10 (Fall 1993): 20-22.
    b. D'Ammassa, Don. *Science Fiction Chronicle* 14, No. 3 (December 1992): 38.
14. *Demons of the Sea* (1992)
    a. D'Ammassa, Don. *Science Fiction Chronicle* 13, No. 9 (June 1992): 34.
    b. Stableford, Brian. "Deep Waters Run Still." *Necrofile* No. 5 (Summer 1992): 8-9.
15. *At Sea* (1993)
    a. D'Ammassa, Don. *Science Fiction Chronicle* 15, No. 5 (March 1994): 33-34.
16. *The Uncollected William Hope Hodgson* (1995)
    a. D[ziemianowicz], S[tefan]. *Necrofile* No. 18 (Fall 1995): 27.
17. *Beyond the Dawning* (1995)
    a. D[ziemianowicz], S[tefan]. *Necrofile* No. 18 (Fall 1995): 27.
18. *Terrors of the Sea* (1996)
    a. Stableford, Brian. "Beneath the Bottom of the Barrel." *Necrofile* No. 22 (Fall 1996): 18-20.
19. *The Boats of the "Glen Carrig" and Other Nautical Adventures* (2003)
    a. De Lint, Charles. "Books to Look For." *Magazine of Fantasy and Science Fiction* 105, No. 6 (December 2003): 24-27 (esp. 25-26).
    b. Green, Roland. *Booklist* 100, No. 1 (1 September 2003): 74.
    c. Kelleghan, Fiona. "Science Fiction and Fantasy." *Washington Post Book World* (24 August 2003): 13.
    d. [Unsigned.] *Publishers Weekly* 250, No. 33 (18 August 2003): 63.

Indexes

A. Names

Adcock, Arthur St. John I.A.15, B.ii.38n; III.D.6, D.1
Adey, Robert I.B.i.8.b
Adrian, Jack I.B.i.8.b
Ahola, Tomás González II.H.i.1
Aickman, Robert I.B.i.102.n
Albrod, Bettina II.I.ii.10.a
Alder, Emily Ruth III.E.2, 3, 4, 5, E.1
Alldis, Brian W. III.E.6
Allie, Scott I.B.i.99.i
Alpers, Hans Joachim II.I.ii.1.a, 2.b, 4.a, 6.a, 13.a, 15.g
Anderson, Douglas A. I.A.62, 64, B.i.5.f; II.B.ii.1.a; III.E.7, 8, 9
Andersson, Martin II.R.ii.9.a
Aramata, Hiroshi II.L.i.3
Arcelli, Tilde II.K.ii.30.a, b
Arellano, Francisco Javier II.Q.i.16
Arthur, Robert I.B.i.17.m, 91.e, 102.p
Ash, Brian III.D.1
Ashley, Mike I.A.61, B.i.5.h, 34.c, 58.c; II.I.ii.10.a; III.B.1, B.1, C.2, D.10, 11, 12

Bacon, Jonathan I.B.iii.43.a, 76.b
Balam, Alaric II.Q.ii.2.a
Balanos, Giorgos II.J.i.1
Baron, Jacques II.G.i.1, 8
Barr, Robert III.G.3.a
Barron, Neil III.D.21
Behrends, Steve III.E.13
Bell, Ian I.A.25; III.B.2, B.1, C.6, D.14, 15, 16, 17, 18
Bell, Joseph III.B.3
Bellomi, Antonio II.K.ii.1.b, 2.b, 3.a, 4.a, 5.a, 6.a, 8.a, 9.a, 11.a, 12.d, 13.b, 15.c, 17.a, 18.a, 19.b, 20.a, 23.a, 24.a, 25.a, 26.a, 27.a, 29.a, 30.f
Benstock, Bernard III.D.7
Berghorn, Rickard II.R.i.3, ii.16.a, 18.c
Bestar, Barbara I.C.1
Betancourt, John I.B.i.33.f

Bigongiari, Diego II.Q.ii.4.a
Birchby, Sid III.D.32, D.19
Blacklin, Malcolm I.B.i.102.y
Blackmore, Leigh III.E.20
Bleiler, E. F. III.D.3, 4, 5
Bloom, Clive III.E.21
Bloom, Harold III.D.6
Bok, Hannes I.A.65
Boronzini, Andrea II.Q.ii.1.a
Borowitz, Albert III.D.7
Borselli, Mauro III.D.8
Boucher, Anthony III.G.10.a
Bould, Mark III.E.76
Boulter, Amanda III.E.21
Boyer, Robert H. I.B.i.44.c
Brendán, Iria II.Q.i.9
Bruno, Jacopo II.K.i.9
Bull, R. C. I.B.i.17.i, 102.l
Bush, Laurence C. III.G.13.a
Busnelli, Paolo II.K.i.3, ii.32.a, b
Butler, Andrew III.E.76

Calabrese, Fabio III.E.104
Cammarota, Domenico II.K.i.4; III.E.22
Campbell, Lori III.E.23
Capper, John Brainerd III.G.6.a
Carimati, Stefania II.K.ii.3.a, 6.a, 9.a, 17.a, 18.a, 23.a, 27.a, 29.f
Carnell, John III.G.2.a
Carson, Dave I.B.i.49.d, g
Carter, Lin III.D.32, D.24, 25, 26, 27
Cartocci, Giauco II.K.i.2
Casas, Mariano II.Q.i.8
Castro, Esperanza II.Q.i.11
Cawthorn, James III.D.9, 10, F.2.b
Ceglie, Vince I.C.6
Čermák, Jan II.B.ii.4.b
Chardome, Émile II.G.i.11, ii.3.a
Charpentier, Annette von II.I.i.3
Chesson, W. H. III.G.4.a
Child, Lincoln I.B.i.102.ff, hh

Christensen, Peter III.D.6, D.28
Cicchetti, Bernardo II.K.ii.21.a
Clauss, Martin II.I.i.7
Coburn, James I.C.2
Conklin, Groff I.B.i.17.g
Cooke, Alan I.C.4
Corben, Richard I.C.7
Cossato, G. II.K.ii.30.e
Crispin, Edmund I.B.i.102.o
Cross, John Keir I.B.i.17.k
Cuddon, J. A. I.B.i.17.p
Currey, L. W. III.B.4
Cusó, Francisco II.Q.i.3, 5

Dalby, Richard I.B.i.36.f, 91.g, 100.d;
   II.F.ii.2.a; III.C.1, D.29, 30
Dalton, Frederick Thomas III.G.9.a
D'Ammassa, Don III.G.2.c, 13.b,
   14.a, 15.a
Dan, Seiji II.L.i.1
Danby, Mary I.B.i.102.dd, 107.r
Daniels, Les I.B.i.102.w, 107.q
David, Michael II.B.ii.1.a
Davide, Ornella Ranieri II.K.i.8
Davidson, Brett III.E.31
Day, Jennifer II.A.i.1
Debra, Juan II.K.ii.16.b
De Carlo, Giuliana II.K.ii.16.d
de la Mare, Colin I.B.i.102.d
De Lint, Charles III.G.19.a
De Nardi, Claudio III.E.74
Derleth, August I.A.18, B.i.15.a, 44.a,
   53.c, 108.b; II.I.ii.7.a, K.ii.22.a;
   III.E.32, 33, 73
De Turris, Gianfranco II.K.i.9;
   III.D.11, D.34, 35
Díaz, Lorenzo II.Q.i.19
Dienel, Traude II.I.i.2, ii.16.a
Diesel, Andreas II.I.ii.11.a, 15.f
Di Marco, Lydia II.K.ii.19.a
Dobson, Roger III.C.1, D.36
Donald, James I.C.2
Dotrice, Michele I.C.4
Dracht, Tonke II.D.ii.1.a
Duperray, Max II.G.i.10; III.E.37, 38
Dziemianowicz, Stefan I.B.i.7.f, 16.c,
   17.t, 36.m, 45.k; III.D.24, F.16.a, 17.a

Eckhardt, Jason I.C.6
Edkins, E. A. III.E.39
Ekholm, Steven II.R.ii.12.a
Ellis, Phillip A. III.E.40
Elwood, Roger I.B.i.7.e, 15.c, 36.c,
   51.f; II.I.ii.5.a
Enfield, Alexander. *See* Haining, Peter
Ernsberger, George I.B.i.102.u
Everts, R. Alain I.A.27-42; III.C.2, D.41

Fabian, Stephen E. I.A.65
Falk, Bertil II.R.ii.10.a
Fanoli, Rita II.K.ii.31.a, b
Feilhauer, Angelika II.I.ii.15.e
Fenner, Phyllis R. I.B.i.23.e
Festa, Frank II.I.ii.8.a, 15.f
Fletcher, Jo I.B.iii.39.g
Flintzberg, Hans II.R.ii.1.a
Formenti, Roberta II.K.ii.30.d
Frank, Jane I.A.60, 61; III.E.42, 43
Franklin, Michael III.D.18, 19
Fransson, Mikeal II.R.ii.2.a
Frederick, J. III.G.4.b
Frederiksson, Karl G. II.R.ii.5.a
Frederiksson, Lilian II.R.ii.5.a
Fruttero, Carlo II.K.i.1, ii.16.d
Fusco, Sebastiano II.K.ii.1.c, 2.c, 10.a,
   11.b, 12.e, 13.c, 16.c, 22.a; III.D.11,
   D.35

Gafford, Sam I.A.1n, 44, 45, 46, 48,
   49, 50; III.C.3, C.6, D.44, 45, 46,
   47, 48, 49, 50, 51, 52, 53
Galdo, Daniela II.K.i.5, ii.1.a, 11.b,
   13.a
Gandolfo, Elvio E. II.Q.i.4
Gecse, Nicu II.O.i.1
Germeraad, R. II.D.i.1
Ghidalia, Vic I.B.i.15.c, 36.c; II.I.ii.5.a
Gianni, Gary I.B.i.36.n, 99.l
Giorgi, Giorgio II.K.i.5; III.E.54
Gissy, Peter II.R.ii.17.a
Goimard, Jacques II.G.ii.4.a, b
Goldsmith, Howard I.B.i.7.e, 51.f
Görden, Michael II.I.ii.12.a
Goss, Michael III.C.1; D.55
Grafton, John I.B.i.17.z
Green, Howard J. I.C.1
Green, Roland III.G.19.b

Greenberg, Martin H. I.B.i.7.f, 16.c, 17.t, 36.g, 76.c
Greene, Hugh I.B.i.53.c; II.I.ii.9.a, b, d, J.ii.15.a
Grenier, Christian II.G.ii.7.b
Gronwald, Werner II.I.ii.7.a
Gross-Hermanns, Annegret II.I.ii.5.a
Gruenberg, Axel I.C.1
Guarriello, Pietro II.K.i.9; III.B.5

Haefele, John III.E.56
Haigh, Wayne I.C.6
Haining, Peter I.B.i.45.e, 46.d, 52.c, 94.d, 107.v
Hansson, Maria II.R.i.3, ii.18.b, c
Haydock, Tim I.B.i.12.i, 17.r
Hays, R. W. III.G.5.a
Heje, Johan III.D.12
Herron, Don III.D.13
Hiller, Arthur I.C.2
Hitchcock, Alfred I.B.i.102.k, 107.f, g, i; II.B.ii.2.a, 4.a, D.ii.2.e, G.ii.8.a, K.ii.30.a, b, 31.a, b
Hoizumi, Hiroshi I.C.3
Hoke, Helen I.B.i.51.e, 102.x, 107.p
Honda, Ishiro I.C.3
Hooper, Walter III.E.70
Hoshi, Shinichi I.C.3
Houdini, Harry I.B.ii.3n, 12n
Hurley, Kelly III.E.57, 58
Hylin, Birgitta II.R.i.3, ii.3.a, c, e

Iannou, Greg I.B.i.102.kk
Itsuji, Akemi II.L.i.4

Jones, Darryl III.E.59
Jones, Stephen I.B.i.49.d, g, 51.h, 102.qq; II.K.ii.14.b; III.D.17
Joshi, S. T. I.B.i.102.ll, C.6; III.C.1.a, C.24, D.60, 73

Kantůrek, Jan II.B.ii.2.a
Katzmarz, Hubert II.I.ii.3.a
Kaye, Marvin I.B.i.93.e
Kelahan, Michael. *See* Dziemianowicz, Stefan
Kelleghan, Roland III.G.19.c
Kernahan, Coulson I.A.2n, 3n, 48, B.ii.17n
Keyha, Andrzej II.N.i.2

Kidd, A. F. III.E.61
Kielty, Bernadine I.B.i.102.g
Kimura, Takeshi I.C.3
Kipling, Rudyard I.B.ii.16n
Klein, T. E. D. III.D.14
Kluge, Manfred II.I.ii.16.a
Koenig, H. C. I.A.17; III.E.62, 63, 64, 74n, 90
Koger, Grove III.G.1.a
Körber, Joachim II.I.ii.14.a, b
Koskela, Pertti II.F.ii.2.a
Kot, G. II.P.i.1.a
Kubo, Akira I.C.3

Lacourbe, Roland II.G.ii.2.a
Lalanda, Javier Martin II.Q.i.10
Lamb, Hugh I.B.i.7.d, 35.f, 66.f, g, 72.h, 99.f, j; II.R.ii.14.a, 17.b
Lankester, Erik II.D.ii.1.b, 2.c, d, 3.b
Lassen, Jeremy I.A.54, 55, 59, 63, 70; III.E.65, 66, 67, 68
Last, Martin III.D.18
Latyseva, N. M. II.P.i.1.a
Lee, Elizabeth I.B.i.102.m
Leiber, Fritz III.E.69
Lévy, Maurice II.G.i.10
Lewis, C. S. III.E.70
Lewis, Gogo I.B.i.51.d
Lippi, Giuseppe II.K.i.9, ii.30.c; III.E.71
Locke, George I.A.22, 26, B.i.45.f, 71.c, 101.c; III.B.6, D.72
Lofficier, Jean Marc II.G.ii.9.a
Lovecraft, H. P. I.A.17n, 42; II.K.i.9; III.D.6, 32, D.44n, 56n, 73, 74
Lowndes, Robert A. W. III.G.11.a
Lucentini, Franco II.K.i.1, ii.16.d
Lundwall, Sam J. II.R.i.2, ii.4.a, b, c, 12.a, 15.a
Luraschi, Abramo II.K.ii.15.b, c

Maartens, Maarten I.B.ii.15n
McDonald, T. Liam I.B.i.7.f
Mackie, Philip I.C.4
McLean, Steven III.E.3
Macnee, Patrick I.C.2
McSherry, Frank D. I.B.i.17.s
Magill, Frank N. III.D.13, 15, 16, 20, 29
Manley, Seon I.B.i.51.d

Marcel, Patrick II.G.i.6.c, 10
Marshall, Gene I.B.i.43.b
Masters, Anthony I.B.i.107.o
May, Hal III.D.31
Mazzeo, Henry I.B.i.107.l
Meachum, Beth III.D.18, 19
Mida II.K.ii.1.b, 2.b, 8.a, 13.b, 20.a, 26.a, 28.b
Miéville, China III.E.75, 76
Miller, Ian I.A.65
Mizuno, Kumi I.C.3
Montanari, Gianni II.K.ii.14.a
Moorcock, Michael III.D.9, 10
Moore, Alan I.C.7
Moroz, A. II.P.i.1.a
Moskowitz, Sam I.A.19, 43, 47, 65, B.i.39.e, 77.b, 102.s; II.K.ii.30.e; III.D.32, D.77, 78, 79, 80, F.5.b
Moslander, C. III.G.1.b
Mühlstrasser, Rudolf II.I.ii.12.a
Müller, Ondřej II.B.ii.4.b

Napier, Alan I.C.1
Natuki, Kenzi II.L.i.6
Nebreda, José Maria II.Q.i.12, 13, 14, 17, 18
Neilson, Keith III.D.15, 16
Nenonen, Kari II.F.i.1
Netherwood, Bryan A. I.B.i.17.n
Newman, Kim III.D.17
Nicholls, Peter III.D.22
Nielsen, Bjarne II.C.i.1
Norton, Alden H. I.B.i.3.d
Notking, R. II.K.ii.16.c

Oanţă, Emilia II.O.i.2
Ogura, Takashi II.L.i.5
Oliver, Francisco Torres II.Q.i.2, 17
Olney, Ross R. I.B.i.107.n
Oščádal, Jan Jam II.B.i.1
Oščádalová, Jana II.B.i.1

Panken, Jef II.D.i.2
Parrish, J. M. I.B.i.102.e
Parry, Michel I.B.i.35.e, 36.d, e, 51.g, 66.e; II.R.ii.6.a, 13.a
Parsons, Jacques II.G.i.2, 4, 6, 7, 8
Pastorino, Diego II.K.ii.14.b
Pattrick, William I.B.i.33.e

Pendennis III.G.4.c
Penzler, Otto III.D.25, 26
Peroutková, Ivana II.B.ii.4.a
Person, James E. III.D.32
Pessina, Héctor R. II.Q.i.1
Piccioli, Maria Barbara II.K.i.9, ii.28.a
Pilo, Gianni II.K.i.4, 5, 6, 7, ii.1.a, c, 2.a, c, 8.b, 10.a, b, 11.b, 12.e, 13.a, c, 16.e, f; III.E.74, 81, 82, 83
Pirie-Gordon, Harry (13th Laird of Buthlaw) III.G.5.c
Pleasence, Donald I.C.4
Polakovics, Friedrich II.I.i.4, ii.2.b, 6.a, 13.a
Pollini, Alfredo II.K.i.2, ii.22.a
Poupard, Dennis III.D.32
Pratchett, Terry III.D.17
Pringle, David III.D.23
Prins, Aart C. II.D.ii.3.a
Pronzini, Bill I.B.i.99.e
Pugi, Jean-Pierre II.G.i.5
Purdom, Edmund I.C.1

Queen, Ellery I.B.i.23.c; III.E.84

Ramone, Jenni III.E.5
Rasmussen, Solveig II.R.ii.6.a, 11.a, 14.a
Raven, Robert I.A.52
Redmalm, Gunnar II.R.i.1
Reilly, John M. III.D.4
Revelstroke, Simon I.C.7
Roberts, Adam III.E.76
Ronson, Mark I.B.i.102.z
Rosén, Knut II.R.ii.17.b

Saarinen, Osmo II.F.ii.3.a
Sadalahto, Markku II.F.ii.1.a, 3.a
Sahl, Habby II.G.i.8
Salcedo, Ruth G. II.Q.i.7
Sánchez, Jorge A. II.Q.i.1, 4
Sandow, James III.G.5.d
Sandrelli, S. II.K.ii.30.e
Sarrantonio, Al I.B.i.76.c
Sauer, Lothar II.I.ii.15.b, d
Sawyer, Andy III.C.1, D.85
Schell, Tilly II.D.ii.2.e
Schinkler, Peter II.R.ii.1.b
Schweitzer, Darrell III.E.111
Searles, A. Langley I.A.17; III.B.7, D.86

Searles, Baird III.D.18, 19
Seehafer, Klaus II.I.ii.2.a
Serdjukova, A. II.P.i.1.a
Shepard, Leslie I.B.i.102.aa
Shorter, Clement K. III.E.87
Siefener, Michael II.I.i.5
Silliphant, Stirling I.C.2
Sinclair, Iain III.E.88, 89
Smith, Andrew III.E.58
Smith, Clark Ashton III.D.32, D.90
Smith, Curtis C. III.D.30
Smith, Peter C. I.B.i.102.v, 107.s
Sōlou, Tetī II.J.i.2
Spiegel, Ingrid II.I.ii.15.a
Spiegel, Walter II.I.ii.15.a
Spurlock, Neal Alan III.E.91
Stableford, Brian II.G.i.6n, H.i.5;
   III.C.1, C.6, 20, 21, 22, 23, 24,
   D.92, 93, 94, F.2.d, 12.a, 14.b, 18.a
Staffilano, Gaetano II.K.ii.14.a
Staley, Thomas III.D.7
Stead, Christina I.B.i.12.f
Steedman, Tony I.C.4
Steinbrunner, Chris III.D.25, 26
Stragliati, Roland II.G.ii.3.b, 4.a, b
Strandberg, Olof II.R.ii.3.a, c
Sullivan, Jack I.B.i.102.ee; III.D.14, 27
Suster, Gerald III.E.95, 96, 97
Sutton, David III.G.2.e
Sutton, Stephen P. I.B.i.102.t
Svensson, Hanna II.R.ii.16.a
Swahn, Sven Christer II.R.ii.11.a
Szumskyj, Benjamin III.E.98

Tamburini, Pico II.K.ii.7.a
Targowska-Grabińska, Małgorzata II.N.i.1
Tasso, Bruno II.K.ii.12.a, b
Tazawa, Yukio II.L.i.2
Tearle, Oliver III.E.99
Teichmann, Wulf II.I.i.1, ii.1.a, 2.a,
   4.a, 15.c, g
Thompson, Diane I.B.i.107.q
Tiburtini, Alessandro II.K.i.7
Tirone, Maria Teresa II.K.ii.2.a
Tosi, Patrizia II.K.ii.4.a, 5.a, 11.a,
   12.d, 19.b, 24.a, 25.a, 29.a
Tremayne, Peter I.A.21, 23; II.A.i.1;
   III.C.1, D.100, 101

Troyanovich, Steve I.B.iii.43.a, 76.b
Truchaud, François II.G.i.3, 7n, 8, 9;
   III.E.102, 103, 104
Tuck, Donald H. III.B.8
Twitchen, Gemma III.E.5
Tymn, Marshall B. III.D.27

Vaarpuu, Tarmo II.E.i.1
Vandenberg, Patricia II.B.ii.3.a
Valentine, Mark I.B.i.36.k; III.C.1,
   C.6, D.105, 106, 107
Valla, Ricardo II.K.i.4
Vallejo, Boris II.K.i.5
van den Broek, C. A. G. II.D.ii.3.a
Van Herp, Jacques III.E.108
Van Hollander, Jason I.A.54, 55, 59,
   63, 64
Van Thal, Herbert I.B.i.107.h, m
Vidinski, Denis II.I.i.6
Vint, Sherryl III.E.76
Voglino, Alex II.K.i.9; III.E.109
Volpatti, Lia II.K.ii.12.a, b

Waedt, C. F. I.B.i.43.b
Wagar, W. Warren III.E.110
Wallace, Jeff III.E.58
Wandrei, Donald III.E.73
Warren, Alan III.E.111
Waugh, Arthur III.E.112
Waugh, Charles G. I.B.i.17.s, 36.g
Weinberg, Robert E. I.B.i.16.c, 17.t, 33.f
Weinstein, Lee III.E.113
Wells, H. G. III.E.3n, 31n, 85n, 94n
Wheatley, Dennis I.B.i.12.d, h, 17.d,
   j, 107.c, j; III.D.32, D.114, 115
White, Tim II.K.i.4
Wilson, Gahan I.B.i.91.h
Winebaum, B. V. III.D.32, F.10.b
Wingrove, David III.D.28, D.6
Winick, L. II.D.i.1
Wolfe, Charles K. III.E.90
Wolfe, Gary K. III.D.6, 29, 30
Wollheim, Donald A. I.B.i.17.h, 45.d,
   72.e, 91.d, 102.h, u

Yano, Kozaburo II.L.ii.1.a

Zahorski, Kenneth J. I.B.i.44.c
Zetterlund, Gösta II.R.ii.7.a
Zoschke, Barbara II.I.ii.15.d

B. Works by Hodgson

"A la recherche du *Graiken*" II.G.i.9
"Ääni yössä" II.F.ii.3.a
"Abitanti di Middle Islet, Gli" II.K.ii.12.a, b, d, e
Adrift on the Haunted Seas: The Best Short Stories of William Hope Hodgson I.A.62
"Adventure of the Deep Waters, An" I.A.62, 64, B.i.94.b, f, g
"Adventure of the Garter, The" I.A.14, 46, 54, B.i.1
"Adventure of the Headland, The" I.A.18, 54, B.i.11.c, d
"Adventure with the Claim Jumpers, The" I.A.54, B.i.2
"After the Years" I.A.60, B.iii.1
"Al largo" II.K.ii.30.c
"Albatro, L'" II.K.ii.1.a, c
"Albatros, L'" II.K.ii.1.b
"Albatross, L'" II.G.i.9
"Albatross, The" I.A.19, 47, 59, 65, B.i.3; II.G.i.9, K.ii.1
All Gothic I.A.51
"Alla ricerca della *Graiken*" II.K.ii.8.a
"Amanda Panda" I.A.14, B.iii.2
"Anello, L'" II.K.ii.10.a, b
"Apprentices' Mutiny, The" I.B.i.4
Aquas profundas (seis relatos de horror) II.Q.i.4
Ar morgezep II.A.i.1
At Sea I.A.45; III.G.15
Attack of the Mushroom People I.C.3n
"Aventure du promontoire, L'" II.G.i.8
"Avventura del promontorio, L'" II.K.ii.4.a

"Ballade" I.A.60, B.iii.3
"Bateau de pierre, Le" II.G.i.8
"Baumoff Explosive, The" I.A.27, 42, B.i.5; II.B.ii.1, G.i.9, ii.1, K.i.6, 9, ii.2, R.i.3
Baumoff Explosive, The I.A.27
"Bells of the *Laughing Sally*, The" I.A.44, 54, B.i.6
"Bestia orribile, La" II.K.i.6

"Beyond the Dawning" I.A.15, 22, 49, 60, B.iii.4
Beyond the Dawning: The Poems of William Hope Hodgson I.A.49; III.G.17
"Bibliophilie" II.G.i.8
"Billy Ben" I.A.14, B.iii.5
Boats of the "Glen Carrig," The I.A.1, 17, 51, 52, 53, 54, 65, 66, 67, B.i.7; II.G.i.2, 7, H.i.1, I.i.1, K.i.2, Q.i.8, 14, 17; III.D.15, D.112n, F.1
Boats of the "Glen Carrig" and Other Nautical Adventures, The I.A.54; III.G.19
Boote der "Glen Carrig," Die II.I.i.1, ii.1.a
Bordercrossings: The Fantasy Novels of William Hope Hodgson I.A.66
Borderlands: Four Horror Fantasies I.A.52
Botes del "Glen Carrig," Los II.Q.i.14
"Boy Billy Boo-Hoo" I.A.61, B.iii.6
"Bridge of Melody, The" I.A.60, B.iii.7
"Bring Out Your Dead" I.A.8, 60, B.iii.8
"Buccaneer Comes Back, The" I.B.i.9.a
"Bullion" I.A.43, 55, B.i.8; II.K.ii.3
"By the Lee" I.A.49, 59, B.ii.1

"Call in the Dawn, The" I.A.18, 54, B.i.101.b, d
"Calling of the Sea, The" I.A.15, 22, 48, 60, B.iii.9; II.I.i.6
Calling of the Sea, The I.A.15; III.G.9
Canots du "Glen Carrig," Les II.G.i.7
"Capt. Gumbolt Charity and the Painted Lady" I.A.13, 64, B.i.29.b, f
"Capt. Jat—The Adventure of the Headland" I.A.13, B.i.11; II.G.i.8, K.ii.4
"Capt. Jat—The Island of the Ud" I.A.13, B.i.12
"Captain Dan Danblasten" I.A.61, 64, B.i.9
"Captain Dang" I.A.49, 64, B.i.10

Captain Gault: Being the Exceedingly Private Log of a Sea-Captain I.A.14; III.G.8
"Captain Jat: An Account of Certain Adventures: The Island of the Ud" I.B.i.12.b
"Captain of the Onion Boat, The" I.A.11, 63, B.i.13
Captain of the Onion Boat, The I.A.6
Cargunka and Poems and Anecdotes I.A.12
Carnacki, cacciatore di spettri II.K.i.3
Carnacki, de spokenjager II.D.i.2
Carnacki, der Geisterfinder II.I.i.7
Carnacki, el cazador de fantasmas II.Q.i.19
Carnacki, el cazafantasmas II.Q.i.10
Carnacki et les fantômes II.G.i.3
"Carnacki, le chasseur de fantômes" II.G.i.10
Carnacki, le chasseur de fantomes II.G.i.11
"Carnacki, the Ghost Finder" [abridgment] I.A.5, 25, 43, 64, B.i.14; II.G.i.10
Carnacki, the Ghost-Finder I.A.9; II.D.i.2, G.i.3, 8n, 11, I.i.7, K.i.3, L.i.2, 6, O.i.1, Q.i.10, 19; III.D.13, D.28n, 65n, 105n, F.5
Carnacki, the Ghost Finder and a Poem I.A.5
Carnacki, vânătorul de fantome II.O.i.1
Casa en el confín de la tierra, La II.Q.i.2
Casa en el confín del mundo, El II.Q.i.7, 16
Casa en el limite, La II.Q.i.1
Casa sull'abisso, La II.K.i.1, 4, 7, 9, ii.16.a, b, c
Casa sull'abisso e altri racconti, La II.K.i.4
Casa sull'abisso a eltri storie del terrore, La II.K.i.9
Casa no confín, A II.H.i.1
"Casa tra i lauri, La" II.K.i.3
"Case of the Chinese Curio Dealer, The" I.A.14, 46, 54, B.i.24.b, c, d
"Case of the Whistling Room, The" I.C.5
"Cavallo dell'invisibile, Il" II.K.ii.15.b, c

"Cavallo fantasma, Il" II.K.ii.15.a
"Cavallo invisibile, Il" II.K.i.3
"Cavallucci marini, I" II.K.ii.23.a
"Chair Exercises" I.B.ii.2
"Challenge to the 'Handcuff King' at Blackburn" I.B.ii.3
"Chambre d'épouvante, La" II.G.i.10
"Chambre qui sifflait, La" II.G.i.3, ii.9.a
"Chevaux marins, Les" II.G.i.8
"Cheval de l'invisible, Le" II.G.i.3
"'Chose' dans les algues, La" II.G.i.8
Chose dans les algues, La II.G.i.1
Chose dans les algues; Deux Adventures de Carnacki, La II.G.i.8
"Chose invisible, La" II.G.i.8
"Cinquième Message, Le" II.G.i.8
"Conqueror, The" I.A.61, B.iii.10
"Conquest" I.A.60, B.iii.11
"Contraband of War" I.A.14, 46, 54, B.i.21.b, c, d
"Cosa invisibile, La" II.K.i.3
"'Cosa' nelle alghe, La" II.K.ii.27.a
"Crew der Lancing, Die" II.I.i.1, ii.2.a, b
"Crew of the *Lancing*, The" I.A.18, 64, B.i.15; II.G.i.8, I.i.1, ii.2, K.ii.5, R.ii.1
Cuentos de alta mar II.Q.i.9
"Cyclonic Storm, A" I.A.61, B.ii.4, 34.d
"Cynic in Hell, The" I.A.60, B.iii.12
"D.C.O. Cargunka—The Adventure with the Claim Jumpers" I.A.13, B.i.2.c
"D.C.O. Cargunka—The Bells of the *Laughing Sally*" I.A.12, 13, B.i.6.d
"Dämonen des Meeres" II.I.i.3.a
"Date 1965: Modern Warfare" I.A.43, 44, 64, B.ii.5
"De la mer immobile" II.G.i.8
"Death" I.A.60, B.iii.13
"Death Cry of Young Genius, The" I.A.60, B.iii.14
Deep Waters I.A.18; II.G.i.1, 8; III.D.20, D.32n, F.11
"Demons of the Sea" I.A.44, 49, 59, 62, 70, B.i.16; II.I.ii.3, R.ii.2
Demons of the Sea I.A.44; III.G.14

"Derelict, The" I.A.11, 21, 52, 57, 59, 62, 65, B.i.17; II.D.i.1, ii.1, F.ii.1, G.i.8, ii.2, I.i.1, ii.4, K.ii.6, Q.i.4, 9, 11, R.i.3, ii.3
Derelict, The I.A.57
"Dernier Voyage du Shamraken, Le" II.G.i.8
"Diamond Cut Diamond with a Vengeance" I.A.64, B.i.18
"Diamond Spy, The" I.A.14, 46, 54, B.i.22.b, c, d
"Ding im Seetang, Das" II.I.i.4, ii.13.a
"Dio, dio, perché non mi aiuti?" II.K.i.6, ii.2.c
"Dödens gudinna" II.R.ii.8.a, b, c
Dom na granicy światów II.N.i.1
Down in the Weeds I.A.50
"Down the Long Coast" I.A.15, 22, 48, 61, B.iii.15
"Downstairs on a Bicycle: A Daring Feat at Blackburn" I.B.ii.6
"Dr. Thomas's Vibration Method versus Sandow's" I.A.47, B.ii.7; III.C.1
"Dreaded Derelict, The" I.A.42, B.ii.8
"Dream of X, The" I.A.8, 20, 64, B.i.19; II.G.i.10, R.ii.4
Dream of X, The I.A.20
Dream of X and Other Fantastic Visions, The I.A.64
"Drowned" I.A.60, B.iii.16
"Drum of Saccharine, The" I.A.14, 46, 54, B.i.25.b, c, d
Dům na rozhraní II.B.i.1
"Dumpley Acrostics, The" I.A.12, 64, B.i.20
"Dying" I.A.60, B.iii.17

"Eight Bells" I.A.15, 22, 48, B.iii.18
"Eloi Eloi Lama Sabachthani" I.A.19, 64, 65, 70, B.i.5.c, g, h, I; II.G.i.9, ii.1.a, K.i.9, ii.2.a, b, R.i.3
"'Emergency Door' of the Sea: 'Out Boats,' The" I.A.61, B.ii.9
"Épave, L'" II.G.i.8, ii.2.a
"Équipage du Lancing, L'" II.G.i.8
"Equipaggio del *Lancing*, L'" II.K.ii.5.a
"Esca di Captain Gault, L'" II.K.ii.7.a
Espectros del mar, Los II.Q.i.6

"Exploits of Captain Gault, The" II.K.ii.7
Exploits of Captain Gault, The I.A.46
"Exploits of Captain Gault: 1. Contraband of War, The" I.B.i.21
"Exploits of Captain Gault: 2. The Diamond Spy, The" I.B.i.22
"Exploits of Captain Gault: 3. The Red Herring, The" I.B.i.23
"Exploits of Captain Gault: 4. The Case of the Chinese Curio Dealer, The" I.B.i.24
"Exploits of Captian Gault: 5. The Drum of Saccharine, The" I.B.i.25
"Exploits of Captain Gault: 6. 'From Information Received,' The" I.B.i.26
"Exploits of Captain Gault: 7. He 'Assists' the Enemy, The" I.B.i.27
"Exploits of Captain Gault: 8. The Problem of the Pearls, The" I.B.i.28
"Exploits of Captain Gault: 9. The Painted Lady, The" I.B.i.29

"Fame" I.A.60, B.iii.19
"Fantasma della Lady Shannon, Il" II.K.ii.13.b
"Fantôme du Lady Shannon, Le" II.G.i.9
"Farewell" I.A.60, 62, B.iii.20
"Fifth Message from the Tideless Sea, The" I.B.i.66.b
"Fifty Dead Chinamen All in a Row" I.A.28, 42, B.i.31
Fifty Dead Chinamen All in a Row I.A.28
"Fight with a Submarine, A" I.A.59, B.i.30
"Find, The" I.A.9, 51, 55, B.i.32; II.C.i.1, D.i.2, G.i.8, K.i.3, R.ii.5
"Finding of the *Graiken*, The" I.A.19, 21, 50, 54, 62, 65, 68, B.i.33; II.G.i.9, K.i.4, 6, ii.8
Finding of the Graiken, The I.A.68
"Fluitende kamer, De" II.D.ii.3.a, b
"Foot Falls" I.A.60, B.iii.21
"Friendship of Monsieur Jeynois, The" I.A.26, 61, 64, B.i.34

"'From Information Received'"
I.A.14, 46, 54, B.i.26.b, c, d
"From the *Blackburn Evening Telegraph*"
I.A.61
"From the Tideless Sea" I.A.11, 18,
29, 42, 50, 54, 56, 62, 65, B.i.35,
66.c, d, f, g, i, j, k; II.G.i.8, K.ii.9,
Q.i.4, 11, R.i.3, ii.6
From the Tideless Sea I.A.29, 56
"Fruit of the Tree of Life, The" I.A.61,
B.iii.22
Fund, Et II.C.i.1
"Fyndet" II.R.ii.5.a
"Gateway of the Monster, The" I.A.5,
9, 51, 55, 65, B.i.36; II.D.i.2, G.i.3,
ii.3, I.i.2, ii.5, K.i.3, ii.10, R.ii.7
"Geheim van de raadselachtige bezoeker, Het" II.D.i.2
"Geisterpferd, Das" II.I.ii.9.a, b, c, d, e
Geisterpiraten II.I.i.4, ii.6.a
Geisterpiraten und andere schauerliche Seegeschicten II.I.i.4
"German Spy, The" I.A.14, 54, B.i.27.
b, d
"Getting Even of 'Parson' Guyles,
The" I.A.13, 64, B.i.37
"Getting Even of Tommy Dodd, The"
I.A.26, 64, B.i.38
Ghost Pirates, The I.A.3, 17, 51, 53, 59,
65, 66, 67, 70, B.i.39; II.E.i.1, G.i.2,
6, I.i.4, ii.6, K.i.5, ii.11, N.i.2, O.i.2,
Q.i.5, 12, 15, 17; III.E.9n, 55n,
61n, 65n, F.3
"Ghost Pirates, The" [abridgment]
I.A.4, 25, 64, B.i.40; II.G.i.10
Ghost Pirates, A Chaunty, and Another Story, The I.A.4
Ghost Pirates and Other Revenants of the Sea, The I.A.59
Ghost Pirates and Others: The Best of William Hope Hodgson, The I.A.70
"Ghosts of the Glen Doon, The"
I.A.43, 55, B.i.41
"Gierende kamer, De" II.D.i.2
"Girl with the Grey Eyes, The" I.A.63,
B.i.42
"Goddess of Death, The" I.A.30, 42,
43, 44, 55, B.i.43; II.R.ii.8

Goddess of Death, The I.A.30
"Gone" I.A.60, B.iii.23
"Graue Meere träumen von meinem
Tode" II.I.i.6
"Graue Zimmer, Das" II.I.ii.5.a
"Grey Seas Are Dreaming of My
Death" I.A.8, 15, 22, 48, 60, 62,
B.iii.24; II.I.i.6
"Grief" I.A.48, 60, B.iii.25
"Grunzende Mann, Der" II.I.i.2
"Gun Drill" I.A.61, B.iii.26

"Habitantes de la Isleta Central, Los"
II.Q.ii.1.a
"Habitants de l'îlot du milieu, Les"
II.G.i.8, ii.4.a, b
"Habitants of Middle Islet, The"
I.A.18, 59, B.i.44; II.G.i.8, ii.4,
I.ii.7, K.i.4, 6, ii.12, Q.i.4, 11, ii.1
"Haunted *Jarvee*, The" I.A.9, 51, 55,
62, 65, B.i.45; II.D.i.2, G.i.3, I.ii.8,
K.i.3
"Haunted *Pampero*, The" I.A.24, 43,
44, 59, 62, B.i.46; II.B.ii.2, G.i.10
Haunted 'Pampero,' The I.A.24
Haunted Pampero, The I.A.43; III.G.13
"Haunting of the *Lady Shannon*, The"
I.A.19, 55, 65, B.i.47; II.G.i.9,
K.ii.13, R.i.3
Haus an der Grenze, Das II.I.i.2, 5
Haus an der Grenze und andere phantastischen Erzählungen, Das II.I.i.2
"Havet utan ebb och flod" II.R.i.3
"Havets fånge" II.R.ii.6.a
"Havets monster" II.R.ii.1.b
"He 'Assists' the Enemy" I.A.46,
B.i.27.c
"Health from Scientific Exercise"
I.A.47, 61, B.ii.10
"Heart Cry, The" I.A.61, B.iii.27
"Heathen's Revenge, The" I.A.49, 55,
B.i.104.c, d
"Heaving of the Log, The" I.A.31,
42, 59, B.i.48
Heaving of the Log, The I.A.31
"Hell! Oo! Chaunty, The" I.A.4, 48,
B.iii.28

"Hemsökelsen i slutet av gatan"
  II.R.i.3
"Hemsökelsen på Lady Shannon"
  II.R.i.3
"Herrenlose, Die" II.I.i.1, ii.4.a
"Hints on Physical Culture" I.B.ii.11;
  III.C.1
"Hlas z temnot" II.B.ii.4.a
"Hlas ve tm☐" II.B.ii.3.a
"Hog, The" I.A.9, 51, 55, 65, B.i.49;
  II.D.i.2, G.i.3, ii.5, I.i.2, K.i.3, ii.14,
  R.ii.9; III.E.98n
"Home-coming of Captain Dan, The"
  I.A.55, B.i.50
"Homeward Bound" I.A.32, 42,
  B.i.89.b, e, f, g
Homeward Bound I.A.32
"Horreur tropicale" II.G.ii.7.a
"Horreur tropicale, L'" II.G.i.9, ii.7.b
Horreur tropicale: Nouvelles, L' II.G.i.9
Horror tropical y otros relatos, Un
  II.Q.i.13
"Horse of the Invisible, The" I.A.5, 9,
  51, 55, 65, B.i.51, C.4; II.D.i.2,
  G.i.3, I.i.9, K.i.3, ii.15, R.ii.10
"Houdini Exhibition, The" I.B.ii.12
"House among the Laurels, The"
  I.A.5, 9, 51, 55, 65, 69, B.i.52;
  II.D.i.2, G.i.3, K.i.3, R.ii.11
House among the Laurels, The I.A.69
"House on the Borderland, The" I.A.2, 17,
  51, 52, 53, 55, 65, 66, B.i.53, C.6,
  7; II.B.i.1, D.i.1, F.i.1, G.i.2, 4,
  H.i.1, I.i.2, 5, J.i.1, 2, K.i.1, 4, 7, 9,
  ii.16, L.i.1, N.i.1, Q.i.1, 2, 7, 16, 17,
  R.i.1, 2, ii.12; III.D.9, 17, 29, D.6n,
  19n, 21n, 23n, 36n, 38n, 54n, 55n,
  85n, 88n, 92n, 96n, 98n, F.2
House on the Borderland and Other Mysterious Places, The I.A.55
House on the Borderland and Other Novels, The I.A.17; III.G.10
House on the Borderland and Other Stories, The I.A.53
"How It Happened" I.A.60, B.iii.29
"How Sir Jerrold Treyn Dealt with the
  Dutch in Caunston Cove" I.A.26,
  64, B.i.54

"How the French Soldier Deals with
  Spies" I.A.61, B.ii.13
"How the Honourable Billy Darrell
  Raised the Wind" I.A.64, B.i.55
*Huis op de drempel can de oneindigheid,
  Het* II.D.i.1
"Huis tussen de laurierheesters, Het"
  II.D.i.2
"Hunger Land, The" I.A.60, B.iii.30
"Huset bland lagerträden" II.R.ii.11.a
Huset vid avgrunden II.R.i.1, 2
"Hvízdavý pokoj" II.B.ii.4.b
"Hylky" II.F.ii.1.a

"I Come Again" I.A.8, 60, B.iii.31
"I den ondes makt" II.R.ii.7.a
"I Have Borne My Lord a Son" I.A.8,
  60, B.iii.32
"If I Were Dead" I.A.60, B.iii.33
Ijigen o nosoku ie II.L.i.1
"Île de Ud, L'" II.G.i.8
Impressionistic Sketches I.A.10
"In Eternity" I.A.60, B.iii.34
"In the Danger Zone" I.A.59, B.i.56
"In the Wailing Gully" I.A.63, B.i.57
"Inn of the Black Crow, The" I.A.26,
  61, 64, B.i.58; II.I.ii.10
"Inquilino dell'ultima casa, L'" II.K.i.3
"Insel des Ud, Die" III.I.ii.11.a
"Inspiration" I.A.60, B.iii.35
"Is the Mercantile Navy Worth Joining?" I.A.44, 61, B.ii.14
"Island of the Crossbones, The"
  I.A.45, 49, 59, 61, B.i.59
"Island of the Ud, The" I.A.18, 54,
  B.i.12.d, e, g, h, i, j; II.G.i.8, I.ii.11,
  K.ii.17
"Isola di Ud, L'" II.K.ii.17.a

"Jack Grey, Second Mate" I.A.47, 59,
  61, B.i.60
"'Jarvee' infestato, Il" II.K.i.3
"Jarvee, Le" II.G.i.3
"Jem Binney and the Safe at Lockwood
  Hall" I.A.26, 64, B.i.61
"Judge Barclay's Wife" I.A.47, 61, 64,
  B.i.62
"Jumping the Claim Jumpers"
  I.B.i.2.b

Kauhujen talo II.F.i.1
"Kind, Kind and Gentle Is She"
  I.A.63, B.i.63
"Lady Shannon, La" II.K.ii.13.a
"Lamie" II.K.i.6
"Last Word in Mysteries, The" I.A.12,
  64, B.i.64
"Listening" I.A.8, 60, B.iii.36
"Little Feet of Maggie Lee" I.A.61,
  B.iii.37
"Little Garments" I.A.8, 60, B.iii.38
"Lost" I.A.5, 15, 22, 48, 60, B.iii.39
Lost Poetry of William Hope Hodgson, The
  I.A.60
"Lost Years" I.A.60
"Love" I.A.60, B.iii.40
"Love Song to the Dead" I.A.60,
  B.iii.41
Luck of the Strong, The I.A.13; III.G.7
"Maarten Maarten's New Novel"
  I.A.47, B.ii.15
"Madre Mia" I.A.48, 60, B.iii.42
"Magic of Kipling, The" I.A.47,
  B.ii.16
"Maiale, Il" II.K.i.3, ii.14.b
La Maison au bord du monde II.G.i.4
*Maison au bord du monde; Les Canots de
  "Glen Carrig"; Les Pirates fantômes, La*
  II.G.i.2
"Maison parmi les lauriers, La"
  II.G.i.3
"Mar de los sargazos, El" II.Q.ii.4.a
"Mar di Sargassi, Il" II.K.ii.8.b
"Mare, Il" II.K.i.6
"Mare di Sargassi, Il" II.K.i.6
"Mare immobile, Il" II.K.ii.9.a
Mares grises sueñan con mi muerte: Cuentos completos de terror en el mar, Los
  II.Q.i.18
*Masters of Terror, Volume 1–William
  Hope Hodgson* I.A.21
Matango I.C.3
Men of the Deep Waters I.A.11; III.G.6
"Menetettyjen lasten laakso" II.F.ii.2.a
"Merciful Plunder" I.A.55, B.i.65
"Middle Islet" II.K.i.4, ii.12.c
"Mimosa" I.A.48, B.iii.43

"Mistero del mar dei Sargassi, Il"
  II.K.ii.19.a
"Mistero del relitto, Il" II.K.ii.19.b
"Monsieur les Vidoques" I.A.61,
  B.iii.44
"Monstre de l'île aux algues, Le"
  II.G.i.8
"More News from the *Homebird*"
  I.A.50, B.i.35.d, f, i, k, l, m, B.i.66;
  II.G.i.8, K.ii.18, R.i.3, ii.13
"Morning Lands, The" I.A.15, 22, 48,
  60, B.iii.45
"Mors Deorum" I.A.60, B.iii.46
"Mostro, Il" II.K.i.6
"Mostro dell'isola delle alghe, Il"
  II.K.ii.29.a
"Mr. Jock Danplank" I.A.55, B.i.67
"Mutiny" I.A.8
"My Babe, My Babe" I.A.8, 60,
  B.iii.47
"My House Shall Be Called the House
  of Prayer" I.A.11, 64, B.i.68
"My Lady's Jewels" I.A.14, 46, 54,
  B.i.69
"My Son! My Son!" I.A.60, B.iii.48
"Mystère de la maison hantée, Le"
  II.G.i.3
"Mystère de l'épave, Le" II.G.i.8
"Mystery of Captain Chappel, The"
  I.A.55, B.i.70
"Mystery of Life, The" I.A.60, B.iii.49
"Mystery of Missing Ships, The"
  I.A.59, B.i.71
"Mystery of the Derelict, The" I.A.18,
  21, 50, 54, 62, 70, B.i.72; II.G.i.8,
  K.ii.19, R.ii.14
"Mystery of the Sargasso, The"
  I.B.i.72.d
"Mystery of the Ship in the Night,
  The" I.A.33, 42, B.i.91.a, j, k
Mystery of the Ship in the Night, The
  I.A.33
"Mystery of the Water-Logged Ship,
  The" I.A.55, B.i.73

Nachtland, Das II.I.i.3
Naito rando II.L.i.3
"Nattlandet" II.R.ii.4.a, b, c, 15.a

Naufragio nell'ignoto II.K.i.2
Náufragos de las tinieblas, Los II.Q.i.8
Nave abandonada y otros relatos de horror en el mar, La II.Q.i.11
"Nave di pietra, La" II.K.ii.25.a
"Navio silencioso, El" II.Q.i.2.a
"Nevermore" I.A.48, 61, B.iii.50
"Night" I.A.60, B.iii.51
"Night and Day" I.A.60, B.iii.52
Night Land: A Love Tale, The I.A.7, 8n, 17, 53, 63, 65, 66, B.i.74; II.G.i.5, I.i.3, K.i.8, L.i.3, Q.i.3, R.ii.15; III.D.10, 16, D.2n, 5n, 6n, 13n, 14n, 17n, 36n, 56n, 68n, 70n, 85n, 110n, F.4
Night Land and Other Romances, The I.A.63
"Night Wind, The" I.A.8, 60, B.iii.53
"9 Letters to Coulson Kernahan" I.A.47, B.ii.17
"Noise in the Night, The" I.B.i.53.c
"Notte squarciata, La" II.K.ii.22.a

"O Parent Sea!" I.A.8, 60, B.iii.54
"Ocean of Eternity, The" I.A.61, B.iii.55
"Ode to a Vase" I.A.60, B.iii.56
"Old French Woman and Her Chickens, An" I.A.61, B.ii.18
"Old Glen Doon, The" I.B.i.41.b
"Old Golly" I.A.34, 42, 43, 59, B.i.75
Old Golly I.A.34
"Old-Time Hands" I.A.60, B.iii.57
"Oltre il futuro" II.K.ii.16.a
"On the Bridge" I.A.11, 45, 59, 62, B.i.80.b, d, e, f
"One Nation Are We" I.A.61, B.iii.58
"Onzichtbare dader, De" II.D.i.2
Orrore dagli abissi II.K.ii.11.a
Orrore del mare, L' II.K.i.6
"Orrore ai tropici" II.K.ii.28.a
"Orrore tropicale" II.K.ii.28.a
"Osynligas häst, Det" II.R.ii.10.a
"Out of the Storm" I.A.19, 59, 62, 65, 70, B.i.76; II.G.i.9, K.i.4, 6, 9, ii.20
Out of the Storm: Uncollected Fantasies I.A.19; II.G.i.9
"Over There" I.A.60, B.iii.59

"Paard van de onzichtbare, Het" II.D.i.2
"Painted Lady, The" I.A.44, 46, 54, B.i.29.c, d, e
Pais de la noche, El II.Q.i.3.c
"Par là entrait le monstre . . ." II.G.ii.3.a
"Passager du 'Pampero,' Le" II.G.i.10
"Passing" I.A.60, B.iii.60
Pays de la nuit, La II.G.i.5
"Pen Picture of How Frenchmen Fight, A" I.A.61, B.ii.19
"Peril of the Mine, The" I.A.47, 61, B.ii.20
"Pfeifende Zimmer, Das" II.I.i.2, ii.16.a
"Phantom Ship, The" I.A.23, 35, 42, B.i.77; II.G.i.10, Q.ii.2
Phantom Ship, The I.A.35
"Physical Culture: A Talk with an Expert" I.A.47, 61, B.ii.21
"Physical Culture versus Recreative Exercise" I.A.47, 61, B.ii.22; III.C.1
"Pillars of the Empire" I.A.61, B.iii.61
"Pilzwald, Der" II.I.ii.15.b, d
Piratas fantasmas, Los II.Q.i.5, 12
Piratas fantasmas y otros cuentos de fantasmas, Los II.Q.i.15
"Pirates, The" I.A.13, 15, 22, 48, B.iii.62
Pirates fantômes, Les II.G.i.6
Pirati fantasma, I II.K.i.5, ii.11.b
Pirații fantomă **II.O.i.2**
"Place of Storms, The" I.A.15, 22, 48, 60, 62, B.iii.63
"Plans of the Reefing Bi-plane, The" I.A.49, 54, B.i.78
"'Poems' and 'The Dream of X'" I.A.8
Poems of the Sea I.A.22
"Poet vs. the Stonemason, The" I.A.47, 61, B.ii.23
"Polvere del tempo, La" II.K.ii.16.b, c
"Poort van het monster, De" II.D.i.2
"Porte, La" II.G.i.3
"Portfolio of Photographs" I.A.61, B.ii.24

"'Prentices' Mutiny, The" I.A.8, 45, 59, B.ii.25
"Problem of the Pearls, The" I.A.14, 46, 54
"Promise, The" I.A.49, 64, B.i.79
"Psychology of Species, The" I.A,12, B.ii.26; III.E.8n

"Quand s'entrouvre la nuit" II.G.i.10
"Quinto messaggio, Il" II.K.ii.18.a

"R. M. S. *Empress of Australia*" I.A.49, B.i.80
"Real Thing, The" I.B.i.81.b
"Real Thing: On the Bridge, The" I.B.i.80; II.K.ii.21; III.C.1, D.12n
"Real Thing: 'S. O. S.,' The" I.A.59, B.i.81
"Red Herring, The" I.A.14, 46, 54, B.i.23.b, d, f, g
"Regarding Similar Names" I.A.47, B.ii.27
"Regeneration of Captain Bully Keller, The" I.A.26, 59, 61, B.i.82
Reino de la noche, El II.Q.i.3
"Relitto, Il" II.K.ii.6.a
"Réservoir de la peur, Le" II.G.i.9, ii.6.a
"Rest" I.A.15, 22, 48, 60, B.iii.64
"Rêve de X, Le" II.G.i.10
"Review of the Totem Question, A" I.A.47, B.ii.28
"Ritrovamento, Il" II.K.i.3
"Ritrovamento della *Graiken*, Il" II.K.i.4
"Riven Night, The" I.A.23, 36, 42, 49, 59, B.i.83; II.G.i.10, K.ii.22
Riven Night, The I.A.36
"Room of Fear, The" I.A.37, 42, 49, 64, B.i.84; II.G.i.10
Room of Fear, The I.A.37
Room of Fear and Other Grues, The I.A.42
"Rösten i morkret" II.R.i.3
Rösten i mörkret och andra skräckfyllda berättelser II.R.i.3
"Rufen des Meeres, Das" II.I.i.6
Rufen des Meeres: Gedichte, Das II.I.i.6

"S.O.S.: The Real Thing" I.A.61, B.i.81.d
"Sailor and His Camera, A" I.A.61, B.ii.29
"Sailormen" I.A.49, 59, B.ii.30
"Scent" I.A.60, B.iii.65
"Scheepswrak, Het" II.D.ii.1.b
"Schicksalsring der Anderson-Familie, Der" II.I.i.2
"Scraps! Scraps!! Scraps!!!" I.A.61, B.iii.66
"Sea-Horses" I.A.11, 18, 38, 42, 58, 64, 70, B.i.85; II.A.i.1, G.i.8, K.ii.23
Sea-Horses I.A.38
Sea Horses, The I.A.58
"Sea of Silence, The" I.A.60, B.iii.67
"Sea Revelry" I.A.61, B.iii.68
"Searcher of the End House, The" I.A.9, 51, 55, 65, 70, B.i.86; II.D.i.2, G.i.3, I.ii.12, K.i.3, R.i.3
"Second Mate of *The Buster*, The" I.A.26, B.i.87
[*Selected Works*] I.A.65
"Selvaggio del mare, Il" II.K.ii.32.a, b
"Senator Sandy MacGhee" I.A.12, 64, B.i.88
"Serbatoio della paura, Il" II.K.ii.26.a
"*Shamraken* Homeward-Bounder, The" I.A.18, 59, 62, 70, B.i.89; II.G.i.8, K.ii.24, Q.i.4, 11
"Sharks of the *St. Elmo*, The" I.A.49, 59, B.i.31.c, d
"Ship, The" I.A.13, 15, 22, 48, B.iii.69
"Ship's Log" I.A.61, B.ii.31
"Ships That Go Missing" I.B.i.71.b, c
"Shoon of the Dead" I.A.48, 60, B.iii.84.c, d
"Shore of Desolation, The" I.A.60, B.iii.70
"Silent Ship, The" I.A.43, 51, 59, B.i.77 f, g
"Silent Ship 'Tells How Jessup Was Picked Up,' The" I.A.3n, B.i.77.b, h
"Sjögräsfolket" II.R.ii.17.a
"Sjögräsmonstren" II.R.ii.17.b
"Skräcken ur djupet" II.R.ii.2.a
"Skräcknatt ombord" II.R.ii.13.a

"Skräkens skepp" II.R.ii.1.a
"Smoke of the Blast, The" I.A.60, B.iii.71
"Smolné Pampero" II.B.ii.2.a
"Smugglers, The" I.A.63, B.i.90
"Sobbing of the Freshwater, The" I.A.8, 15, 22, 48, 60, B.iii.72
"Song of the Great Bull Whale, The" I.A.8, 11, 15, 22, 48, B.iii.73
"Song of the Ship" I.A.15, 22, 48, 60, B.iii.74
"Southern Lights" I.A.60, B.iii.75
"Speak Well of the Dead" I.A.8, 48, 60, B.iii.76
Spectral Manifestations I.A.25; III.G.12
"Spectres Pirates, Les" II.G.i.10
Spectres Pirates et six autres récits fantastiques, Les II.G.i.10
"Sphistyashchaya kamnata" II.P.i.1
Spiti sta synora tou kosmou, To II.J.i.2
Spiti tēs avyssou, To II.J.i.1
"Spookschip Jarvee, Het" II.D.i.2
"Spuk auf der Jarvee, Der" II.I.ii.8.a
"Stanza che fischiava, La" II.K.i.3
"Stanza col fischio, La" II.K.ii.31.a, b
"Stem in de nacht, De" II.D.i.1, ii.2
Stem in de nacht: Griezelverhalen, De II.D.i.1
"Steinerne Schiff, Das" II.I.i.4
"Stimme aus der Nacht, Die" II.I.ii.15.a
"Stimme des Ozeans, Die" II.I.i.6
"Stimme in der Nacht" II.I.i.1, ii.15.c, e, f, g
Stimme in der Nacht: Unheimliche Geschichten II.I.i.1
"Stone Ship, The" I.A.13, 18, 21, 59, 62, 65, 70, B.i.91; II.G.i.8, I.i.4, K.ii.25, Q.i.4, 11
"Storm" I.A.15, 22, 48, 60, B.iii.77
"Storm, The" I.A.42, 43, 44, 64, B.i.92
"Sul ponte" II.K.ii.21.a
"Svinvarelsen" II.R.ii.9.a

Tales of Land and Sea I.A.26
"Tempesta, La" II.K.i.4, 9
"Ten Months at Sea" I.A.49, B.ii.32

Terra dell'eterna notte, La II.K.i.8
"Terrible Derelict, The" I.A.39, 42, B.i.72.b, h, i
Terrible Derelict, The I.A.39
"Terror of the Water-Tank, The" I.A.19, 21, 55, 65, B.i.93; II.G.i.9, ii.6, K.i.5, 6, 9, ii.26
"Terrore ai tropici" II.K.i.4
"Terrore della cisterna, Il" II.K.i.5, 9
Terrors of the Sea I.A.47; III.G.18
"Thing in the Weeds, The" I.A.18, 54, B.i.94; II.G.i.8, I.i.4, ii.13, K.ii.27
"Thing Invisible, The" I.A.4, 9, 51, 55, 65, B.i.95; II.D.i.2, G.i.8, K.i.3
"Thou and I" I.A.60, B.iii.78
"Thou Living Sea" I.A.15, 22, 48, 60, 62, B.iii.79
"Thou, Who Art Jesus' Mother!" I.A.60, B.iii.80
Three Gothic Horror Tales I.A.67
"Thresher, The" I.A.60, B.iii.81
"Through the Heart of a Cyclone" I.A.61, B.ii.33
"Through the Vortex of a Cyclone" I.A.11, 44, 61, 62, B.ii.34; III.E.11n
"Thy Wandering Soul" I.A.60, B.iii.82
"Timely Escape, A" I.A.43, 63, B.i.96
"To God" I.A.60, B.iii.83
"To My Father" I.B.iii.84
"Totems for Authors" I.B.ii.35
"Totems for Authors" I.B.ii.36
"Trade in Sea Apprentices, The" I.A.47, 61, B.ii.37
"Trading with the Enemy" I.A.46, 54, B.i.97
"Tramp! Tramp!" I.A.61, B.iii.85
Trilogía del abismo II.Q.i.17
"Trimming of Captain Dunkan, The" I.B.i.98
"Tropical Horror, A" I.A.19, 21, 59, 62, 65, 70, B.i.99; II.G.i.9, ii.7, I.ii.14, K.i.4, 6, ii.28, Q.i.13, R.ii.16
"Tropischer Schrecken" II.I.ii.14.a, b
"Tropisk skräck, En" II.R.ii.16.a
"Two Letters" I.B.ii.38

"Ultimo viaggio dello Shamraken, L'" II.K.ii.24.a

Umi fukaku II.L.i.5
Uncollected William Hope Hodgson, The I.A.48; III.G.16
"(Untitled)" I.A.60, B.iii.91
"Ur *Huset vid avgrunden*" II.R.ii.12.a
"Vaisseau fantôme, Le" II.G.i.10
"Valley of Lost Children, The" I.A.40, 42, 43, 44, 64, B.i.100; II.F.ii.2
Valley of Lost Children, The I.A.40
"Varco del mostro, Il" II.K.i.3
"Vendetta, La" II.K.ii.13.c
"Verghe d'oro!" II.K.ii.3.a
"Verlaten Schip, Het" II.D.i.1
"Verrat, Le" II.G.i.3, ii.5.a
"Verro, Il" II.K.ii.14.a
Viirastuspiraadid II.E.i.1
"Visslande rummet, Det" II.R.ii.18.a, b, c
"Voce nella notte, Una" II.K.ii.30.a, b, d, e, f
"Voce nella tempesta, Una" II.K.ii.20.a
"Voice in the Dawn, The" I.A.62, B.i.101; II.G.i.8, J.ii.29
"Voice in the Night, The" I.A.11, 18, 21, 52, 59, 62, 65, 67, 70, B.i.102, C.2, 3n; II.B.ii.3, D.i.1, ii.2, F.ii.3, G.i.8, ii.8, I.i.1, ii.15, K.ii.30, L.i.4, ii.1, Q.i.4, 11, ii.3, R.i.3; III.E.100n
"Voice of One Crying in the Wilderness, The" I.A.60, B.iii.86
Voice of the Ocean, The I.A.16, 22, 48, B.iii.87; II.I.i.6
"Voix dans la nuit, La" II.G.i.8, ii.8.a
"Voix dans la tempête, Une" II.G.i.9
"Vondst, De" II.D.i.2
"Voz en la noche, Una" II.Q.ii.3.a
"Vraket" II.R.i.3, ii.3.a, b, c, d, e
"Vrakets hemlighet" II.B.ii.14.a
"Vreselijke varken, Het" II.D.i.2
"Výbušnina Baumoff" II.B.ii.1.a

Wandering Soul: Glimpses of a Life, The I.A.61
"Waterloo of a Hard-Case Skipper, The" I.A.45, B.i.103
"Ways of the Heathens, The" I.A.41, 42, B.i.104
Ways of the Heathens, The I.A.41
"We Two and Bully Dunkan" I.A.13, 59, 70, B.i.105
"Weed Men, The" I.A.50, B.i.7.d, e, g; II.R.ii.17
"What Happened in the Thunderbolt, The" I.A.26, 64, B.i.106
"When the Sea Gets Cross" I.A.61, B.ii.39
"Whistling Room, The" I.A.5, 9, 51, 55, 65, B.i.107, C.1, 5n; II.B.ii.4, D.i.2, ii.3, G.i.3, ii.9, I.i.2, ii.16, K.i.3, ii.31, P.i.1, R.ii.18
"Who Make Their Bed in Deep Waters" I.B.iii.88
Widmowi piraci II.N.i.2
"Wild Man of the Sea, The" I.A.43, 59, 62, B.i.108; II.K.ii.32
William Hope Hodgson: A Centenary Tribute I.A.23
"Wirtshaus zur schwarzen Krähe, Das" II.I.ii.10.a
"World of Dreams, The" I.A.60, B.iii.89
"Wrack am Höllengrund, Das" II.I.ii.7.a
"Wrak, Het" II.D.ii.1.a
"Wrecked" I.A.60, B.iii.90
"Writers of Ghost Stories" I.A.49, B.ii.40

Yûrei karyûdo Carnacki II.L.i.2
Yûrei karyûdo Carnacki no zikenbo II.L.i.6
Yuro no koe II.L.i.4

C. Periodicals

Adventure I.B.i.3.a, 60.a, 62.b, 81.b
Alfred Hitchcock's Mystery Magazine
   I.B.i.102.ii, 107.u
All Around Magazine I.B.i.17.c, 71.a,
   80.c
Allt I fickformat II.R.ii.3.b
Antiquarian Book Monthly Review
   III.E.18
Argosy (UK) I.B.i.12.e, 23.d, 62.c,
   68.d, 72.d, 89.e, 102.f, 107.d
Argosy All-Story Weekly I.B.i.65.a
Arkham Collector I.B.iii.39.d, 84.b
Arkham Sampler I.B.ii.38.a
Armchair Detective III.E.28, F.5.a
Author I.B.ii.23.a, 27.a, 28.a, 35.a,
   36.a

Blackburn Times I.B.ii.12.b
Blackburn Weekly Telegraph I.B.ii.6.a, 21.a
Blue Book Magazine I.B.i.66.a, 72.c,
   93.a, 102.a
Blue Magazine I.B.i.96.a
Book and Magazine Collector III.E.30
Booklist III.G.19.b
Bookman (London) I.B.ii.15.a, 16.a;
   III.G.1.c, 3.b, c, 4.d, 5.e, f, 6.b, 7.a,
   9.b
Bookman's Journal & Print Collector
   III.E.116
Books and Bookmen III.G.2.f
Boston Transcript III.G.8.a
British Fantasy Society Newsletter
   III.G.2.e
British Weekly III.G.5n

Canada in Khaki I.B.i.30.a, 56.a
Cassell's Magazine I.B.ii.10.a
Chicago Sun Book Week III.G.5.d
Choice III.G.4.e
Cornhill Magazine I.B.i.68.a, 81.a,
   100.a, ii.34.a
Country Life III.G.4n

daedalos II.I.ii.3.a
Daily Express III.G.5n
Damned Thing I.B.i.102.jj; III.E.52
DAST-Magazin II.R.ii.10.a

Empire Magazine I.B.i.45.a
Etchings & Odysseys I.B.i.83.d, 84.a
Eternauta, L' II.K.ii.28.a
Everybody's Magazine I.B.i.103.a
Everybody's Weekly I.B.i.8.a

Famous Fantastic Mysteries I.B.i.7.b,
   17.e, 39.c
Fantastic Novels Magazine III.G.5.b
Fantastik II.G.ii.6.a
Fantasy Commentator III.B.7, D.86
Fantasy Crossroads I.B.iii.88.a
Fantasy Fan III.E.62
Fantasy Review III.G.2.g, 12.a
Fantasycon III.E.54

Giallo d'Epoca II.K.ii.30.d
Glasgow Herald III.G.6n
Globe III.G.5n
Gothic Imagination, The III.E.4
Grand Magazine I.B.i.57.a, 73.a, 90.a,
   99.a, ii.14.a, iii.73.b

Herne, L' III.E.108
Horizons du fantastique III.E.38
Humo II.D.ii.2.b

Ideas I.B.ii.20.a
Idler I.B.i.36.a, 51.a, 52.a, 86.a, 107.a;
   III.G.3.a
Interdisciplinary Humanities III.E.99
Irish Studies Review III.E.59

Jules Verne-Magasinet II.R.ii.4.a
Jury: Tidskrift för deckarvänner II.R.ii.5.a

Kring aftonlampan II.R.ii.8.c

Lancashire Life III.E.101
Lektyr II.R.ii.8.a
Library Journal III.G.2.h
Liverpool Courier III.G.5n, 6n
London Magazine I.B.i.1.a, 21.a, 22.a,
   23.a, 24.a, 25.a, 26.a, 27.a, 28.a,
   29.a, 35.b, 62.a, 66.b, 69.a, 85.a,
   97.a, iii.72.b
London Times III.G.6n
Luna Monthly III.G.1.b

Magazine of Fantasy and Science Fiction III.G.19.a
Magazine of Horror I.B.i.107.k
Manchester Courier III.G.4n
Mellan fantasi och verklighet II.R.ii.8.b
Mike Shayne Mystery Magazine I.B.i.95.d
Millemon di Estate II.K.ii.19.a
Min värld II.R.ii.18.a
Minotauren II.R.ii.9.a, 18.b
Monthly Story Magazine I.B.i.35.a
Morning Leader III.G.4n
Morning Post III.G.4n
Mysterious Traveler Mystery Reader I.B.i.107.e

Nash's Magazine I.B.i.13.a, 102.b
Nash's Weekly I.B.i.5.a
Nation III.G.8.b
Nautical Magazine I.B.ii.37.a
Necrofile III.G.2.d, 13.a, 14.b, 16.a, 17.a, 18.a
New Age I.B.ii.5.a
New Dimensions I.B.i.83.b
New Magazine I.B.i.3.b, 95.a
New Worlds III.G.2.b
New York Herald Tribune Weekly Book Review III.G.10.c
New York Times Book Review III.G.2.i, 8.c, 10.b
Northern Daily Telegraph I.B.ii.3.a, 12.a
Nyctalops III.E.113

Occult Review III.G.4.a
Omen II.I.ii.11.a
Opta II.G.ii.1.a, 7.a
Orient Express II.K.ii.21.a

Pall Mall Gazette III.G.4.c
Penny Pictorial Weekly I.B.ii.2.a
People's Favorite Magazine I.B.i.9.a
Phantagraph III.E.63, 74, 90
Planète III.E.104
Playboy I.B.i.102.j
Popular Magazine I.B.i.37.b
Premier Magazine I.B.i.45.b, 46.b, 71.b, 101.a
Psycho II.K.ii.32.a
Publishers Weekly III.G.19.d

Pulpdom I.B.i.102.nn
Putnam's Monthly I.B.i.76.a, 89.a, ii.34.b

Re in Giallo, Il III.E.104
Reader and Collector III.E.33, 39, 64, 69, 84, 90
Red Magazine I.B.i.2.a, 6.a, 11.a, 12.a, 17.a, 18.a, 33.a, 34.a, 37.a, 38.a, 41.a, 42.a, 50.a, 54.a, 55.a, 58.a, 59.b, 61.a, 63.a, 67.a, 70.a, 82.a, 87.a, 91.a, 106.a
Riverside Quarterly III.E.19
Rod Serling's "The Twilight Zone" Magazine I.B.i.102.bb; III.E.9
Rod Serling's "The Twilight Zone" Magazine Special I.B.i.102.gg
Royal Magazine I.B.i.43.a

San Francisco Chronicle III.G.10.a
Sandow's Magazine I.B.ii.7.a, 11.a, 22.a; III.E.29n
Sargasso III.E.2, 20, 31, 40, 43, 56, 91, 107
Saturday Review of Literature III.G.5.g
Saturday Westminster Gazette I.B.i.80.a
Science Fantasy III.G.2.a
Science Fiction Chronicle III.G.2.c, 13.b, 14.a, 15.a
Science Fiction Collector III.B.1
Sea Stories Magazine I.B.i.4.a, 16.a, 41.b, 108.a
Shadow I.B.i.77.a, 83.a, ii.6.b; III.E.41
Short Stories I.B.i.2.b, 6.b, 12.b, 46.a, 59.a, 73.b, 75.a, 91.b, 92.a, 94.b
Son of WSFA Journal III.G.4.b
Speciale Weird Tales II.K.ii.12.c
Spectator III.G.2.j, 5.h
Sphere III.E.87
Springfield Republican III.G.8.d
Startling Mystery Stories III.G.11.a
Story-teller I.B.i.72.a, 94.a
Strand Magazine I.B.ii.34.d
Studies in Weird Fiction III.C.1.a, D.13, 14, 53
Super Science and Fantasy Stories I.B.i.17.f
Super Science Stories (Canadian) I.B.i.39.d

Suspense I.B.i.102.i

Terror Tales I.B.i.76.d
Times Literary Supplement III.G.1.d, 2.k, 4.f, 5.c, 6.a, 9.a
To-day's Magazine I.B.i.68.b

Urania II.K.ii.16.a

Vanity Fair III.G.4.g
Veckorevyn II.R.ii.3.d

Washington Post Book World III.G.2.l, 19.c
Weird Fiction Review III.E.44, 45
Weird Tales I.B.i.5.b, 33.b, 49.a, 93.b, 99.b; III.E.79
Weird Tales (Canadian) I.B.i.49.b
Westminster Gazette I.B.ii.9.a, 13.a, 18.a, 19.a; III.G.5n
Wide World Magazine I.B.ii.25.a
Wilson Library Bulletin III.G.1.a
Windsor Magazine I.B.i.89.b
Wormwood I.B.ii.26.b; III.E.8, 98

General Index

Adams, Guy 134
"Adventure of the Headland, The" 52, 79
Adventures of Captain Kettle, The (Hyne) 150-51
Aldiss, Brian 180, 182
Amari, Richard 135
Arkham House 7, 40
Arnold, Matthew 184
Aroca, Alberto Lopez 134
Ashley, Mike 8
At the Mountains of Madness (Lovecraft) 74, 193
Author 46

BFI Companion to Horror, The (Newman) 133
Ballard, J. G. 180
Barlow, R. H. 198-204
Barrie, J. M. 50
"Baumoff Explosive, The" 54, 62, 83
Baxter, Stephen 173
Beck, Martin 11
Beddoes, Thomas Lovell 37
Begg, Paul 66-67
Bell, Ian 7, 16, 90
Belle Rosalie, La 59-60, 66-67
Bellamy, Edward 30
Benson, A. C. 28
Benson, E. F. 31, 119
Benson, R. H. 28
Benton, Thomas Hart 199
Beresford, J. D. 54, 171
Berkeley Square (film) 193
Berruti, Massimo 8, 198, 199
Bethe, Hans 183
Bid for Fortune, A (Boothby) 88
Birkhead, Edith 37

Blackburn Standard and Weekly Express 12, 16
Blackburn Star 23
Blackburn Times 19-20
Blackburn Weekly Telegraph 14-15
Blackwood, Algernon 28, 31, 34, 35-36, 51, 74, 81, 85, 88, 131, 194, 196, 201
Boats of the "Glen Carrig," The 27, 34, 35, 36, 42, 47, 48, 50, 51, 57, 93, 94, 95, 96, 97, 98, 100-101, 103, 104, 105-6, 108, 124, 194, 199, 200, 201, 202, 203
Bookman (London) 27-28, 29-30, 31, 32-33, 86
Boothby, Guy 88
Bradley, Dr. 18, 19, 20, 22
Bramah, Ernest 84
Brandon, Ruth 24
British Weekly 30
Brown, Raymond Lamont 57n1
Bulwer-Lytton, Edward 175
Burnley Express 21
Buss, Reinhard J. 65

"Call in the Dawn, The" 75
Calling of the Sea, The 33
Campbell, Joseph 92
Captain Gault 33, 41, 74, 87, 126-28, 150-56
"Captain of the Onion Boat, The" 124
Cargunka, and Poems and Anecdotes 33, 152
Carnacki: Ghost-Finder: The New Adventures (Meikle) 134
Carnacki: Heaven and Hell 134

Carnacki, the Ghost-Finder 30–31, 35–36, 39, 40, 41, 51, 84–91, 131–45, 152, 199, 200, 201, 202
Carnacki, the Ghost-Finder, and a Poem 30, 33
Carter, Lin 118–19
Cartmel, Andrew 134
"Case of the Curio Dealer, The" 154–55
Century of Horror Stories, A (Wheatley) 39
Chambers, Robert W. 196
Childhood's End (Clarke) 184
Clarke, Arthur C. 184
Clegg, Richard 21–22
Coleridge, Samuel Taylor 56, 80
Collected Fiction 7, 73
Collins, Wilkie 85
"Colloquy of Monos and Una, The" (Poe) 184
"Colour out of Space, The" (Lovecraft) 80
"Conceptual Investigation of Love, A" (Newton-Smith) 158
Consolations in Travel (Davy) 48
Corley, M. S. 134–35
Country Life 29
Crawford, F. Marion 31
Credulities Past and Present (Jones) 56, 58
Crowley, Aleister 135
Cunningham, Allan 56, 66, 69

Daily Express 30
Daily Star (Blackburn) 12, 16
Daily Telegraph 32
Dante Alighieri 189
Davy, Humphry 48
Darwin, Charles 183
de la Mare, Colin 37, 39
Degeneration (Nordau) 184
"Demons of the Sea" 58, 78–79, 203
"Derelict, The" 32, 39, 54, 57, 80–81, 113–15
Derleth, August 86, 199, 200, 202, 203
Dim-Remembered Stories (Berruti) 198, 199
Dodds, Georges T. 153
"Dover Beach" (Arnold) 184
Doyle, Sir Arthur Conan 141, 151
"Dr. Thomas' Vibration Method *versus* Sandow's" 15
Dracula (Stoker) 85
Drake, H. B. 193
Dream of X, The 54
Dunsany, Lord 169, 170
Dwyer, Bernard Austin 203
Dyllington, Anthony 86

Eddison, E. R. 177
Einstein, Albert 190
"Eloi, Eloi, Lama Sabachthani." *See* "Baumoff Explosive, The"
Eureka (Poe) 48, 184
Everts, R. Alain 7, 91, 117, 152

Faig, Kenneth W., Jr. 199
Famous Fantastic Mysteries 38, 40
Fantasy Fan 7
Farnsworth, Gilbert 154
"Fifth Message from the Tideless Sea, The." *See* "More News from the Homebird"
"Find, The" 86, 155
"Finding of the *Graiken*, The" 77
Flammarion, Camille 184
Flying Dutchman, The (Wagner) 56, 68
"Foreign Devils" (Cartmel) 134
472 Cheyne Walk (Kidd-Kennett) 134
Frank, Jane 126
Freeman, R. Austin 89
"From Information Received" 155
"From the Tideless Sea" 32, 46, 57, 76, 124
Fuseli, Henry 137

"Gateway of the Monster, The" 82, 86, 87–88, 89–90, 134
Gernsback, Hugo 170
"Ghosts of the *Glen Doon*, The" 58, 78
Ghost Pirates, The 27–28, 35, 38, 39, 42, 48, 50–51, 52, 58, 63–70, 77, 94, 95, 96, 99, 100, 101, 106–7, 108, 199, 200, 201, 203
Ghost-Stories of an Antiquary (James) 28
Globe 30
Gnaedinger, Mary 38
"Goddess of Death, The" 46, 83
Greene, Hugh 140
"Grief" 108

"Habitants of Middle Islet, The" 62
Hambly, Barbara 134
Hardeen, Theodore 17, 18
Hardman, George 20
Harmsworth, Alfred 46, 54
"Haunted *Jarvee*, The" 82, 86, 89
"Haunted *Pampero*, The" 77-78
Haunted Pampero, The 69
Helmholtz, Herman von 183
Herald (Glasgow) 32
Heron, E. and H. 85
Hill of Trouble, The (Benson) 28
Hodgson, Bessie 38, 54, 117-18
Hodgson, Chad 118
Hodgson, Chris 110
Hodgson, Lissie 117-18
Hodgson, Samuel 45, 118
Hodgson, William Hope: as detective writer, 41, 84-91, 133; early reviews of, 27-33; as novelist, 27-30, 34-35, 36-37, 41-42, 47-51, 52-54, 64-70, 92-109, 118-20, 146-49, 157-65, 169-81, 184-91, 193-96, 198-203; and physical culture, 13, 14-16, 45, 46, 118; as poet, 33; as sailor, 14, 45, 110-11; and the sea, 56-72, 74-81, 106-7; as short story writer, 30-33, 35-36, 37, 41, 46-47, 51-52, 54, 56-63, 73-83, 84-91, 111-15, 120-28, 131-44, 150-56; in World War I, 7, 38, 40, 54, 117-18
"Hog, The" 51, 82, 86, 90, 91, 102, 132
Hornig, Charles D. 201
Hornung, E. W. 84, 153
"Horse of the Invisible, The" 82, 86, 137, 140-44
Houdini, Harry 11-26, 87
Houdini the Myth-Maker (Woods-Lead) 16
Hound of the Baskervilles, The (Doyle) 88-89
"House among the Laurels, The" 82, 86
House on the Borderland, The 27, 28, 34-35, 36, 40, 42, 48-50, 51, 52, 53, 56, 91, 93-94, 95, 96, 97-99, 101, 102, 103-4, 105, 106, 108, 115, 146-47, 148, 149, 157-66, 169-75, 176, 177, 184-91, 194, 195, 199, 200, 201, 203
House on the Borderland and Other Novels, The 7
Howard, Robert E. 170
Hull Daily Mail 21
Hurley, Kelly 57n2, 136
Hyne, C. J. Cutliffe 52, 150-51, 153

Idler 51, 81, 85-86, 136, 140
In the Sargasso Sea (Janvier) 46
"Is the Mercantile Navy Worth Joining" 14
"Island of the Ud, The" 39, 52, 79

Jacobs, W. W. 151
James, M. R. 28, 31, 42, 170
Janvier, Thomas A. 46
Jesus Christ 54, 62, 138
John Silence—Physician Extraordinary (Blackwood) 74, 81, 85, 86
Jones, William 56, 58
Joshi, S. T. 8, 157, 193, 194, 198n1, 200
"Judge Barclay's Wife" 124-26

Kalish, William 22
Katz, Nathaniel 133
Kelvin, Lord 49, 183
Kennett, Rick 134
Kermode, Frank 190
Kidd, A. F. (Chico) 134
"Kind, Kind and Gentle Is She" 122-24
Kipling, Rudyard 62
Klein, T. E. D. 133
Knox, Ronald 88
Koenig, H. C. 7, 34, 194, 198n1, 200, 202, 203
Kristeva, Julia 135-36

Lassen, Jeremy 152
"Last Lord of Helvellyn, The" (Cunningham) 66, 67, 69
Last Man, The (Shelley) 104
Lead, Brian 13, 16
Le Fanu, J. Sheridan 85
Lewis, C. S. 118
Libra Nos 69
Lindsay, David 184

Liverpool Courier 31, 32
London Magazine 46, 54, 152, 154
Looking Backward (Bellamy) 30
Lost Continent, The (Hyne) 151
Lost Valley and Other Stories, The (Blackwood) 31
Love's Knowledge (Nussbaum) 158
Lovecraft, H. P. 7, 36, 37, 41, 42, 53, 56, 74, 80, 88, 89, 95n4, 115, 118, 131, 146, 157–58, 164, 193–97, 198–203
Luck of the Strong, The 32–33, 39, 154
Lumen (Flammarion) 184

Machen, Arthur 151, 169–70
MacNaughton, Frank 12
"Madre Mia" 108
Malory, Thomas 179
Manchester Courier 29
Marryat, Frederick 56, 68
Martin, John 37
"Matter of Fact, A" (Kipling) 62
Maturin, Charles Robert 171, 175
Meikle, William 134
Melmoth the Wanderer (Maturin) 171, 175
"Memory, A" (Barlow) 198–204
Men of the Deep Waters 31–32, 39
Mendel, Gregor 183
Mirror of Shalott, A (Benson) 28
"Monkey's Paw, The" (Jacobs) 151
Monthly Story Magazine 46
Moonstone, The (Collins) 85
Moorcock, Michael 170, 180
Moore, Thomas 69
More Ghost Stories of an Antiquary (James) 31
"More News from the *Homebird*" 46
Morning Leader 29
Morning Post 29
Morris, William 177
Moskowitz, Sam 7, 15, 16, 23, 53, 61, 69, 90, 110, 154
Muir, Percy 37
Murray, Wayne 134
Music for Thomas Carnacki 135
"My Lady's Jewels" 126, 128, 155–56

"Mystery of the Derelict, The" 32, 46, 76
"Mystery of the Water-Logged Ship, The" 78

New Magazine 86, 136
New Worlds 170
Newman, Kim 134
Newton-Smith, W. 158
Night Land, The 28–30, 35, 36, 39–40, 41, 42, 52–54, 56, 74, 83, 87, 90, 91, 92, 93, 94, 95, 96–97, 98, 99, 100, 101-3, 104, 108–9, 115, 118–20, 128, 133, 135, 144, 147–49, 152, 169, 175–80, 185–91, 193–97, 198–204
"Nightmare, The" (Fuseli) 137
Noble, Edward 151
Nordau, Max 184
Northern Daily Telegraph 13, 16, 19, 21
Northern Mythology (Thorpe) 64
Nussbaum, Martha C. 157–59

Occult Review 29
O'Donnell, Elliott 85
"Old Golly" 58–59
"On the Bridge" 32
Onions, Oliver 31
Orczy, Baroness 84
"Out of the Storm" 47, 51, 62–63, 74, 80
Out of the Storm 16, 54, 110

"Painted Lady, The" 154
Pall Mall Gazette 29
"Parliament of Owls, A" (Meikle) 134
Pearson, Arthur 46
Phantom Ship, The (Marryat) 56, 68
Pirates of the Caribbean (film) 68
"Plans of the Reefing Bi-Plane, The" 154
"Plattner Story, The" (Wells) 188
Pleasance, Donald 140
Poe, Edgar Allan 32, 48, 85, 146, 169, 184
"*Poems*" and "*The Dream of X*" 33
Prince Zaleski (Shiel) 88
"Problem of the Pearls, The" 155
Purple Cloud, The (Shiel) 49

Queen, Ellery 133, 140

Rappoport, Angelo S. 56, 61, 65
Red Magazine 54, 87
Rengade, Jules 46
Rime of the Ancient Mariner, The (Coleridge) 56, 63, 67, 80
Rimel, Duane W. 201, 203
Rivals of Sherlock Holmes, The (Greene) 140
"Riven Night, The" 58, 60-62, 63, 83
Rohmer, Sax 155
Rokeby (Scott) 68
Room in the Tower, The (Benson) 31
"Room of Fear, The" 83
Rowland, Marcus L. 136
Royal Magazine 46
Russ, Joanna 182
Russell, Alan K. 140n5
Russell, W. Clark 151

Sandow's Magazine 15
Sargasso 8
Sargasso Sea 46, 75-76
Saturday Review of Literature 27
Sauer, Carl 199
School of Physical Culture 11, 13, 15, 20, 45, 118, 178
Schuberth, Charles 12
Schultz, David E. 193
Schweitzer, Darrell 179n3
Scott, Sir Walter 68
"Sea Horses" 32
"Searcher of the End House, The" 82, 86, 91
Sense of an Ending, The (Kermode) 190
"Shadow out of Time, The" (Lovecraft) 193-97
Shadowy Thing, The (Drake) 193
"Shamraken Homeward-Bounder, The" 47, 58, 60
Shaw, A. E. 21, 22
Shelley, Mary 184
Shiel, M. P. 28, 49, 54-55, 88, 171
"Silent Ship, The" 69-70, 77
Silverman, Kenneth 22-24
Sime, S. H. 42
Sinclair, Ian 133-34
Sleeper Awakes, The (Wells) 30
Sloman, Larry 22

Smith, Clark Ashton 131, 194, 200, 201, 202
"Smugglers, The" 120-22, 126
Society for Psychical Research 85
Society of Authors 45-46
Some Facts in the Case of William Hope Hodgson (Everts) 91
"Spectre of New Haven, The" (Begg) 66-67
Stableford, Brian 133, 171, 174, 189
Stapledon, Olaf 42, 184, 190
Star Maker (Stapledon) 184
"Stone Ship, The" 33, 54, 74, 77
Story of the Days to Come, A (Wells) 30
"Strange High House in the Mist, The" (Lovecraft) 164
"Supernatural Horror in Literature" (Lovecraft) 7, 35n1, 37, 53, 157
Superstitions of Sailors (Rappoport) 56, 65
"Sussex Vampire, The" (Doyle) 89, 140
Suster, Gerald 84
Symons, Julian 91

Tale of Terror, The (Birkhead) 37
Telling, Mike W. 12
"Terror of the Water-Tank, The" 46-47
Terrors of the Sea 154
They Walk Again (de la Mare) 37, 39
"Thing in the Weeds, The" 52, 74, 76-77
"Thing Invisible, The" 74-75, 82, 86, 136-40, 141
Thomson, William. *See* Kelvin, Lord
Thorpe, Benjamin 64
"Through the Vortex of a Cyclone" 32, 60
"'Till A' the Seas'" (Barlow) 198, 202
Time Machine, The (Wells) 30, 49, 146, 169-81, 182, 184-91
Time Ships, The (Baxter) 173
Times (London) 31
Tolkien, J. R. R. 170
Tomlinson, H. M. 151
"Towards an Aesthetic of Science Fiction" (Russ) 182

"Trading with the Enemy" 154
Traditional Tales of the English and Scottish Peasantry (Cunningham) 56, 66
Tremayne, Peter 90
"Tropical Horror, A" 46, 75
Turn of the Screw, The (James) 74

Unseen Thing, The (Dyllington) 86

Valentine, Mark 132–33
"Valley of Lost Children, The" 50, 83
Vanity Fair 29
Verne, Jules 46
"Voice in the Night, The" 32, 37, 39, 47, 73, 79–80, 111–13, 124
Voice of the Ocean, The 33
Voyage sous les flots (Rengade) 46
Voyage to Arcturus, A (Lindsay) 184

Wagner, Richard 56, 68
Wandering Ghosts (Crawford) 31
War of the Worlds, The (Wells) 170
Weinstein, Lee 131–32
Wells, H. G. 7, 30, 46, 54, 146, 169–81, 182–92, 193
"Wendigo, The" (Blackwood) 74
Westminster Gazette 30
Wheatley, Dennis 37, 39
"Whistling Room, The" 31, 39, 82, 84, 86, 89, 91, 132, 134
Whitechurch, Victor L. 84
Whitehead, Henry S. 201
Widdershins (Onions) 31
"Wild Man of the Sea, The" 59
William Hope Hodgson: Voyages and Visions (Bell) 7
"Willows, The" (Blackwood) 194, 201
Winthrop, John 66
Woman in White, The (Collins) 85
Woods, Roger 13, 16, 20, 21, 22
Wooley, Natalie H. 203
Worm Ouroboros, The (Eddison) 177
"Written in Passing Dead-man's Island" (Moore) 69

www.ingramcontent.com/pod-product-compliance
Lightning Source LLC
Chambersburg PA
CBHW060109170426
43198CB00010B/831